HERBERT R. NORTHRUP, Ph.D.

Chairman, Department of Industry,
Wharton School of Finance and Commerce,
University of Pennsylvania

COMPULSORY ARBITRATION AND GOVERNMENT INTERVENTION IN LABOR DISPUTES

COMPULSORY ARBITRATION AND GOVERNMENT INTERVENTION IN LABOR DISPUTES

An Analysis of Experience

HERBERT R. NORTHRUP, Ph.D.

Chairman, Department of Industry,
Wharton School of Finance and Commerce,
University of Pennsylvania

1966

LABOR POLICY ASSOCIATION, INC.

Acknowledgements

Many people have aided in the making of this book but none so much as my secretary and administrative assistant, Mrs. Margaret E. Doyle. Mrs. Marie P. Spence also helped in the typing with her usual accuracy and efficiency. Mr. Arthur Donner, a Ph.D. candidate at the University of Pennsylvania did some of the background research. Mrs. Marjorie C. Denison made up the index.

The following publishers and journals kindly permitted republication of materials: Richard D. Irwin, Inc.; *Labor Law Journal*, published by Commerce Clearing House, Inc.; *The Journal of Industrial Relations*, published by the Industrial Relations Society of Australia; *British Journal of Industrial Relations*, published by the London School of Economics and Political Science; the *International Labour Review*, published by the International Labour Office; *Industrial Relations*, published by the Institute of Industrial Relations, University of California; the *Industrial and Labor Relations Review*, published by the New York State School of Industrial and Labor Relations, Cornell University; and the *Journal of Business of the University of Chicago*. In addition, materials originally developed in collaboration with both Dr. Gordon F. Bloom and Professor Richard L. Rowan have aided in the writing of this book.

Herbert R. Northrup

June 10, 1965.

Foreword

THE ADVOCATES of compulsory arbitration—that is, government-imposed settlements—of the terms of employment in collective labor contracts, come from one or more of three groups:

1. Those who are concerned with the "public interest" in the consequences of collective bargaining.

2. Those who are so over-matched in collective bargaining, who find the scales so loaded against them, that bargaining has become a sham.

3. Those who believe in bringing government further into control of the details of economic life, including the fixing of wages and prices.

The basic aim of the well-meaning supporters of compulsory arbitration is strike avoidance. This has become a matter of public concern as federal policies and labor union practices have enlarged the area of labor disputes and thus have aggravated the effect of such disputes upon the public.

The increasing show of interest in the subject of compulsory arbitration, and its repeated proposal as a cure, in one form or another, in each strike crisis, has not been matched by knowledge of its usefulness or effectiveness. Dr. Herbert R. Northrup, in *Compulsory Arbitration and Government Intervention in Labor Disputes,* supplies the knowledge and understanding needed. He states and analyses the experiences of the free nations which have tried it in whatever degree, including our own. He especially examines the generally misunderstood and often misrepresented Australian system. His conclusions, based upon his analyses of the facts, should take the naive nonsense out of consideration of this backdoor approach to a government "incomes policy" or wage control.

Dr. Northrup says: "In a free-market economy the strike performs a function for which there is no adequate substitute. The prospective costs of a strike to the two parties involved is the restraining influence which induces moderation and accommodation. The employer risks loss of business and profits; the union risks loss of jobs by its members, loss of membership, and loss of the strike itself. The pressures of these risks, the extent of them, and the weighing of them by those involved, pretty much determine the bargaining behavior of the parties and their dispositions to settle. To the extent that they may be relieved of risks, the inducement to settle is diminished. When an extreme position holds little or no risk, but serves as a means of bringing in an arbitrator who will certainly grant a considerable part of the demand, whatever it may have been, the rewards all go to the intransigent. There is little point in being prudent or reasonable.

"When the right to strike is withdrawn, as in compulsory arbitration legislation, the incentive to agree declines sharply. If the parties are not faced with the full consequences of refusing to settle, their desire, determination, or even ability to settle dwindles. This has occurred under each and every law or procedure, federal and state, legal and extra-legal, that has existed.

"The result is not strike control, but settlement avoidance. Fearing that to settle will mean a less attractive 'package' than an arbitrator would give, that it will be a sign of weakness, or that it will cause criticism by rivals or fellow officers or managers, unions and companies prepare for the arbitration procedure instead of for collective bargaining and private settlement. The aim is to force intervention. The more adamant, obdurate, and intransigent the parties, the more pressure upon the arbitrator. The pay-off is likely to be greatest to those willing to take the most extreme positions.

"Thus emergency dispute and arbitration laws create their

own rationale, and behavior becomes tailored to the laws. The laws create the emergencies which must be arbitrated, and the laws become 'necessary' to deal with them."

The conditions which have produced the drift or the drive toward government interventions in labor disputes, including compulsory arbitration of disputes over the making of contracts, are the results of faulty government labor policies. Now government is being asked to treat the effect, not to remove the cause; and, ironically, the treatment proposed is guaranteed to perpetuate the disease and to spread it, not to cure it.

Crises which develop in labor disputes are devised and intended to bring pressure upon the public, and through the public upon the government. It is secondary action on a colossal scale. It is not aimed primarily at the employers who are the formal target. It is an arm-twisting technique, and the arm that is twisted is that of the public.

There would be no "emergencies" 1) if government quit subsidizing strikes and strikers; and 2) if government kept its hands off and permitted the normal risks of strikes and striking to exercise their restraining influence upon the parties; in short, if government would permit its proclaimed basic labor policy of bona fide collective bargaining, observed too often in the breach, to function without constraint, and if government performed effectively one of the few, simple, elementary functions for which governments are constituted, that is, keeping the peace.

Inevitably, we are going in one of two directions in this country as a consequence of the evolution of our labor policies. Either we shall continue with more government "settlements" dictated by political considerations, not economics; or we must move in the direction of reducing the area of conflict so that widespread public damage cannot be caused by these private economic controversies.

There are many ponderous philosophical arguments against government interventions and political settlements; the elementary, practical argument is that they do not work, while private settlements do.

WILLIAM INGLES, *President*,
Labor Policy Association, Inc.

Table of Contents

PART I

INTRODUCTION

1 The Issues of Intervention

THE WAGES, HOURS, and working conditions of those who work for others in a modern society are usually established in one of five ways:

1. The employer or employer group may set the terms;
2. The employee or employee group may set the terms;
3. Employers and employees, bargaining individually or through organizations, may set the terms;
4. The state may establish the terms by totalitarian controls such as exist in Communist nations, or by less stringent regulation of various types—for example, the Australian compulsory arbitration system;
5. A combination of numbers 3 and 4 may exist in various proportions, such as has developed in the United States and Canada.

In a free society like that of a western democracy, unilateral determination of wages, hours, and working conditions by employer or employee groups is never either absolute or satisfactory. The conditions for the rapid expansion of unionism in the United States from 3 million in 1934 to a total of 17 million in 1964, were established by the tremendous government support for union growth and after 1940, the rapid expansion of the American economy. But the basic desire to unionize on the part of employees undoubtedly derived from their general feelings of dissatisfaction with unilateral determinations of conditions of employment and their association of such unilateral employer determinations with the mass layoffs and insecurity of the Great Depression.

Unilateral employee or union determination of conditions of employment is likewise unsatisfactory, especially to the other party —the employer. It exists on an unorganized basis in very tight labor markets where a particular or scarce skill can command its own price. It also exists where a bargaining power is heavily weighted on the organized employee side. This occurs in various service and transportation industries in which a shutdown causes a non-recoverable business loss, or in a building construction, in which the contract must be completed in a specified period to avoid severe financial loss. In many of these industries, the employers are small, poorly financed, and short of both cash and credit, and easy prey to both economic and more physical pressures, whereas the unions are large, financially well-heeled, and capable of exerting tremendous economic and more directly devastating pressures. In such industries, existence in many areas on the part of the business requires acquiescence in union determination of wages, hours, and working conditions.

The dissatisfaction with unilateral determination of wages, hours, and conditions of employment has resulted in systems of joint determination which vary widely from area to area, industry to industry, and country to country. But joint determination by labor and management has not been the panacea which its proponents promised. Large segments of the public have clamored for improvements of the resulting collective bargaining systems, and demanded that government intervene and regulate the methods, systems, or even results to provide either conduct or results more satisfactory to those desiring improvement. Likewise, when either the unions or management have seen an opportunity for gain, each has sought to aid the government machinery and legislation. The result today in all democratic countries is a mixed system of private and government regulation and controls, with the private under constant attack from those who would increase government regulation. What is not considered is (1) whether more government regulation will accomplish the end of peaceful settlement, and (2) what effects will the intrusion of the government have on the willingness of the parties to settle, the means of settlement, or on the settlement itself.

Strikes are messy events. It is no wonder that mankind in an industrial society has looked for ways and means to avoid them. The question is only partially whether strikes can be avoided. The question is also whether the cure is worse than the problem. The answer depends, of course, on a number of value judgments.

But judgments should be based upon facts and experience. In this area, both are available. In the United States and in other democratic countries a wealth of data and experience has been amassed. Indeed, so great has been the search and experimentation for ways and means of determining by peaceful means the wages, hours and working conditions of employees and so varied the techniques utilized, that no one today can plead ignorance of the consequences of proposals for methods designed to produce peaceful settlement of labor disputes.

This book has a limited objective: an examination of the effects of government intervention as an inducing or compelling agent to obtain peaceful settlement where the government forces the parties to submit their dispute to third parties for either recommendations or decision, or penalizes the parties for declining to agree to such submission. The concern is primarily with the United States experience, but the situation in nearly all other democratic countries of size has been examined in order to test the principles derived from American experience. The purpose is to make available to managers, legislators, union representatives, and students this experience in summary and comprehensible form so that the debate over issues can be based upon fact, and legislation will not promise what it cannot deliver.

Judgments are freely made throughout the book, but, it is believed, they are thoroughly grounded on facts and the author's 25 years of experience as a teacher, researcher, and practitioner. Part II of the book is devoted to compulsory arbitration experiments,

Part III to other forms of mediation, and Part IV to analyses, conclusions, and recommendations. The appendices include a number of articles by outstanding scholars on labor relations and government intervention abroad, as well as three detailed accounts of our own state experience by the author and two of his associates.

PART II

COMPULSORY ARBITRATION

CHAPTER

2 Nature
And
Background

If COMPULSORY SETTLEMENT of labor disputes is the goal, the issues must be determined by someone—and this means compulsory arbitration—the determination of wages, hours, and working conditions by a third party other than representatives of employers and employees, and provisions requiring that such determination be final and binding for a specified period of time. Compulsory arbitration statutes set forth a procedure for invoking arbitration, for selecting the arbitrator (either on an ad hoc, or case-by-case basis, or establishment of a permanent arbitrator or arbitration board), and usually also provide methods of enforcement of awards and penalties for refusal to abide by them. Many statutes also attempt to set forth criteria or standards to guide arbitral decisions.

The free world has had considerable experience with compulsory arbitration. It has been tested in the United States during both World Wars, and by several of the states during postwar periods;

and it has become a way of life in Australia, New Zealand, and, to a lesser extent, in South Africa; and it has been adopted by India and most of the emerging nations. In addition, many European countries adopted compulsory arbitration during World War II and retained these wartime controls for a considerable period thereafter. More recently, in the United States, by administrative enlargement of powers, something approximating compulsory arbitration is being attempted by the National Labor Relations Board, which already has statutory authority to determine representation and jurisdictional disputes—that is disputes over which union, if any, shall represent a given group of employees, and which union or employees shall do work over which more than one group claims jurisdiction.

The Support for Compulsory Arbitration

Compulsory arbitration has been adopted in different areas for a variety of reasons. During wartime, interruptions in the flow of goods and materials to the troops could not be tolerated. Consequently, compulsory arbitration was instituted for this very practical reason. Compulsory arbitration was kept in force in many countries after World War II because of the need to control wages and prices while the devastation was overcome by rebuilding. As prosperity returned to Britain, Holland, and other countries, however, the system of compulsion was either disregarded or formally ended.

The United States abandoned compulsory arbitration as an instrument of government policy at the close of hostilities in 1945, but instituted a series of intervening techniques, including fact finding and seizure (see Figure I for definitions) which culminated in the national emergency procedures of the Taft-Hartley Act. Meanwhile, the great strike wave of 1945-1946 combined with public and employer support aimed at reducing union power led to the enactment of strike control laws in eleven states, eight of which provided for compulsory arbitration.

Likewise in the United States, the threat of a nationwide rail strike, the failure of the fact finding procedure of the Railway Labor Act either to preserve collective bargaining or to evolve a substitute framework for settlement, and the refusal of the President to permit a nationwide railway strike resulted in 1963 in the

Figure I

DEFINITIONS

MEDIATION AND CONCILIATION are used interchangeably to mean an attempt by a third party, typically a
government official, to bring disputants together by persuasion and compromise. The mediator or conciliator is not
vested with power to force a settlement.

STRIKE-NOTICE laws require the union and company
to notify each other and certain public officials a specified
number of days prior to striking or locking out.

STRIKE-VOTE laws require an affirmative vote of either
the union members or the employees in the bargaining unit
before a strike may be called.

FACT FINDING involves investigation of a dispute by
a panel, which issues a report setting forth the causes of a dispute. Usually, but not always, recommendations for settling
the dispute are included in the report. Laws requiring fact
finding usually provide that the parties maintain the status
quo and refrain from strikes or lockouts until a stipulated
period after the fact finders' report has been made. Once
the procedure has been complied with, however, the parties
are free to strike and to lock out.

COMPULSORY ARBITRATION requires the submis-
sion of an unsettled labor dispute to a third party or board
for determination. Strikes or lockouts are completely forbidden, and the arbitrator's decision is binding on the parties
for a stated length of time.

SEIZURE involves temporary state control of a business
which is, or threatens to be, shut down by a work stoppage.
Strikes or lockouts are forbidden during the period of seizure, which lasts until the threat of work stoppage is abated.

first federal peacetime compulsory arbitration act, outside of the limited area of representation, jurisdictional, and grievance disputes.[1]

The railroad arbitration law of 1963, like the post-World War II state acts, was supported by management—in this case railway management—and opposed by railway unions. Many elements, although certainly not all, of the employers in all of the transportation industries—airlines, truck, and maritime—support compulsory arbitration. Some of these managements operate under federal subsidies, directly or indirectly, and apparently feel that the federal government will reimburse them for wage increases granted by government boards and thus assure them profitable operation without labor difficulties. Many employers, particularly in the maritime and trucking industries, feel also that the unions are so strong and their ability to withstand a strike is so limited, that under compulsory arbitration their position cannot be seriously worsened.

Those railway and airlines employers who look with favor on compulsory arbitration have an additional reason. Under the fact finding procedures of the Railway Labor Act, which are discussed in Chapter 5, a situation has developed in which political pressures effectively require that management accept the recommendations of fact finders just as if they were the awards of arbitration boards; but if unions are dissatisfied they have not hesitated to pressure for, and usually obtain, greater benefits than those recommended by fact finders. Hence, these railway and airline managements feel that compulsory arbitration already exists for them and that their position would be improved if unions, like managements, were required to accept the results of government boards.

In contrast to the situation in the transportation industries, and to that in various states in the post-World War II period, compulsory arbitration in Australia, New Zealand, and India, as well as in some of the emerging countries, was adopted primarily as a means of supporting trade union growth and power. To be sure, other factors were present, particularly a desire to avoid industrial strife. But the basic support has come from legislators representing labor parties and from other union adherents. In New Zealand, for example, when the Conservative Party came to power in 1932, the compulsory feature of the law was set aside, only to be reinstituted a few years later when the Labor Party regained authority.

India likewise instituted compulsory arbitration in order to generate union growth. An additional factor is the belief in India, and in many emerging countries, that controls are necessary to spur economic growth, or that arbitration is necessary to further economic development or social or socialistic aims.

In South Africa, intervention in industrial relations is also designed to maintain basic governmental policy—in this case strict segregation of the races. The South African system controls effectively the competition of colored with whites for the better jobs, keeps the wages of white workers at a high level, and thereby gains the support of the white workers for the racial restrictions as well as for restrictions on actions by unions or employers.

In all countries, arbitration statutes usually contain fulsome praise for the institution of collective bargaining and settlement of disputes by the parties themselves. Indeed, the encouragement of collective bargaining is often one of the stated aims of proponents of compulsory arbitration. Yet opponents of compulsory arbitration have repeatedly charged that the very existence of the arbitration machinery encourages the very opposite of collective bargaining. For parties are, say the critics, inevitably tempted to refuse to settle or even to compromise either in the hope that the arbitrators will grant a demand or that any compromise in pre-arbitration bargaining will prejudice the compromising party's position before the arbitrator. The result, say critics of arbitration, is that the arbitration machinery becomes hopelessly entangled with a myriad of minor disputes which cause delays, dissatisfaction, and eventually strikes or demonstrations against the machinery itself.

In the United States, unions are the main bulwark supporting the expanding role of the National Labor Relations Board into determinations regarding the bargaining process, and very close to the bargain itself. The role of the NLRB in determining representation disputes has wider support, but the policy of the Board to make direct determinations in this area, now becoming common, without an objective election among affected employees, has support only among extreme union partisans. On the other hand, the compulsory arbitration of jurisdictional disputes clearly has far greater employer than union backing.

We thus find that compulsory arbitration legislation has been enacted and is supported for the following reasons:

1. To insure uninterrupted production in wartime;

2. To further the economic or social aims or policies of government;

3. To curtail strikes and/or union power in general or in crucial industries;

4. To enhance union growth or power;

5. To support collective bargaining.

Obviously, all of these aims cannot be met at once, for some are inconsistent with others. It is clearly not possible both to curtail union power and to enhance it; or to encourage and to discourage collective bargaining; but in addition, national or social aims may run counter at times—at least in theory—either to union or employer rights or aspirations. Consequently, it must be assumed that some of the divergent groups who have supported or opposed compulsory arbitration legislation have seen results which both surprised and disappointed them. The record of compulsory arbitration in action needs to be examined in order to determine whether such legislation

1. insures industrial peace;

2. enhances or reduces union power and growth;

3. supports national economic and social policies of various types;

4. encourages or discourages collective bargaining.

The only way to accomplish this is to examine and to evaluate the record. The remainder of the book will attempt to do just that, not only for compulsory arbitration, but as well for other forms of government intervention which have been advocated or approved by some of the same arguments utilized with respect to compulsory arbitration.

NOTES

1. The statements and facts set forth in this introductory chapter will be supported by evidence and sources in the detailed analysis to follow.

3 Two United States Experiences

THE UNITED STATES has had relatively limited experience with compulsory arbitration. The two principal areas where it was tried were during World War II and in several states between 1947 and 1952. This chapter examines the background and history of these experiences in the light of the criteria set forth in Chapter 2.

WARTIME ADJUSTMENT MACHINERY

Except for the railroad industry and for occasional *ad hoc* Presidential intervention, federal intervention designed to postpone or to prevent strikes prior to 1946 was largely a wartime phenomenon.[1] The needs of war production, combined with the psychological necessities of uniting for the war effort, mean that no industrial strike can be tolerated in wartime. During both World War I and World War II, therefore, compulsion substituted for voluntarism in the settlement of labor disputes. To lessen the degree of compulsion, prominent roles in wartime adjustment machinery were given to representatives of labor and industry. Nonetheless, the factor of compulsion remained, and the difficulty of restoring voluntary collective bargaining after compulsory controls are lifted is well illustrated by the great strike waves of both 1919-1920 and 1945-1946. Moreover, the principles and precedents developed by war labor agencies have had permanent influence on peacetime policy.

The World War I Labor Board

The industrial strains created by World War I—higher prices, expanding industry, and labor shortages—caused considerable unrest and strife even before the United States entered the conflict. To devise remedies, President Wilson called a conference of labor and industrial leaders to formulate a national industrial relations policy. The conference, after ten weeks' deliberation, agreed on an eight-point program, including a pledge of no strikes or lockouts, the freedom of workers to organize and bargain collectively, and the maintenance of the *status quo* on the question of the closed and the open shop. To effectuate these policies, the National War Labor Board of World War I was created in April 1918. The Board was composed of five industry, five labor, and two public members.[2]

The World War I Board was in existence for approximately one year. Although its guiding rule was the maintenance of the *status quo* in industrial relations generally, it had the effect of encouraging unionism and collective bargaining. Through it, the American Federation of Labor won official governmental recognition on a par with employers' associations; through it, peaceful collective bargaining was encouraged;[3] and under its benevolent aegis and the tight labor market of the era, union membership grew to a pre-New Deal high of five million.

The World War I Board was able to settle all cases referred to it with the exception of three, which were referred to President Wilson, who, as a means of enforcing the Board's awards, either took over plants or threatened to draft workers and bar them from war jobs. In view of the national emergency, labor and management generally showed a patriotic willingness to abide by the Board's awards.

With the end of the war, strikes flared up throughout the country. At the height of the strike wave, President Wilson convened a National Industrial Conference, composed of labor, industry, and public groups, to formulate principles for a "genuine and lasting co-operation between capital and labor." The conference broke down on the issue of union recognition. Industry declined to yield on this issue, and unions had neither the government support nor the power to alter managerial opposition. Without either, union membership declined steadily during the decade that followed.

The National Defense Mediation Board

As the defense program got under way in 1940, strikes in crucial industries gave rise to increasing concern. On March 19, 1941, President Roosevelt created the National Defense Mediation Board to adjust labor disputes in defense industries. This tripartite agency had no authority to order settlement, but it soon began to issue public recommendations which resulted in government seizure if they were not accepted by unions or management. When the Mediation Board declined to award the union shop in a case involving the United Mine Workers, the CIO labor members withdrew. President Roosevelt then set up a special arbitration board which granted this demand. By this time, hostilities had begun.

The National War Labor Board of World War II

On January 12, 1942, the National War Labor Board of World War II was established by executive order. In June 1943, it was given statutory backing by the War Labor Disputes Act, passed by Congress over the President's veto. During the previous October, the Board had been assigned wage control under the Stabilization Act. To aid in administering its functions, the WLB also established thirteen regional boards and several industry commissions. Its jurisdiction included virtually all American industry, except rail and air carriers subject to the Railway Labor Act.

The War Labor Board initially attempted to decide each industrial dispute case on its merits. Gradually, however, it developed official policies on virtually every issue under dispute between the parties. It attempted to maintain peace in settling disputes by using three basic approaches: (1) appeal to the legal framework governing industrial relations in wartime; (2) appeal to historical precedent, whenever possible; and (3) compromise.

The WLB used the "legal framework" method most frequently in wage cases. The Stabilization Act and the executive orders issued thereunder set forth the law. Hence, when a proposed increase exceeded the Little Steel Formula (the permissible legal wage increase), the War Labor Board had merely to cite a higher authority as the basis of its decision.

The appeal to historical precedent as a basis for maintaining industrial peace is well explained by the following quotation:

> Where an arbitrator's decision is based on historical precedent, especially if this historical pattern has been created and/or perpetuated by collective bargaining, neither party to the dispute can logically accuse the arbitrator of attempting to innovate in the field of industrial relations. Where the parties are convinced of a negative fact that the arbitrator is not trying to impose any "revolutionary" change on either of them, the first step in avoiding conflict has already been taken. And when, in addition, the positive part of the arbitrator's action is molded along historical lines, the parties are very likely to go along with the decision.[4]

Thus the War Labor Board refused to disturb North-South wage differentials, or historical differentials between two plants of the same company located in different parts of the country, or even local differentials between two neighboring plants. Likewise, the WLB refused to alter union or closed shop contracts voluntarily agreed to by management.

When the WLB had neither law nor historical precedent to guide it, compromise always remained. The best example is, of course, found in the issue of union security. The principle of maintenance of membership is an obvious compromise between the closed and the open shop. Likewise, compromise guided the War Labor Board when it acceded to unions' demands for such "fringe" issues as paid vacations, paid holidays, and night-shift bonuses, but denied demands for paid sick leave and compulsory health and welfare funds.

Since changes in wages invariably affect industrial relations, the stabilization duties of the War Labor Board were closely interrelated with its job of maintaining industrial peace. The War Labor Board realized this quite clearly. For example, its attempt to eliminate interplant wage inequities was based not so much on stabilization principles (although the extent of the adjustments permissible under this concept was regulated by stabilization) as by a belief, as expressed by Chairman George W. Taylor, that "the absence of a proper internal rate alignment may often be more destructive of employee morale than interplant differences."[5]

But wage stabilization was not only related to peaceful labor relations; it often worked at cross purposes with it. The denial of a voluntary application for wage increases, jointly submitted by an employer and a union, usually caused unrest in a plant, and sometimes a work stoppage. Such stoppages were directed not against employers but against the War Labor Board.

Because of this conflict between wage stabilization and labor peace at a time when the latter was considered paramount, compromise was often permitted to weaken stabilization. For example, when a substantial general increase demand of the CIO Steelworkers was denied, a variety of fringe issues such as improved vacations, night-shift bonuses, and the elimination of interplant inequities was used to mollify the union. In sum, stabilization was made flexible to suit the immediate needs of labor peace.

Enforcement of Settlement

The War Labor boards of both World War I and World War II were set up by Presidential executive orders, and therefore had, legally, only "advisory" power. In fact, however, defiance of the orders (legally, advice!) of these agencies could not be tolerated if general respect for the procedures was to be maintained. Hence, utilizing wartime emergency powers, Presidents Wilson, Roosevelt, and Truman were forced to handle compliance by decree and use, or potential use, of the armed forces.

The problem in World War I was minor. Only three cases of defiance of the War Labor Board of that period occurred. "Two were cases of company defiance and resulted in government seizures. The third was a defiant strike which led to President Wilson's famous 'work-or-fight' order. The workers returned to their jobs."[6]

Seizure in World War II became the recognized method of enforcing orders of the National Defense Mediation Board, the War Labor Board, and railway labor agencies, although in three cases other sanctions were also employed (for example, loss of material priorities for companies, loss of draft deferments for strikers). A total of forty seizure cases occurred during World War II, in addition to the four in the pre-war Defense Mediation Board period.[7]

Government seizure, as noted in Figure I, involves temporary government control of a business. Nationalization is not contemplated. In the absence of specific legislation the legal basis for seizure rests in the wartime and emergency powers of the executive to prevent a breakdown of essential services to the community.[8]

In 1943, Congress passed the War Labor Disputes Act over President Roosevelt's veto. This law provided a statutory basis for seizure, but many wartime and postwar seizures were made under executive emergency power without reference to the wartime law, which expired by its own terms on June 30, 1947.

The Heritage of the War Labor Board

The National War Labor Board of World War II rendered decisions for all industry on every conceivable aspect of industrial relations. For many years, its decisions have served as a guide for rulings in labor disputes. The WLB established the historical precedents and the legal framework for arbitrators to follow, and both labor and management still turn to the WLB's rulings for precedents in solving disputed questions. And this will continue to be true whether the War Labor Board's decisions have been "sound" or not, primarily because the scope of such decisions includes all industry and all phases of industrial relations.

Likewise, War Labor Board decisions have furthered certain union goals which became increasingly prominent in postwar years. They include the following: (1) that a "responsible" union deserves union security; (2) that paid vacations, paid holidays, paid sick leave, group health insurance, night-shift bonuses, and other benefit issues are proper union objectives; (3) that unions should have a voice in the establishment of benefit plans, and that such plans are a proper sphere of collective bargaining; (4) that wage rate structures should be simplified so as to eliminate intraplant differences; and (5) that similar occupations in neighboring areas should be similar compensated.

That union growth and power was enhanced under the wartime

arbitration system seems incontrovertible. Union membership rose from 8.7 million in 1940 to 14.3 million in 1945. In 1940, union security agreements—that is, provisions requiring union membership as a condition of employment—were found in 40 percent of all union contracts; by 1946, 65 percent of such agreements included union security provisions.[9] Although wage stabilization undoubtedly curbed wage increases and prevented employers and unions from bidding up the price of labor, the benefits won and the precedents opened for further benefits greatly enhanced the position, power, and prestige of unions.

The strike record during World War II was mixed. The percentage of employees involved in strikes was low in 1942, but for the other war years about average for prewar and postwar years (except for the abnormally high year of 1946). The number of stoppages was also not typically different than the average pre- or postwar year. But the duration of strikes and the man days idle were substantially less than the pre- and postwar peacetime average.

Thus even in wartime strikes do occur under a compulsory arbitration system. But the strikes are likely to be of short duration. For their purpose is usually either to force management to settle a grievance or to attract the attention of the authorities. The latter situation often results from rising discontentent over the inevitable delay which must occur as a case winds its way through a government bureaucracy. More than one-half of the dispute cases submitted to the War Labor Board of two large samples studied took at least ninety days to process, and another 25 percent took six months or more.[10] Delay created unrest; demonstrations get attention. Moreover, such wartime strikes had little risk. They generally could be certain that they would be ordered back to work quickly and just as quickly welcomed back in the shop. The fear that they would suffer privation by being out on strike for a long period was negligible. In later chapters,[11] we shall note the similarity in this respect of the American wartime experience with that under the Australian compulsory arbitration system, and to some extent also with the developments under the United States Railway Labor Act.

Another reason for delay in the settlement of wartime dispute cases—and hence for unrest and resultant quickie stoppages—was the tendency of management and unions to load the War Labor Board with issues, often of great complexity, rather than to settle them without availing themselves of government intervention. In discussing issues of case processing, a historian of the WLB noted "that hundreds of cases and thousands of minor issues were tossed into the lap of the Board for final determinations that might have been bargained by the parties. . . . One or both sides frequently desired to pass on the effort of effectuating an agreement to the Board, and the risk and blame as well. Negotiations were often viewed as something of a farce, since rules of the Board greatly restricted the area for give-and-take . . . [most] important . . . in lengthening case processing time was the multiplicity and complexity of the issues involved in the typical dispute case. One case alone might easily have 25, 50, or even more, separate issues that had to be independently heard, analyzed, and finally decided. Many of these issues were exceedingly complex (such as intraplant inequity problems) and required the most careful consideration before a fair and equitable judgment could be reached. This demanded time—in the hearing, by the panel, by the wage stabilization division, and by the Board itself."[12]

The effect of the War Labor Board on strikes, collective bargaining, and public policy was profoundly felt in the immediate post-World War II period. After four years of setting terms and conditions of employment, the federal government was reluctant to retire from the field. In addition, large sections of management and labor found it difficult to return to collective bargaining. Moreover, many unions and many employers were anxious to "teach the other a lesson." This, combined with the pent-up resentment of wartime, did much to make 1946 the greatest strike year of American history in terms of man-days lost from work.

Both labor and management were surprised at the duration of some of the 1946 strikes. During the war, such strikes as occurred were, as noted, usually "quickies." The emphasis was on uninterrupted production to the exclusion of all else. Union leaders found in the postwar period that management resistance was much greater, particularly when loss of business was compensated for by rebates of wartime excess profits taxes. On the other hand, those employers who felt that unions could not survive postwar strife miscalculated badly. One result of the postwar strike wave was a more realistic appraisal of the effectiveness, costs, and results of strikes on the part of both labor and management.

Another wartime heritage to which the 1946 strikes gave sharp emphasis was the increasing public concern with stoppages of work which interfered with "essential" services or even inconvenienced a portion of the population. Wartime hysteria over strikers was carried over into the postwar period. Moreover, a number of unions exhibited unparalleled irresponsibility and lack of understanding of public sentiment in striking essential services. One result was the election of a Congress with a Republican majority in 1946, which enacted the Taft-Hartley law; and another result was an increasing concern of state legislatures with "emergency" labor settlement machinery, including the arbitration laws discussed in the next section of this chapter.

War Labor Board—Evaluation Summary

In terms of the Criteria established in Chapter 2, the War Labor Board of World War II appears to have furthered national goals by accomplishing a reasonably effective job of stabilizing wages and maintaining labor peace. On the other hand, strikes did occur— usually of a short duration. These strikes were largely localized and aimed at calling attention to delays in, or dissatisfaction with, the War Labor Board procedure. A notable exception, of course, as anyone familiar with the period can recall, was the action of John L. Lewis and the United Mine Workers in calling strikes which affected a whole industry and which were not quickly ended.

Despite relative effectiveness in labor peace and wage stabilization, union power was clearly enhanced, judged by membership gains, gains in union security or compulsory unionism contracts, and gains in obtaining a union voice in fringe benefits and other areas in which union influence had been slight. Despite postwar legislative setbacks, unions emerged from the war far more powerful by any reasonable criterion than they were in 1940.

Finally, collective bargaining was profoundly affected by the War Labor Board. There was a strong tendency for representatives of unions and of management to refrain from bargaining and to dump all significant—and many insignificant—contract issues into the lap of the WLB. The ability to settle atrophied. When the war ended, the great rash of strikes in 1945 and 1946 was in part attributable to this reliance on the WLB and the failure of the parties to appreciate that such reliance was no longer available as a crutch against their own failure to deal realistically with their own problems. Concomitant to this failure was the miscalculation of unions and management as to each other's capacity to withstand work stoppages and the consequent likely duration of such stoppages.

The War Labor Board operated in a period of extreme national emergency. Experiences under it are useful in assessing how compulsory arbitration works in practice, but conclusions must necessarily be softened by the knowledge that during a more typical era, results could be different. For this reason, we now turn to the post-World War II period in the several states which tried compulsory arbitration for a four-year peiod.

STATE COMPULSORY ARBITRATION LAWS

American states have experimented with compulsory arbitration for short periods after both World Wars.[13] In each period, state laws for banning strikes and providing for compulsory arbitration were enacted following bitter strikes which affected key industries. The post-World War I experiment occurred in Kansas, where a general compulsory arbitration law was enacted in 1920, and rendered inoperative by court decisions in 1923 and 1925,[14] after an interesting, controversial career.[15]

Among the industries affected by the strike wave in 1946 were a number of public utilities, including electric light and power and gas operations. As a result, 11 states enacted emergency legislation in 1947. Eight of the laws provided for compulsory arbitration.[16] A majority of these laws became inoperative as a result of a 1951 Supreme Court decision striking down the Wisconsin law as in conflict with the Taft-Hartley Act, but meanwhile, valuable experience was accumulated.[17]

The Indiana Law

A majority of these laws were modeled on the Indiana statute. This law covered privately owned companies supplying electric power, gas, water, telephone, and transportation (exclusive of railroad and air) services to the public. It exhorted parties to settle their disputes by collective bargaining. In the event a strike was threatened, and the Governor believed severe hardship to the public would occur, he was required to appoint a conciliator who attempted to mediate the dispute. If mediation proved unsuccessful within a thirty-day period, the dispute was referred to a board of arbitration. No strikes, lockouts, or other use of force were permitted once a conciliator was appointed. The Governor could, however, decline to appoint a conciliator if he believed no hardship would endure, and then no prohibition on strikes or lockouts was in force.

The Indiana law featured great care in outlining the duties, functions, and limitations of the Board of Arbitration. It was a public board, selected from a panel chosen by the Governor, and had the power of subpoena, and of administering oaths. It was directed where rates of pay and other conditions of work were in dispute, to establish same comparable to those established by other public utility employers for workers of the same skills in the area where the dispute existed, or if no comparable public utility employer or employees existed in the area, to make the same comparison with adjoining labor market areas within the state.

The standards feature of the Indiana law attracted considerable attention; and was the basis for the adoption of similar laws in Florida, Wisconsin, Michigan,[18] Pennsylvania, and Nebraska. As in Indiana, these laws had considerable employer and conservative support, and were opposed by pro-union groups.

New Jersey did not go the "Indiana route." As originally enacted in 1946, the New Jersey law provided for a combination of fact finding and seizure. The statute declared that heat, light, power, sanitation, transportation, communication, and water were essential and that an interruption of these services was a threat to public health and welfare. To avoid such interruption, a panel was set up by labor and industry representatives through the State Board of Mediation. If the parties did not settle their disputes, members of the panel were appointed to hold hearings and make recommendations for settlement to the Governor. If a strike still threatened, the Governor was empowered to seize the facilities. No penalties before or after seizure were provided.

When this procedure did not stave off a threatened strike of telephone employees, the New Jersey legislature added a compulsory arbitration provision after seizure with severe fines and jail terms for violations. Later the jail terms were eliminated and the fines reduced. Standards were added to the New Jersey law after a state court decision requiring such guides as a condition of constitutionality, and the provisions for fact finding before seizure were later eliminated by the legislature as unnecessary. The constitutionality of the New Jersey law was not passed on by the courts after the Wisconsin case was decided by the Supreme Court. The law, however, has not since been invoked.[19]

Minnesota Hospital Act

Minnesota had enacted a comprehensive fact finding law in 1939, which applies to public utilities among other industries.[20] Then in 1947, the state enacted amendments providing for compulsory arbitration for wage and hour issues in charitable hospitals only. Only hospitals in Minnesota are thus subject to arbitration.

Impact of the State Arbitration Laws

It is difficult to assay the impact of these state laws in terms of our basic criteria. Strikes were generally absent from industries covered by these laws in the period in which they operated, i.e., 1947-1952, but strikes were also relatively uncommon in such industries in other states during these years, and have also been uncommon in the affected states since the laws became inoperative. Union power may have been enhanced by these laws to judge from the fact that the most use of them occurred in those situations were unions were attempting to make gains not readily achievable by collective bargaining, as the analysis below on the effects of the laws on bargaining demonstrates. On the other hand, some unions evidently felt that the laws were having the opposite effect, for the successful legal attacks on these state laws were made by unions in all cases.

Little material is available on the effect of these laws on economic policy, except a general feeling, buttressed by some factual evidence that state public regulatory commissions which control public utility rates, seemed to be more prone to grant rate adjustments to utilities if a state arbitration board had ordered a wage increase than if such a wage increase had been bargained.[21] The net effect, if carried to an extreme, would surely end collective bargaining for it would not pay a utility to grant adjustments if only ordered adjustments were rate compensable. And, of course, why a wage increase should cost more if ordered than if bargained is an aspect of economic policy not easily explained or understood.

As to the effect of these arbitration laws on collective bargaining, the evidence is much clearer. All the state compulsory arbitration laws contained pronouncements favoring settlement of disputes by collective bargaining. Most such laws also provided for attempts at settlement by conciliation or mediation, with the express hope that compulsory arbitration would not need to be utilized except rarely and then only for cases in which the disputed issues are exceptionally difficult to resolve.

What actually occurred is in part demonstrated by the data in Table 1. In Wisconsin, Indiana, and New Jersey, for example, the administrators of the laws did not hesitate to use them in disputes in which covered industries were involved even though the prospective disputes would not have been of major proportion. Disputes sent to arbitration involved small Rural Electrification Administration cooperatives, accounting employees of telephone companies, and bus operators in small cities. Compulsory arbitration was used, as the Supreme Court stated in the decision invalidating the Wisconsin law, not as "emergency" legislation but as "a comprehensive code for the settlement of labor disputes between public utility employers and employees."[22]

Moreover, the willingness of these states to invoke compulsory arbitration encouraged its use. The belief of some unions and employers that they can do better under arbitration than they could

TABLE 1

ARBITRATION CASES BY STATE AND INDUSTRY, 1947ᵃ–1952

State	Total Cases	Urban Transit	Communi-cation	Electric Light and Powerᵇ	Gas	Water Works
Florida............	4	3			1	
Indiana............	29	14	8	6		1
New Jersey.........	25	3	9	3	9	1
Pennsylvania........	9	(ᶜ)	(ᶜ)	3	6	
Wisconsin..........	40	2	10	24	4	
Total cases						
	107	22	27	36	20	2

ᵃ All laws enacted in 1947; all statistics from dates of enactment.
ᵇ Includes gas utilities operated in conjunction with electric light and power.
ᶜ Jurisdiction of Pennsylvania law does not include these industries. Data on usage follows those set forth in New Jersey Governor's Committee on Legislation, *Report to Governor Robert B. Meyner*, pp. 33–40, except for Pennsylvania, where records of the State Labor Relations Board show two additional cases.

under collective bargaining resulted in perfunctory negotiations and hasty applications for the invocation of arbitration. And the unwillingness of the state administrators to oppose this tide encouraged it.

Wisconsin REA

Special conditions in the electrical industry in Wisconsin and in the gas industry in New Jersey brought increased case loads in those states. By and large, unions and management in the two industries have compiled an excellent record of peaceful settlement without recourse to outside agencies. In Wisconsin, however, a basic dispute over whether Rural Electrification Administration cooperatives should pay rates comparable to private electric utilities accounted for most of the disputes in the electric industry there. And in New Jersey disputes in the gas industry involving competitive rival AFL, CIO and independent unions resulted in nine out of the 25 arbitration board appointments.

Urban Transit

If a union asks a ten-cent increase and a company offers eight cents, the union can refuse the compromise, go to arbitration and point out that the company has already offered eight cents. Then the arbitrators are under great pressure to give, instead of eight cents, a few cents more—in other words, to compromise the company's offer upwards. If this happens once, it is most unlikely that the company the following year will make any offer for fear of seeing that offer used as a springboard for further concessions in an arbitration proceeding. The situation may then snowball; neither party is willing to bargain for fear that any bargaining will be used against it in later arbitration procedure. Such an impasse appears to typify present-day industrial relations in the urban transportation industry in the states surveyed.

The Amalgamated Association of Street, Electric and Motor Coach Employees, the dominant union in urban transportation, has from its inception stated that one of its objectives is "to encourage the settlement of all disputes between employees and employers by arbitration." For more than 50 years, this union has "made it obligatory for local divisions to offer arbitration to the employer where other means of settlement failed. . . . The International (union) has exercised strict control over the making of collective agreements and has attempted to have incorporated in them all a clause that would provide arbitration not only in case of disputes arising out of the agreement but also in the event that a new agreement could not be negotiated to replace an expiring one. By 1905 . . . arbitration was provided in the majority of . . . agreements then in existence."[23]

Post-World War II strike-control legislation, therefore, found this union thoroughly favorable to arbitration as a means of settlement and, in addition, extremely competent and well staffed to win arbitrations.

Not that the Amalgamated Association welcomed strike-control legislation; in 1919, it had emphatically opposed the Kansas compulsory arbitration law, and since 1947 it has led the fight to invalidate state strike-control laws. Local divisions of the Amalgamated attempted to secure management agreement for voluntary arbitration in those states in which compulsory arbitration existed. In some instances, this occurred, but often management representatives declined on the grounds that management's interests were better protected by arbitrating under state laws.

Whether engaged in voluntary or compulsory arbitration, however, it has become fairly common for the parties in the urban transportation industry to prepare for arbitration rather than for collective bargaining. As a result, it is not unusual for the parties in this industry to certify for arbitration, whether voluntary or compulsory, 20 to 40 issues, some of which have obviously been left in by either the Amalgamated Association or the employer in order to improve their chances of winning their really basic demands.

For this industry, it appears that voluntary arbitration has been used as a substitute for collective bargaining. And for a short period compulsory arbitration replaced voluntary arbitration.

Telephone Industry

Although the history and present situation of labor relations in the telephone industry have been quite different from those in urban transportation, the policies of the Communication Workers of America (CIO), the dominant union in the telephone industry, also contributed to the use of governmental strike-control machinery. Perhaps because it was a relatively new organization which did not attain the bargaining power enjoyed by some other large unions, CWA apparently determined that it could secure more favorable results through fact finding and arbitration than through collective bargaining. Thus, although CWA maintained official opposition to compulsory arbitration, it actually indicated a preference for such means of settlement.[24]

The Pennsylvania Situation

The Pennsylvania arbitration law is similar to that of Indiana and Wisconsin, except for (1) a last-offer strike vote provision and (2) its narrow coverage which excludes transportation and communication. The last-offer strike vote provision was modeled on the provision in the Taft-Hartley Act and has had similar results. Of the nine votes, eight resulted in rejections of company last offers. The ninth occurred just before the Korean War wage freeze went into effect, and the employees feared that to reject it would deprive them of a wage increase throughout the emergency period.[25]

Under the Pennsylvania law, employees send a case to arbitration by refusing the employer's last offer. In theory, this was a tailor-made provision to encourage arbitration because it invited an arbitration award above the rejected employer's last offer. Actually, Pennsylvania had fewer arbitrations than Indiana, Wisconsin, and New Jersey. There are several reasons for this:

(1) One study found that bargaining relations in most Pennsylvania utilities were sufficiently satisfactory to both labor and management that neither desired to force invocation of the law. The fact that three of the nine cases involved one gas utility gives some support to this viewpoint.

(2) Another reason is that the Pennsylvania act was apparently administered with a conscious effort to discourage the use of arbitration. As one industrialist put it: "You have to go to Harrisburg and camp on the Governor's doorstep for about two weeks and even then he probably won't invoke the law. By that time, the parties usually get so disgusted that they settle the thing themselves."

Probably most important in reducing the number of arbitrations in Pennsylvania is the limited coverage of the statute. For the industries which are covered in Indiana, New Jersey and Wisconsin (but excluded in Pennsylvania) include urban transit and telephone. These industries have been involved in almost one-half the state arbitrations. Moreover, in Pennsylvania, there was no problem of rural electrification wage rates as existed in Wisconsin nor interunion competition in gas plants as existed in New Jersey. Hence the industrial and union factors in Pennsylvania weighed against utilizing the law instead of collective bargaining.

The Florida Situation

Florida did not utilize its law very much, apparently because the opportunity did not arise as for any other reason. The degree of unionism was then lower in Florida, and most disputes which did occur in covered industries did not involve the law. The bitterest, that pertaining to the Miami transit industry, occurred after the *Wisconsin* decision, and caused the Florida law to be struck down by the courts.[26]

The Nebraska Situation

Table 2 summarizes the experience under the Nebraska law. This act is similar to the Indiana type legislation, but it is administered by a permanent three-man Court of Industrial Relations, and it covers all local transportation and public-owned utilities in addition to the coverage of the Indiana type law. The willingness of Nebraska's court to invoke its law when local truckers and taxicab drivers are involved is certainly difficult to justify on the basis of emergency dispute legislation.

Table 2

Arbitration in Nebraska by Industry
1947-1962

Total cases	15	
Taxicab companies	5	
Power districts	5	
Urban transit	3	
Motor freight companies	2	

Source: Letter dated March 14, 1962 from Court of Industrial Relations, State of Nebraska.

Nebraska's power industry is entirely public-owned. The coverage of these government installations by an arbitration law is both unique and interesting in its attempt to provide a means of settlement where employees clearly have no protected right to strike.

Hospital arbitration in Minnesota

As already noted, the arbitration law of Minnesota applies only to charitable hospitals and not those operating for profit. In addition, only "any unsettled issue of maximum hours of work and minimum hourly wage rates" is subject to arbitration, although strikes or lockouts over any issue are forbidden. This latter feature has been strongly criticized by employee groups, who claim that wages won in arbitration can be balanced by unilateral hospital withdrawal of benefits, but this fear has apparently not been realized.

Despite their criticism of the Minnesota arbitration law, hospital employees have not hesitated to use it. The law has been invoked by both professional and nonprofessional hospital workers in Minnesota in recent years in a number of cases. The American Nurses' Association (a professional society which has established a collective bargaining program for its members), as well as unions of nonprofessional hospital workers, realize that they can do better through arbitration than through the use of their limited economic strength. It is noteworthy that surveys have found hospital employees in Minnesota to be more completely unionized than those in most other areas.[27] It is interesting to note that unions trying to organize hospitals in New York have recently successfully supported compulsory arbitration in that state. Organization in Minnesota hospitals is thus being built upon arbitration without collective bargaining over new agreements, having previously existed to a significant degree.

State Arbitration Laws—Evaluation Summary

Little evidence is available about the impact of these state laws in terms of the criteria established in Chapter 2, except for the impact on union power and collective bargaining. Certainly these laws did not decrease union power. The effect on bargaining was direct and profound. Laws designed to protect the public from emergencies were invoked to arbitrate the most minor disputes involving situations where public inconvenience was, at worst, slight. It is noteworthy that the invalidation of these laws invoked little protest and only perfunctory attempts to secure federal legislation which would have revalidated them.

Perhaps the main accomplishment of state arbitration laws was to demonstrate, especially to their industry and management sponsors, how these laws work out in practice. The hope that union power would be diminished proved ill-founded. The impact on collective bargaining discouraged both unions and management. The invalidation of these laws, which were utilized mostly where no great public interest can be found, saw, after their invalidation, no public outcry of a need for reinstatement or additional protection.

NOTES

1. The materials relating to wartime arbitration are based largely on Herbert R. Northrup and Gordon F. Bloom, *Government and Labor* (Homewood: Richard D. Irwin, Inc., 1963), Chapter 13, by permission of the publisher and courtesy of the co-author.

2. For a discussion of the World War I experience, see Alexander Bing, *War-Time Labor Disputes and Their Adjustment* (New York: E. P. Dutton & Co., 1921); and U. S. Department of Labor, Bureau of Labor Statistics, *National War Labor Board*, Bulletin No. 287 (Washington, D. C.: U. S. Government Printing Office, 1922).

3. The World War I Board also pioneered in such questions as representation elections, appropriate bargaining unit, majority rule, etc., and thus established precedents for various NRA boards and the National Labor Relations Board.

4. J. Shister, "The National War Labor Board: Its Significance," *Journal of Political Economy*, Vol. LIII (March 1945), pp. 39-40.

5. George W. Taylor, "Wage Regulation in Post-War America," *American Economic Review*, Vol. XXXIV (March 1944), Supplement), p. 188.

6. Ludwig Teller, "Government Seizure in Labor Disputes," *Harvard Law Review*, Vol. LX (March 1947), p. 1020.

7. Nineteen of these seizure cases arose from employer noncompliance, 21 from union noncompliance. See W. E. Chalmers, "Voluntarism and Compulsion in Dispute Settlement," in *Problems and Policies of Dispute Settlement and Wage Stabilization during World War II*, Bulletin No. 1009 (Washington, D. C.: U. S. Department of Labor, Bureau of Labor Statistics, 1950), p. 59.

8. We shall analyze experiences under government seizure in Appendix B.

9. Data on union membership, union security and strikes for the United States are taken from official compilations of the U. S. Bureau of Labor Statistics.

10. *Termination Report of the National War Labor Board* (Washington, D. C.: U. S. Department of Labor, 1946), Vol. 1, p. 486.

11. See below, Chapter 4.

12. E. B. McNatt, "Problems of Case Processing," in *Problems and Poli-*

cies of Dispute Settlement and Wage Stabilization . . . op. cit., pp. 331, 333, 335.

13. The material on state arbitration laws is based upon Herbert R. Northrup and Richard L. Rowan, "Arbitration and Collective Bargaining: An Analysis of State Experience," *Labor Law Journal,* Vol. XII (February 1963), pp. 178-191, by permission of the publisher and courtesy of the co-author. The full article is reprinted as Appendix A.

14. *Wolff Packing Co. v. Court of Industrial Relations,* 262 U. S. 522 (1923); 267 U. S. 552 (1925).

15. For a careful history of the Kansas law, see D. Gagliardo, *The Kansas Industrial Court,* University of Kansas Publications, Lawrence, Kansas, 1941.

16. New Jersey, Indiana, Florida, Wisconsin, Pennsylvania, Michigan, Nebraska, and Minnesota.

17. *Amalgamated Association v. Wisconsin Employment Relations Board,* 340 U. S. 383 (1951). The legal issues involving state and federal laws are discussed in Chapter 11 and Appendices A-D.

18. The Michigan law was quickly found unconstitutional by the state courts because of a procedural defect. *Local 170, Transport Workers' Union v. Gadela,* 34 N.W. (2d) 71 (1948). A previous Michigan fact finding statute then became operative again. It is discussed in Appendix C.

19. The seizure aspect of the New Jersey law is discussed in Appendix B.

20. See Appendix C.

21. The author made a field survey in 1951 among utilities affected by these laws. Most felt quite strongly that their prospects for rate increases would be enhanced by a state board ordered wage increase. See also the comment of a New Jersey public utility commissioner, reported in the *Newark Evening News,* January 31, 1951, p. 2, which strongly supports this view.

22. See Note 18 above.

23. E. P. Schmidt, *Industrial Relations in Urban Transportation* (Minneapolis: University of Minnesota Press, 1937), p. 194.

24. See the report of CWA Vice-President A. T. Jones to the 1950 CWA Convention, as summarized in "Daily Labor Report," No. 124, June 27, 1950, pp. A-6, A-7. Another indication of the desire of CWA officials to use strike-control machinery was their unsuccessful attempts to bring Western Electric workers within these laws in Florida and Wisconsin.

25. See Chapter 7, Table 4, for Taft-Hartley experience.

26. Henderson v. Florida ex rel. Lee, 65 So. (2d) 22 (1953).

27. Cited in H. Parker, "The Laws Governing Labor-Management Relations in Michigan Hospitals," *Labor Law Journal,* Vol. XII (October 1961), p. 973, n. 9.

4 Key Foreign Experiences

Foreign experience is frequently cited for support by both the proponents and opponents of government intervention in labor disputes. There exists for many countries a documented and factual analysis as to how these foreign systems work and what environmental factors have contributed to their development and problems. A number of such studies are reproduced in Appendices E and N. In this chapter, we summarize the compulsory arbitration experience, particularly of Australia and New Zealand, with a shorter summary of the South African system and some comments on the spread of compulsory arbitration to the underdeveloped countries.[1]

Compulsory Arbitration in Australia

Superficially, few countries seem to provide a better setting than Australia for the development of good industrial relationships. The Australian population of ten million is still relatively homogeneous, concentrated largely in less than a dozen cities, has a single language, a high level of literacy, and a significant middle class. Differences in standards of living between states and within each state are small, while work methods vary very little from one place to another.

From the middle of the nineteenth century a vigorous trade union movement has existed in Australia. Today, about 60 percent of wage and salary earners belong to unions. Organization among the employers has been equally advanced. The position can be summed up that there are no substantial areas of employment anywhere in Australia in which group relations between employers and employees do not exist, whatever the nature of those relations may be. But the entire system of unionism and collective bargaining is structured on the basis of complex state-federal compulsory arbitration machinery which has spurred the growth of unionism, but has failed to bring industrial peace to the country.

"Compulsory arbitration has, of course, been a feature of the industrial relations systems of Australia and New Zealand for a very long time. In these countries it was introduced (at a time when trade unionism was very weak) in the belief that it would foster the organization of labour, and at the same time ensure that wage earners received a fair reward for their labours."[2] Thus does the eminent British labor economist, B. C. Roberts, explain the genesis of compulsory arbitration in these two countries.

In Australia, the conditions of work of all but a small minority of workers (and those mostly in agriculture) have been regulated for the better part of a half century by awards of federal and state arbitration and conciliation machinery and state wage boards. Under federal law and the law of four of the states (New South Wales, Queensland, South Australia, and Western Australia) intervention takes the form, for the greatest part, of conciliation and then arbitration through industrial courts. In the two remaining states (Victoria and Tasmania) it is effected through the agency of a number of wage boards, each assigned to a defined trade or group of trades. There is no organic connection between federal and state industrial tribunals (that is, no system of appeals), but in the event of a conflict the federal tribunal awards prevail.[3] At present, federal awards regulate the employment of slightly more than 40 percent of the workers subject to awards or determination.

In the federal sphere only the Commonwealth Arbitration Court and the Commonwealth Conciliation Commissioners operate to regulate wages, hours of work, and employment conditions of members of national or interstate unions. The state tribunals, on the other hand, regulate the wages and other conditions of workers who are members of intrastate unions.

In addition to federal and state tribunals, there are an appreciable number of special tribunals which have been created to deal with wages and related matters in particular cases. Some of these special tribunals, such as the Public Service Arbitration, function at the federal level, while the Western Australian Coal Industry Tribunal functions at the state level. In this complex system there is no doubt as to which jurisdiction is the most significant.

"Despite constitutional limitation upon its powers, the Commonwealth Arbitration Court has developed into the most important and influential tribunal in Australia. Not only do federal awards cover approximately 40 percent of all workers, but as already mentioned, tribunals in several states are obliged to incorporate federal wage standards in their respective awards, while most of the tribunals usually follow the federal standard very closely."[4]

The Commonwealth Arbitration Court Machinery and Union Control

Since the passsage of the Commonwealth Court of Conciliation and Arbitration Act of 1904, Australian labor unions have been under a form of public control and regulation. Under this Act a registered union is given a virtual monoply in its trade or industry to represent workers during collective bargaining processes. The chief objective of the Act was to encourage the organization of representative bodies of employers and employees and their registration under the Act.[5] The jurisdiction of the Court has been interpreted very liberally, and practically all national labor unions have found it advantageous to register under it.

Australian workers have sought their ends through political means. The Labour Party has long been either in power, or narrowly out of authority. But, as we shall note below, there has been a corresponding neglect of local union and shop leadership development. One result has been the short strike, also discussed below. A related factor has been intense Communist infiltration and leadership at the local level. The register system is not only an attempt to control jurisdictional and representation disputes; it is also aimed at controlling Communist infiltration. Parenthetically, it clearly *limits* freedom of association. For it denies workers a choice of unions—they must usually choose the registered organization, or be denied the use of government machinery upon which the unions depend. And it increases the dependency of unions on government while eliminating competitive unionism which, like all competition, can be a spur to improvement.

"Only a registered union can have the benefits of the Act, and those benefits are of great importance. A registered union can make claims against employers with respect to wages, hours, working conditions, and other industrial matters, and if agreement cannot be reached by negotiation, the employer can be required to appear before a Conciliation Commissioner or the Court for a compulsory conference. If agreement cannot be reached with the aid of conciliation the Commissioner or the Court will proceed to settle the dispute by arbitration, make an award which lays down minimum standards which are legally enforceable against the employers. . . . In order to obtain these advantages, however, a union becomes subject to a considerable amount of regulation and control by the Commonwealth Arbitration Court and its Registrar."[6]

The Act has been amended from time to time, with the amendments of 1949 and 1951 proving of particular interest. In the former case a labor government, and in the latter case a liberal government attempted to put more teeth into the Act so that fraud and irregularities might be prevented in those unions under Communist control. By 1951 the Act had been amended to require secret ballot voting and union elections held under the auspices of the Court when any group of union members requested it. However, union elections under Court auspices have not provided the complete solution to Communist domination, since in some unions Communist elements have been freely elected.

Some of the most interesting interventions into union internal affairs have been concerned with the improper expulsion or suspension of union members. The Court may disallow a union rule which imposes unreasonable conditions, such as an exesssive initiation fee, or in the case where the Court terms union rules as "tyrannical or oppressive," it may de-register the union.[7] This has been done in a few cases. In Australia, as in the United States, government support of unions has been followed by government control.

Bargaining Weapons, Strikes, and Benefits

Although the right to utilize strikes and lockouts varies among jurisdictions, these rights have certainly been severely limited in Australia. For example, the South Australian Industrial Code contains a flat prohibition on strikes and lockouts, with penalties to enforce this code. The Queensland Industrial Conciliation and Arbitration Act specifies that all strikes are illegal unless authorized by a secret ballot conducted by the registrar of the Court. The New South Wales legislation allows only certain types of strikes while the Tasmanian wages board directly forbids strikes and lockouts.[8]

Under the Commonwealth machinery, the strike or lockout is illegal once a union is registered. But strikes remain a frequent occurrence. Studies by Professors Kenneth Walker,[9] James W. Kuhn (see Appendix E), Arthur Ross, and Paul Hartman,[10] as well as the annual data published by the International Labour Office,[11] all confirm frequent occurrence of stoppages despite the existence of the compulsory arbitration system and the fact that most of these strikes are illegal.

Moreover, in recent years work stoppages have been increasing in number in Australia. In 1959, Mr. Ian Sharp of Melbourne wrote in *The Journal of Industrial Relations* (the Australian professional journal in this field) "that the number of disputes per year since 1950 has been mainly in excess of the number in years prior to that date and has been considerably higher than the pre-war level, even allowing for population growth and increase in industrial establishments. Furthermore, whatever decline there has been in the number of disputes has occurred almost entirely in the coal mining industry. If that industry, which has been under particular economic stress in recent years, is excluded, it becomes clear, beyond doubt, that the number disputes has been increasing quite sharply."[12]

This trend has continued. In 1963, the number of strikes in most major groupings increased over the previous year and again in 1964, the latest year for which data are available, the statistics show that there was a considerable increase in the level of industrial disputes over the previous year.[13] There are several reasons for this. First of all, in years past, a number of key unions were dominated by left-wing or Communist elements and either refused to register, or paid no heed to registration obligations. These unions have been concentrated in mining and longshore, which, in Australia, as in many other countries, have had a record of frequent industrial stoppages.[14]

Most significant, however, in the Australian strike situation is the effect of the compulsory arbitration machinery on the risk of strikes to strikers and on the character and stability of local union leadership. It was noted in Chapter 3, that during World War II, a large number of strikes occurred in the United States which lasted only a short period. The wartime compulsory arbitration system was punctured by these stoppages which employees engaged in with the knowledge that no risk of long idleness was involved. Government machinery would promptly return them to work.

So it is in Australia. Stoppages in most years are more frequent relative to labor force, than in any other country. Moreover, these strikes involve a large percentage of employees—20 percent year after year. But the strikes are of a short duration. Workers protest against awards of the arbitration courts, or often because the legalistic red tape involved in processing a case consumes so much time. But the stoppage ends quickly, for its purpose is usually to get attention, not to make a major economic gain.

Lack of effective local, or often national, union leadership and organization is another reason for the poor strike record of Australia. With a union movement heavily dependent upon government and political support, with the most able union leaders siphoned into political work, and with the experience that disputes will end up before a government board anyway, there is little incentive to attract promising persons into local union activity and even less incentive to settle at the local level. The failure of the Australian system to distinguish between disputes over new agreements (interest disputes) and disputes over grievances or contract interpretation (rights disputes) aggravates this problem because it means that any significant dispute of either kind is likely to be decided by a government tribunal rather than at a bargaining session.

The disinterest in local organization and in service to the rank and file has also aided Communist infiltration at the shop level. This has undoubtedly contributed to the rash of strikes which over the years has featured the Australian labor relations scene, along with its compulsory arbitration system.

In recent years, the separation of the national union leadership from the rank and file has become almost formalized by the creation of local shop councils to handle local union work. These have been condemned as Communist inspired by top union leadership, but apparently are not always so. The councils have constituted a challenge to the union "establishment" by taking strike action without union approval.[15]

The interest of the rank and file in shop councils indicates the remoteness of dispute settlement in Australia from the union member. "Thus while strike action is still something in respect of which the rank and file of unions generally have a direct say, the remedying of grievances and the termination of disputes through the public machinery of conciliation and arbitration has become dependent not on rank and file judgment and action, but on the services of specialists in that field, be they union officials, industrial advocates, or barristers."[16]

Although the number of strikes and worker participation therein is annually often twice the rate as in the United States, the *duration* of strikes in Australia is so much shorter. Only one-half as many man days per worker are lost from strikes in Australia as in the United States. Proponents of the Australian system have hailed this statistic as a great accomplishment of the Australian system. Perhaps it is. But when a breakdown does occur, as it has frequently in some industries, defiance has resulted in either ignoring the law or in the drastic penalties far beyond de-registering—violence, the use of troops, stiff fines, etc., to break the strike. The latter are spectacular. But the usual procedure is to ignore the violation of law, for, in fact, penalties are rarely enforced. After a careful analysis of experience, it was concluded that "the threat of severe penalties does not seem to have improved the prospect of eliminating work stoppages . . . nor was the . . . law on this subject . . . enforced, nor expected to be enforced in the great majority of cases."[17]

Concluding Remarks—Australia

Compulsory arbitration has had a profound influence on trade union development in Australia. Compulsory arbitration induced unorganized employees to organize, induced employers to negotiate

The following article appeared in the *New York Times*, February 2, 1965.

WALKOUT BY MINERS HURTING AUSTRALIA; DISPUTE BROADENS

BY TILLMAN DURDIN

Special to The New York Times

SYDNEY, Australia, Jan. 32—A labor dispute at the Big Mount Isa copper, lead and zinc mines in northwest Queensland is having increasingly serious national repercussions.

Mines and related operations of the Mount Isa Company constitute the largest single industrial enterprise in northern Australia. A United States concern, the American Smelting and Refining Company, has a majority interest in the Mount Isa Company.

The drastic emergency orders issued last week by the Queensland government to deal with the dispute over pay and other matters have failed to promote a settlement. The mines have not been operating since the middle of December and workers decided at a meeting today not to end the walkout.

The company had hoped that enough workers would report tomorrow to permit mining to restart. Because of the workers' decision, the company plans to halt work being done outside the mines on Tuesday.

This means that 700 men, in addition to several thousand miners, will not be working and that virtually every company activity at Mount Isa will come to a halt.

The Mount Isa mines produce most of Australia's copper needs and a large part of their output is sold abroad. The labor dispute is costing the mining company and the Australian economy millions of dollars a week.

The Queensland government's emergency orders empowered the police to arrest without warrant anyone trying to interfere with the resumption of work at the mines. The police were also authorized to prevent anyone who might be considered likely to prejudice the resumption of work from going to Mount Isa.

The emergency orders were meant to block contact between the mineworkers and rebel labor leaders, who are leading the dispute in defiance of regular officials of the Australian Workers Union.

The orders are considered so drastic, however, that union officials and most other labor elements in Australia have swung in behind the Mount Isa miners.

Many labor leaders have termed Queensland's action "Gestapo tactics." Moderate labor officials charge that the orders have played into the hands of the Mount Isa rebels, including the Communists who are said to be in the background.

before an arbitration tribunal, and induced white collar and government employees to organize. Australia has thus become one of the most highly unionized countries in the western world, but the union organization at the local level has been neglected in the process. Today, more than 60 percent of the employed labor force is in trade unions, largely because of the artificial creation of the arbitration system. Certainly, the system has enhanced union power, but has made it utterly dependent on government.

There is some indication that the trade unions are growing restless under the regulations imposed upon them. For example, "The president of the Australian Council of Trade Unions advised visiting students from Asian countries, 'Don't allow your workers' organizations to become shackled as we have become in Australia, through too much legalizing of the system.' "[18]

As to the effect on collective bargaining, all evidence points to the tendency to paralyze the propensity to settle and thus to bring to the arbitration courts a myriad of disputes which under a freer bargaining system would be settled by the parties themselves. In recent years, the red tape delays and tangled legalistic approach have induced a few industries and unions to settle their own disputes.[19] The fact that this is so novel as to cause detailed comment is illustrative of the state of collective bargaining in Australia.

There can be no doubt that the Australian arbitration system has not succeeded in eliminating strikes and lockouts. It may have shortened strikes, but it certainly has increased their number. Any one who believes that the existence of a compulsory arbitration system will either curb unionism or will eliminate or reduce the number of strikes would be well advised to make a realistic study of Australian experience.

One analyst has credited the Australian arbitration system with reducing work hours to forty per week and raising the level of real wages. He argues that these improvements have not been achieved at the expense of the economic well-being of the country.[20] He does not deal with the question of whether the improvements would have been greater or less under a freer collective bargaining system.

On the other hand, Professor K. F. Walker notes that the Australian compulsory arbitration has certain built-in rigidities. "On a rising market arbitration prevents the workers from obtaining full advantage of their economic power due to the keen demand for labor. On a falling market arbitration obstructs employers from obtaining the full advantages of their economic power due to the scarcity of jobs and the weakness of trade unions through abnormal unemployment."[21] There seems to be general agreement that these rigidities exist in Australia and that another effect is to narrow skill differentials so that the unskilled are over priced relative to the skilled. That such a rigidity reduces the incentive to progress up the occupational ladder seems certain.

Finally, there has been some criticism of the role of the Commonwealth Arbitration Court's wage determination policy and national economic policy. Because of the nature of the Court's powers it is invariably involved in general reviews of the state of the national economy. Yet the Court appears to conduct its operations outside the framework of general economic policy and without channels of communication between it and policy-making agencies.

Compulsory Arbitration in New Zealand

Compulsory arbitration in New Zealand actually antedates the Australian system, dating from 1894. As already noted, a prime purpose of the law was the encouragement of unionization, as well as the maintenance of industrial peace. Compulsory arbitration has thus been in effect in New Zealand for almost 70 years, with only a break of four between 1932 and 1936 when it was abolished before being reinstituted. A small country, New Zealand does not have the complicated federal-state relationships in arbitration as does Australia.

As in Australia, unions must register to be assured of a noncompetitive jurisdiction and to take advantage of the law. Also, as in Australia, the New Zealand Court has jurisdiction over such matters as union financial records and fairness of union elections. In addition, however, New Zealand prescribes *compulsory union membership*. All workers covered by agreement must by law join the union which represents them. This aspect of the law dates from an enactment of the Labour Government of 1936.[22]

Perhaps because of its less industrialized character, New Zealand has escaped from some of the turmoil which features the Australian scene. Communist infiltration has made little progress, and historically the land has been relatively strike free. The smallness of the country mitigates the separation of shop and union with the system of arbitration. Recently, however, the incidence of strikes has risen rather sharply, particularly in manufacturing.[23] Whether this reflects a growing discontent with the situation remains to be determined.

Strikes are outlawed under compulsory arbitration in New Zealand. The principal penalty, de-registration and loss of compulsory membership, however, can be withstood by a strong union with a staunch voluntary following, and are rarely used.

"The penalties provided in the Act for illegal stoppages are seldom invoked, the main object of restoring a good working relationship between the parties being somewhat incompatible with the extraction of penalties. One of the strongest penalties against strikes is the power of the Minister of Labour in certain circumstances to cancel the registration of an offending union or to cancel its award or industrial agreement. As with the other penalties this power is seldom used."[24]

Compulsory arbitration in New Zealand is part of one of the most complete state welfare systems in the world. The main expenditures of the New Zealand government are for welfare (Britain and the United States are depended upon for defense), with state pensions, health, house mortgages, and most types of insurances provided. Extremes of income is avoided and wage differentials narrowed by the compulsory arbitration system.[25] Productivity is relaxed and not high at the work place.[26]

New Zealand since World War II has been a relatively prosperous country, with its magnificent sheep herds providing a key to its economic well-being. But this was not always so. In 1932, during the severe depression, the Conservatives came to power and abolished compulsory arbitration because the Arbitration Court was artificially keeping union strength and wage levels too high for the national wellbeing. Four years later, however, the Labour Party, back in power, reinstituted compulsory arbitration and added compulsory union membership. Since then, the system has been retained as a pillar of this welfare state.

A feature of the New Zealand system, to which proponents point with pride, is that 75 percent of the disputes are usually settled by conciliation (mediation) without resort to the arbitration machinery. But a more careful analysis shows that the awards of the arbitration Court are made in key cases in such detail that the main task of the conciliator is to show the parties the path upon which they must tread and to point out to them the results that are inevitable if they take the trouble to go to arbitration. Hence, conciliation in New Zealand is something quite different than mediating a dispute in the vast, complicated economy of the United States.

New Zealand has a population about the size of, but much more homogeneous than, Detroit. Its people are apparently tuned to a welfare capitalism and state-dependent unionism. Its experience is interesting, but much less appropriate for United States comparison than is Australia's—which is likewise a much smaller and simpler economy than ours.

Other Compulsory Arbitration Systems

Besides Australia and New Zealand, a number of other countries have experimented with forms of compulsory arbitration. In this section, a brief resume is given of the South African situation, and of that in various underdeveloped countries.

South Africa

South Africa has a low strike incidence by any international comparison. The reasons appear to be in its racial policies and growth economy.

The unions are composed largely of white workers who occupy the skilled jobs, the white-collar jobs, and to a large extent, the supervisory jobs. The white unions bar Negroes and collaborate with the government in return for policies which preclude colored worker competition for jobs. Unskilled whites occupy posts in the state and local governments, on the state-owned railways, and to a lesser extent, in manufacturing—wherever sheltered jobs exist. A shortage of manpower provides a constant demand for white labor.[27]

The Suppression of Communism Act of 1950 has been a constant source of second thought to leaders who may be contemplating action likely to incur government disfavor. Anyone can be incarcerated and charged as a Communist without any rights whatsoever, even to a trial.

Employers are almost exclusively white and well-organized, showing little hostility to white unions or unwillingness to bargain collectively. The agreements and the laws require registration and make it very difficult for rival unions to organize. In addition, strikes are illegal on matters covered by an agreement during its currency or if the issue in dispute is not so covered before the parties have met to consider the matter. Voluntary arbitration may be resorted to but is ultimately compulsory in the case of the workers engaged in essential services which are widely defined. There are other limitations and constraints on strikes, for the government fears that a strike may induce white and Negro labor collaboration.

The continued uncritical propagation of industrial peace as an unmixed blessing has almost certainly had a significant if indeterminate effect on the general willingness to strike . . . whites have thrived not on industrial militancy but on economic expansion and racial restrictions.[28]

African workers are forbidden to organize, poorly paid, and bear the brunt of racially discriminatory policies. Police and soldiers are used to break up any strikes or collective action and break them up brutally. Systematic hostility is against any unionization of the non-white majority. Moreover, by using migrants from other areas in the mines, chemicals, explosives, and iron and steel industry, who are in South Africa for just a given period, any attempt at racial solidarity is broken up. It would appear that industrial peace will prevail as long as the present government combination of restriction and industrial development also prevails.

The Underdeveloped Countries

In the underdeveloped countries of Africa, Asia, and various island areas, labor movements are largely creations of government. There strength without government support is negligible. In such situations, compulsory arbitration has frequently been established. India, for example, instituted such arbitration in order to build up unionism.[29]

In many of the underdeveloped countries, compulsory arbitration has been instituted also because of the belief that strikes are inconsistent with national goals. Actually, governments in newly independent countries of Africa and Asia "fear strikes for both political and economic reasons. Where political opposition has been eliminated they are afraid that industrial unrest may be provoked and strikes used as a means of overthrowing their rule."[30]

Moreover, as several observers have pointed out,[31] the leaders of these countries have a naive concept of the working of the free market system and an equally naive overestimation of the ability of civil servants to accomplish economic goals and to regulate economic activity. Equating modern capitalism with the colonial monopolies and cartels which they encountered as subject nations, they see socialism and independence as almost synonymous concepts. The regulation of enterprise to them also requires the regulation of unionism and industrial relations. Despite repeated failures to achieve their goals, regulation of economic activity increases rather than decreases, and with it more stringent controls over industrial relations. "It would be difficult to prove from the history of the more advanced countries that the prevention of strikes by law would have resulted in an increase in the rate of economic growth. However, the fact that the case for making strikes illegal is not based upon any proven economic analysis is not likely to influence governments that have decided not to tolerate industrial stoppages."[32]

Not only is there no proof that compulsory arbitration contributes to economic growth in the underdeveloped countries, but rather there is a strong presumption and some evidence that it is usually exactly the opposite. Roberts, for example, believes that "the effects of bottling up grievances that would otherwise have led to strikes results in the slowing down of adaptation to change and to the adoption of modern organizational methods and other injustices of industrial development. The pressures generated by strikes may have a stimulating effect that is more beneficial to economic growth than a deterrent to it.[33]

In India, "A clear pattern of the determination to control and regulate the level of wages and the wage structure through the authority of the state on principles of fairness and equity is now evident.[34] But the economics of growth, and "fairness and equity" to wage earners often require different policies. Repeatedly, governments in India and in countries once ruled by the British, have found that "compulsory arbitration has enabled unions to force them to make larger concessions to workers in essential industries than was justified on the grounds of economic policy."[35] In such instances, the giving of concessions is regarded as less an evil than would exist if settlements were permitted by collective bargaining, again without either reasoned theory or demonstrated proof.

Given the state of their economies, of industrial development, and of unionism, the situation and experience of the underdeveloped countries provided little experience of use to the United States—except perhaps further proof that compulsory arbitration is no panacea for such economies either.

NOTES

1. The basic research for this chapter was performed by Mr. Arthur Donner, formerly my research assistant.

2. B. C. Roberts, *Labour in the Tropical Countries of the Commonwealth* (Durham, N. C.: Duke University Press, 1964), p. 324.

3. Orwell Foenander, "The Achievement and Significance of Industrial Regulations in Australia," *International Labour Review*, Vol. LXXV (February 1957), pp. 105-106.

4. D. W. Oxnam, "Industrial Arbitration in Australia: Its Effects on Wages and Unions," *Industrial and Labor Relations Review*, Vol. IX (July 1956), p. 615.

5. *Ibid.*, p. 252.

6. *Ibid.*, p. 253.

7. *Ibid.*, p. 257.

8. K. F. Walker, *Industrial Relations in Australia* (Cambridge, Mass.: Harvard University Press, 1956), pp. 31-32.

9. *Ibid.*, passim.

10. Arthur M. Ross and Paul T. Hartman, *Changing Patterns of Industrial Conflict* (New York: John Wiley & Sons, Inc., 1960), pp. 141-160.

11. See, e.g., *Yearbook of Labour Statistics*, 1964 (Geneva: International Labour Office, 1965), pp. 37 *et seq.*

12. Ian Sharp, "Some Features of the Australian Industrial Relations Scene," *The Journal of Industrial Relations*, Vol. 1 (April 1959), p. 5.

13. J. R. Kerr, "Industrial Relations 1963-1964," *The Journal of Industrial Relations*, Vol. 6 (November 1964), pp. 173-174; *Ibid.*, "Industrial Relations, 1964-65," *loc. cit.* Vol. 7 (July 1965), page 112.

14. Ross and Hartman, *op. cit.*, pp. 147-148.

15. Kerr, *op. cit.*, pp. 173-175.

16. Sharp, *op. cit.*, p. 3.

17. Charles P. Mills, "The Enforcement of Penalties Against Strikes," *The Journal of Industrial Relations*, Vol. II (April 1960), p. 41.

18. Quoted by L. S. Merrifield, "Regulation of Union Elections in Australia," *Industrial and Labor Relations Review*, Vol. X (January 1957), p. 269.

19. See, e.g., F. T. deVyver, "The Melbourne Building Industry Agreement," *The Journal of Industrial Relations*, Vol. I (April 1959), pp. 7-19.

20. Foenander, *op. cit.*, pp. 110-113.

21. Walker, *op. cit.*, p. 4. See also, E. L. Wheelwright, "The Dilemma of Margins," *The Journal of Industrial Relations*, Vol. II (April 1960), p. 50.

22. A detailed account of the New Zealand system is found in N. S. Woods, *Industrial Conciliation and Arbitration in New Zealand* (Wellington, N. Z.: R. E. Owen, Government Printer, 1963).

23. *Yearbook of Labour Statistics*, 1964, p. 601.

24. Woods, *op. cit.*, p. 13.

25. See G. H. Sorrell, "The Determination of Wages in New Zealand," *The Journal of Industrial Relations*, Vol. V (October 1963), pp. 120-134.

26. C. J. V. Murphy, "Traveler in Small Utopia," *Fortune*, Vol. LXXI (May 1965), pp. 238, 242.

27. See Garfield Clack, "Industrial Peace in South Africa," *British Journal of Industrial Relations*, Vol. I (February 1960), pp. 94-106, which is reproduced in Appendix M.

28. *Ibid.*

29. Roberts, *op. cit.*, p. 324; see also, Paul L. Kleinsorge, "Singapore's Industrial Arbitration Court: Collective Bargaining with Compulsory Arbitration," *Industrial and Labor Relations Review*, Vol. XVII (June 1964), pp. 556-565.

30. Roberts, *op. cit.*, p. 323.

31. *Ibid.*, Elliot J. Berg, "Socialism and Economic Development in Tropical Africa," *Quarterly Journal of Economics*, Vol. LXXVIII (November 1964), pp. 549-573, and John C. H. Fei and Gustav Ranis, *Development of the Labor Surplus Economy: Theory and Policy* (Homewood: Richard D. Irwin, Inc., 1964).

32. Roberts, *op. cit.*, p. 324.

33. *Ibid.*, pp. 323-324.

34. A. J. Fonseca, *Wage Determination and Organized Labour in India* (London: Oxford University Press, 1964), p. 101.

35. Roberts, *op. cit.*, p. 327.

CHAPTER

5 From Fact Finding to Arbitration

THE RAILWAY LABOR ACT provides the framework for the most comprehensive control of labor relations and labor disputes on the American scene, and the most detailed experience with fact finding procedure. The present basic law, the Railway Labor Act of 1926, as amended in 1934 and 1951, is an outgrowth of legislative experimentation and government intervention which dates back to the 1880's.[1] In 1936, the air transport industry was brought under the Act; and in 1963, arbitration of two aspects of the dispute involving work rules was ordered by a special and limited amendment to the Act. After a brief summary of the Act, this chapter contains an analysis of its main features.[2]

RAILWAY LABOR ACT—BACKGROUND AND SUMMARY

Being dissatisfied with the then existing governmental intervention machinery which followed government operation of the railroads during World War I, railway management and unions agreed on a bill which became the Railway Labor Act of 1926. This Act made it the duty of the parties to exert every reasonable effort to "make and maintain agreements concerning rates of pay [and] working conditions," and to attempt to adjust all differences by peaceful methods. A five-man, nonpartisan Board of Mediation was created, which attempted mediation if the parties could not agree among themselves. The board was further instructed to urge voluntary arbitration if mediation proved unsuccessful. If arbitration was refused and the dispute was such as "substantially to interrupt interstate commerce," the Board of Mediation was instructed to notify the President, who could create special emergency boards to investigate and publish findings. During the pendency of these various proceedings and until thirty days after the report of the emergency board, neither party was to alter "the conditions out of which the dispute arose" except by mutual agreement. The parties, however, were under no legal obligation to accept the recommendations of the emergency board.

The Act of 1926 also provided that "boards of adjustment shall be created" by the parties for the purpose of handling disputes arising out of the interpretation of agreements. Under the provision the boards established by the operating brotherhoods under the Transportation Act of 1920 continued in operation. In the case of the nonoperating groups, however, negotiations between the carriers and the unions broke down as to whether the boards should be regional or local in scope. Some three hundred adjustment boards were established, but many not until several years after 1926; and for many classes of employees, no boards were set up. Moreover, the adjustment machinery provided no means to break deadlocks, and since the boards were all bipartisan in character, deadlocks occurred with increasing frequency, so that by 1934, when the adjustment boards were abolished, some 2,500 disputes remained to be adjudicated.[3]

The Railway Labor Act of 1926 also provided (Section 2, Third): "Representatives, for the purpose of this Act, shall be designated by the respective parties in such manner as may be provided in their corporate organization or unincorporated association, or by other means of collective action, without interference, influence or coercion exercised by either party over the self-organization, or designation of representatives by the other." No specific machinery for the determination of employee bargaining representatives was contained in this law, however; nor did it compel carriers to deal solely with the representative of the majority. The Act also contained no specific penalties for carriers which violated prohibitions against interference with the free choice of representatives by employees, as guaranteed by Section 2, Third. The Supreme Court, however, ruled that such interference was subject to the injunctive process.[4]

The period 1926-1934, during which railway labor relations were conducted under the 1926 legislation, was featured by peace on the rails. Only two strikes occurred, and but ten emergency boards were appointed, half of the latter during the last year of the Act's operation. The increased threats to railway labor peace during the last year of the Act's unamended incumbency have been attributed to inherent defects in the legislation.[5] A more realistic analysis, however, would probably find the causes of unrest in the Great Depression and the general political upheaval which took place after 1933.

The 1934 Legislation

Whatever its merits, the 1926 Act was found defective by the railway unions on several counts. They desired national adjustment boards with effective machinery for breaking deadlocks and for enforcing awards; they desired specific penalties, in addition to the injunctive process, to prevent carriers' influence over the choice of employees' representatives; they desired formal machinery by which bargaining agents could be selected; and they desired drastic changes in the personnel of the Board of Mediation, which had fallen from their favor. All these objectives they achieved by the 1934 amendments to the Railway Labor Act, which were backed by the railway unions, assisted materially by the late Joseph B. Eastman, then Federal Coordinator of Transportation, and which were bitterly opposed by the carriers.

The amended Railway Labor Act maintains the basic structure of the 1926 legislation insofar as mediation, arbitration, and the appointment of emergency boards are concerned. The main difference in this respect is that the five-man Board of Mediation was abolished and replaced by a three-man National Mediation Board.

The 1934 amendments established the National Railroad Adjustment Board, which has jurisdiction over grievances and disputes arising out of the interpretations of agreements. The Adjustment Board is a bipartisan agency composed of thirty-six members, half of whom are selected and compensated by the carriers, and half by unions "national in scope." (Thus, smaller organizations of workers have no representation on the Adjustment Board.) The work of the Adjustment Board is divided into four divisions, each of which has jurisdiction over certain crafts. If a division deadlocks, referees are appointed by the National Mediation Board or by the division if it can agree on a selection.

The 1934 amendments also provided elaborate safeguards for the free choice of employee representatives by setting forth a list of unfair labor practices similar to those contained in the National Labor Relations (Wagner) Act. Enforcement is different from the Wagner Act, in that violations are punishable by criminal penalties and prosecution is under the jurisdiction of the Department of Justice. These penalties, of course, supplement the employees' right to use the injunctive process.

Prior to 1951, union security and check-off provisions were outlawed under the Railway Labor Act, but in that year Congress amended the law to permit such agreements. Most of the industry then acceded to union demands to grant the union shop and the check-off.

In 1936, the air transport industry was brought under all the provisions of the Railway Labor Act except those pertaining to the National Railroad Adjustment Board. That agency's jurisdiction is confined to the railway industry. Provision is made, however, for a National Air Transport Board when the National Mediation Board deems it desirable; but thus far there has been no demand for the establishment of such an agency.

ANALYSIS OF THE RAILWAY LABOR ACT— THE DISPUTES PROCEDURE

The Railway Labor Act is thus a comprehensive code of labor legislation which (1) established definite provisions for the conduct of negotiations and provides for the postponement of strikes or lockouts until a variety of government intervenor techniques have occurred; (2) provides for compulsory arbitration of grievance disputes before a national, publicly supported bipartisan board; (3) provides for a method of selecting bargaining representatives and proscribes employer unfair labor practices; and (4) applies the principles and practices of the Act (except for compulsory arbitration of grievances) which were developed in the railroad industry to a new industry—air transportation. What have been the results?

Required Collective Bargaining

Section 2, First, of the Railway Labor Act establishes "the duty of all carriers, their officers, agents and employees to exert every reasonable effort to make and maintain agreements concerning rates of pay, rules, and working conditions and to settle all disputes" peacefully. Ensuing paragraphs of the same section set forth a procedure for collective bargaining which includes (1) written request for a conference relating to a dispute served by one party on the other; (2) written reply by the second party, setting a time and place mutually agreeable for a conference; (3) requirement that the conference be held within twenty days after the receipt of the original notice at a location "upon the line of the carrier," except that the time and place may be altered by mutual agreement; and (4) prohibition of unilateral changes in contracts except in the manner prescribed in the Act.

Thus the first basic element in the Railway Labor Act's disputes settlement is the obligation of the carriers to make and to maintain collective agreements which, by custom, are written agreements. Corollary to this obligation is a second one—the duty to dispose of disputes quickly and peacefully.

The National Mediation Board, the Railway Labor Act's mediation agency, has placed much stress on the policy pronouncement and the procedure for collective bargaining embodied in the Act. The Board as well as many other authorities have argued that the Act's stated policy and procedure encourage collective bargaining and collective agreements which, it believes, are "primarily" responsible for the alleged (and not proved) "peaceful nature" of collective bargaining in the railroad industry.[6]

Undoubtedly, the Railway Labor Act has encouraged the making of collective agreements, particularly in the earlier years of its existence, when collective bargaining was so much less universally accepted. Few will also deny, however, that the National Labor Relations (Wagner) Act also resulted in a substantial increase in collective agreements. Is the strike record under the Railway Labor Act superior to that in many other industries because the Railway Labor Act makes it the duty of unions and employees to settle disputes peacefully, whereas the Wagner Act did not deal with labor-management disputes? One may well doubt that policy pronouncements have so compelling an influence. Rather, it seems wiser to conclude that although this portion of the Railway Labor Act has probably been of some value in maintaining industry peace, its influence has not been nearly so significant as the Mediation Board claims.

Mediation

If the parties are unable to settle a dispute by collective bargaining, they may seek mediation by the National Mediation Board, or the Mediation Board "may proffer its services in case any labor emergency is found by it to exist at any time." We shall discuss the role of mediation as an intervention technique in Chapter 9. Here we are concerned with the role of mediation by an agency established for the special benefit of one industry.

On the basis of statistics which show that mediation has settled far more cases than other forms of intervention, both the Mediation Board and many of the observers who have studied the Railway Labor Act have concluded that mediation is the most important and most effective method of intervention under the Act. There is no doubt that the National Mediation Board and its staff have enjoyed the respect and confidence of the parties in the railway industry, and to a lesser degree (as will be discussed below) in air transport as well. The availability of a mediation service which enjoys good relations with the parties is surely an aid to peaceful settlement. To that extent the National Mediation Board and its employees have performed a real service in aiding industrial peace.

On the other hand, statistics of cases settled, and arguments based thereon, do not distinguish qualitatively among cases. A dispute involving all the standard unions and railroads and one involving three train dispatchers on a single road receive the same weight. Actually, very few nationwide railroad wage cases have been settled

by mediation since 1936. In an industry like the railroads where national collective bargaining settles basic wage issues, it would be
surprising indeed if most of the cases requiring government intervention were not settled by mediation. Hence, the fact that mediation is used more than any other form of government intervention
does not mean that it is either the most satisfactory or the most successful, but rather that it is the method most useful for minor controversies when the major issues have been disposed of.

One should not infer from this discussion that mediation is un-
important in railway labor disputes. Quite the contrary is true. The
existence of a mediation agency having the respect of the parties
has aided immensely in bringing about peaceful settlement of numerous cases. Some of these cases conceivably might have erupted
into stoppages if such competent or influential mediation were not
present. Undoubtedly also, mediation under the railway Labor
Act has prevented minor disputes from becoming major ones.
Again, however, this does not make mediation the most effective or
most important method of settlement, especially in view of the fact
that mediation is not utilized very much where big issues or national disputes are involved, except as a step toward the appointment of an emergency board.

One other aspect of the availability of a special mediation agency
deserves mention. On several occasions in its annual reports the
National Mediation Board has noted that it is too frequently requested to mediate without any genuine attempt at settlement having been made by the parties themselves.[7] This, as will be noted below, is partially, if not largely, the result of the parties getting ready
for an emergency board instead of bargaining. It is also the result
of the very availability of a special agency, the National Mediation
Board, which the parties feel is there to serve them, to assist them,
or otherwise to suit their purposes of strategy, rather than just to
mediate.

Voluntary Arbitration

If the National Mediation Board is unable to settle a dispute by
mediation, it must request the parties to arbitrate. Either or both
may refuse to do so without penalty. If, however, both agree, Sections 7, 8, and 9 provide detailed procedure for the establishment
of an arbitration board and for the conduct and enforcement of the

arbitration. An award issued under this procedure is final and binding on the parties, as it is filed in the nearest federal district court and becomes a court order. It is enforceable as such unless overturned on one or more of the following three grounds: that either the award or the proceedings were not in conformity with the requirements of the Act; that the award did not conform nor confine itself to the stipulations of the agreement to arbitrate; or that fraud or corruption affected the results of the arbitration.

Under the Railway Labor Act, voluntary arbitration boards may be composed of either three or six members, who are evenly divided between those chosen by unions, those chosen by carriers, and those representing the public. Public members are selected by the partisan members or by the National Mediation Board if the partisan members are unable to agree. Arbitration boards may be reconvened to interpret any section of an award on which the parties disagree.

Arbitration under the Railway Labor Act is not utilized with great frequency. During the period 1926-1934, a total of 538 disputes were settled by arbitration, but most of these disputes were over contract interpretation or involved unsettled grievances. Since 1934, such disputes have been handled by the National Railroad Adjustment Board, as will be discussed later in this chapter.

Between 1934 and June 30, 1964, when arbitration of disputes involving contract interpretation and arbitration of disputes arising from proposed contract changes have been processed separately, only 285 cases of the latter type were submitted to arbitration boards, an average of less than 10 per year for the railroad and air transport industries combined, with their multitude of carriers and unions.[8]

The reason for this lack of interest in voluntary arbitration appears to be the existence of other means of settlement. Minor disputes have been settled mainly either by the parties or by mediation. This is, of course, all to the good, since the responsibility for settlement is directly on the parties. On the other hand, major disputes (as well as many minor ones) have tended to go to emergency boards rather than to arbitration boards. The reason for this is rather obvious. As the late Professor Sumner H. Slichter pointed out, "it is easier for the representatives on one side or the other to . . . refuse to arbitrate if an immediate result is not a strike or a lockout, but the appointment of an emergency board which has no authority to make a binding award."[9]

Emergency Boards—The Record

If the parties, or one of them, reject arbitration, and the dispute threatens, in the opinion of the Mediation Board, to deprive an area of essential transportation, the Board notifies the President, who may then appoint an *ad hoc* emergency board to hear the dispute and make recommendations for its settlement. The emergency board has 30 days in which to make its report (unless, as is frequent, its time is extended), during which, and for 30 days thereafter, the parties are required to maintain the *status quo*. After that, there are no legal restrictions on the parties.

Between 1926 and 1934, when the Act was amended, only two minor strikes occurred, and only ten emergency boards were appointed. In at least one case a board's recommendation was disregarded by a carrier, but no strike occurred, although the resulting grievances did cause a stoppage in 1936.

Five of the ten boards appointed during this period were created in the fiscal year 1933-1934. The fact that as many boards were appointed during the last year of the unamended Act as in the previous seven years is attributable to the increased organizing activity begun in that period and the disputes resulting therefrom, and also to the greater willingness on the part of President Roosevelt, as compared to his predecessors, to appoint emergency boards.

Of the ten emergency boards appointed prior to July 1934, nine involved relatively minor cases concerning small segments of the railroad system, and only one involved a regional case of major importance. Between 1933 and 1935 the Federal Coordinator of Transportation, an office established in the early 1930's to reexamine all federal transportation policies, took over the handling of most important railway labor disputes. Nationwide negotiations between carriers and unions were mediated by the Federal Coordinator and frequently by the President himself. In a period of turmoil in industrial relations the major disputes were thus handled outside the framework of the Railway Labor Act.

In 1937 the railway unions negotiated a general wage increase with the carriers with the help of mediation by the National Mediation Board. The following year, as a result of the recession, the

carriers made a demand for a 15 percent nationwide wage reduction. The case went to an emergency board, which recommended
that the demand be denied. The carriers acquiesced in the settlement. This was the last major dispute prior to 1941.

It was in the period 1933-1941 that the Railway Labor Act
achieved its reputation as a "model law." This reputation was
based on an alleged relationship between railway labor peace and
the procedures of the Railway Labor Act compared with strife in
industry generally where this Act did not apply. A more sophisticated analysis would point to the absence of great organizing
drives and new unionism on the railroads at a time when industry
generally was involved in the difficult task of adjusting to unionism for the first time.

The tone of wartime labor relations on the railroads was set by
the 1941 dispute, in which all the standard railway unions demanded substantial increases and an emergency board was appointed to hear the case on a national basis. The recommendations
of the board did not meet the unions' desires. They appealed to
President Roosevelt; he reassembled the board and, in effect, put
pressure on the carriers and the board to grant further increases,
which was done.

During the war and immediate postwar period, similar developments were common. The 1943 diesel case, the nonoperating employee disputes of the same year, the 1943-1944 case involving operating employees, the Illinois Central case of 1945, and the 1946
and the 1947 wage cases were the most important of those which
featured union repudiation of emergency board decisions, threatened or actual strikes, and usually government seizure, culminating
on several occasions with more favorable terms to the unions than
were recommended by the boards. Further union repudiations of
emergency board recommendations were involved in the Pacific
Electric, and the Chicago-Milwaukee interurban cases. Some of the
emergency boards were appointed from the National Railway Labor Panel, which was established during World War II so that
emergency boards could be created without a union strike vote,
but otherwise the procedure was consistent with the provisions of
the Railway Labor Act.[10]

But the climax came in 1946, when the Engineers and Trainmen
struck all the nation's railroads after rejecting both an emergency

board recommendation and a proposal by President Truman which, as had become the custom, modified upward the recommendations of the fact finders. The strike, which shut down nearly all railroads, lasted for two days and ended on the President's terms as he was asking Congress for a drastic strike law to deal with the emergency. In 1947, three unions—the firemen, conductors, and switchmen—precipitated a crisis by refusing an emergency board award. Using his unexpired war powers, President Truman seized the railroads to prevent a strike, but this time declined to improve the emergency board recommendations. After a time the unions capitulated and settled. Labor relations on the railroads continued in somewhat of an upheaval for the next several years, with strikes by the locomotive firemen over the extent and number of firemen (actually helpers) to be carried by diesel engines, and by the switchmen, trainmen, and others over the forty-hour week. In addition, numerous difficulties arose because of unsettled grievances pending before the National Railroad Adjustment Board, as will be discussed below.[11] During the latter part of the 1950's, however, the bigger cases were settled without great difficulty, although strikes resulting after recommendations of emergency boards had been rejected continued to occur on some railroads. This was a period in which unions could not count on favorable intervention from the White House. Moreover, as traffic and employment declined on the railroads, the carriers became more insistent on the elimination of obsolete work rules and featherbedding practices, and the weaknesses of the unions' case on these issues discouraged them from invoking the emergency board procedure.[12]

In its report involving a dispute between the larger railroads and the conductors' and trainmen's unions in 1955, an emergency board recommended a detailed study and review of the railroad industry's wage structure for the operating classifications, noting that this had not been done since World War I. James P. Mitchell, Secretary of Labor in the Eisenhower administration, succeeded in obtaining agreement between the railroads and the five operating unions to set up a tripartite commission, which was done by Presidential executive order. As with an emergency board, recommendations of the commission were not to be binding on the parties.

The Presidential Railroad Commission made an exhaustive study and report after a year spent in hearing evidence, having special studies made, and observing the matters at issue. It recommended many changes in existing practices, many favorable to employees, but also the elimination of wasteful practices and unproductive jobs, including the use of "firemen" on yard and switch diesels.[13] The carriers accepted the recommendations, but the unions did not. President Kennedy declined to throw the full weight of his office behind the Railroad Commission's recommendations. Instead, he told the parties that the Commission report was a basis for further negotiations. To the unions, this was a message to hold out for further concessions, such as they were used to obtaining in the Roosevelt-Truman eras after rejecting an emergency board report. Moreover, this action of the late President was consistent with his handling of other disputes. For example, the Order of Railroad Telegraphers struck the Chicago and North Western Railway. The issue was the demand of the union for a veto over job abolishments. An emergency board had recommended liberalized unemployment, retraining, and severance payments instead, which the carrier was willing to accept. The President demanded "sufficient concessions" from both sides to get an agreement. A few days later the parties agreed to arbitrate, giving the union another "bite at the apple," although the arbitrator, in effect, sustained the carrier's position. At the same press conference at which the late President disregarded the recommendations of a statutory board established pursuant to the Railway Labor Act, he threw the full weight of his office behind the recommendation of a panel which he created without legislative sanction to handle a dispute in the areospace industry, and which recommended a voting procedure in regard to the union shop to the dismay of the companies and to the joy of the unions.[14]

The Kennedy policy of intervention in railway labor disputes in behalf of unions is further illustrated by the Florida East Coast Railway case. Here an emergency board requested by management was refused because the issue was whether the railroad should put into effect rates of pay agreed to by other railroads. After a strike was called, the Secretary of Labor set up a special extralegal inquiry board which recommended reinstatement of the strikers and institution of national rates. When the company declined, an emergency board was appointed which also failed to settle the strike. The issues since then have been in court litigation with operations (except passenger operations) continuing with non-strikers.

Compulsory Arbitration Act of 1963

When the railway unions and the carriers did not solve the rules disputes analyzed by the Presidential Commission, President Kennedy set up a regular emergency board to rehear the issue. This board made recommendations embodying several concessions to the unions. Again the carriers accepted and the unions rejected the recommendations.

There then followed a series of interventions by the Secretary of Labor, the President, the President's Labor-Management Advisory Committee, and several members of Congress, with a Supreme Court Justice at least in the wings. The unions continued to make, then to postpone, strike threats, while refusing any settlement. The carriers threatened to put revised work rules into effect, as a counter tactic, while advocating compulsory arbitration as the only solution. Finally, Congress enacted a law on August 23, 1963, providing for compulsory arbitration of the diesel firemen and crew consist issues. No strike on this issue was permitted for two years after an award was issued. The remainder of the issues were required by the law to be held in status quo pending negotiations by the parties with the right to strike suspended on such issues till early 1964.

The arbitration board provided for the eventual elimination of the firemen—by a process of attrition—a more liberal procedure than had been proposed either by the Presidential Commission or by the emergency board. For the crew consist issue, the award provided for a settlement for road service, but referred yard issues to local negotiation and eventual arbitration. Almost two years later, the Arbitration board was still busy interpreting its award. The railroads have, however, made substantial reductions in the number of firemen in service. As a result, the threat of the Brotherhood of Locomotive Firemen and Enginemen to revive the issue when the two-year time limit provided in the arbitration law expires in February 1966, does not seem serious.

By early 1965, it was apparent that there would be no settlement on the issues which Congress referred back to the parties. To avert a strike, President Johnson called the parties to Washington and, with the aid of two special mediators, Professor George W. Taylor and Mr. Theodore Kheel, obtained a settlement under which "the railroads failed to achieve any significant revision" of the other work rules which they were attempting to change.[15]

Emergency Boards and Arbitration—Analysis

From the time the Railway Labor Act was amended in 1934 to June 30, 1964, emergency boards were appointed to hear 159 cases (of which about 35 were air line cases), and 58 additional boards were selected from the National Railway Labor Panel. These boards considered some cases involving nearly all the nation's railroads, as well as some involving one issue on a small, localized carrier. The record indicates three conclusions: (1) The appointment of emergency boards had become commonplace; (2) recommendations of emergency boards at critical times have been handled with political expediency; and (3) the procedure has severely inhibited collective bargaining.

1. The thinking which went into the creation of the Railway Labor Act assumed that the emergency boards would be appointed only in rare instances of genuine emergency. In other cases where disputes were not settled by collective bargaining or mediation, it was felt that arbitration would be utilized.[16] The late Dr. William M. Leiserson, for many years Chairman of the National Mediation Board, emphasized this thinking when he declared that emergency boards were merely an extension of arbitration, with public opinion the force to secure compliance.[17] The union view is that such boards provide "a basis for negotiation."[18]

Actually, to term emergency boards "arbitration" boards is as much a misnomer as to term them "fact finding" boards, because public opinion usually is not nearly as effective as proponents of this view believe. It is correct that one reason why public opinion has not turned the emergency board procedure into an effective, binding-award-making mechanism is that far too many boards have been appointed. This was especially true when Presidents Roosevelt and Truman, partially because of the necessities of war, commenced appointing "emergency" boards to hear the most trivial disputes. Yet the ease with which many unions disregarded the recommendations of these boards during the war years, when a railroad strike was unthinkable, indicates that public opinion cannot bind participants.

It is, moreover, not practical to assume that any strict limit can be kept on the number of emergency boards which are to be appointed. As long as the emergency board procedure is available, one side or the other will create the "emergencies" if the possibility of gaining a better settlement exists. When that occurs, the pressure on the President, or whoever must appoint such boards, from well-meaning citizens and newspaper headlines to prevent the "emergency," plus added pressure from labor or industry to aid the emergency creator, usually results in the appointment of a board, the establishment of a precedent, and an ever-increasing number of "emergencies" and boards. In addition to railway labor experience, ample evidence to support this analysis is found in our Taft-Hartley experience (Chapter 7), in the state experience discussed in Appendix C, as well as in the experience of other countries which have utilized similar machinery—for example, Canada (Appendix L).

2. Great opportunities to make the Railway Labor Act's emergency procedure work have been lightly jettisoned. When President Roosevelt, first in 1941, and then repeatedly throughout the war years, assisted the railroad unions to gain additional benefits over and above emergency board recommendations, he set the tone for over a decade of railway labor relations. The failure of the late President Kennedy to place the full weight of his office behind the impressive findings of the Presidential Railroad Commission, and his lack of endorsement of the recommendations of other emergency boards, reactivated and accelerated the "platform" approach to emergency board procedure—that is, use of the board recommendations as a departure point for further benefits.

This is, of course, not surprising if viewed in the context of political power, instead of industrial relations. The Railway Labor Act, and especially the 1934 and 1951 amendments, stand as testimony to the ability of the railway unions to achieve goals via the political route when the procedures of the Act fail to accomplish desired ends.

3. Preparing for an emergency board proceeding and bargaining collectively are quite different approaches to the task of either winning gains or achieving agreement. If one is doing the former,

it is often wiser to ask for more than expected, in both amounts and quantity of demands, in the hope that the emergency board will recommend the maximum possible. Why bargain away anything when it might be granted? This is what has happened in the railway industry. The parties usually go through the procedure of the Act with little or no intention of yielding on anything till the emergency board stage is involved—and then too often not till after the emergency board recommendations are issued.

Consider, for example, the comment of the emergency board in a 1948 case:

The board was not asked, on this conversion rule issue, to resolve a question of principle. It was made, instead, the target for a barrage of conflicting arguments about a lot of little details. We were asked to find the answers to all these quibbles in a mass of evidence and testimony which covered 230 pages of exhibits and 150 pages in the record. This was to be done, within a 2-week period, as 1 little piece of a job which included the disposition of 36 other issues on the basis of well over 12,000 pages of testimony and exhibits.[19]

Fourteen years later, another emergency board gave this succinct summary of what passes for collective bargaining in the railroad industry:

The [union] Organizations, by letter dated September 25, 1961, invited the Carriers to meet on the issues. The Carriers replied on October 5, 1961 that they would consider the matter later. Five days later, the Organizations invoked mediation.

The parties after a strike vote had been taken, met in Washington, D. C., January 10, 1962 in what was or should have been intended as an effort to negotiate or otherwise settle the issues confronting them.

It should be noted and noted well that the principals involved in the matter, which is a labor dispute of the greatest magnitude and importance to the Nation, conferred with each other but four times in as many months.

The Organizations declined the National Mediation Board's proffer of arbitration; the Carriers, after the case had been closed out, advised the National Mediation Board they were agreeable to arbitration, providing a proper arbitration agreement could be reached. The certification of this dispute to the President and the appointment of this board then followed.

The board convened in Chicago, Illinois, on March 6, 1962 to hear the positions and arguments of the parties. Hearings were held there and in Washington, D. C. on a total of fifteen days. The transcript of these hearings consists of 2,649 pages and the board received 24 exhibits from the Organizations and 26 from the Carriers, as well as data supplied by the parties at the board's request.

In addition, the board met with representatives of the parties in many sessions in Chicago and Washington in an effort to mediate the issues which separated them. Our efforts in this regard were unavailing. The will to agree was not present. . . .

It bespeaks a traditional failure to meet problems and an unwillingness to grapple with them without invoking the aid of outsiders. . . .[20]

Little need be added to this summary except to point out that the absence of bargaining before an emergency board is appointed not only insures the appointment of a large number of such boards, and therefore aids in making public opinion an ineffectual enforcement measure, but creates the real emergency—if such can occur—*after* the emergency board has reported and one of the parties has declined to accept the recommendations. This usually brings the Mediation Board back into the situation; or the Secretary of Labor, or Congress, or the President, or, as in 1963, all enter the picture, with either pressure on the carrier to accept the emergency board recommendations or pressure on the carrier to grant more in order to induce the union to accept peaceful settlement. In such cases the emergency procedure may even create the emergency—for if it were not in existence, the parties would have to settle the disputes themselves, as they do in most other industries.

In this respect, emergency board procedure may be less in the public interest than compulsory arbitration. Both inhibit collective bargaining. But compulsory arbitration at least affords a substitute method of settlement, whereas the railroad emergency board procedure, or other so-called "fact-finding" arrangements, do not, but merely invite further intervention to settle the problem. But before a final assessment of the Railway Labor Act procedure is made, other aspects of the law must be analyzed.

NATIONAL RAILROAD ADJUSTMENT BOARD

The great majority of collective bargaining contracts—probably more than 90 per cent—provide that disputes arising over contract interpretation are to be determined by arbitration. The contract usually provides for a means of appointing arbitrators if the parties cannot agree on a selection. Only in the railway industry has Congress provided for compulsory arbitration of such disputes, and established an agency, the National Railroad Adjustment Board, "the only administrative tribunal, federal or state, which has ever been set up in this country for the purpose of rendering judicially enforceable decisions in controversies arising out of the interpretation of contracts."[21] The NRAB was created by the 1934 amendments to the Railway Labor Act and marked the return of the settlement of grievances on a national basis which had prevailed during World War I and which the railroads refused to continue in the interm period. The NRAB consists of thirty-six members, one-half chosen by the carriers, and one-half by unions "national in scope" and free from carrier domination. It is divided into four divisions and is actually four separate boards rather than a single agency.

Although in some cases other unions have more members or more contracts, only the standard (mostly AFL-CIO affiliated, plus a few older independent) unions have been designated "national in scope" or otherwise permitted to participate in the selection of employee representatives. This has proved a decided advantage to these unions in competitive organizing situations.[22]

When a Division of the NRAB cannot agree on a case, a referee is appointed either by the Division or, if it cannot agree, by the National Mediation Board.[23] If they so desire, carriers and unions can set up system regional boards, or special boards to hear their cases, instead of referring them to the NRAB. This has been done in a number of instances, sometimes because of the long wait for a decision on the part of the NRAB, on other occasions because of the desire of a nonstandard union to select its own employee representatives.

Procedure of the NRAB

Cases may be submitted to the NRAB by one or both of the parties, but 80 percent are submitted by the standard unions.[24] Neither notice nor a right of hearing is given to any individual or organization which might be affected, other than the carrier or union involved, although awards of the NRAB have been enjoined or otherwise collaterally attacked on many occasions because of this lack of elementary due process.[25] The fact that the Divisions operate in secrecy without stenographic records, reporters, or other outsiders present, accentuates the problems of due process or lack thereof.

When a Division issues an award, judicial review is provided only by the losing party refusing to put it into effect and the winning party instituting enforcement proceedings by suit in federal court. For years the operating unions frustrated this process by an agreement among themselves not to take such cases to court, but to threaten a strike. In addition, strike threats aimed at by-passing the NRAB altogether became increasingly common. The net effect was to invoke the Railway Labor Act's disputes procedure, and often emergency board proceedings. In some years, such cases were the leading cause of emergency boards being created.[26]

Legal proceedings may finally have checked this extra-legal activity and enforcement. If a case is before the NRAB, the courts will enjoin a strike and require the union to rely solely on NRAB procedures.[27] If the NRAB has issued a decision, the courts will enjoin a strike aimed at enforcing an award, making judicial review a real instead of an empty route.[28] Of course, it is conceivable that a union can threaten to strike over an alleged wage matter, when the real underlying issue is still under NRAB jurisdiction. Thus legal processes might still be frustrated.

Case Load and Issues

From its inception in 1934 to June 30, 1964, the NRAB had received a total of 61,916 cases. Of these, more than two-thirds were First Division cases—that is, those involving engineers, firemen, trainmen, conductors, or other such operating employees.[29] Now these employees provide less than one-half of the NRAB's work. Unfortunately, this has not been a real decline, since about 20,000 cases between 1951 and 1964 were referred to special regional or system boards of adjustment set up because of the awesome case load and the as high as ten-year backlog of the First Division. Had these cases been docketed by the First Division, it would have received about 80 per cent of the NRAB's cases in this period, too.

Although the number of grievances received by the Second, Third, and Fourth divisions is not small, these divisions do keep reasonably current. Not so the First. Despite the creation of many special boards to alleviate its load, it continues to maintain a four- to six-year backlog of cases. The number of cases involved and the length of time required to decide them are unprecedented and unique in American industrial relations practice. There are several reasons for this.

In the early days, when precedents were established, the unions clearly won the advantage, both in terms of numbers of claims sustained[30] and in the nature of the decisions, which the late Professor Sumner H. Slichter termed "among the strangest in the annals of industrial relations."[31] The unions were able to install the principle that each and every bit of work is "owned" by a craft or class of employees and that any deviation therefrom was at the carriers' risk. No matter how long a carrier had the practice of doing something differently, that carrier was liable—often as far back as the 1920's—for deviating from a practice deemed correct by a referee and five union representatives who made up a majority of the First Division. Thus, through the Adjustment Board the unions were able to apply, nationally, restrictive rules which obtained on one railroad, despite the wide variety of different conditions and history of bargaining which prevail on many railroads.

The carriers, however, refused to concede precedent, while the unions attempted to expand precedent as widely as possible. Moreover, to the outsider, the awards are written with such "telegraphic brevity"[32] that what was meant and what was not meant by an award is often difficult to determine, let alone apply as precedent. Hence the decision in one case still does not cause others to be decided on the basis of an outstanding award.

In recent years the carriers have succeeded in reversing the First Division box score and now win most cases, partly because they have already lost on the basic issues, and the interpretations sought by the unions are simply beyond any possibility of credibility; and partly because the carriers are now better and more thoroughly represented. This has not, however, reduced the grievance flow or backlog. It appears that union representatives still process cases they are certain to lose, but find it easier to "send to Chicago" than to settle and thereby possibly alienate some constituents.

The changing box score of the First Division and the court rulings which have estopped extra-legal enforcement of awards have lessened the railway brotherhoods' opposition to regional and system boards of adjustment to relieve the First Division's case load. Many have been appointed, but the only effect is to increase the number of cases, for as soon as these boards are formed, a flood of cases is generated which maintains a four- to six-year backlog of the First Division.

The real basis of the First Division's backlog seems to be three-fold: (1) the arthritic condition of the settlement process on the railroads in the light of the grave decisions and problems, and the long history of having governmental decision machinery available; (2) the already noted substitution of national machinery and prec-edents as a decision-making guide without regard to local varia-tions and with assured retroactivity; and (3) financing of the costs of grievance settlement by the taxpayers instead of by the parties.

No industry faces more severe problems than those with which railway employers and unions must grapple. The carriers require relief from the oppressive work rules, which have often been ex-panded and reinforced by NRAB awards, if they are to achieve solvency and to meet the competition of rival carriers. The unions, with a membership decimated by unemployment, and dominated by old men desirous of working out their lives as nearly as possible in a manner to which they have grown accustomed, stand firm against change, and hope for more favorable governmental inter-vention to maintain the *status quo*. Both are so inured to govern-mental solutions that the need to step up to their problems is rarely given serious mutual consideration. The failure to settle grievances where most of them should be settled—at the local level—is just one aspect of a total situation.

In the final analysis, the single most significant factor which (when all else fails) forces unions and companies to settle their dis-putes over contract interpretations is absent from the railroads. Only in this industry does the taxpayer support grievances settle-ment. "An arbitration rate of one per year for every 220 employees would bankrupt most local unions and would be a serious financial burden to most international unions and employers at the usual cost of private arbitration."[33] The NRAB procedures cost local unions nothing, and national unions and carriers only the salaries of their representatives on the divisions. All other costs are met by the payers. In the fiscal year ended June 30, 1964, the NRAB cost the taxpayers $830,483. When system, regional, or special boards of ad-justment operate, the taxpayer pays the referee. There is no more basic reason for the failure to reduce the backlog of cases on the First Division than this. In the other divisions the issues are not so sharp, so that the availability of public support has not created so drastic a result. Nevertheless, as the Presidential Railroad Commission stated: "There is no reason for the public to continue to support from public funds"[34] grievance settlement in this industry any more than in any other. The "unique" National Railroad Adjustment Board requires many reforms—but none would be so important as to withdraw taxpayer support and to compel the parties to support their own industrial relations system, as do labor and management in every other industry in the United States.

REPRESENTATION DISPUTES

Besides the disputes machinery and the compulsory arbitration of grievances and contract interpretations, the Railway Labor Act also provides machinery for the settlement of representation matters—that is, disputes over what union, if any, is entitled to represent a given group of employees—and for the prevention of unfair labor practices. Because the manner in which representation disputes are handled affects the maintenance of labor peace, we shall deal briefly with this aspect of Railway Labor Act procedure.[35]

Section 2, Ninth, of the Amended Railway labor act requires the National Mediation Board to investigate representation disputes and determine, by secret ballot or other means, which organization or individual, if any, represents a "craft" or "class." By requiring that the bargaining unit be a craft or class, Congress limited the discretion of the Mediation Board to define the bargaining unit (and the freedom of employees to organize on other bases). Outside of specifying that the principle of majority rule should hold, Congress left the procedure and methods for determining bargaining agents, as well as the definition of "craft" or "class," to the Mediation Board.

As of June 30, 1964, the Mediation Board had decided 3,665 representation disputes. In recent years, about 60 of these have occurred per year, with a substantial number involving the air line industry.[36] The Mediation Board has been very careful to define "craft" or "class" to match the jurisdictional claims of the standard unions. The net effect has been to assist these unions to eliminate and/or to resist raiding attempts from nonstandard organizations.[37] This has been defended by the Board on the ground that it encourages stability and therefore labor peace. The Board's policy is understandable in view of its prime concern, as a mediation agency, with the maintenance of peaceful collective bargaining. This favoritism of one group of unions over another is, as already noted, a feature of the Railway Labor Act and much of its adminintration.

A more serious question, perhaps, is whether Congress should have confined the bargaining unit to craft or class. The declining employment in the industry and the changing character of jobs has not left either crafts or unions in the same status as was the case in 1954. The Presidential Railroad Commission pointed out that the existence of five standard craft unions among the operating groups made employee relations problems in all aspects more difficult of solution.[38] Thus the confinement of the bargaining unit to a craft or class, plus the adherence to union jurisdictional claims as a basis of determining craft or class, may also tend to retard solutions to problems which must be solved if peaceful collective bargaining is to exist.

As to procedure, the Mediation Board at first acted very informally, and actually published no rules of procedure until it was forced to do so by the Administrative Procedures Act of 1946. In this early period the Board tended to certify unions on the basis of card authorizations obtained by unions. Its members and staff were, on occasion, otherwise not too careful to observe reasonable rules of conduct or to preserve rights of nonunion employees, nonstandard unions, or especially of Negro railroad employees against whom many standard railway unions have discriminated for many years.[39] More recently, Mediation Board procedure has been tightened up somewhat.

There remain, moreover, significant differences between National Labor Relations Board and National Mediation Board representation proceedings which illustrate shortcomings in Mediation Board procedure. Unlike the NLRB, the Mediation Board does not put "No union" on the ballot, so that employees who want this preference can obtain it only by not voting. The Mediation Board will not certify a union if 51 percent of those eligible do not vote. The NLRB certifies on the basis of a majority of those voting. The NLRB procedure encourages voting; the Mediation Board procedure does not. Since the Railway Labor Act, unlike the Taft-Hartley Act, makes no provision for decertification elections, this in effect reduces the nonunion potential. The Mediation Board does not make the employer a party to representation proceedings, thus effectively denying him a voice either in handling cases, in determining the bargaining unit, or in petitioning for an election, all of which rights the employer enjoys under the Taft-Hartley Act.

The Mediation Board's policies thus further union organization even if only a minority of employees desire a union. For if one more than 50 percent of the employees vote, and 26 percent favor one of two unions, it will be certified. The Mediation Board quite frankly states that its "ballot was drafted to permit employees to secure some form of representation."[40] This is an interpretation of the Railway Labor Act quite inconsistent with the repeated assurances of the framers of the law to the effect that "employees shall be free to join any labor union of their choice and *likewise be free to refrain from joining any union if that be their desire...*"[41] Nevertheless, court challenges to this form of ballot, or to the policy of excluding employers from a voice in bargaining unit determination have been unsuccessful.[42] The National Mediation Board's policy of promoting unionism even though a majority of employees do not desire to be represented continues unchecked.

A final difference of interest here between the Taft-Hartley act and the Railway Labor Act is that supervisors, including the yard and road superintendents, stationmasters, and other management personnel, are "employees" under the latter law but would be excluded by the former. The fact that the Railway Labor Act furthers the unionization of managerial personnel has been severely criticized, because it interferes both with managerial effectiveness and with freedom of association of the rank and file who are placed in the same bargaining unit with their bosses.[43]

APPLICATION OF RAILWAY LABOR ACT TO AIR TRANSPORT

The air transport industry was placed under the Railway Labor Act in 1936 at the behest of the Air Line Pilots' Association, then the only unionized group in the industry, supported by the American Federation of Labor. The industry was neither in favor nor opposed. Since then, the industry has grown tremendously and has become quite thoroughly unionized. The record indicates that it is at least questionable to attempt to transfer both a system of collective bargaining and a method of government control developed in one industry to another.

The disputes procedure in the air line industry has had the same effect on collective bargaining as it has had on the railroads. The ability to get an emergency board appointed has inhibited collective bargaining and has resulted in more crises after the emergency board procedure has been exhausted. The first air line emergency board was appointed in 1946; but in recent years, they have been appointed with increasing frequency. About thirty-five air line emergency boards had been appointed as of June 30, 1964, with the number showing decidedly increasing trends in recent years.

Despite the increased number of air line emergency boards, it is difficult to find one case where a real emergency, or even a serious inconvenience, existed. Air lines do not generally bargain as a group, and never have bargained industry-wide. In most cases, at least two lines serve an area, so that a strike involving one does not mean no air transportation. And almost always, other forms of transport are available. Since the appointment of an emergency board does not and has not meant the end of strikes, the practice of appointing them in air line cases seems dubious.

Voluntary arbitration under the Railway Labor Act has been utilized by the unions and the air line industry to an increasing degree. But such arbitration would be equally available if the industry were not covered by the Act, and is also used by many other industries, some more, some less, without being covered by the Railway Labor Act.

Mediation as provided under the Railway Labor Act has certainly been of service to the parties in air transport, but this is limited by the fact that nearly all mediators have had their major experience in the railroad industry. As one executive of a large air line stated: "The mediators know their business, but usually they are so steeped in solutions worked out in the railroad industry that they feel all we have to do is what is done there. I doubt that this attitude is helpful."[44]

It is difficult to believe that the Federal Mediation and Conciliation Service could not supply mediation facilities equal to those now supplied. Because of the varied conditions to which FMCS mediators are exposed, it is not improbable that such mediators would be receptive to special problems of the industry without relating them to solutions developed in just one industrial environment.

In the representation area a firm case exists against the decision which brought the air line industry under the Railway Labor Act. For in so doing, Congress decreed that employees must organize by craft or class. In other industries, organization proceeded on a basis determined by employees and, in turn, resulted from various factors inherent in labor market and industrial conditions. Even on the railroads the craft or class rule was not decided till after it was largely a fact.

By limiting employee organization to craft or class, federal policy created a number of problems and aggravated others. For example, one result has been to establish separate bargaining units of each and every class of flight crews—pilots, flight engineers, radio operators, and navigators, and stewards or stewardesses. All but the first and last have become, or are becoming, technologically obsolete. Their organization into separate unions aggravates the technological displacement problem because the demise of the craft means the demise of the union. Several strikes of flight engineers have resulted from the attempts of a union to save itself after the problems of its members were at least reasonably met.

The craft or class problem on the air lines has been aggravated by the rigidity of the National Mediation Board's interpretations and rulings. Basically, the Board applies regulations and policies developed on the railroads, and these are often of questionable applicability on the air lines.[45] It is difficult to see how this phase of the Railway Labor Act has contributed constructively to air line employee relations.

The air line industry and unions therein may be directed by the National Mediation Board under Section 205 of the Railway Labor Act to set up an eight-man bipartisan National Air Transport Adjustment Board. No action has been taken, however, and none is advocated by either side. For all the unions and all carriers in this industry to agree upon two representatives is not likely. Moreover, each group has observed the operations of the National Railroad Adjustment Board, emulation of which is not likely to be consider desirable.

Grievance settlement in the air line industry has instead followed the more common and satisfactory method. Each air line and union which bargain collectively have established procedures to settle grievances. When they cannot agree on an arbitrator, they usually ask the National Mediation Board to make the appointment. Arbitrators so appointed are compensated by the parties, not by the government.

EVALUATION

The Railway Labor Act involves the most complete form of government control of collective bargaining which has been developed for American industry in peacetime. It is noteworthy that the industries involved are also regulated in a variety of other ways— including supervision of pricing, business routes and location, and rights to initiate or abandon service.

The experience of the Railway Labor Act raises the serious question of whether the government can control collective bargaining without being forced into a position of complete dictation. As the situation now exists, the emergency board procedure has caused the parties to cease bargaining in order to await the appointment of a board. Then a crisis is likely to arise *after* the board has been appointed. Collective bargaining is further inhibited by the Act's machinery to settle grievances and contract interpretations. Grievance arbitration at public expense, excessive retroactivity and the subversion of local practice to national rules and interpretations have combined to stimulate grievance disputes but to paralyze grievance settlements. Unrest, strife, and litigation are the results.

That the Railway Labor Act has enhanced union power should not be surprising. The present law is largely designed to give the standard railway unions what they desire, and it is administered obviously and consciously with that intent. Representation dispute cases are carefully handled to insure success for the standard unions, as are the rules and regulations of the National Railroad Adjustment Board. In all facets of the Act, promotion of collective bargaining has been interpreted to mean enhancement of the position of the standard railway unions.

Despite the fact that the strike record in the railway or air line industries is not a bad one compared with others (although it is no better than the record in other utilities) the Railway Labor Act can claim little credit. Serious threats to public inconvenience have been settled by other forms of intervention—usually *ad hoc* Presidential, once by compulsory arbitration, and sometimes by a myriad of public officials getting into the act. Perhaps if the collective bargaining inhibiting procedures of the Act did not exist, fewer crises would have been created. *Certainly almost no major dispute since 1941 has been settled without intervention beyond the Act's procedures.*

It is difficult to believe that the Railway Labor Act serves the public interest on national economic or social objectives. By requiring unions and companies to bargain on a craft basis, by enhancing the power of a few unions, and by promoting bargaining representation on a minority basis, it encourages narrow, rather than broad interests and discourages adjustment to change. At a time when transportation policy requires cost reduction and managerial flexibility, the Railway Labor Act encourages adherence to old, high cost rules, precedent, and the saddling of a new industry and technology with the mistakes of an older one.

The subjection of collective bargaining in the air line industry to the rigidities and inhibitions built into the Railway Labor Act can only be termed a sad error of public policy. This would be true even if the Railway Labor Act had worked beyond criticism in the railroad industry, where it reflects to some extent a codification of practice. But the structure and problems of the air lines require a collective bargaining system tailored to its own needs, not those of a different industry. The same might be said concerning suggestions often made to place other industries under the Railway Labor Act—suggestions usually based on little research as to how the Act works in practice.

In ending this chapter, it might be well to note that the Railway Labor Act is, in effect, special-privilege legislation. It confers rights and duties dissimilar to those conferred on the parties in other industries. The railroad industry and unions are specially treated in most other social legislation, including social security, unemployment, and health and safety legislation. The rationale has always been the "special nature" of the business and employment conditions.

On the other hand, each industry has its special conditions. Does the railroad industry deserve this special privilege?

Some analysts believe so. One observer, for example, found nine conditions which differentiated railroad employment from that in other industries.[46] Professor William Gomberg, in commenting upon these points, noted that far from being unique characteristics, they exist, often in greater severity, in many other industries which overcame equally difficult problems.[47] Perhaps the very existence of special-privilege legislation has so conditioned the parties in the railroad industry to governmentally imposed solutions that they cannot be expected to face up to their problems. The air lines may well be headed in the same direction under the impetus of the Railway Labor Act. On this basis alone, it is difficult to believe that the Railway Labor Act serves either the economic or social objectives of our country.

NOTES

1. Some of the material in this chapter is based upon Herbert R. Northrup and Gordon F. Bloom, *Government and Labor* (Homewood: Richard D. Irwin, Inc., 1963), Chapter 12. It is used here by permission of the publisher and courtesy of the co-author.

2. References will be made to the "standard" railway unions in this chapter. These unions include the Brotherhood of Locomotive Engineers, the Brotherhood of Locomotive Firemen and Enginemen, the Order of Railway Conductors, the Brotherhood of Railroad Trainmen, and the Switchmen's Union in the operating end; and the Brotherhood of Maintenance of Way Employees, the Order of Railroad Telegraphers, the Brotherhood of Railway and Steamship Clerks, Freight Handlers, Express and Station Employees, the American Train Dispatchers' Association, the Brotherhood of Railroad Signalmen, the Brotherhood of Railway Carmen, the International Association of Machinists, the International Brotherhood of Electrical Workers, the Brotherhood of Boilermakers, Shipbuilders, Welders, and Helpers, and the Brotherhood of Firemen and Oilers in the non-operating part of the industry. The last four include unions which now have only a small portion of their membership in the railroad industry; the remainder draw most of their members from the railroad industry. All are AFL-CIO affiliates except the Engineers, Conductors, and Signalmen, which are independent.

3. William H. Spencer, *The National Railroad Adjustment Board*, Vol. VIII, No. 3, of "Studies in Business Administration" (Chicago: University of Chicago Press, 1938), pp. 11-12.

4. *Texas and New Orleans Railroad Co. v. Brotherhood*, 281 U. S. 548 (1930).

5. For an endorsement and elaboration of this viewpoint, see H. S. Kaltenborn, *Governmental Adjustment of Labor Disputes* (Chicago: Foundation Press, 1943), p. 52.

6. Kaltenborn, op. cit.

7. See, e.g., National Mediation Board, *Twenty-Sixth Annual Report* (Washington, D. C.: U. S. Government Printing Office, 1960), p. 27.

8. Statistics from annual reports of National Mediation Board.

9. Summer H. Slichter, "The Great Question in Industrial Relations," *New York Times Magazine*, April 27, 1947, p. 5.

10. For a history of railway labor relations during this period, see Herbert R. Northrup, "The Railway Labor Act and Railway Labor Disputes during Wartime," *American Economic Review*, Vol. XXXVI (June 1946), pp. 324-343.

11. See below, pages 67-72.

12. For a history of disputes during this period, see David M. Levinson, "Railway Labor Act—The Record of a Decade," *Labor Law Journal*, Vol. III (June 1952), pp. 13-29; and Jacob J. Kaufman, "Emergency Boards under the Railway Labor Act," *Labor Law Journal*, Vol. IX (December 1958), pp. 910-920, 949.

13. *Report of the Presidential Railroad Commission* (Washington, D. C.: U. S. Government Printing Office, February 1962).

14. From President Kennedy's news conference of September 12, 1962, as transcribed in the *New York Times, September* 15, 1962, p. 12. See also the editorials in the *New York Times* for September 15, 1962, and in the *Washington Post*, September 16, 1962. It should be noted that the vote procedure in the aerospace case did not obtain the union shop for the unions because the employees voted it down.

15. J. J. Kaufman, "The Railroad Labor Dispute: A Marathon of Maneuver and Improvisation," *Industrial and Labor Relations Review*, Vol. XVIII (January 1965), p. 210.

16. See, *e.g.*, the comments of union spokesmen advocating the original 1926 law, reproduced in Kaufman (note 12, above), pp. 911-912.

17. William M. Leiserson, "Public Policy in Labor Relations," *American Economic Review*, Vol. XXXVI (May 1946), p. 345 (*Papers and Proceedings of the Fifty-eighth Annual Meeting of the American Economic Association*, Cleveland, January 24-27, 1946).

18. This was the actual comment of a union official upon receiving a recommendation of an emergency board in 1948.

19. *Report of the Emergency Board in re* [*Certain Railroads*] . . . *and the Brotherhood of Locomotive Engineers, et al.* (Washington, D. C., 1948).

20. *Report to the President by the Emergency Board* . . . *in re* [*Certain Railroads*] *and* . . . *Eleven Cooperating Railway Labor Organizations* (Washington, D. C., May 3, 1962).

21. Lloyd H. Garrison, "The National Railroad Adjustment Board: A Unique Administrative Agency," *Yale Law Journal*, Vol. XLVI (1937), p. 567.

22. Herbert R. Northrup and M. L. Kahn, "Railroad Grievance Machinery: A Critical Analysis," Part I, *Industrial and Labor Relations Review*, Vol. V (April 1952), pp. 370-372. The Secretary of Labor has the duty to determine if a union is eligible. The Brotherhood of Sleeping Car Porters is one nonstandard union found eligible, but the other unions do not permit it representation on the Third Division.

23. The Second Division has always been able to agree on referees, the Fourth generally, the Third occasionally, and the First, which decides 70-80 percent of the cases, almost never. The First Division has jurisdiction over operating employees, the Second over shop employees, the Third over

all nonoperating groups except shop, waterborne, and supervisory, and the Fourth over waterborne employees of railroads, supervisory and miscellaneous groups.

24. Although the Railway Labor Act seems to authorize submission by individuals, the union representatives, with few exceptions, vote not to hear them. This creates a procedural deadlock which there is no way to break, so they do not get heard. The First and Second divisions do not accept cases of nonstandard unions, but the Third and Fourth do. However, most nonstandard unions will not submit cases to a Board whose union members are controlled by rivals.

25. For a list of cases, see Northrup and Kahn, *op. cit.*, pp. 373-74. Individual authorization, usually obtained through union constitutions and membership applications, is also required for an award to be binding upon employees. Merely being the bargaining agent does not confer the right to represent employees before the NRAB. *Elgin Joliet & Eastern Railway Co. v. Burley*, 325 U. S. 711 (1945).

26. In 1949-1950, for example, six of eleven emergency boards were actually concerned with matters properly within the jurisdiction of the NRAB, and one 45-day strike occurred. The Mediation Board noted that a "great amount of time of the [Mediation] Board and its mediators was spent in preventing strikes in such situations." See National Mediation Board, *Sixteenth Annual Report* (Washington, D. C.: U. S. Government Printing Office, 1950), pp. 24-25.

27. *Brotherhood of Railroad Trainmen v. Chicago River Industrial Railroad Co.*, 353 U. S. 30 (1951). The courts will not enjoin a strike if the case has not been submitted to the NRAB, even though the matter is within the NRAB's jurisdiction (*Manion v. Kansas City Terminal Railway Co.*, 353 U. S. 927 [1956]); but presumably, to obtain an injunction, the carrier may merely submit the matter to the NRAB.

28. *Denver and Rio Grande Western Railroad Co. v. Brotherhood of Railroad Trainmen*, 185 F. Supp. 369 (1960).

29. Data are from Garth L. Mangum, "Grievance Procedures for Railroad Operating Employees," *Industrial and Labor Relations Review*, Vol. XV July 1962), pp. 474-499; and National Mediation Board, *Thirtieth Annual Report* (Washington, D. C.: U. S. Government Printing Office, 1964).

30. Mangum, *op. cit.*, p. 491.

31. Sumner H. Slichter, *Union Policies and Industrial Management* (Washington, D. C.: Brookings Institution, 1941), p. 195, n. 80. The courts have been equally caustic about NRAB awards. See Northrup and Kahn, *op. cit.*, Part II, *Industrial and Labor Relations Review*, Vol. V (July 1952), pp. 549-555, for analysis of awards and court citations.

32. Mangum, *op. cit.*, p. 496.

33. *Ibid.*, p. 499.

34. *Report of the Presidential Railroad Commission*, p. 185.

35. For an analysis of the Railway Labor Act's unfair labor practice procedure, see Herbert R. Northrup, "Unfair Labor Practice Prevention under the Railway Labor Act," *Industrial and Labor Relations Review*, Vol. III (April 1950), pp. 323-340.

36. Data from National Mediation Board annual reports.

37. Herbert R. Northrup, "The Appropriate Bargaining Unit Question

under the Railway Labor Act," *Quarterly Journal of Economics*, Vol. LX (February 1946), pp. 250-269; and J. J. Kaufman, "Representation in the Railroad Industry," *Labor Law Journal*, Vol. VI (July 1955), pp. 437-440, 508-512. The National Mediation Board has published three volumes containing its representation cases and decisions (*Determinations of Craft or Class of the National Mediation Board* [Washington, D. C.: U. S. Government Priting Office, Vol. I, 1948; Vol. II, 1953; and Vol. III, 1961.]).

38. *Report of the Presidential Railroad Commission*, pp. 184-185.

39. For cases in point, see Herbert R. Northrup, "The Appropriate Bargaining Unit . . ."; and *ibid.*, *Organized Labor and the Negro* (New York: Harper and Bros., 1944), pp. 58-62. The fact that many railway unions have historically denied Negroes membership rights means that the careless policies of the Mediation Board in the early years of its existence contributed substantially to union racial discrimination.

40. National Mediation Board, *Administration of the Railway Labor Act by the National Mediation Board*, 1934-1957 (Washington: Government Printing Office, 1958), pp. 18-19.

41. U. S. House of Representatives, Committee on Interstate and Foreign Commerce, 23rd Congress, 2nd Sess., Report on HR 9861, 1934, p. 2. HR 9861 became the 1934 amendments to the Railway Labor Act. In a like vein, see the comments of Joseph P. Eastman, then Federal Coordinator of Transportation and draftsman of the House of Representatives hearings on this bill and the comments of the late Senator Wagner of New York on the S.3266 (the companion bill in the Senate) at page 12 of *Hearings on S.3266*, U. S. Senate, Committee on Interstate Commerce, 1934.

42. *National Mediation Board* v. *United Air Lines*, 85 S. Ct. 1192 (1965).

43. E. Dale and R. L. Raimon, "Management Unionism and Public Policy on the Railroads and Airlines," *Industrial and Labor Relations Review*, Vol. XI (July 1958), pp. 551-571; and Northrup, "The Appropriate Bargaining Unit. . . ."

44. Interview, August 1962.

45. See, for example, cases involving clerical and store and stock clerks, C-1693, C-2252, C-2389, and R-1706.

46. Jacob J. Kaufman, "Logic and Meaning of Work Rules on the Railroads," *Proceedings of the Fourteenth Annual Meeting, Industrial Relations Research Association*, 1961, pp. 378-388. Dr. Kaufman serves as consultant to the Switchmen's Union and other railroad union groups.

47. William Gomberg, "Discussion," *ibid.*, pp. 413-416.

6 The National Labor Relations Board's Trend To Arbitration

THE NATIONAL LABOR RELA-tions Act was enacted in 1935 because of the refusal of American employers to recognize unions freely chosen by employees. The purpose of the original Act, known as the Wagner Act, was to provide a peaceful method of determining whether employees desired a union (or which union, if any, where competing unions are involved) to represent them for the purposes of collective bargaining. In other words, Congress decided that this issue should not be left to economic power, but should be determined by a presumably impartial agency on the basis of the wishes of the employees involved.

In 1947, when the National Labor Relations Act was amended by the Taft-Hartley amendments (by which name it is now known), Congress provided that disputes over which union group does what work—that is, jurisdictional disputes—would, like representation disputes, be subject to National Labor Relations Board determination.

The Taft-Hartley Act thus provides for the arbitration of two classes of disputes which are discussed in this chapter. In addition, however, the Taft-Hartley Act contains various proscriptions against employer and union conduct which in recent years have been utilized by the NLRB to expand its control of the collective bargaining process to such a degree that the Board is very close to determing collective bargaining content. The nature of this administrative expansion and its portent are also analyzed in this chapter.

Representation Disputes

The Wagner Act gave the National Labor Relations Board almost *carte blanche* and no guidelines to determine whether a group of employees desired a union to represent them. If a majority did, the Act required that the union be certified as the representative of all the employees in a bargaining unit and that the employer must bargain with the union as the exclusive representative of *all* the employees in the bargaining unit.

To handle representation cases, the NLRB evolved certain principles and practices over the years, some of which were altered by the Taft-Hartley amendments. In general, the NLRB holds elections so that employees can determine for themselves whether a union is desired. The union or unions, and "no union" are on the ballot.

It is not the purpose here to discuss representation procedures or problems essentially,[1] but rather to emphasize why arbitral determination of representation disputes may be justified in a free economy, and, second, to show even so how such dispute machinery may be utilized to enhance union power.

The question of whether a union should represent an employee is basically not for unions or management to determine—rather, it is for the employees to determine directly. The unions and management should certainly have the right to try and to persuade (without coercion) employees to their respective points of view on the subject. But in the final analysis only employees can determine the question of whether they desire representation. A fair election is therefore a proper solution. For economic power can easily be on the side of the employer or of the union, but the wishes of the employees may be to the contrary.

For example, employees in an isolated mill town may fear to express their preference except in a secret election. Here the power of the employer is likely to be overwhelming, but the preferences of the employees may not be in accord with that power. Likewise, in New York City, the power of a union to picket or boycott an employer into submission may or may not be significant as to the wishes of the employees involved. Public policy, therefore, rejects both employer interference or the long held position of organized labor that it should bargain for people without their authorization.

But like all government machinery which is established in the best of faith, the representation machinery of the National Labor Relations Board soon became both a center of controversy for conflicting views and a vehicle for political enhancement of union power. Bargaining units were determined to suit union organizing convenience; foremen and supervisors were placed in the same bargaining unit with employees that they supervised; unions which lost elections picketed and boycotted employers (and employees) despite their repudiation at the polls; and the NLRB restricted the right of employers to communicate their views to employees.

All these abuses the Taft-Hartley Act sought to correct, but administrative rulings have all but whittled away many of the safeguards written into the law by Congress. For example, despite a clear statement of the right of free speech in the Taft-Hartley Act, the NLRB has repeatedly set aside elections because employers pointed out that union membership may involve risks as well as privileges, and duties as well as rights;[2] and despite a clear provision in the Taft-Hartley Act that extent of organization should not be the sole criterion in determining bargaining units, the NLRB has done just that by carving up insurance companies and retail stores to suit union interests. Recently, the United States Supreme Court remanded some of these cases to the NLRB with the order that it explain its reasoning.[3]

Under its present practice, therefore, in passing on petitions for the establishment of craft units or the severance of craft or craftlike groups from existing larger units, the Board does not follow any automatic rules, but instead utilized "the case-by-case analysis based upon such factors as the desires of the parties, bargaining history, similarity of skills, job functions and working conditions, common supervision and or interchange of employees, type of industry, organization of the plant, and whether any union seeks to represent the technical employees separately."[4]

The same case-by-case approach typifies the attitude of the present Board toward most problems involving the appropriate bargaining unit. While there is merit in such attention to the particular details of each case, it is also important to both management and labor that rules and precedents evolve in this important field, so that there can be advance planning and stability in employee relations. The Board has been making bargaining unit determinations for almost thirty years, so one would expect that by now there would be some established pattern in Board decisions on this subject. On the contrary, so sweeping is the present Board's re-examination of its basic policies that bargaining unit decisions are in a complete state of flux, and important precedents topple day after day. A careful examination of these cases will hardly find even one which can be termed anything but favorable to unionism. The resultant turmoil, of course, in no way contributes to the peaceful determination decreed by Congress. Nor does it give the employee the careful voice which the procedure was created to accomplish.

More recently, the NLRB has shown signs of forcing employers to recognize unions on the basis of signed authorization cards. Anyone familiar with the facts of industrial relations knows that such cards are often signed by the employee to "get the organizer off his back." Moreover, the card usually states that it is for the purpose of obtaining an election. Despite this flimsy evidence, employers have been forced to deal with unions on the basis of a card check, and in one key case even though a union subsequently lost an election.[5] It is difficult to imagine a more fundamental disregard of a law which is written in terms of *majority* rule. That Congressional reform is necessary to prevent gerrymandering bargaining units, to protect free speech, and to insure free elections, seems obvious.

Jurisdictional Disputes

Section 8 (b) 4 of the Taft-Hartley Act made it an unfair labor practice for a union to engage in or to encourage any strike or refusal by employees to use, manufacture, transport, work upon, or handle goods if an object of such action was, among other things, to force or require an employer to assign particular work to employees in one union or craft rather than to employees in another union or craft. This clause was intended to outlaw the so-called "jurisdictional strike." Such strikes, growing out of controversies as to which craft has the right to perform a particular job, were particularly common in the construction industry and evoked widespread public criticism. As a direct result of the enactment of the Taft-Hartley law, the building trade unions set up machinery to adjust jurisdictional disputes among the various crafts.

A union which engages in this activity commits an unfair labor practice and renders itself liable in damages to anyone whose business or property is injured as a result of the strike. Moreover, the NLRB must hear and "determine" such cases itself unless, within ten days after the charge had been filed, the parties agree to voluntary adjustment of the dispute. The NLRB can seek an injunction in situations where such relief is appropriate.

At first, the NLRB religiously refrained from making determinations of work assignments in jurisdictional dispute cases coming before it. In 1961, however, in the Columbia Broadcasting case,[6] which involved a dispute between a union of television technicians and a union of stage employees over which union would control the work of providing electric lighting for television shows, the United States Supreme Court held that the NLRB could not "duck" this responsibility imposed upon it by Congress and that it must make an affirmative award of disputed work in such cases. Since then a steadily increasing number of cases have come before the NLRB for determination—1,626 in the 1964 fiscal year alone.[7] Two conclusions are apparent.

It is, first of all, clear that when the NLRB refused to make determinations, which the Supreme Court found contrary to law, unions, especially in the building trades, were settling these issues among themselves. The building trades unions established a voluntary arbitration agency after the Taft-Hartley Act was passed, and it apparently worked quite well. But unions in other industries did not, thus precipitating the Supreme Court case.

Once the NLRB had to hear these cases, however, those building trades unions which did not win their cases before the voluntary tribunal, refused to abide by the awards and thus forced the NLRB to hear the case. Thus again, the mere existence of a government agency of last resort invited parties to utilize it.

As for the decisions of the NLRB in jurisdictional claims, there has been considerable controversy. The intent of the law seems to have been that in case of a dispute, the employer's assignment would be determinate; but if he were neutral the NLRB could decide on other factors. The NLRB, however, has assumed the right to cast aside employer assignments and decide cases on "area practice" or other criteria, although employer preference is usually the decisive factor.[8]

In view of these developments, it would appear that a new procedure is in order. If Congress desires to condemn jurisdictional strikes, a simple, three-prong policy would accomplish this. Strikes over jurisdictional issues can be prohibited. If they occur, they can be made subject to immediate injunctive relief by any one affected. And unions should be required to submit such disputes to peaceful determination by any machinery that they desire where the employer is neutral. But where a work assignment is made by the employer, that should be controlling. The NLRB does seem an inappropriate agency to handle such cases.

"Good Faith" Bargaining

The National Labor Relations Board is charged with the duty of arbitrating representation and jurisdictional disputes; but its greatest incursion into the bargaining process is made under the guise of a seemingly innocuous provision which makes it an unfair labor practice for an employer "to refuse to bargain collectively with the representatives of his employees duly chosen pursuant to other provisions of the Act." This provision, Section 8 (5), was added to the Wagner Act after some debate among its sponsors, for it differs from the other four unfair labor practices which proscribe specific practices of discrimination because of union membership, because of testimony given under the Act, because of employer attempts to dominate a union, or because of other restraint or coercion in defiance of rights guaranteed under the Act. In 1947, the Taft-Hartley Act made the "good faith" bargaining Section 8 (a) (5) and added a similar provision, 8 (b) (3) applicable to unions.[9]

Wagner Act Interpretation

Interpretation of Section 8 (5) must be viewed against the backdrop of anti-union hostility which existed at the time the Wagner Act was adopted. It would serve no useful purpose to promote the organization of unions in response to employee wishes if employers would not meet with union representatives and discuss wages, hours, and other working conditions. And many employers in those early years would not talk to a union representative unless compelled to do so by a court of law. This attitude reflected the strong emphasis on private property rights and individual initiative which characterized our industrial development prior to the thirties. One can visualize the purple rage of a self-made tycoon who has worked himself up by his own bootstraps to a position of authority over thousands of employees and is suddenly told that a union business agent who is not even one of his own employees wants to sit down with him to tell him how to run his business!

This section of the law was inserted to require employers to meet and negotiate with representatives of their employees. It is clear from the legislative history of the Act that Congress did not intend to compel employers to agree to anything; it did want to assure that they would at least sit down and bargain. The language of this section was the subject of violent criticism, both by management and by union spokesmen. Employers objected to the fact that the obligation to bargain was imposed only on them and not on unions. Furthermore, they criticized the manner in which the NLRB established criteria as to what was "good-faith" bargaining, claiming that such rules, in effect, required employers to come to an agreement contrary to the original statutory purpose. Unions criticized the lack of any effective enforcement procedure under this section. When confronted by a violation of this section of the law, all the Board could do was to issue an order requiring the employer to bargain collectively with the representative of his employees. If an employer was determined to resist union organization, he could draw out the administrative proceedings by demanding a full hearing before the Board, disregarding the Board's order, and appealing the NLRB decision to the courts. Two or three years might elapse before a final order would be handed down which the employer would obey. During this entire period the employer was in a position to weaken the union by refusing to meet with it and ignoring the demands of its representatives. Obviously, many local unions would disintegrate during such a long period when subjected to strong employer pressure.

Nevertheless, despite its ambiguous language, and despite its weak enforcement provisions, the good-faith bargaining requirement was an essential part of the original Wagner Act. Although many employers sought means to avoid its strictures and were brought before the Board on unfair labor practice charges, many more employers abided by its provisions and therefore enabled the statutory purpose to become a reality. Without this section as an integral part, the Wagner Act would have been less effective in promoting collective bargaining between labor and management through unions representing employees. Whether or not this statutory language serves a useful purpose today is another question.

Taft-Hartley Interpretation

In years to come, historians may look back upon the Taft-Hartley Act as the first major step down the road to compulsory arbitration of labor disputes. This is a rather surprising statement because the Act itself, as will be noted in Chapter 7, is notoriously weak in handling even national emergency disputes. Nevertheless, it is true that the Act has injected government into every vital aspect of union-management relations, and history demonstrates that once government commences to control a field of human endeavor, its scope of influence always grows. The Act has involved government in the negotiation of collective bargaining agreements, the content of collective bargaining agreements, the administration of union-management relations under such agreements, and strike settlements as discussed in Chapter 7. In the following discussion, we shall consider the impact of the Taft-Hartley law on the first three of the above mentioned phases of the collective bargaining process.

The Taft-Hartley Act itself spelled out what employers and

unions could and could not include in labor contracts with respect to welfare plans, union security clauses, and checkoff of union dues. There is no need to analyze these provisions here. But beyond the clear words of the statute, the NLRB has utilized the "good-faith" bargaining provisions contained in the Act to lay down rules respecting the content and conduct of collective bargaining negotiations. The development of the law on the subject of what constitutes bargaining in good faith provides a revealing example of how a simple statutory precept has been used as a wedge for government intervention in collective bargaining. The question is no longer: "Should the government intervene at the bargaining table?" We have gone too far down the road of regulation to retrace our footsteps to completely free collective bargaining. The government, in the person of the National Labor Relations Board, is already at the bargaining table. The question now is simply: "How great should its influence be?", and whether as advocated by NLRB members and staff, it should be expanded.

The Control of Bargaining Tactics

The original Section 8 (a) (5) of the Wagner Act provided merely that it was an unfair labor practice for an employer to refuse to bargain collectively with representatives of his employees. Congress was primarily concerned that employers bargain with collective bargaining representatives. How they bargained once they sat down together was not then considered a problem requiring government interference. As Senator David I. Walsh, then Chairman of the Senate Committee on Education and Labor, stated: "When the employees have chosen their organization, when they have selected their representatives, all the bill proposes to do is to escort them to the door of the employer and say, 'Here they are, the legal representatives of your employees.' What happens behind those doors is not inquired into, and the bill does not seek to inquire into it."[10]

However, anti-union employers sought to weaken this provision by listening to union demands and rejecting all of them. As a consequence, the National Labor Relations Board, with the sanction of the courts, found it necessary to establish a series of rules as to what constituted bargaining in good faith. For example, it held that there had to be a "common willingness among the parties to discuss freely and fully their respective claims and demands and, when these are opposed, to justify them on reason."[11] Furthermore, the Board held that an employer could not simply listen and reject all union demands, but had to make counter proposals.[12]

While some affirmative action by the NLRB was undoubtedly necessary to make the bargaining provision of the Wagner Act effective, many employers claimed that the NLRB frequently went too far and used the threat of an unfair labor practice charge to compel employers to accede to union demands. Thus, in the course of the Congressional hearings preceding enactment of the 1947 Taft-Hartley amendments of the Wagner Act, it was stated that the National Labor Relations Board had "gone very far, in the guise of determining whether or not employers had bargained in good faith in setting itself up as the judge of what concessions an employer must make and of the proposals and counterproposals that he may or may not make."[13]

The Taft-Hartley amendments enacted by Congress in 1947 sought to counteract the pro-labor provisions contained in the Wagner Act. With respect to good-faith bargaining, two important changes were made. In the first place, Congress added a new Section 8 (b) (3), which made it an unfair labor practice for a labor organization or its agents to refuse to bargain collectively with an employer. This provision was intended to impose an obligation to bargain in good faith upon unions, which had in many cases adopted the same kind of "take it or leave it" attitude which the NLRB had condemned in management in the early years of administration of the Wagner Act.

In the second place, a new provision, Section 8 (d), was added, applicable to both unions and employers alike, which sought to define the obligation to bargain collectively. As the United States Supreme Court has pointed out: ". . . it remains clear that Section 8 (d) was an attempt by Congress to prevent the Board from controlling the settling of the terms of collective bargaining agreements."[14]

Section 8 (d) states:

. . . to bargain collectively is the performance of the mutual obligation of the employer and the representative of the employees to meet at reasonable times and confer in good faith with respect to wages, hours, and other terms and conditions of employment, or the negotiation of an agreement, or any question arising thereunder, and the execution of a written contract incorporating any agreement reached if requested by either party, but such obligation does not compel either party to agree to a proposal or require the making of a concession. . . .

A number of labor authorities contend that this statutory language is inherently self-contradictory. Professor Archibald Cox, recently the United States Solicitor General, for example, suggests that the statutory duty to bargain must either simply require recognition and the formalities of negotiation, or else it must require that plus the making of objectively reasonable proposals.[15] The NLRB has generally held that bad faith in bargaining depends upon a totality of conduct and, despite the statutory language which states that concessions are not required, has tended to view a refusal to make a counterproposal as evidence of bad faith. Thus, it appears that the NLRB has tended to lean in the direction of the second of Professor Cox's viewpoints. Moreover, the Board has continued to amplify the good-faith bargaining requirement by regulating various aspects of the collective bargaining process.

Thus, for example, the NLRB has over the years marked out certain actions as constituting per se violations of the good-faith requirement of the law. A refusal to sign a written agreement,[16] or unilateral changes in wages during negotiations,[17] or the withholding of information on wages and hours necessary for collective bargaining[18] have all been held to be per se indications of bad faith. In this manner the NLRB has attempted to set up standards of conduct which negotiators must follow behind closed doors.

Furthermore, the Board has seemingly adopted the notion that it is its function to attempt to maintain "laboratory" conditions for the bargaining process. It has therefore condemned attempts by unions or employers to use economic pressure during negotiations on the ground that this would disrupt the negotiations process. For example, in one case,[19] during the course of negotiations between a large insurance company and a union representing insurance agents, the agents refused to write new contracts, slowed down in their work, and adopted various tactics to harrass and embarrass the company. The NLRB ruled that such tactics constituted an unfair labor practice on the part of the union, but on appeal the United States Supreme Court disagreed.

The Court, in its decision, criticized the NLBR for its attempts to regulate the bargaining process. It stated that it was the intent of Congress that the parties approach bargaining with the proper attitude, but "apart from this essential standard of conduct, Congress intended that the parties should have wide latitude in their negotiations, unrestricted by any governmental power to regulate the substantive solution of their differences." The Court held that the use of economic pressure was not inconsistent with bargaining in good faith. "We see no indication that Congress has put it to the Board to define through its processes what economic sanctions might be permitted negotiating parties in an " 'ideal' or 'balanced' state of collective bargaining." Expressing a fear reminiscent of employer charges in the pre-Taft-Hartley era, the Court noted that if the Board could regulate the use of bargaining tactics under the guise of policing the good-faith requirement, it would be in a position to exercise considerable influence on the substantive terms of bargaining.

The General Electric Case

Nevertheless, the NLRB has not been deterred from its path of regulating tactics in bargaining to an extent certainly not envisioned by the writers of the Taft-Hartley Act, and apparently, at least to the layman, in contradiction to the policies laid down by the United States Supreme Court. The latest and most extreme version of the NLRB's action along these lines is the *General Electric* case.[20] In this instance the company, in 1960, followed its usual policy of offering a complete package of what it thought fair and proper to the unions with which it deals, after several weeks of negotiations.[21] Later, the company modified its offer in several ways, and most of the unions accepted it as the basis for a three-year contract. The International Union of Electrical Workers, however, following the leadership of its later deposed president, James B. Carey,[22] who had declared "I owe GE a strike,"[23] declined the offer, struck, but returned on substantially the pre-strike terms three weeks later.

Carey's union then filed a "refusal to bargain" charge. Four and one-half years *after* this union (and over 100 others) signed three-year agreements with General Electric, and eighteen months *after* these parties peacefully arrived at three year successor agreements, the NLRB ruled that GE was guilty of an unfair labor practice by refusing to bargain in good faith! The NLRB's reasoning is particularly extraordinary because it also found that (1) GE was not seeking to eliminate the union as a bargaining agent; (2) GE was at all times willing and even anxious to sign a new agreement; (3) GE did not engage in individual bargaining, as such; (4) GE's conduct at the bargaining table was not unlawful; and (5) GE's communications to its employees constituted legally protected activity. Then the NLRB applied its "totality of conduct" doctrine, added up all the legalities, and produced an illegality.

This the NLRB did principally by finding that communications to the employees by the company "froze" the company's stance at the bargaining table despite the fact that the company altered its offer several times and despite the clear wording of the Taft-Hartley Act which prohibits the NLRB from interfering with communications which bear no taint of coercion or promise of betterment. The NLRB also charged that the company derogated the President of the International Union of Electrical Workers, whereas the company pointed out that it merely communicated the truth of this person's actual words and conduct at the bargaining table.[24] Six months after the NLRB decision, this person in question, James B. Carey, resigned his presidency after the United States Department of Labor disclosed that his "re-election" had been fraudulent and that he had actually lost by 23,000 votes.

The NLRB's decision in this case is now on appeal before the courts. If it is sutained, it can only mean that agreements not satisfactory to union officials are not agreements at all, but unfair labor practices. Hence, the NLRB will have the right to pass upon content to determine whether it is fair—a definite step to, if not initial arrival at, compulsory arbitration.

The Lockout as a Tactic

The lockout is the employer's counterpart of the strike. Yet the NLRB has done everything possible to restrict its use. As a result, despite legislative sanction, the lockout has been so circum-

scribed by the NLRB that employers who use it must be on guard
against detailed legal attack.[25]

First of all, it has been generally established that to lock out
to forestall unionization is an unfair labor practice. The NLRB
then attempted to proscribe lockouts where the employer temporarily replaced employees in order to operate, but the courts
overruled this view. Repeatedly, the NLRB has attempted to
penalize employers who locked our employees as a bargaining
tactic without any anti-union motive, but many of these NLRB
decisions have been overturned by the courts.[26] As the U.S.
Supreme Court stated in the *Brown* case:[27]

"We begin with the proposition that the [Taft-Hartley] Act does
not constitute the Board as an 'arbiter of the sort of economic weapons
the parties can use in seeking to gain acceptance of their bargaining
demands'. . . . In the absence of proof of unlawful motivation, there
are many economic weapons which an employer may use that either
interfere in some measure with concerted employee activities, or
which are in some degree discriminatory and discourage union membership, and yet the use of such economic weapons does not constitute conduct that is within the prohibition of [the Act]. . . . Specifically,
he may in various circumstances use the lockout as a legitimate economic weapon . . . we hold that a lockout is not an unfair labor practice
simply because used by an employer to bring pressure to bear in support of his bargaining position after an impasse in bargaining negotiations has been reached."

Despite this posture of the United States Supreme Court, the
NLRB continues to attempt to limit, as much as possible, the use
of this key employer tactic.[28]

Co-Determination—The Control of Bargaining Content

Besides regulating how bargaining should be conducted, the
NLRB, with an assist from the courts, also regulates what may be
bargained, again utilizing Sections 8 (a) (5) and (b) (3), the
"good faith" bargaining sections as the wedge. The result is an
ever expanding area of managerial prerogatives opened to union
challenge, but a corollary protection of items from management
challenge which unions believe are solely their right to decide.
This is accomplished by dividing subjects into three areas: (1)
Mandatory; (2) Prohibited; and (3) Nonmandatory but lawful.

Mandatory Subjects of Bargaining

Under the Wagner Act the subjects over which there was a duty to bargain were defined by the NLRB and the courts through interpretation of the statutory language which refers to "bargaining in respect to rates of pay, wage, hours . . . or other conditions of employment." In the famous Inland Steel case[29] the Court held that even such matters as pensions and compulsory retirement were encompassed by this statutory language. Since that time, such varied issues as merit increases, group insurance, Christmas bonuses, rentals for company housing, and stock purchase plans have been held to be within the scope of collective barganing.[30]

Employers ask with some concern where are the limits to the matters over which there is a statutory obligation for them to bargain. They fear that the continually broadening view of what is encompassed by "wages, hours, or other conditions of employment," plus the Board's tendency to require counterproposals as part of the totality of conduct constituting good-faith bargaining, is gradually whittling away managerial preorgatives, and subjecting them to either co-determination by unions or arbitration by the Board.

This problem is graphically illustrated by the decisions of the NLRB on the subject of subcontracting. In March 1961, the NLRB held, in the Fibreboard Paper Products case,[31] that an employer had no obligation under the Taft-Hartley Act to bargain with a union representing its maintenance employees concerning the *company's decision* to contract out maintenance work. Subsequently, in April 1962, after a change in membership of the Board, this ruling was overturned, and the Board held that an employer must bargain with the union representing his employees regarding a decision to subcontract bargaining unit work, even if the *decision* to subcontract was motivated solely by economic considerations. Such a decision, the NLRB said, falls within the statutory phrase "other terms and conditions of employment" and is a mandatory subject of collective bargaining.[32] The Board emphasized, however, that the obligation to bargain did not prevent the employer from going ahead with a decision to subcontract made for valid business reasons. The Supreme Court affirmed the NLRB's ruling.[33]

The full significance of this decision is not yet clear. Does the Board mean that the employer can make up his mind, and then simply go through the motions of talking it over with the union, or must he actually "bargain"? Employers generally take a dim view of the Board's action. They contend that if the law requires them to talk about an issue with union representatives, it is almost impossible to avoid some compromise on it. The result will be new provisions on subcontracting in collective bargaining agreements, and managerial freedom to adjust to changing economic circumstances will be further restricted. As Professor Charles O. Gregory states: "The difference between this and a direct statutory command from Congress that certain matters be included in contracts is only one of degree."[34]

Nor was the Supreme Court's decision clarifying. For the court seemed to this layman to confuse bargaining over the *details* of subcontracting—that is, how much subcontracting, what allowances might be paid to workers displaced by subcontracting, etc. —with bargaining over the *decision* to subcontract. That the NLRB requires management to do the latter appears irrefutable. This in turn means that union agreement—that is, co-determination, must occur or else the union may ask the NLRB to set aside management's decision—in short, unions have a right to arbitral re-determination of a management decision.

A similar situation exists in plant closings. We have already noted how the NLRB has repeatedly attempted to thwart employers' use of the lockout as a tactical weapon. Going a step further, the NLRB attempted to assert the right to determine whether companies could go out of business.[35] The U.S. Supreme Court ruled that an employer "has an absolute right to terminate his entire business for any reason he pleases," but may not terminate part of it for anti-union purposes.[36] But this leaves the NLRB the right to determine whether a multiplant employer has closed one plant for anti-union purposes. If the NLRB so decides, then presumably it can order the plant reopened. Thus the NLRB becomes the final arbitrator of the right to cease doing business at a particular location!

The extent to which the NLRB has managed to inject itself into managerial decision making as the final arbiter is made clear by examining in combination the implications of the subcontracting and plant closing decisions with those of the *General Electric* case. For not only are all management decisions now subject to union co-determination, but management cannot reach an impasse with the union for this is obviously not "good faith" bargaining. How can it be? A failure to agree is obviously worse than an agreement, but in the *General Electric* case, it was ruled that an *agreement* followed by a new agreement three years later did not exonerate the company from a charge of bad faith! One must therefore not only reach agreement, but also an agreement satisfactory to the NLRB!

Prohibited Subjects of Bargaining

Under the Wagner Act the substantive terms of collective bargaining contracts were almost entirely free of statutory regulation. The Taft-Hartley amendments, however, prohibited bargaining concerning certain matters even if both labor and management were agreeable to the inclusion of such provisions in a contract. Thus the amended Act made it an unfair labor practice for an employer or a union to enter into or to effectuate closed shop or preferential hiring agreements. Congress, in effect, stated that public policy considerations superseded the wishes of the parties concerned when they bargained over such issues.

Nonmandatory Subjects of Bargaining

Congress has thus stated that the parties must bargain over certain issues and cannot bargain over others. What about all the issues which do not fall in these two categories—are they free of regulation?

Assume the following set of facts: An employer bargaining with a union insists, as a condition to entering into any contractual agreement, that such agreement contain (a) a "ballot" clause calling for a pre-strike secret vote of employees, both union and nonunion, as to the employer's last offer; and (b) a "recognition" clause which excludes as a party to the contract the international union which had been certified by the NLRB as the employees' exclusive bargaining agent and substitutes for it an uncertified local union.

Now, it can be argued that the second demand involves an illegal objective, since the Taft-Hartley Act requires the employer to bargain with the certified representative of the employees, and the employer circumvents this purpose by substitution of an un-certified local. But what about the first demand—is there anything wrong with that? The employer's argument, of course, is that he is interested in avoiding strikes resulting from hasty action by the employees and therefore wants to make sure that employees have time to consider his last offer and to vote for or against it by secret ballot.

This set of facts came before the NLRB in the Wooster Division of Borg-Warner Corporation case and subsequently was appealed all the way to the Supreme Court.[37] The Supreme Court upheld an NLRB order that the employer's insistence upon either clause was violative of the good-faith requirement of Section 8 (a) (5) of the amended NLRA. Justice Burton, speaking for the majority, stated that neither clause related to a matter which under the amended Act was a subject of mandatory collective bargaining. He enunciated the view that the parties could talk about other things, but if they *insisted* on inclusion of such matters in a contract, it violated the good-faith requirement of the law!

Justice Harlan, speaking for the minority, raised some penetrating questions concerning the practicality of the majority position. He agreed with the majority as to the employer's insistence upon the recognition clause, but disagreed on the matter of the secret ballot clause. He stated:

> . . . I am unable to grasp a concept of "bargaining" which enables one to "propose" a particular point, but not to "insist" on it as a condition of agreement. The right to bargain becomes illusory if one is not free to press a proposal in good faith to the point of insistence. Surely adoption of so inherently vague and fluid a standard is apt to inhibit the entire bargaining process because of a participant's fear that strenuous argument might shade into forbidden insistence and thereby produce a charge of an unfair labor practice. . . .

The Court could have decided that the ballot clause was a mandatory subject of bargaining falling within the meaning of the statutory language "wages, hours, and other terms and conditions of employment." This position would have given the parties the maximum latitude over subjects which could be included in collective bargaining. Specifically, it would mean that the employer could bargain to an impasse on the issue of the ballot clause. By the same token, it would mean that a union could bargain to an impasse on issues which employers in future cases might feel should not be included in normal collective bargaining negotiations. Furthermore, once an issue is determined to fall in the mandatory bargaining category, the power of government can be brought to bear to force a recalcitrant party to negotiate on this subject. As a practical matter, once an issue falls in the mandatory class, it is only a question of time before it becomes embodied in written contracts, for it is almost impossible to bargain in good faith on an issue in accordance with Board standards and not be led into compromises and settlements with respect to it. From this point of view the Court, in the Borg-Warner case, by refusing to hold that the ballot issue fell within the mandatory class, could have set a precedent which would tend to slow the invasion by unions of the critical area of managerial prerogatives. For while, in this case, it was the employer who was pressing an unusual demand, it is usually unions who try and expand the scope of bargaining. Actually, of course, the Court has adopted a schizophrenic approach because it has given general approval to the NLRB union program of expanding the scope of bargaining into managerial prerogatives while at the same time estopping managerial attempts to invade "union prerogatives."

Instead of deciding that the Borg-Warner demand for a free ballot was a mandatory subject of bargaining, the Court concluded that bargaining to an impasse on the ballot clause was per se an unfair labor practice, even though the trial examiner had made a finding that the company had bargained in good faith. This approach effectively narrows the area of permissible collective bargaining. It places the government in the position of more or less preserving the *status quo* as to what is a bargainable issue. The Court, in effect, says to the parties: "This issue does not seem to fall within the statutory language referring to 'wages, hours, and other terms and conditions of employment,' and therefore you cannot press this demand too far." Ironically, however, the Court says this only about management's demands! Not only is this approach one-sided, but it also brings the government further into the bargaining process, for there is little significant difference between having the government tell parties what they *must* bargain about and what they *cannot* bargain about. In either case the government exercises a major control over the substantive content of collective bargaining, and sets up the NLRB as the final arbitrator.

Moving Directly to Arbitration

Having moved so closely to compulsory arbitration without statutory basis except in the limited area of representation and jurisdictional disputes, it is not surprising that NLRB spokesmen have indicated how a statutory basis could be accomplished to expand even further the Board's drive for compulsory power. This was foreshadowed by the brief of the General Counsel in the General Electric case, which stated:[38]

"Thus the General Counsel contends that GE's avowed opposition to third party intervention either by way of mediation or arbitration, two processes which are accepted and even preferred methods of resolving differences between employers and unions, is clear evidence of the closed-mind bargaining alleged herein."

Then in a formal law review article, the Solicitor of the NLRB, Mr. William Feldesman proposed a plan to encourage what he calls "voluntary arbitration" by use of the NLRB powers. Under his plan, if either party offered arbitration, the other would be penalized by not accepting. Thus the NLRB could enjoin a strike if an employer requested arbitration and the union declined to accept and the employer might receive tax benefits; but if a union proposed arbitration, and the employer declined, economic strikers could not lose their jobs and would receive unemployment compensation benefits. Mr. Feldesman concludes: "Practical encouragement of voluntary arbitration through the balancing of rights under the familiar legal rubric of the federal collective bargaining statute would appear to be clearly in the public interest."[39]

Obviously, arbitration would not be voluntary, nor would collective bargaining exist under this plan. For example, let us suppose that a mythical union, the United Current Workers, is negotiating with a mythical company, the General Current Corporation, under Mr. Feldesman's proposal. The union demands an end to company communication, no contracting out, co-determination over new plant construction, and a 45-cent wage and benefit package. The company rejects these demands, makes a counter offer and advises its employees of the economic consequences of the union demands. The union proffers arbitration, but the company declines to put the future of its enterprise into the hands of a group of academicians who have no responsibility for the future of the business. The union strikes, and after three weeks the strike is settled on terms approximating those offered by the company.

After the strike the union files an unfair labor practice. Four and one-half years later, the NLRB finds that the company did not bargain in good faith because of its "totality of conduct." Meanwhile the union members received protection against replacement during the strike as well as unemployment benefits and the union continued to accumulate a strike fund which it never had to pay out. The number of strikes which would follow union demands to arbitrate and the increasing bankruptcy of state unemployment conpensation funds which would result are easy to envision.

Or, consider the case where a company requests arbitration. "No," says the union official, "I owe this company a strike." The company requests an injunction against the strike, but the union files a charge claiming that the company did not bargain in good faith. Because of the union charge, the NLRB would then plead neutrality—and decline to request the injunction. Four and one-half years later, the NLRB might exonerate the company, but meanwhile it may have gone out of business.

The Need for Reform

Despite the obvious inequities and completely destructive nature of this proposal, it, like other NLRB programs, is put forward to "strengthen collective bargaining." What are the real remedies for the NLRB attempt to substitute its decisions for the collective bargaining process?

Insofar as representation disputes are concerned, there is obvious need for Congress to act to insure free speech, fair bargaining units, and fair secret ballot elections—not card checks. Such action must be in the form of the clearest language, for the NLRB's present membership has developed a keeness unexcelled in reading Congressional intent to suit its purposes.

The tendency of the NLRB to utilize Section 8 (a) (5) to curb management bargaining power, to promote union objectives, and, indeed, to move generally toward a system of co-determination from one of managerial right to manage, or from a demand and response type of bargaining, has shown a marked increase since 1961 when appointments of the Kennedy Administration assumed control of the NLRB. The extreme positions taken by the New Frontier-controlled NLRB, and the gyrations in NLRB policy over the years have resulted in several suggestions for reform. Among those have been life appointments for NLRB members, transfer of NLRB functions to the courts, and abolition of Section 8 (a) (5) and 8 (b) (3).

Of these three proposals, only the last reaches out to the heart of the problem. Life appointments could be "bad," as well as "good," appointments from many points of view; and the courts could take the government as far into the bargaining process as the NLRB has done. The need is to remove to *raison d'etre*—not to alter the method.

Returning Collective Bargaining to the Parties

The GE case points up what many scholars of the law have become convinced[40]—the need to protect collective bargaining from the steady encroachments of the National Labor Relations Board, and to return the NLRB to its originally conceived role of determining peacefully representation disputes and proscribing discrimination relating thereto. The consensus is that the way to accomplish this is to delete the refusal to bargain section—8 (a) (5) and (b) (3)—entirely from the law, and to confine the activities of the NLRB entirely, as expressed by Professor William Gomberg, a veteran of twenty years in the labor movement to "1. The promulgation of rules and procedures for holding representation elections; 2. Formulating adequate remedies for those workers who are the victims of discriminatory discharge or layoff prompted either by union or employer."[41]

In agreement with Professor Gomberg are the distinguished scholars[42] who comprised the Committee for Economic Development's Independent Study Group. They concluded:[43]

"The requirement to bargain . . . has been succeeded by a flood of litigation and an increasingly complex set of regulations stemming from amendments of the original provisions and from interpretations by the NLRB and the Courts. The efficacy of the process . . .—to compel the parties to bargain in good faith—is at best doubtful. . . .

"The subjects to be covered by bargaining, the procedures to be followed, the nuances of strategy involving the timing of a 'best offer' . . . are best left to the parties. Indeed the work load of the National Labor Relations Board and of the parties could be substantially reduced by returning the issues to the door of the employer or union where Senator Walsh wisely left them."

If such reform is not accomplished, the NLRB will continue to be used as, in Gomberg's words, "a whipping boy for the frustration of a party to the bargain who refuses to face the consequences of overplaying his hand and then goes running to papa government."[44] In view of the extreme position of the General Counsel in this case as to what constitutes good faith bargaining, its general acceptance by the trial examiner, and the fact that such a position is likely to be taken again against a company less equipped to protect itself than is General Electric, the danger to collective bargaining and free enterprise inherent in the NLRB's steady intrusion into the bargaining sphere is as obvious as it is urgently in need of reform.

NOTES

1. See, e.g., Herbert R. Northrup and Gordon F. Bloom, *Government and Labor* (Homewood, Ill: Richard D. Irwin, Inc., 1961), Chapters 2-7.

2. On this subject, see Kenneth C. McGuiness, *The New Frontier NLRB* (Washington: Labor Policy Association, Inc., 1963), Chapter V; and Herbert R. Northrup, *Boulwarism: The Labor Policies of the General Electric Company* (Ann Arbor: Bureau of Industrial Relations, University of Michigan, 1964), Chapter 12. See also Sylvester Petro, *How the NLRB Repealed Taft-Hartley* (Washington: Labor Policy Association, Inc., 1958).

3. *National Labor Relations Board v. Metropolitan Life Insurance Co.,* U. S. Supreme Court, April 5, 1965.

4. From speech by NLRB member Gerald A. Brown at Institute on Labor Law, Duke University Law School, Durham, North Carolina, February 9, 1962.

5. *NLRB v. S.N.C. Manufacturing Co.,* U. S. Court of Appeals, District of Columbia, May 14, 1965. Despite serious doubts of the fairness of the authorization cards, the court enforced this order, a most extraordinary decision.

6. *National Labor Relations Board v. Radio and Television Broadcast Engineers' Union,* 364 U. S. 573, 81 S. Ct. 330 (1961).

7. Data from NLRB.

8. For studies of NLRB decisions in the jurisdictional areas, see Charles T. Schmidt, Jr., "What is the Current Status of Work Assignment Dis-

putes," *Labor Law Journal*, Vol. XVI (May 1965), pp. 270-293; and J. S. David, "Jurisdictional Disputes Since the CBS Decision," *New York University Law Review*, Vol. XXXIX (June 1964), pp. 657-685.

9. Much of the ensuing discussion is based on Northrup and Bloom, *op. cit.*, Chapter 5, and Northrup, *Boulwarism*, *op. cit.*, Chapter 11.

10. *Congressional Record* 7660, 74th Congress, 1st session, May 16, 1935.

11. *National Labor Relations Board v. George Pilling & Son Co.*, 119 F. (2d) 32, 37 (3d Cir. 1941).

12. *Rex Manufacturing Co., Inc.*, 24 LRRM 1653.

13. U. S. House of Representatives, Committee on Education and Labor, *Labor Management Relations Act*, 1947, Report No. 245, 80th Congress, 1st session (Washington, D. C.: U. S. Government Printing Office, April 11, 1947), p. 19.

14. *National Labor Relations Board v. Insurance Agents International Union, AFL-CIO*, 361 U. S. 477, 487; 80 S.Ct. 419 (1959).

15. Archibald Cox, "The Duty to Bargain in Good Faith," *Harvard Law Review*, Vol. LXXI (June 1958), p. 1416.

16. *National Labor Relations Board v. Highland Park Manufacturing Co.*, 110 F. (2x) 632 (4th Cir. 1940).

17. *General Motors Corp.*, 81 NLRB 779, enforcement granted 179 F. (2d) 221 (2d Cir. 1950).

18. *National Labor Relations Board v. F. W. Woolworth Co.*, 352 U. S. 938, 77 S.Ct. 261 (1956).

19. *National Labor Relations Board v. Highland Park Manufacturing Co.*, 110 F. (2d) 632 (4th Cir. 1940).

20. *General Electric Co.*, 150 NLRB No. 36, December 16, 1964.

21. A full description of General Electric's labor relations policies is found in Northrup, *Boulwarism*, loc. cit.

22. Mr. Carey resigned in March 1965 after the U. S. Department of Labor disclosed that he had actually been defeated for re-election by 23,000 votes, not re-elected as his self-chosen tellers had reported three months before.

23. For source, date, etc. of this comment, see Northrup, *op. cit.*, p. 68.

24. See *ibid.*, pp. 82-84 for excerpts from the Carey conduct.

25. See Bernard D. Meltzer, "Lockouts under the LMRA: New Shadows on an Old Terrain," *University of Chicago Law Review*, Vol. XXVIII (Summer 1961), pp. 614-628.

26. See, *e.g.*, *American Ship Building Co. v. NLRB*, and *NLRB v. Brown*, U. S. Supreme Court, March 29, 1965.

27. *Loc. cit.*, note 26.

28. See the *Daily Labor Report*, May 6, 1965, p. A-1, in which the NLRB is reported to be requesting the Second Circuit Court of Appeals to narrow the scope of its interpretation of the cases cited in note 26, above.

29. *Inland Steel Co. v. National Labor Relations Board*, 170 F. (2d) 247 (7th Cir. 1948).

30. See Leon M. Despres and Samuel D. Golden, "The Duty to Bargain," *University of Illinois Law Forum* (Spring, 1955), p. 15.

31. 47 LRRM 1547.

32. *Town & Country Manufacturing Co.*, 49 LRRM 1918.

33. *Fibreboard Paper Products Corp. v. NLRB*, U. S. Supreme Court, December 14, 1964.

34. C. O. Gregory, *Labor and the Law* (2d ed. New York: W. W. Norton Company, Inc., 1961), p. 413.

35. *Darlington Co.*, 51 LRRM 1278.

36. *NLRB v. Darlington Mfg. Co.*, U. S. Supreme Court, March 29, 1965.

37. *National Labor Relations Board v. Wooster Division of Borg-Warner Corp.*, 356 U. S. 342, 78 S.Ct. 718 (1958).

38. General Counsel's Brief, in Case 150 NLRB, No. 36, p. 246.

39. William Feldesman, "Another Approach to Strikes: Inducements to Voluntary Arbitration," *George Washington Law Review*, Vol. XXXIII (December 1964), pp. 457-466.

40. Professor George W. Taylor, for example, whose views on collective bargaining are excerpted at great length in the General Counsel's brief for the General Electric case, has long held the belief that Sections 8 (a) (5) and 8 (b) (3) have no place in the Taft-Hartley Act, unless possibly applied only to the initial contract bargaining between the parties.

41. William Gomberg, "Government Participation in Union Regulation and Collective Bargaining," *Labor Law Journal* XIII (November 1962), pp. 946-947.

42. The members included Professor Taylor, Dr. Clark Kerr, President of the University of California, Mr. David L. Cole, and Professors Douglas V. Brown of Massachusetts Institute of Technology, and Philip Taft of Brown, among others.

43. Independent Study Group, *The Public Interest in Collective Bargaining* (New York: Committee for Economic Development, 1961), pp. 81-82.

44. Gomberg, *op. cit.*, p. 944.

PART III

GOVERNMENT INTERVENTION IN
OTHER FORMS

CHAPTER

7 The Search for a Policy: *Federal Intervention, 1945-1965*

WHEN WORLD WAR II ENDED, the return to collective bargaining was made difficult by the reliance of both industry and unions on government intervention and the failure of either to realize that postwar strikes would be long-drawn-out affairs, not the "quickies" which featured eruptions during wartime. There resulted a series of executive and Congressional improvisations culminating in 1947 with the passage of Title II of the Taft-Hartley Act.

This chapter reviews the experience of the postwar period, examines the effectiveness of the Taft-Hartley Act in the light of our criteria, and analyzes also extra-legal disputes activities of the federal government since 1945.

Post-World War II Fact and Seizure

Several efforts were made by both President Truman and the Congress to cope with major strikes in the period between the end of World War II and the passage of the Taft-Hartley Act in 1947. Both the President and the Congress leaned heavily on the procedures of the Railway Labor Act as a model for their proposals and activities, but both also advocated and strove to utilize more stringent measures when the more modest ones seemed to fail.

The President, obviously dismayed by the postwar strike wave, sought to abate it by the appointment of fact finding boards, some set up by himself, others by his Secretary of Labor. These operated similarly to those under the Railway Labor Act, but without statutory basis. Their recommendations were not always acceptable, but with some "sweetening," usually after a White House conference in the manner of the Railway Labor Act Workings in this period (see Chapter 5), they usually provided a basis of settlement. A Committee appointed by the governor of New Jersey to review emergency dispute laws was favorably impressed with these extra-legal boards, maintaining that they helped to avoid strikes in some cases or helped to curtail them in others.[1] On the other hand, representatives of the industries involved, and probably most management personnel, felt that these boards were created as a result of "labor's easy access to the White House," and that the "boards' recommendations . . . were unduly generous to labor."[2]

Congress, too, favored the fact finding approach. Two bills, Ball-Burton-Hatch, and Case, which received serious attention, were modeled in part on the Railway Labor Act. Congress passed the Case bill in May 1946 (on the very day on which the railroad unions went out on a nationwide strike), but President Truman successfully vetoed it. The Ball-Burton-Hatch proposal, which did not get out of committee, added a compulsory arbitration feature to the Railway Labor Act procedure.

When fact finding did not succeed and White House conferences also failed, President Truman used his seizure powers which he retained under wartime emergency powers in effect through mid-1947. On nine occasions after the Japanese surrender, he seized properties, with the coal mines and the railroads the most frequent industries involved. In both the second 1946 coal strike and the 1947 railroad dispute, seizures were accompanied by injunctions, ordering the termination of the strike in the former and barring a strike in the latter. When John L. Lewis and the United Mine Workers defied the injunction secured by the federal government, both were heavily fined. On appeal, the United States Supreme Court upheld the fine, ruling that the coal miners were "government employees" during the period of the seizure and that therefore the Norris-La Guardia Anti-injunction Act[3] did not apply to such "government employees."[4] The Court ruled thus although seizure had resulted in only the most nominal government operation, with the coal mine owners designed as "government managers" of the mines, and with profits accruing to the private owners, although losses were assumed by the federal government.

War and postwar seizure was not always objectionable to unions, however. For example, in one of the dramatic confrontations between the government and John L. Lewis's United Mine Workers which occurred in this period, the mines were seized, and then the famous agreement between Lewis and Secretary of the Interior Julius Krug set up the welfare payments on the basis of a royalty per ton of coal mined. "When this kind of settlement is made, employees as a group are not required to work under unsatisfactory terms, but the position of the employers is most unenviable. Only by embracing a settlement to which they were not a party can they secure control of their plants."[5]

EMERGENCY DISPUTES AND THE TAFT-HARTLEY ACT

The emergency disputes provisions of the Taft-Hartley Act were shaped by wartime and postwar events. The Republican Party won control of Congress in 1946 on a platform which stressed labor reform. Although the chief attention of Congress was directed toward amending the Wagner Act, there was considerable interest in strike control in view of the big strike wave of 1946 and the general public disquiet with labor strife.

The postwar experience had, however, given some pause to those who advocated stringent strike control. The late Senator Robert Taft, Republican leader in the Senate, led the fight which prevented the adoption of President Truman's "draft labor" bill, aimed at ending the 1946 railroad strike.[6] The costly Krug-Lewis coal mining agreement pointed up the dangers of government seizure to management proponents. And the experiences under fact finding boards appointed by President Truman, as well as the war and postwar record of the Railway Labor Act, discouraged too faithful emulation of the Railway Labor Act's procedures. The product was a series of compromises which left labor free to strike after a delaying procedure, provided for fact finding boards but denied such boards the right to make recommendations, tried to make certain that employees really wanted to strike, and then required the President to request Congressional action if he believed more authority to deal with a situation was required. The result, like most compromises, has pleased very few, been administered quite differently under different administrations, and remained in effect because of lack of agreement on proposed changes, not because of lack of proposals for change.

Emergency Strike Provisions of Taft-Hartley

Title I of the Taft-Hartley Act provides that a sixty-day notice be required for changes in labor-management contracts. These notices have become perfunctory and, as will be examined in Chapter 9, affect primarily the intervention activities of mediation services.

Title II of the Taft-Hartley Act also provides that the President appoint a "board of inquiry" to investigate and to report on the issues of a dispute where he believes that such threatened or actual dispute "will, if permitted to occur or to continue, imperil the national health or safety. . . ." The board of inquiry is required, after public hearings if it so desires, to report to the President, setting forth the pertinent issues in dispute and the positions of both parties, but the report "shall not contain any recommendations."

Upon receiving the report, the President may then direct the Attorney General to petition a federal district court for an injunction to prevent or to terminate a strike or lockout. If the injunction is granted, the conditions of work and pay are frozen for the time being, and the parties are obliged to make every effort to settle their differences with the assistance of the Federal Mediation and Conciliation Service. If these efforts fail, at the end of 60 days the board of inquiry, which the President reconvenes when the injunction is granted, is required to make another public report to the President, also without recommendations for settlement, which includes the current status of the dispute, the positions of the parties, and "the employer's last offer of settlement." The National Labor Relations Board is then required within 15 days to poll employees as to whether they would accept the last offer of employer and to certify the result to the Attorney General within five days. The injunction must then be dissolved. By this time, 80 days have elapsed since the first application for an injunction. If the majority of workers refuse the employer's last offer, then the President may submit a complete report to Congress with or without recommendations for action, but the employees are free to strike or the employer to lock out once the injunction is dissolved. Table 3 shows that, as of June 1, 1965, boards of inquiry had been appointed, under this section, on 24 different occasions. In 11 cases a strike vote on the employer's last offer was taken; and in five cases, strikes occurred after the machinery of the Act had been completely utilized.

Presidents and Industries

An examination of the data in Table 3 shows that President Truman was a major invoker of the Act, utilizing it ten times in five years, seven of which came in the first year of its existence. President Kennedy might have surpassed this record, for he invoked Taft-Hartley emergency procedure six times in about three years, where as President Eisenhower utilized this procedure only seven times in eight years. It could be argued that times were more difficult for labor peace in the Truman and Kennedy administrations than in Eisenhower's. Given, however, the propensity of Presidents Truman and Kennedy to utilize extra-legal emergency provisions in addition, and often in preference, to those of the Taft-Hartley Act, as will be recounted later in this chapter, one must conclude that these presidents had a greater willingness to invoke emergency procedure, just as they frequently demonstrated a greater willingness to utilize government intervention in other aspects of the economy, than did President Eisenhower.

In short, the more "interventionist" the president, the more are parties likely to secure that intervention by pushing their disputes to what are conceived as emergency situations. And as is

TABLE 3

EMERGENCY DISPUTES UNDER THE TAFT-HARTLY ACT, 1947–APRIL 1, 1963

Administration	Year	Industry, Company, and Union	Results
Truman	1948	1. Atomic energy, Oak Ridge, Tennessee (Union Carbide Company versus Atomic Trades and Labor Council, a local federation of AFL unions)	Agreement reached after Act had run its course and "last" offer rejected, on basis of an offer superior to "last" offer. No strike before or after Act was invoked.
	1948	2. Meatpacking (Swift, Armour, Cudahy, Morrell, and Wilson companies and United Packinghouse Workers)	Strike ended by agreement after board of inquiry made its report, but before injunction was issued.
	1948	3. Bituminous coal industry (most of industry and United Mine Workers)	Strike settlement by appointment of Senator Bridges of New Hampshire as neutral member of pension board. Meanwhile, John L. Lewis and United Mine Workers disobeyed court injunction and were heavily fined by district judge for contempt of court.
	1948	4. Telephone (American Telephone and Telegraph Company versus American Union of Telephone Workers [now Communication Workers of America])	Dispute settled without a strike after board of inquiry was appointed, but before hearings were held.
	1948	5. Maritime and longshore industry (all unionized shipping companies, plus Pacific stevedoring industry, and all shipping unions plus International Longshoremen's and Warehousemen's Union)	Shipping dispute settled after injunction but prior to last-offer vote except on West Coast. International Longshoremen's and Warehousemen's Union ordered a boycott of vote, and no longshoremen voted. Then a ten-week strike occurred before settlement was reached on the West Coast.
	1948	6. Bituminous coal (industry and United Mine Workers)	Agreement reached by parties prior to strike and prior to report of a board of inquiry.

Truman (continued)	1948	7. Longshore industry (East and Gulf Coast stevedoring firms and International Longshoremen's Association)	Act invoked and injunction issued before strike. Last-offer vote held and rejected. Agreement negotiated but rejected by membership. After two-week strike, improved agreement accepted by membership.
	1949–50	8. Bituminous coal industry (most of industry and United Mine Workers)	Sporadic strikes over four-month period led to board of inquiry appointment. When injunction failed to end strike, government moved for contempt, but court ruled government had failed to produce evidence of contempt. At this point, parties negotiated a new agreement as President Truman was asking Congress for authority to seize mines.
	1951	9. Copper and nonferrous metals industry (Phelps-Dodge, Kennicott, Anaconda, American Smelting and Refining, and smaller companies, and Mine, Mill and Smelter Workers' Union)	After a strike, union declined offer to call it off and submit it to National Wage Stabilization Board, then a board of inquiry was appointed and an injunction issued, ending strike. All major firms settled with the union during the 80-day period, but eight smaller companies did not. Employees in these companies rejected last offer. Record does not indicate terms of settlement in these companies.
	1952	10. Atomic energy (American Locomotive Company, Dunkirk, New York, plant and United Steelworkers)	Strike halted after initial board of inquiry report and injunction. Agreement reached prior to end of 80-day period.
Eisenhower..............	1953–54	11. Longshore industry (East and Gulf Coast stevedoring companies and two factions of International Longshoremen's Association)	Dispute essentially involved attempt of AFL to replace racket-ridden International Longshoremen's Association, which it disaffiliated, with a new affiliate in port of New York. After two representative elections, several strikes, contempt proceedings, and fines, old ILA group won out by narrow margin, won a contract, and eventual AFL reaffiliation.

TABLE 3 (Continued)

Administration	Year	Industry, Company, and Union	Results
Eisenhower (continued)......	1954	12. Atomic energy (Union Carbide Company, Oak Ridge, Tennessee, and United Gas, Coke and Chemical Workers)	Short strike was followed by board of inquiry report and injunction. "Last" offer rejected, but as in 1948, better offer than "last" one resulted in agreement without strike.
	1954	13. Atomic energy, Oak Ridge, Tennessee (Union Carbide Company and Atomic Trades and Labor Council, a local federation of AFL unions)	Board of inquiry, same as No. 12, reported no threat of stoppage. Issues settled on basis of agreement reached in No. 12.
	1956–57	14. Longshore industry (East and Gulf Coast stevedoring companies and International Longshoremen's Association)	Strike over economic issues and union demand for industry-wide agreement resulted in board of inquiry, 80-day injunction, considerable litigation, rejection of employers' "last" offer, and another strike of one week in New York and longer in other ports until agreement was reached.
	1957	15. Atomic energy, Portsmouth, Ohio (Goodyear Rubber Company and Oil, Chemical and Atomic Workers)	After short strike, board of inquiry was followed by 80-day injunction and rejection of employers' "last" offer. The day after the injunction was dissolved, the parties reached agreement on a better offer than the "last" one.
	1959	16. Longshore industry (East and Gulf Coast stevedoring employees and International Longshoremen's Association)	Strike was followed by board of inquiry, 80-day injunction, and rejection of last offer. Agreement was then reached on new contract.
	1959–60	17. Basic steel industry (major steel producers and United Steelworkers)	Strike began in July. In October, board of inquiry set up, and injunction granted after Arthur Goldberg, then union counsel, contested view that health and safety were

Eisenhower (continued).......			involved. Before injunction expired, agreement was reached through pressure and mediation by Vice President Nixon and Secretary of Labor Mitchell. Four small companies did not agree, and their employees rejected "last" offer. A few strikes occurred before eventual settlement.
Kennedy...........	1961	18. Maritime industry (East and Gulf Coast shipowners, plus a few Pacific Coast ones, and National Maritime Union and other unions)	Strike resulted in board of inquiry and 80-day injunction. Settlement was reached during 80-day period in all disputes, except that of one company, whose employees rejected "last" offer.
	1962	19. Maritime industry (Pacific Coast shipowners and Seafarers' International Union and other unions)	Board of inquiry followed by injunction ended strike. Settlement was reached for new contract during 80-day period.
	1962	20. Aerospace industry (Republic Aviation, Farmingdale, New York, and International Association of Machinists)	Board of inquiry and injunction ended strike. Settlement was reached for a new contract during 80-day period.
	1962–63	21. Longshore industry (East and Gulf Coast stevedoring employees and International Longshoremen's Association)	Despite "preventive mediation" by federal mediators, strike occurred when contract expired without any change of position by parties on issues involving automation and work crews. After board of inquiry, 80-day injunction, and last-offer vote rejection, strike began again two days before Christmas. After a strike of about one month, President Kennedy appointed an extralegal board headed by Senator Wayne Morse which in effect imposed a settlement too generous for the union to reject and which was reluctantly accepted by the employers.

TABLE 3 (Continued)

Administration	Year	Industry, Company, and Union	Results
Kennedy (continued)........	1962	22. Aerospace industry (Lockheed Aircraft Company, California, and International Association of Machinists)	After Lockheed refused to permit a vote on union shop, as recommended by an extra-legal Presidential board, union struck, and President invoked the Act. Union accepted Lockheed's offer of contract without union shop prior to last offer vote because of indications that employees would vote favorably on company offer.
	1963	23. Aerospace industry (Boeing Aircraft Company, Seattle, Washington, and elsewhere, and International Association of Machinists)	After Boeing refused to accept a union shop recommendation of an extralegal board appointed by President Kennedy, the President invoked the Act to prevent a strike. Dispute settled eventually without union shop after last offer vote rejected.
Johnson...............	1964–65	24. Longshore Industry (East and Gulf Coast and International Longshoremen's Association)	Despite extensive federal "preventive mediation" and research on facts, no bargaining occurred on strike deadlines. President Johnson invoked law and obtained 80-day injunction in late 1964. Agreement reached before strike deadline, but rejected by New York membership. Strike began on January 10, 1965, in New York and spread to all Atlantic and Gulf ports. New York members accepted agreement on second vote, but strike continued as other ports negotiated. President Johnson intervened in February and strike called off in all settled ports. All ports back at work by end of February.

SOURCE: U.S. Department of Labor, Bureau of Labor Statistics, *National Emergency Disputes Under the Labor Management Relations (Taft-Hartley) Act, 1947–October, 1960* Report No. 169 (Washington, D. C.: U.S. Government Printing Office, 1961); records of National Labor Relations Board and Federal Mediation and Conciliation Service.

noticeably true under the Railway Labor Act, the more friendly the administration is to labor, the more unions are likely to push their demands to a stage where intervention by that friendly administration is assured. Thus, despite the abhorrence with which unions have officially regarded the Taft-Hartley Act, certain of them have not hesitated to push for its use where the prospects for satisfactory results appeared good.

From an industry analysis, the most invocations have occurred in longshore, atomic energy, and coal. The last all occurred in the early years when coal strikes were both more frequent and more critical than under the conditions of the 1960's. After John L. Lewis and the United Mine Workers were both fined for contempt of an injunction in 1948, the coal operators apparently believed that the Taft-Hartley Act was their "equalizer." When, however, in the 1949-1950 case, the courts ruled that the government had to prove its charges by evidence which it had not done, earnest bargaining replaced seeking government intervention. Since then, the parties in this industry have settled their disputes without strikes or fanfare as the market for their product and employment in the industry have continued to plunge downward.

Five disputes in the atomic industry, and three in the aerospace companies, make up a defense industry total of seven. In most of these cases, extra-legal procedures, which are discussed later in this chapter, were also utilized. The attitude of the federal government toward strikes and/or labor relations in facilities in which the government is the sole, or almost sole, customer, and in which the products are required for, or utilized in, the nation's defense effort, remains a critical problem of public policy which will be left for the discussion of major issues and problems later in this book.[7]

The East and Gulf Coast longshore industry remains the most persistent utilizer of Taft-Hartley emergency procedure. Faced with serious problems of automation, the International Longshoremen's Association has countered until recently with a refusal to discuss change intelligently, while the employers have been almost as intransigent in discussing their responsibilities under change. In the 1962-1963 dispute, the *New York Times* noted that "ever since negotiations began . . . both sides have proceeded with certainty that there would be no real bargaining until after the President had been compelled to invoke his power to order the longshoremen back to work in the public interest." More accurately, there was no bargaining even after the "last" offer was turned down and the strike resumed.

To many observers, it seemed that if the late President had not felt "compelled" to invoke the Act's machinery immediately after the strike began in October, the parties might have been stunned into moving toward settlement. Instead, the real "emergency," if it occurred, started when the Act's machinery had been completed. That this union and this industry have created emergency after emergency in order to use the Act's machinery as part of their negotiating tactics appears obvious. The action of President Kennedy in appointing an extra-legal board, and that board's most generous award—39 cents in wages and benefits over two years, almost double the employers' last offer—in effect rewarded the union for its intransigence and irresponsibility.

As part of the 1963 settlement, the parties agreed to have the United States Department of Labor make detailed studies of hiring practices and manpower usage in the principal Atlantic and Gulf ports. Despite the wealth of data, the parties, again in 1964, did no bargaining until their strike deadline was reached—and again Presidential intervention—this time by President Johnson—produced an 80-day injunction as soon as a strike occurred. On this occasion, however, revolts occurred against the do-nothing practices of both management and union representatives. Management representatives of automated companies, particularly Sea/Land Services, and up-and-coming union leaders like John Scotto of Brooklyn, forced a reversal of traditional policies. The result was a four-year agreement in the Port of New York providing for gradual elimination of featherbedding practices and regularization of employment, as well as substantial wage and benefit gains.

Nevertheless, the New York City rank-and-file, lacking effective communication and distrustful of any agreement negotiated at "headquarters," voted down the deal. After considerable communication, a new vote resulted in an acceptance. But the strike which began in New York on January 10, 1965, after the first vote continued in all Atlantic and Gulf ports for a month until negotiations took place in other ports outside of New York. President Johnson then intervened, and the union finally let all ports which had settled return to work, with all ports finally settling later in February. Hopefully, the new agreement and the new forces within port management and labor will result in the parties accepting their responsibility and their bargaining *before* the Taft-Hartley process is set into motion. Such self-help could be greatly enhanced if the President would not so readily invoke the machinery of the Act.

The Last-Offer Vote

Of all the procedures in the Act, the least successful is the last-offer vote. With few exceptions it has been utilized to gain the unions more. They have simply told their memberships to vote "no" and they will obtain more, *and this has happened in all twelve cases in which a last-offer vote occurred*, more often without a strike than with one. It also happened in eight of the nine cases in which a vote was held under a similar procedure of the Pennsylvania Utility Arbitration Act (see Table 4). The only

TABLE 4

LAST-OFFER VOTES: EXPERIENCE UNDER TAFT-HARTLEY AND
PENNSYLVANIA LAWS TO JANUARY 1, 1963

Law	Number of Votes	Last Offer Accepted	Last Offer Rejected
Taft-Hartley Act....................	12	0*	12
Pennsylvania Utility Arbitration Act...	9	1†	8

SOURCE: National Labor Relations Board and Pennsylvania State Labor Relations Board.
   * In one case the employees rejected a subsequent and higher offer after the "last" offer had been rejected; in the West Coast longshore case the union asked employees to boycott the vote; no one voted from this group.
   † Vote conducted on January 24, 1951, just prior to 1951 Korean War wage freeze. Employees feared that to reject it would mean freezing existing wages.

exception occurred the day before the Korean War wage stabilization program was scheduled to become effective in 1951. The workers voted to accept for fear of having their wages frozen at pre-last-offer levels.

This is to be expected. An offer, once made, is rarely withdrawn, so why not vote "no" and probably get more?

Actually, there have been two cases in which the last-offer vote served the purpose of inducing agreement. Professor George W. Taylor has noted that the steel industry settled in 1960 partially because the "last" offer was about to be rejected, according to all forecasts.[8] And in the Lockheed case (No. 22, Table 3) the union settled without the union shop because it feared that the employees would not support its insistence on this demand in the last-offer vote. In most cases, however, this provision induces unions not to settle because they might get more after a last-offer vote, or to the extent that it induces employers to hold back until after the last-offer vote, it retards instead of inducing settlement.

Other Criticisms Widespread

Criticisms of the Taft-Hartley emergency procedure have not been confined to the last-offer provision, although on that there is probably close to unanimous agreement that it serves little constructive purpose. Presidents Truman, Eisenhower, and Kennedy have all proposed changes in the procedure, as have numerous labor, industry, and public groups. The proposals have run the full gamut from complete repeal of any form of national emergency procedure to the substitution of complete compulsion —for example, compulsory arbitration—for the present procedure.

Before proposals for change in the Taft-Hartley Act are analyzed, it is appropriate to continue our examination of experience —for nearly all proposals for change have been tried by federal or state governments, or in other countries.

AD HOC EXTRA-LEGAL INTERVENTION

Besides legal procedures for intervention in so-called "emergency strikes," many presidents have acted without benefit of specific legislation, especially to handle singular situations. Thus, in the Pullman strike of 1894, President Grover Cleveland dispatched troops to maintain "law and order," although the governor of Illinois (and most close observers) found no breakdowns of law. In the anthracite coal dispute of 1902, President Theodore Roosevelt put heavy pressure on the industry to arbitrate its dispute. And, as already noted, Presidents Franklin D. Roosevelt and John F. Kennedy repeatedly put pressure on railway management to accept settlements beyond the scope of Railway Labor Act fact finding recommendations.

The establishment of the National Defense Mediation Board and the National War Labor Board by executive orders was also "extra-legal," although undoubtedly within the broad framework of presidential war powers. Following the end of hostilities, as we have already noted, President Truman and his Secretary of Labor followed a policy of appointing fact finding boards, doing so in about fifteen cases.

When the Taft-Hartley Act was passed, President Truman utilized the emergency procedures of that law seven times in one year—still a record (see Table 3). After his re-election in 1948 on a program which included repeal of Taft-Hartley, his propensity to invoke it declined sharply. In 1949, he persuaded the steel industry to agree to submit its dispute over pensions and welfare to an extra-legal board favored by the United Steelworkers because it did not have the bonus which labor attached to Taft-Hartley procedure, *and because such a board could issue recommendations*—which it did, favorable to the union. After a short strike the union won the noncontributory pensions (as well as a contributory welfare plan) which it had requested.

Emergency Disputes and the Korean War

When the Korean War broke out, labor unions proposed that special tripartite emergency machinery be set up to handle both wage stabilization and disputes which interfered with war production. Industry countered by citing the availability of Taft-Hartley machinery to handle labor disputes, but labor wanted no part of Taft-Hartley.

When the Wage Stabilization Board was established in the early fall of 1950, it had no power to intervene in dispute cases but was confined to stabilization matters. In February 1951, however, labor members of the tripartite Wage Stabilization Board walked out as a result of a dispute over allowable wage adjustments. When the WSB was reconstituted some six weeks later, labor had won its demand that the WSB be given power over emergency disputes as well as over wage stabilization.

The WSB did not become involved in many disputes because labor and industry were in general agreement that labor peace was important to both, and industry offered only token resistance to substantial wage increases. The one big case which was referred to the WSB, the steel case, ended whatever usefulness the WSB had, both as a disputes agency and as a wage stabilizer. The Wage Stabilization Board awarded a substantial increase to the CIO Steelworkers, with industry members dissenting; the industry declined to accept the increase without large price increases, which the government at first would not authorize. When the union struck, President Truman blamed the industry and seized it under his "inherent powers." Truman, in a speech to the country, stated that steel production was essential or we would "have to stop making shells and bombs that are going directly to our soldiers . . . in Korea . . . delay our atomic energy program . . . stop making engines for Air Force planes . . . bring our defense production to a halt and throw our domestic economy into chaos."[9]

At this point the industry appealed to the courts. Despite the claim of the government that seizure was "necessary to avert a national catastrophe" and that the President was acting constitutionally to avoid a "grave emergency," the United States Supreme Court ruled that President Truman's seizure was unlawful.[10] The industry was turned back to its private owners, and when they failed to accede to the union demand that the full WSB award be put into effect, the union struck. Public pressure was brought upon President Truman to invoke the Taft-Hartley Act, but he declined to do so on the ground that this would punish the union, which had already postponed a strike longer than the 80-day Taft-Hartley waiting period, rather than the industry, which President Truman held to be at fault. The strike lasted about two months, when it was settled by granting the WSB award to the workers and by granting substantial price increases to the industry.

The fact that a strike in the basic steel industry could last 55 days in the midst of the Korean War without any of the dire consequences predicted by President Truman when he seized the industry, or by numerous commentators before and since in similar or less critical circumstances, is of major importance in any discussion of emergency disputes procedure.

Eisenhower Cabinet Intervention

President Eisenhower eschewed the fact finding route of his

predecessor and repeatedly made public statements emphasizing his desire to keep the government's hands out of key contract settlements. But although intervention by the Eisenhower administration was far less prevalent than that of its two predecessors, *it was felt in some key instances, especially in the steel industry.* "In 1956, the political architects of the steel settlement were Secretary of the Treasury George M. Humphrey and Secretary of Labor James P. Mitchell. Again the companies were under pressure. They capitulated and improved their offer to the point where an agreement that would quickly end the dispute was possible."[11]

In 1959 the Vice President functioned as the "pressurizer," again with industry as the heavy recipient. "Technically, there was no retreat from this nonintervention position, not, at least, so far as the President himself was concerned. The political pressure emanated from the Vice-president, who happened also to be the Republican heir apparent . . . the man who could be the next occupant of the White House. . . ."[12]

President Eisenhower did appoint one extra-legal board—the Presidential Railroad Commission—which, as noted in Chapter 5, was agreed to by the carriers and unions, and made a monumental study of railway labor relations. And as will be discussed below, the Eisenhower administration also kept the atomic energy panel alive.

Kennedy Fact Finding and Defense Contracts

Special boards and commissions again became an important focus of labor relations under the Kennedy administration. Despite the appointment of one extra-legal agency—after Railway Labor Act procedure had been exhausted—it still required a long strike to break the deadlock involving flight engineers on Eastern Airlines. In 1962, also, the principal West Coast aerospace companies were persuaded by direct presidential intervention to submit disputes over compulsory union membership to extra-legal fact finding boards, and then in the case of some to submit the union shop issue to an employee vote—which the unions lost. When Lockheed Aircraft declined to permit the vote, its dispute was then brought under the Taft-Hartley Act—and eventually settled by the parties. Boeing's dispute also went to a Taft-

Hartley panel, and then to eventual settlement by bargaining aided by mediation.[13]

Another, and already noted extra-legal intervention by the Kennedy administration was the appointment of the board headed by Senator Wayne Morse which awarded the extraordinarily generous settlement to the longshoremen in 1963.

The most direct—and at the same time undocumentable—type of intervention that was attributed to the Kennedy administration was through the use of defense contracts. Government business has become a significant source of work and profit in many industries. In aerospace, it is the bulk of both. When Lockheed Aircraft declined to accept an extralegal board's recommendation for an election to determine the union shop issue, the Defense Department announced, in effect, that its contracts were being especially reviewed and placed on an *ad hoc* basis.[14]

To what extent similar pressures have determined contract allocation it is impossible to know. Certainly, however, some officials in the aerospace and other defense industries believed that any opposition to Kennedy administration labor policies threatened government contract possibilities.[15] Certainly, also, it is difficult to discover any intervention by the Kennedy administration which did not seem to be at the behest of or in favor of unions, even though as in the aerospace instance, the results did not favor unions.

Johnson Power Mediation

It is too early to judge the policies which will be followed by the Johnson administration, but certainly a trend is evident. At critical times, President Johnson has intervened; at others he has allegedly provided intervenors with the necessary power to effectuate a settlement. When the railroad union threatened a strike in 1964, the President utilized the services of two expert special mediators, Dr. George W. Taylor and Mr. Theodore Kheel, but the pressure to settle was applied by the President. He persuaded the railroads to give up most of their demands and then allegedly promised to have their tax structure reviewed.

In the 1965 longshore strike, the President intervened after a month's stoppage and pressured the union into calling off the strike by threatening the reinstitution of a National Labor Relations Board case which could have upset the joint port bargaining in the industry.

The 1965 extension of the steel contract late in April was heralded as a mediation triumph of William Simkin, Director of the Federal Mediation and Conciliation Service. It no doubt was. But rumors were also rife in Washington that Mr. Simkin was able to advise the union that if it did not extend the contract, the President would not support repeal of Section 14(b) of the Taft-Hartley law—the section which permits states to outlaw compulsory unionism. In view of the President's mastery of the political and pressure arts, one cannot discount these rumors.

When the final contract negotiations for the 1965 agreement were held, it was obvious that Mr. I. W. Abel, newly elected president of the Steelworkers, was not anxious to take the responsibility to agree to any settlement. At the same time it appears that the steel industry felt that government intervention would ease their problem of edging prices upward. Under these circumstances mediation was not successful even in the hands of a skilled mediator like William Simkin.

The President then intervened on several fronts. First he sent Senator Wayne Morse, who was last remembered as the author of the extraordinary high 1963 longshoremen's settlement, and Undersecretary of Commerce Leroy Collins, who publicly stated he had no experience in labor relations, as special mediators. After they reported that they were unable to settle the dispute, the President called the parties to Washington and "mediated it personally." As a matter of fact, Mr. Johnson imposed the settlement. It was the highest one in recent years in the steel industry but the Council of Economic Advisors which had publicly issued a report stating what steel could afford to pay, anointed this settlement with its blessings as "within the area of the guidelines."

We thus had what amounted to compulsory arbitration in the White House. First the Council of Economic Advisors announced what steel should pay and then the President imposed a settlement close to that announcement. Given the backdrop of the 1959 strike and the 55 day strike during the Korean War, it is difficult to justify the President's acts in the name of "emergency." Perhaps the best comment concerning the President's action is that he completed the settlement in time to face the cameras at 6:30

P.M. Eastern Daylight Time—the standard hour for nationwide news broadcasts.

PERMANENT EXTRA-LEGAL AGENCIES

It will be recalled that the first case for which the emergency provisions of the Taft-Hartley Act was invoked, as well as several subsequent cases, involved the atomic energy "industry." Although there is actually no atomic "industry" as such, except for the production of fissionable and special nuclear material, the annual reports of the Atomic Energy Commission show that over 125,000 persons are employed by the AEC and its construction and operations contractors in many locations throughout the country on a great variety of jobs and operations. Particularly in the early days of atomic development, great concern was expressed that there be no interruption in work at vital atomic installations. After the first Taft-Hartley national emergency case in 1948, President Truman appointed a committee headed by William H. Davis, former Chairman of the War Labor Board. From this committee, which reported in 1949, came the creation of what appears to be the first permanent extra-legal agency to handle emergency disputes—the Atomic Energy Labor Relations Panel, later reorganized and renamed the Atomic Labor-Management Relations Panel.[16]

Atomic Labor-Management Relations Panel

The original atomic panel was set up by executive order of President Truman in 1949 with Davis as Chairman, and with the panel lodged in the Federal Mediation and Conciliation Service. It attempted to handle disputes which the parties could not settle themselves in an informal manner, and refused a number of cases when advised by the Atomic Energy Commission that national defense was not affected. Often, however, it acted as a fact finding agency, making recommendations or, if the parties agreed, acting as an arbitration panel. Both the awards and the recommendations of the panel were handled as informally as possible, in line with procedure espoused by Davis. A total of 61 cases came before this panel from its inception in 1949 until January 1953.[17]

When President Eisenhower took office, Davis and the members of his panel resigned, both as a matter of form and as an expression of belief on the part of Davis that the time had come to withdraw special disputes machinery from the atomic labor picture. The President, however, revised and renamed the panel, and transferred it to the Atomic Energy Commission from the FMCS. Cyrus Ching, former head of FMCS, was named chairman, a post which he still holds.

The procedure under Ching became more formalized. Jurisdiction was not asserted until the FMCS certified the case as being one which could not be resolved by the parties through mediation. The FMCS was required to check beforehand with the Atomic Energy Commission and to verify that a stoppage would vitally harm the atomic energy program. After it takes jurisiction of a case, the Ching panel usually issues formal recommendations; but unlike fact finding boards in other jurisdictions, Ching panels never publish the facts as they see them nor do they issue any other bases for their recommendations. This procedure has continued, although some cases since 1957 have been handled informally also.

The elimination of cases not considered harmful to the atomic energy program cut down the jurisdiction of the panel. Nevertheless, the Ching panel handled 27 cases during its first three years, demonstrating a "quick-trigger" attitude toward intervention out of line with the policy of the Eisenhower Administration toward labor disputes. Things then settled down between 1957 and 1962 with an average of less than three cases per year coming to the attention of the Panel.[18]

The advent of the more intervention minded Kennedy Administration saw an increase in the Panel's business. Intervention by the Secretary of Labor in Oak Ridge, Tennessee, and Hanford, Washington, followed by panel hearings resulted in recommendations favorable to unions.[19] An upsurge of cases followed, with 10 in 1962, 8 in 1963, and 5 in 1964.

The activities of the Atomic Panel do not preclude further intervention nor have strikes been eliminated. In one case a Taft-Hartley emergency board was appointed after the atomic panel recommendation was rejected, a last-offer vote was held, and a settlement was made superior to the "last" offer.[20] In other cases, strikes have been called and occurred without apparent damage to the atomic energy program.[21] In the decade beginning in 1954, the Atomic Energy Commission lists a total of 21 strikes occurring in various aspects of the program.[22]

This raises the question of why the Atomic Labor-Management Panel continues to exist. In 1957, that question received a searching answer from the Secretary of Labor's Advisory Committee on Labor-Management Relations in Atomic Energy Installations, under the chairmanship of David L. Cole. It recommended that the panel "taper off" its activities because most of the conditions which induced its creation no longer existed.

The Advisory Committee felt in 1957 that it was then "appropriate to treat labor-management relations at atomic energy installations in the same manner as those in other industries, including those which produce vital military and defense items for the government." Failure to do this, the Advisory Committee noted, would mean a continuation of the tendency on the part of the parties in the industry "to rely more and more" on "alternatives to the pressures of collective bargaining . . . provided by the government." For example, "at the installations in which resort to the panel has been most frequent, notably Oak Ridge, Paducah, and Sandia, the ability to reach agreement through negotiations seems to have been weakened, and the panel has considered it necessary to issue detailed recommendations in practically all cases in which it intervenes."

Mediation has likewise suffered from the existence of the panel, according to this Advisory Committee report. "The availability of the panel procedure has impaired the effectiveness of the Federal Mediation and Conciliation Service. The knowledge that the panel can be caused to appear detracts from the continuity and effectiveness of the services of the mediator."[23]

The view of the Cole committee is supported by both industry and union spokesmen with experience in the atomic energy field. A labor relations official of the Nuclear Division of the Union Carbide Company wrote:[24]

"We have a good frame of reference upon which to make comparisons of this dispute and strike record. In the privately owned plants of Union Carbide, in the United States and Canada, there are approximately 36,000 manual workers; and approximately 20,000 are represented by unions in collective bargaining. The same industrial relations practices, bargaining methods and procedures, and methods of wage determination are in effect in both the private plants and the government-owned plants. In the past four years (1960 through 1963), the number of man-days lost in the unionized privately owned plants, with no disputes-settlement panel, was 690,000, or .14 percent; while the number of man-days lost in the atomic energy installations was 874,000, or .67 percent. Thus, it has been our experience in UCC that work stoppages are more prevalent where a disputes panel is available than in a situation where it is not available.

* * *

The availability of a disputes-settlement panel is like an ever-present shadow over the bargaining table. It allows the parties to avoid the difficult decision-making process, which is necessary in meaningful negotiations. It creates a tendency for each side to hope that they can get a better deal from the panel than they can get from their adversary in collective bargaining."

In the same vein are the remarks of a vice-president of the International Association of Machinists:[25]

". . . the possibility exists during every negotiation that the panel will intercede. Thus the influence of a third party is always present—a third party which I call the Ghost at the Bargaining Table . . . His shadowy presence has caused bargaining to be done in an aura of hypocrisy. . . ."

Despite this adverse criticism of experts, of industry and of labor, the Atomic Labor-Management Relations Panel had neither tapered off nor showed any signs of so doing. Without specific Congressional sanction, it is continuing to operate, and even showing a tendency to handle an increased case load as its need grows ever less.

The Missile Sites Labor Commission

In 1960 the United States Senate Committee on Government Operations, under the chairmanship of Senator John L. McClellan, began an investigation of work stoppages, wage practices, and labor conditions at missile sites and bases. The Committee uncovered a situation involving excessive work stoppages, waste, and practices which came very close to outright extortion. Jurisdictional strikes among craft unions and between craft and industrial unions, competition for labor among various governmental procurement agencies, featherbedding work duplication, low productivity and excessive overtime, and a strike record many times worse than the national average were the order of the day at installations, including that at Cape Canaveral, Florida, the most important missile test center. There, man-days lost amounted to 5.5 to 6 percent of total man-days worked—many times the national average.[26] Meanwhile, it appeared that the missile program was being seriously impeded.

Senator McClellan advocated strong legislative action to bar strikes. To head this off, President Kennedy, in May 1961, appointed a tripartite Missile Sites Labor Commission, headed by the Secretary of Labor, with the director of the Federal Mediation and Conciliation Service as vice chairman. It appeared quite obvious to the heads of the unions, particularly those in building construction who were especially involved in the repeated work stoppages, that Congress was in a mood to act if the situation did not improve.

Continuing surveillance by the McClellan Senate Committee on Government Operations and the work of the Missile Sites Labor Commission, together with better coordination among the government procurement agencies, appear to have brought a semblance of order to labor relations at missile locations. The FMCS has done outstanding work by assigning key mediators to these areas, and having them work out problems with labor and management at the local level. The national officers of the building trades unions exerted more firm control over local business agents, some of whom seemed uninhibited in their desire to achieve the most fantastic wages for the least work.[27] Strikes declined and some of the worst uneconomic practices were brought under control.

Another factor which improved the labor situation after the establishment of the Missile Sites Labor Commission was the easement of pressure by government agencies on contractors to settle at all costs in order to avoid stoppages. The knowledge on the part of union business agents and workers that peace at any price was the order of the day was a continuing invitation to the calling of strikes and other harassments. Moreover, there was evidence that some contractors were purposely overcharging jobs and furthering uneconomic practices, both of which were an invitation to similar practices on the part of unions. With the formation of the Missile Sites and Labor Commission came better regulations and control by the government agencies to prevent such practices.[28]

The extra-legal Missile Sites Labor Commission has been criticized by at least two observers for its failure to adhere to national labor policy as expressed in the Taft-Hartley Act. One noted that the Commission had issued directives resolving jurisdictional disputes in situations where "assent of the parties was not obtained," thus, "disregarding applicable provisions" of the Taft-Hartley Act, and in effect, overriding "the functions and power entrusted by Congress to the National Labor Relations Board and to the courts. . . ."[29]

Professor John R. Van de Water has called attention to the case of the electronic products subcontractor whose employees voted overwhelmingly in an NLRB election against union affiliation, but were forced off a missile base by a strike because they had so voted. Whereas an NLRB injunction against such a strike and boycott was in order, the Missile Sites Labor Commission intervened and asked the parties to "be mature"—which resulted in the work being done in a manner acceptable to the strikers.[30]

One may well ask whether, even on defense installations, executive improvising should replace action prescribed by duly enacted law.[31] Meanwhile, the extra-legal Missile Sites Labor Commission, like its atomic counterpart, appears headed for a long life. However, the business of the Commission is dwindling as sites become completed, so that its jurisdiction may be confined to such large installations as Cape Canaveral and Vandenberg.

CONCLUSION AND EVALUATION

The search for a national policy to handle emergency disputed at the federal level has been, since 1945, a combination of improvisation, executive temperament, and utilization of a compromise law which satisfies few and has had limited success. In terms of our criteria, the following judgments appear in order.

Insofar as the promotion of industrial peace is concerned, the success has been limited, although strikes since 1946 have not been a major problem. Serious strikes have occurred in steel, longshore, and in defense industries after invocation of the procedures of the Taft-Hartley law and after various *ad hoc* intervening techniques.

There is doubt that the intervention reduced the threat or duration of the stoppages in several cases. In other cases, a careful analysis at least raises the question of whether the emergency would have existed at all if it had not been invited by the existence of the emergency procedure. This seems especially the case in the longshore industry under the Taft-Hartley Act and is obviously the case today insofar as industries under the jurisdiction of the Atomic Panel. Moreover, the steel strikes of 1952 and 1959 raise the question of whether the hysteria generated by such strikes is not completely unfounded. A later chapter will analyze this question in depth.

In the case of the missile sites, industrial peace was furthered. It remains to be seen whether bureaucratic and political considerations will keep the Missile Sites Commission alive beyond its usefulness, so that someday, like the Atomic Panel, it will become an emergency creator instead of an emergency dispeller.

There can be little doubt that these improvisations, as well as the Taft-Hartley procedure, have not encouraged collective bargaining in balance, but like the Railway Labor Act, tend to substitute policies on the part of the parties aimed at invoking the government machinery instead of settling disputes. Again, this is especially true of the Atomic Panel, the longshore industry under Taft-Hartley, and the *ad hoc* panels of the Kennedy Administration. On the other hand, before the Missile Sites Commission was appointed, collective bargaining was already subverted by uninhibited union power, indifferent cost-plus conscious contractors, and unwise governmental procurement.

Undoubtedly, the net effect of intervention has been the enhancement of union power. The character of the intervention, the relations between the government and the unions (except in the Eisenhower Administration) and the push on the part of unions to invoke intervention, and the character of the settlements all point in this direction. That is not to say that industry has been blameless. In both steel and longshore, for example, some managements seem to prefer government dictation to collective bargaining. Nevertheless, the manner in which the intervention rate rises in relation to the intensity of pro-unionism in the White House seems conclusive—and the results achieved document the obvious.

Again, we must note that the Missile Sites Commission certainly reduced local union power. But it did so by enhancing national union leadership.

We may thus conclude that, in balance, the promotion of industrial peace was limited, union power enhanced, and collective bargaining discouraged. All these conclusions are relative and do not involve major institutional changes. Insofar as another national goal is concerned—the maintenance of a stable price level—the period is mixed. Considerable inflation, undoubtedly caused or enhanced by wage increases beyond the advance in productivity occurred between 1945 and 1957. Since then the price level has been relatively stable. The conclusion is that basic economics have been controlling. When employers could no longer afford to grant wage increases because the market would not permit price increases, their resistance stiffened, the rate of wage increases declined, and prices leveled off. Collective bargaining policies cannot fly in the teeth of the hard facts of economics—a fact which gives pause to those who see in emergency disputes machinery a cure-all for economic ills or a method of economic improvement.

NOTES

1. New Jersey Governor's Committee on Legislation Relating to Public Utility Labor Disputes, *Report to Governor Robert B. Meyner* (Trenton, 1954), p. 13. David L. Cole, who served on some of these fact finding boards, was Chairman of this Committee.

2. Industrial Relations Counselors, Inc., *Emergency Disputes: A National Labor Policy Problem*, Industrial Relations Monograph No. 138 (New York, 1961), p. 23.

3. For an analysis of the Norris-LaGuardia Act, see Herbert R. Northrup and Gordon F. Bloom, *Government and Labor* (Homewood, Ill.: Richard D. Irwin, Inc., 1963), Chapter 2. It is appropriate to note here also that most of the material in the analysis of disputes machinery since 1945 is from Chapter 13 of *Government and Labor*, with the courtesy of the publisher and the co-author.

4. *United States* v. *United Mine Workers*, 67 S.Ct. 677 (1947).

5. George W. Taylor, "Is Compulsory Arbitration inevitable?" *Proceedings of the First Annual Meeting, Industrial Relations Research Association*, 1948, p. 76.

6. As noted in Chapter 5, President Truman's proposal to draft strikers and subject them to severe penalties was quickly enacted by the House of Representatives, but was referred to committee in the Senate on the motion of Senator Taft, where it was allowed to die quietly. The strike was called off as the President was addressing the Congress and requesting his bill.

7. See below, pp. 127-135.

8. George W. Taylor, "The Adequacy of Taft-Hartley in Public Emergency Disputes," *The Annals*, Vol. CCCXXXIII (January 1961), p. 79.

9. *New York Times*, April 10, 1952.

10. *Youngstown Sheet and Tube Co. v. Sawyer*, 343 U. S. 579 (1952).

11. John Perry Horlacher, "A Political Science View of National Emergency Disputes," *The Annals*, Vol. CCCXXXIII (January 1961), p. 90.

12. *Ibid.*

13. For an analysis of the aerospace cases, see Northrup and Bloom, *op. cit.*, Chapters 8 and 13.

14. See, for example, the Defense Department statements in the *Daily Labor Report*, November 26, 1962. Lockheed, among other things, is the principal contractor in the highly successful Polaris program.

15. Interviews, November-December 1962. Needless to note, these accusations were often not precise, but the feeling was certainly almost unanimous among company officials who would talk about it—always with a pledge of secrecy. They pointed to the Lockheed case, to awards of contracts to one company which agreed to an agency shop, and to the loss of a key contract by another company which rigorously held to its anti-union-shop position. Actually, no one on the outside, as the author is, is in the position to know the truth or falsity of these whispered charges. They are noted only because of the fact that since many persons in industry believed them to be true, their conduct in key labor relations cases was probably affected by this belief. Some of the difficulty lies in the change in Defense Department procurement policies initiated by Secretary of Defense Robert McNamara in which labor relations are not necessarily involved. Nevertheless, the feeling in industry of a relation of labor policies and success in obtaining defense contracts has been very strong. (See the editorial in *Fortune*, "What the Hell Do Those Fellows Want?" Vol. LXVII [February 1963], pp. 81-82.) Senator Lausche (Dem., Ohio) introduced a bill in the Senate on March 4, 1963, barring duress by federal agency officials in labor relations matters pertaining to defense contracts. The Senator stated flatly that this was occurring. (*Daily Labor Report*, March 4, 1963, p. A-2.)

16. Also on the basis of this Panel report, certain keystone principles of atomic industry labor relations were agreed to, including making security risks a nonbargainable issue, not subject to the grievance procedure.

17. See J. J. Bambrick, Jr., and A. A. Blum, *Labor Relations in the Atomic Energy Field*, Studies in Personnel Policy, No. 158 (New York: National Industrial Conference Board, 1957), p. 29.

18. Data on the Ching Panel activity is based upon annual reports issued by the panel for its first three years (but not thereafter); a pamphlet entitled *Maximizing the Effectiveness of Collective Bargaining within the Atomic Energy Program*, issued by the Atomic Energy Commission in April 1965; and the *Industrial Relations Newsletter*, published monthly by the Atomic Energy Commission.

19. In the Hanford Case, e.g., the panel recommended substantially more liberal terms than General Electric had offered or had granted to unions in other plants of the company.

20. This was Case No. 12, Table 3.

21. For example, in the 1962 case involving Dow Chemical and the Den-

ver Metal Trades Department, the unions accepted the panel's recommendations, but the company instead requested further negotiations. Whereupon the unions threatened a strike, and the Secretary of Labor requested that the parties meet with him in Washington. There, Dow acceded and agreed to accept the panel's recommendations. Then the membership rejected a settlement. A strike began and lasted for 26 days before a settlement was reached.

22. *Maximizing Effectiveness of Collective Bargaining, op. cit.,* Table 1, p. 42.

23. *Report of the Secretary of Labor's Advisory Committee on Labor-Management Relations in Atomic Energy Installations* (Washington, D. C.: U. S. Government Printing Office, 1957). The conclusions and recommendations are reprinted in Bambrick and Blum, *op. cit.,* pp. 45-47.

24. T. E. Lane, "Special Government Dispute Panel," *Labor Law Journal,* Vol. XV (July 1964), p. 418.

25. P. L. Siemiller, "Special Government Dispute Settlement Panels," *Labor Law Journal,* Vol. XV (July 1964), pp. 422-423.

26. "Work Stoppages at Missile Bases," *Report of the Committee on Government Operations,* U. S. Senate, 87th Congress, 2d session, Report No. 1312 (Washington, D. C.: U. S. Government Printing Office, 1962), p. 11. Two volumes of Hearings, plus an Index, were also published by the Committee in 1962.

27. Consider this testimony relating to Vandenberg Air Force Base: "The lowest paid [plumber earned] . . . $402 and the highest $733. The average weekly earnings . . . was $451. The lowest paid [electrician] received $413 for the week, and the highest $670 . . . the average . . . was $510. . . . The commanding general at Vandenberg . . . is a major general. His total pay and allowances for 25 years' service, including his quarters allowance and his subsistence allowance, amounts to $365 a week. Each and every one of the plumbers and steamfitters and electricians made more than the commanding general." The report, "Work Stoppage at Missile Bases," pp. 7-8, also found that laborers made more than colonels, and semiskilled workers made more than Dr. Wernher von Braun, the missile expert.

28. W. S. Price and Armin Behr, "Control of Uneconomic Practices at Government Sites: A Comparative Study of Two Government Panels," *Labor Law Journal,* Vol. XV (August 1964), pp. 519-531.

29. H. L. Browne, "The Missile Sites Labor Commission and the Derogation of the Taft-Hartley Act," *American Bar Association Journal,* Vol. XLVIII (February 1962), pp. 121-124.

30. John R. Van de Water, "Labor Law and National Defense," *Labor Law Journal,* Vol. XIII (August 1962), pp. 617-618; see also *ibid.,* "Applications of Labor Law to Construction and Equipping of United States Missile Bases," *Labor Law Journal,* Vol. XII (November 1961), pp. 613-624.

31. How complicated extralegal intervention may become is illustrated by developments at the Nevada Test Site of the Atomic Energy Commission. Since both a missile test site and atomic energy were involved, the two extralegal agencies avoided a jurisdictional dispute by establishing a third such agency—The Nevada Test and Space Site Construction Labor Board —to look into certain uneconomic and inefficient practices there. The results largely ended in failure to end the offending practices. See Price and Behr, *op. cit.,* pp. 531-537.

PART

III GOVERNMENT INTERVENTION IN OTHER FORMS

CHAPTER

8 Three Key Experiences

THE STATES have experimented with almost every form of government intervention in labor disputes. Besides mediation, they have tried strike notices and strike votes, fact finding, compulsory arbitration, seizure of industrial plants, and choice of procedures. In addition, as on the Presidential level of the federal government, governors or lesser state officials have often intervened in labor disputes without benefit of specific legislation. In Chapter 3 we discussed in summary state experiences with compulsory arbitration. In Appendices A-D, the state legislation dealing with compulsory arbitration, seizure, fact finding, and strike notices and strike vote are analyzed in detail. In this chapter are summarized three key state experiences: fact finding in Minnesota, seizure in Virginia, and choice of procedures in Massachusetts.[1]

Fact Finding in Minnesota

Minnesota has had about as much experience with fact finding as any other state. Under a law enacted in 1939, the state first attempts to settle a dispute by mediation. If that fails, the state conciliator suggests that the parties agree to arbitrate. If the parties fail so to agree, and if the dispute is in an industry affected with the public interest, "which includes, but is not restricted to, any industry, business or institution engaged in supplying the necessities of life, safety, or health, so that a temporary suspension of its operation would endanger the life, safety, health or well-being of a substantial number of people of any community," the conciliator must notify the governor, who may appoint a tripartite commission "to conduct a hearing and make a report on the issues involved and the merits of the respective contentions of the parties to the dispute."

The commission's report must be submitted to the governor after 25 days, and may be publicized by the governor. Strikes and lockouts are prohibited for 30 days after the governor is notified of the "public interest" dispute, in order to give the commission time to report. If the governor does not appoint a commission, strikes and lockouts are permitted five days after he is notified instead of 30 days thereafter.

This procedure is, of course, very similar to that of the Railway Labor Act, which was enjoying its unearned reputation as a "model law" when the Minnesota legislation was first enacted. An examination of the Minnesota experience indicates some of the same ills which befell its prototype on the railroads—overutilization, inhibition of collective bargaining, lack of the parties' respect for fact finding recommendations, and lack of public interest in supporting those recommendations.

The Minnesota law began at a difficult time because, soon after its enactment, came the defense program and then World War II. Early in this emergency period the conciliator adopted a policy of considering any industry to be "affected with the public interest" if the employer was materially engaged in the production of defense items. Between 1940 and 1945, 167 commissions were appointed—70 between July 1, 1941, and June 30, 1942. If the commission's recommendations were not accepted, the case might be referred to the National War Labor Board.[2] In any case the war period provides no real guides to the Act's effects.

After World War II an overeagerness to permit Minnesota's unions and employers to utilize the Act persisted for several

years. An annual average of 43 commissions was appointed between 1946 and 1949. Hotels and restaurants, manufacturing of
every description, laundries, and optical firms were found to be
"affected with the public interest." After analyzing the first decade of the Minnesota law (including the war years), Professor
Stieber found "considerable evidence . . . to indicate that fact finding procedure, as practices in Minnesota, has hindered free collective bargaining." He found a tendency for the same unions and
employers to appear before fact finding commissions each year,
for a high percentage of rejection of fact finding commission reports, and for the conciliator and/or the governor then to step in
and usually effectuate a settlement by compromise between what
the commission recommended and what the party holding out
had demanded.[3]

Stieber's analysis, of course, is quite consistent with our analysis of the Railway Labor Act. If the parties learn to expect that a
fact finding board or commission will be appointed, they soon
toss everything into the commission's lap rather than settle anything in collective bargaining. The fear is that anything conceded
in bargaining or mediation will be used as a springboard for
further concessions before the commission. If, however, the commission poorly gauges the relative strength of the parties, or turns
in a report which either or both parties reject, the real emergency
occurs. For here, both collective bargaining and the emergency
procedure have been exhausted, and nothing has been settled.

If, at this stage, a conciliator or governor or other public official is available to seek a settlement by putting pressure on one
party to make further concessions, the tendency of the party
seeking additional concessions to reject a recommendation of a
fact finding commission is further encouraged. Between 1946 and
1949, 45 percent of the cases for which fact finding commissions
were appointed were settled on the basis of "modification by
further conciliation," whereas only 23 percent were settled on
the basis of the commissions' reports.

By 1950 the administrators of the Minnesota law were determined to improve the effectiveness of the fact finding commission procedure by giving "a more strict interpretation of the legislative intent.[4] The following year the conciliator pointed with
pride to the fact that "there has been a continued decrease in the

number of disputes referred to fact finding commissions. This section of the law has been given a more strict interpretation in an attempt to make it more effective."[5]

After 1950, there was a steady reduction in the use of fact finding commissions. There are several reasons for this; one is the aforenoted new policy of the law's administrators. Certainly, they are correct in stating that the more commissions appointed, the less will be their effectiveness. During the first ten years of the Act, public opinion did not rise to support commission recommendations, nor did strikes decrease relative to other areas or states.[6] If the fact finding commission is to be of valuable service, it must be utilized most sparingly.

Another reason for the declining use of fact finding commissions in Minnesota since 1950 has been the general lack of serious strike situations. The most important stoppages in Minnesota since then have been steel or mine strikes under national bargaining, in which the state has been helpless to intervene. The 1950's were a decade of relative labor peace in Minnesota, as in the rest of the United States.

Finally, like most states with strike control laws which have not been ultimately tested in the courts, Minnesota is loath to bring about a final test of constitutionality by forcing the issue through the appointment of fact finding commissions which are unacceptable to the parties. Most appointments in recent years have not been opposed by the parties. In such instances, of course, with compulsion lacking, fact finding has its greatest opportunity to achieve—actually through a sort of advanced mediation—an acceptable settlement. This is a far cry from the traditional theory of fact finding which assumes that an impartial commission can, by discovering the facts and publicizing them, induce the parties to agree to a rational settlement.[7]

SEIZURE IN VIRGINIA

Virginia adopted seizure in the post-World War II period as a technique to control strikes in industries deemed essential. Laws providing for state seizure and operations to prevent strikes were passed on three occasions, the most significant being the Virginia Public Utility Labor Relations Act, initially passed in 1947, and amended in 1952.

The 1952 Virginia law is written with the clear intent of providing for "the continuous, uninterrupted, and proper functioning and operation of public utilities engaged in the business of furnishing water, light, heat, gas, electric power, transportation, or communication, or any one or more of them, to the people of Virginia . . . declared to be essential to their welfare, health, and safety." Although the 1947 law made some attempt at promoting dispute settlement by the parties, with the governor's aid available, the 1952 law makes no mention of the collective bargaining process except as it may affect the parties themselves. The law is not a dispute-settling device. Its only intent is to provide service to the people while the parties attempt to settle their differences.

When there is a threat of a strike or interruption in the operation of any public utility, as mentioned above, the governor makes an investigation to determine whether or not the stoppage "will constitute a serious menace or threat to the public health, safety or welfare." If he determines that such will be the case, he notifies the parties that at the time of stoppage, he will take immediate possession of the utility.

After the governor issues a proclamation of intention to seize the utility, he must ascertain what jobs are essential to operate the utility and whether present jobholders are willing to fill these jobs during government operation. Any employee who is willing to work during state operation must declare that fact and then is entitled to do so; those who do not wish to do so may remain away from their jobs during state operation without penalty. "The status of no person as an employee of the utility shall be affected by either his acceptance of employment by the state or by his refusal of such employment."

If a stoppage occurs and the governor takes possession, strikes, lockouts, picketing, etc., are forbidden and subject to severe penalties. Wages and conditions of employment must be maintained at the levels existing when negotiations were commenced. Seizure remains in effect until the governor is satisfied that the utility is capable of "normal" operation and "the public interest so requires."

The Virginia law goes beyond the seizure provisions of New Jersey by providing that "after payment of proper operating expenses and reimbursement of the State for all expenses incurred in preparing to operate same . . . eighty-five percentum of . . . net income shall be paid to the utility as compensation for the temporary use of its business, facilities, and properties." Fifteen percent of net income is thus retained by the state. In addition to the compensation paid to the state, costs incidental to the operation of the utility which are incurred by the state are charged to the company as part of its operating expenses. In case of a loss the state takes nothing. It neither furnishes money to provide a profit nor assumes any part of the loss as its obligation.

The Virginia Public Utility Labor Relations Act was enacted following a threatened strike in an electric utility. Besides electric light and power, however, the law covers water, heat, gas, communication, and transportation not subject to the federal Railway Labor Act. Of the 11 seizures which had occurred as of April 1962, nine involved urban transit units and the Amalgamated Association of Street, Electric and Motor Coach Employees, and the other two have involved telephone companies and the Communication Workers of America.

Like all innovating legislation, Virginia's seizure law has raised some problems. In the first place, it is conceivable that in time of high employment, it would not be possible to replace personnel who exercised their right not to work for the state during the seizure period. However, in the 11 seizures to date, this problem has not arisen.

A second problem under the Virginia law concerns the role during seizure of the State Corporation Commission, the state public utility regulating body. In one case the Commission was placed in the anomalous position of having before it an application for a rate increase from a utility which had been seized and operated by the Commission. The utility maintained that the increase was needed to pay a wage increase so as to settle the dispute and repossess its properties. The Commission managed to postpone action until after seizure was terminated. Since, however, the Virginia Act does not require that seized utilities be operated by the Commission, this problem is easily avoidable.

Another problem which might arise under the Virginia law is the reaction of a union to a wage-cut request by management during a period of economic depression. A union could refuse to take the cut or to arbitrate the dispute, and threaten to strike. This would involve state seizure with its statutory ban on changes in wages and conditions of work. Utility employees, "as the law now stands . . . could remain employed by the Commonwealth indefinitely. Their wages might be greatly out of line, the utility might be shoved into bankruptcy by the distorted costs of labor, but as long as the workers remained adamant the law could not touch them."[8]

A principal criticism of the administration of the Virginia law is that it has been invoked in relatively minor disputes. In a real sense, none of these disputes were actual emergencies. The fact that the law has not been invoked since 1952 may reflect a realization that such minor disputes do not deserve state intervention. Or it may merely be that Virginia desires to avoid litigation over the constitutionality of its law.

Another unusual aspect of the Virginia law is that it could guarantee a minimum increase to employees. If seizure is to cost a public utility 15 percent of profits, why not give that amount to employees in the form of wages and avoid the problems of a state take-over? Certainly, it would seem that a union which felt seizure was a possibility would not consider settling for less. Of course, the reluctance of the state to invoke the Act in recent years has no doubt curbed any union policy based on this theory.

Despite these criticisms, one must conclude that the Virginia approach deserves careful consideration as an attempt to afford the public protection without intruding the state into the bargaining process.

"CHOICE OF PROCEDURES" IN MASSACHUSETTS

Because of the tendency of emergency laws to become a substitute for collective bargaining, a school of thought has emerged which advocates giving the chief executive a "choice of procedures" to utilize so that those who are pushing an interruption of a vital service are not able to compare settlement by collective bargaining with settlement under governmental direction.[9]

The choice-of-procedures theory has been written into law in Massachusetts, as a result of a report by a tripartite committee appointed in 1947 by the then Governor, Robert Bradford, to survey the labor legislation of the state. This committee, of which the late Professor Sumner H. Slichter was Chairman, made a unanimous report covering numerous phases of labor law which were almost entirely adopted into law. Among them is included this unique statute governing strikes affecting public health and safety.

The "Slichter law," as it is known, applies to the "production and distribution of food, fuel, water, electric light and power, gas, or hospital or medical services." It provides that in the event of a threatened stoppage in these industries which the governor finds would endanger the health or safety of any community, he may do one of two things:

1. He may require the parties to appear before a governor-appointed moderator, who must be "an impartial person skilled in industrial relations," and show cause why the dispute should not be submitted to voluntary arbitration. The moderator's job is to induce the parties to arbitrate, or to make public the reasons for their refusal to do so. He is forbidden by law to review the merits of the dispute. An arbitration submission or the moderator's report is required within 15 days of the governor's proclamation of an emergency, during which time no changes in conditions of work and no stoppages are permitted.

2. Or the governor may request the parties to submit the dispute to a tripartite arbitration board. This board is required not only to decide the issues, but also to "fix in its recommendations the date, prospective or retroactive, as of which its recommendations shall be made effective and in so doing shall consider evidence as to the responsibility of either party for delaying the settlement or rejecting arbitration."

If neither of these methods is successful in avoiding a stoppage, or if the dispute "is of such a nature that these procedures cannot be applied thereto," the governor is required to declare the existence of an emergency during which he may either (1) "enter into arrangements with either or both parties" to continue to produce or to distribute sufficient essential services "to safeguard the public health and safety" or (2) seize the business and operate it "for the account of the person operating it immediately prior to the seizure;" or, if such person elects within ten days after seizure, he may waive the proceeds during seizure and receive instead "fair and reasonable" compensation for the appropriation and use of his property for which he may sue the state. But in determining this compensation, the courts are directed to take into account the fact that a labor dispute existed which interrupted, or threatened to interrupt, private operation of the plant "and the effect of such . . . upon the value to the petitioner of the use" of the facility.

During the emergency seizure, all federal and state labor legislation remains in effect. Conditions of employment, however, may be altered by the governor upon recommendation of a tripartite arbitration board appointed by him. "Such recommendations will be based on the conditions in existence in the industry affected." Strikes, lockouts, or supporting activities to such are forbidden during the emergency period.

An interesting and novel concept in the law is the "show cause" procedure before the moderator as to why the dispute should not be submitted to arbitration. This procedure was designed to encourage voluntary arbitration by the parties themselves, with the idea that no union or company would like to have a finger pointed at it charging that it would rather endanger the community than arbitrate. Moreover, if arbitration is refused, a penalty may be imposed by compulsory arbitration in the form of prospective or retroactive application of the award.

The "show cause" procedure may have another and, paradoxically, contrary merit. A demand, for example, may, in the eyes of one of the parties, be so extreme or so lacking in conformity with existing practices that he feels arbitration involves an impossible risk. But the party refusing to arbitrate has a forum to which he can explain and attempt to justify what the public might otherwise consider as pure disregard of its interests.

The Slichter law attempted to meet all contingencies arising under seizure. Profits and losses go to the private owners unless they elect compensation for use instead. In the latter event, they risk a lesser figure, since their compensation must consider losses which might have occurred if a stoppage were effective. Labor legislation remains in effect. And unlike the Virginia legislation, wages can be raised or lowered by an arbitration board if the governor so desires.

On the other hand, altering conditions of work during seizure has its dangers. Permanent and costly concessions can be made to a union which an employer must accept in order to secure the return of his property. The fact that any contractual changes must be in accord with existing industry conditions does afford protection against startling innovations, but the danger of costly changes is not completely removed.

Experience with the Slichter Law

The Slichter law has been invoked six times and has not been invoked since 1953. How has it worked in practice?

A careful study of the law found that the health and safety of any community in Massachusetts had not been imperiled since the passage of the law, but neither had such peril occurred in neighboring states which did not have any emergency legislation.[10] This same study also found indications that the final settlement in four of the cases was about the same as would have occurred under collective bargaining. In two of the cases, however, it noted that the final settlement was probably higher, being more than the unions were willing to accept for settlement at one point.[11]

There seems to be general agreement that the Slichter law has not disrupted collective bargaining. This has been attributed by one author to restraint in administration.[12] *Fortune* magazine noted that the unions were beginning to utilize the law to gain greater benefits when the then Governor, Christian Herter, was advised by the authors of the law to choose not to invoke the law,[13] even in situations where it previously had been utilized. This seems to have stabilized the situation.

A more practical reason for withholding use of the law has been the political situation in Massachusetts. The Slichter law was enacted by a Republican administration and has been invoked only by Republican governors. Although the labor members of the Slichter committee supported it, the law did not have union support and was opposed by the Democratic Party in the state. Professor Slichter told the author several years before he died that the law could always be more successful under governors who were opposed to it, because they would invoke it only reluctantly. The fact that Massachusetts has had few governors favorable to the Slichter law may indeed be a factor explaining its limited encroachment on collective bargaining.

Whether choice of procedures in fact creates the uncertainty that in theory it is supposed to, so as to discourage its being substituted for collective bargaining, remains a question. Certainly, as administered by Governor Herter in 1953—at least until he stopped invoking the law—it did not. To be sure, the threat of seizure authorities disbursing company cash has given management considerable pause and acts as a spur for management to settle. No such incentive to unions has been demonstrated. Herein is one of the great weaknesses of the law.

Concluding Remarks

The three state experiences discussed show great ingenuity, but all must be regarded as having achieved less than their objectives. The Minnesota fact finding law inhibited collective bargaining but provided little if any protection against strikes. The Virginia law, despite its interesting provisions and lack of settlement procedures, was invoked only in minor disputes having minimal public impact. The Massachusetts legislation proved no choice except between seizure and inaction—and unions found it helpful in enhancing their power, although this was limited by the failure of pro-union governors to invoke the law. This chapter raises the question whether collective bargaining can function under any form of government intervention.

NOTES

1. The material in this chapter is based on Herbert R. Northrup and Gordon F. Bloom, *Government and Labor* (Homewood: Richard D. Irwin, Inc., 1963), Chapter 14.

2. J. W. Stieber, *Ten Years of the Minnesota Labor Relations Act* (Minneapolis: University of Minnesota, Industrial Relations Center, 1949), p. 23.

3. *Ibid.*, pp. 22-23.

4. State of Minnesota, Division of Conciliation, *Annual Report, 1949-1950* (St. Paul, 1950), p. 9.

5. *Ibid., Annual Report,* 1950-1951 (St. Paul, 1951), p. 27.

6. Stieber, *op. cit.*, pp. 17-23.

7. For a different view of the Minnesota law, see Joseph Lazar, "Tripartitism in Minnesota," *Industrial Relations,* Vol. II (February 1963), pp. 119-126; and for a criticism of Professor Lazar's view, see this writer's comment, *ibid., October* 1963, pp. 125-129, and Lazar's reply, *ibid.,* pp. 129-131.

8. *Richmond News-Leader*, editorial, August 26, 1949.

9. Among the supporters of this approach have been Archibald Cox, Solicitor-General, and W. W. Wirtz, Secretary of Labor in the Kennedy-Johnson Administrations. See the article by Mr. Wirtz in I. Bernstein, *et al* (eds.), *Emergency Disputes and National Policy* (New York: Harper and Brothers, 1955), pp. 149-165.

10. George P. Shultz, "The Massachusetts Choice-of Procedures Approach to Emergency Disputes," *Industrial and Labor Relations Review,* Vol. X (April 1957), p. 363.

11. *Ibid.*, pp. 364-365.

12. *Ibid.*, pp. 365-370.

13. "Boston Roulette," *Fortune,* February 1961, pp. 190, 193.

CHAPTER

9 Federal and State Mediation

COLLECTIVE BARGAINING is a method of setting the terms and conditions of the employment process by negotiation between representatives of an employer or employer group, on the one hand, and of a unionized employee group or groups on the other. Before agreement is reached, strife or strikes may occur. Mediation and conciliation are used interchangeably to denote intervention by a third party who, without power to compel agreement, attempts by persuasion, compromise, etc., to assist the parties to come to an agreement.[1]

A famous mediator and arbitrator has written that "mediation is inseparable from collective bargaining; it is an integral part of dispute settlement, and it can exert an important influence on government's role in labor relations. It potentially bears on how union or industry power is exercised and, thus, becomes an important factor in deciding whether additional regulating legislation is needed."[2]

This quotation not only points up the importance of mediation as an intervention process, but it also illustrates the views of many authorities who think of mediation and collective bargaining as almost one and the same; others regard mediation as an "adjunct to collective bargaining."[3] We believe that it is more accurate to look upon mediation as a form of intervention because mediation involves the introduction of a third party into the bargaining process. Once the mediator enters, bargaining is never the same as it was before he came.

To be sure, the government—or at least its shadow—is never absent from the bargaining table. There are always restrictions, or potential ones, on the parties. There is always the threat of intervention by one level of government or another. But once that intervention takes place, the situation changes. The constraints are there and visible, and must be considered by the parties. If this remains collective bargaining, it is a different kind of bargaining than it was before the mediator entered. To call it simply by the name of the pure process is likely to be confusing rather than descriptive.

Nor can mediation be considered as merely an "adjunct to collective bargaining," that is, a supplemental assistant. Again, to be sure, it is often that; and in its most constructive form, mediation is utilized to carry the parties to agreement when they are almost there by themselves. This, however, requires that mediation be utilized at precisely the right time and in the right way. But if mediation is introduced too early, the mediator can become an obstacle to overcome. Likewise, mediation too often or too regularly introduced can induce the parties to save a little to give to the mediator. In such instances, mediation is no adjunct but a hindrance. In any case, mediation is intervention and can only be correctly understood as such. For however clever the mediator, he is helping to do what the parties should have the courage to do themselves—settle their differences. The better he does it, the less the parties will need him; the more the parties rely on mediation, the greater will be the propensity for more complete intervention to come in, particularly as mediation, like an old hat, loses its novelty and charm.

The Mediation Agencies

By far the largest and most important and active mediation agency is the Federal Mediation and Conciliation Service, headquartered in Washington, D.C., with offices throughout the land. The Taft-Hartley Act requires in Section 8 (d) that unions and company notify the FMCS (and any appropriate state agency) at least 30 days before a contract expires if no new agreement has been achieved. Hence, the Service is aware of possible strikes. The FMCS may be called into a dispute by either labor or management, or it may proffer its services. It has, however, no authority to force itself upon an unwilling employer or union. Of course, as a federal agency, it carries with it the prestige of the government, so that refusal to participate in a conference called by the Service is not usual.

Besides the federal service, nearly all the states also maintain mediation activities. Most of the states, however, do not engage aggressively in this function, but provide that the state labor department, or similar agency or person, may assist in the solution of labor disputes. When that is the case, most mediation activities in a state are left to the federal service.

State mediation received a substantial boost when the aforementioned section of the Taft-Hartley Act required notice of an impending dispute to state as well as to the federal mediation agency. In addition, the Taft-Hartley Act directed the FMCS to refrain from mediating disputes which have a minor effect on interstate commerce and authorized the FMCS to work out "suitable procedures" for cooperation with state and local services. Desirous of settling problems within their states and conscious that an active role in seeming to maintain labor peace and stability projects a good political image, many state administrations have, since 1947, developed active mediation agencies. Other states have expanded their mediation services merely by doing an effective job. The most active state agencies are Connecticut, Massachusetts, New York, New Jersey, and Pennsylvania in the east; Michigan, Minnesota, and Wisconsin in the midwest; and California in the west. North Carolina has the most active mediation service in the south. Illinois and Indiana are also quite active in the midwest.

In addition to federal and state mediation, some municipalities have established agencies. The most active one is that of New York City. The reasons for the activity of this city agency depend upon the fact that within New York City the mayor is in many ways a more powerful figure than the governor of the state. Many of the disputes which occur in New York City are directly involved in city activities. For example, construction, hauling, fuel, sand, and gravel, etc., all involve city licenses to do business or other direct or indirect relations with the city government. Moreover, whereas the state and federal mediators are usually merely mediators, the city labor relations head is apparently empowered to and, in fact, does speak in the name of the mayor. Consequently, many disputes in New York are not settled until the mayor's voice is heard through his labor division.

The Jurisdiction Question

The Taft-Hartley Act, as noted, encouraged the development of state mediation agencies, and specifically provides that both state and municipal mediation bodies may exist side by side with the federal service. Jurisdiction is thus concurrent, not exclusive. Despite many efforts, including the recent establishment of a code of conduct agreed to by federal and state agencies,[4] no agreement has ever been reached between the federal and state agencies as to their relative jurisdiction. The fact of the matter is that no agreement is likely because each bureaucracy desires as much activity as possible in order to justify its staff and budget, and undoubtedly because both federal and state officials believe that their particular agency is best suited to perform the mediation function. The result is often aggressive mediation intervention which inhibits collective bargaining instead of promoting peaceful settlement, and which furthers duplication of service and wastes taxpayers' money.

The blame for the failure of federal and state mediation agencies to achieve accord is the fault of both. The federal service enters a vast number of cases involving small industry and few employees, which by any objective criterion do not have a "substantial" impact on interstate commerce. The state agencies often attempt to assert jurisdiction in cases involving such vast multistate enterprises as General Motors or United States Steel, which clearly do have an effect on interstate commerce.

Part of the problem has resulted from the increasing competence of state agencies. Before the Pennsylvania service was reorganized in 1958, the FMCS could, without protest, take jurisdiction over almost any dispute in the commonwealth. Now, Pennsylvania has a much abler staff who want to assert their jurisdiction, but FMCS personnel are loath to give up areas handled in the past. In other states, too, the problem has grown more acute as the effectiveness of the state personnel has improved.

In Indiana the governor has been sending out letters announcing the availability of the Indiana Mediation Service and, in effect, inviting industry and labor to use state instead of federal mediators. In other areas an informal "first come, first served" arrangement is in effect. One mediator termed this sort of thing "mediation ambulance chasing."[5]

Another reason why state mediators attempt to assert jurisdiction in clearly major interstate situations is likely to be their frustration over the fact that the most important disputes affecting the people and industries of their states are really beyond their power to act. Consider this comment by the Minnesota Division of Conciliation:

> . . . there are many instances in which neither the union nor the employer file a petition for conciliation with this office. Particularly where industry-wide bargaining covers employees in several states and where the negotiations are carried on in a location outside the State of Minnesota is this true. Nevertheless, such cases can, and sometimes do have a tremendous impact on the economy within the state. By way of illustration, the steel negotiations affecting over 14,000 employees in the Iron Range area can be cited as an outstanding example.[6]

An official who is charged with keeping the peace likes to be able to handle breaches; his rewards, his staff, and his general standing are usually more favorable the busier he is and the better the strike record looks. This, of course, is the kernel of the problem. Moreover, mediators are often prodded by public figures who want their administrations to receive credit for settlement. "Those intimate with the problem recognize an increasing awareness of the 'exploitability' of labor disputes. Strikes make headlines; the bigger the strike, the bolder the headlines. Strike settlements bring public acclaim to the peacemaker. 'Agreement reached at the office of . . .' are pleasant words to read on the front page of today's paper."[7]

In some areas, difficulties are further complicated by having more than two jurisdictions represented. Where a dispute crosses state lines, two state agencies and the FMCS may all have a hand in the dispute. In New York City there have been several occasions when the FMCS, the State Board, and the New York City Labor Division were all involved. In one case three state agencies, the New York City agency, and the FMCS all participated. Yet few would claim that mediation is made more effective because of the number of mediators.

The reason why this jurisdictional hodgepodge has not resulted in open fighting among the agencies is that it has been disguised from the public by an uneasy accommodation known as "the duet" or, in New York City, "the trio." What this means in practice is that in virtually all significant cases, when a dispute arises in states—for example, Connecticut and Michigan, and in the Boston area of Massachusetts—two mediators appear on the scene, one state and one federal. Usually, the mediators are friendly toward each other and sometimes work well as a team. Sometimes, they are downright antagonistic and work at cross purposes. Either way, it gives both agencies an opportunity to service the entire jurisdiction, and avoids at least the outward manifestations of hostility among agencies whose prime job is the furtherance of labor peace.

A spokesman for the Connecticut State Board of Mediation has commended the formal mediation duet as practiced in his state as an ideal solution of the jurisdictional question which recognizes the jurisdictional interest of all concerned and which provides sound mediation.[8] Others have been highly critical of dual mediation as a bureaucratic solution which, in effect, amounts to mediation featherbedding and which wastes taxpayer dollars without increasing the effectiveness of mediation.[9] No one has ever found that mediation effectiveness has been improved by adding to the number of mediators. Rather, the net effect has been a race on the part of the rival mediators to intervene, and unnecessary mediation and intervention.

COMPULSORY AND PREVENTIVE MEDIATION

In 1959, when the Landrum-Griffin bill was before Congress, Joseph F. Finnegan, then Director of the Federal Mediation and Conciliation Service, and later Chairman of the New York State Board of Mediation, asked Congress to consider making it an unfair labor practice for a union or company representative to refuse to attend a mediation meeting called by the FMCS. This proposal is not new, having been suggested at one time or another by state and federal officials and private citizens over the years. It has not been adopted, however, by any jurisdiction. The Minnesota law, which comes closest to this position, is not administered in practice with any compulsory mediation features.

The argument behind these proposals was recently suggested to the writer by a member of a state agency. "The parties," he said, "are often surprised with what we can do to bring them to settlement. Our files bulge with letters attesting to this fact. On the other hand, too often, they think that to ask for, or even to accept, mediation is a sign of weakness. Perhaps Mr. Finnegan's suggestion goes too far. But I would require the parties to accept mediation if the chairman of our Board or the director of the FMCS assigned a mediator to assist them."[10]

Unfortunately, there is another side of the problem. Assigning a mediator does not produce mediation. The old story of leading the horses to water but not being able to make them drink, is applicable here. Combined with this fact is the pressure which would be put on officials to assign mediators. It is bad enough now. We know of at least one international union which makes it a practice to demand mediation almost as soon as it starts negotiations with a major concern. This company is strong enough to handle its own situation and knows it. The minute the mediators walk in, the company's chief negotiator states to the union and management committees something like this: "Gentlemen, I want you to meet federal mediators Jones and Smith. They are certainly welcome to join us. They will be the first to tell you that they have no authority to force a settlement, or otherwise to substitute government fiat for our deliberations."

Mediation has never contributed much to these negotiations. If the presence of the mediator were made compulsory, the company would not change its policy. The mediators might come even earlier, but their effectiveness would be no greater.

Compulsory mediation is not likely to be effective mediation. As the Independent Study Group authorized by the Committee on Economic Development noted: "Extensive experience with mediation has disclosed two facts of primary importance about it.

The first is that mediation works best when the parties themselves decide that it would be helpful. The second is that the individual mediator must command the respect and have the confidence of the parties. When an unqualified or unwanted man is thrust upon the parties, not only is he less likely to be successful, but confidence in mediation as a whole may be shaken."[11]

Preventive Mediation

In its annual report for 1957 the Federal Mediation and Conciliation Service stated that "the basic industrial relations policy of the United States (as expressed in Section 201 of the [Taft-Hartley] Act) can be effectuated only if, in addition to dispute mediation, the mediators of the Service make an active effort to identify and help solve disruptive labor relations when the parties are not engaged in crisis bargaining . . . and the advantage of industrial peace can be more readily seen by both parties."[12] The FMCS defines "preventive mediation" as the "providing of advice and counsel to parties as needed and wanted by them." This means that the mediator may enter the case even before bargaining starts, or remain concerned with a case long after a strike has ended, working with the parties to identify causes of friction or to attempt to improve attitudes, practices, or other factors which might contribute to industrial peace.

The current director of the FMCS is a firm believer in preventive mediation and has requested additional personnel in order to staff his program of attaching mediators to potential dispute areas before strikes erupt.

On the face of it, preventive mediation seems like a sound idea. Why wait till the parties get into trouble before mediating their disputes? Cannot early entrance into the situation enhance opportunities for settlement by locating, as former President Eisenhower suggested, the "fever spots" of discord before they erupt into economic warfare?[13] The answer seems to be that the advocates of this technique have forgotten the basic fact that mediation is a form of intervention, and that therefore it is not the same as collective bargaining.

Preventive mediation means early intervention. Sometimes this can be helpful, but only if collective bargaining has already broken down. To intervene prematurely otherwise is more likely to insure failure of both collective bargaining and mediation.

The early entrance of the mediator upsets the power balance. With the consequences of either intransigence or ignorance— i.e., the strike—still in the distance, the early entrance by the mediator often results in a hardening of positions, instead of a realistic appraisal of the situation. Moreover, in such a situation the mediator can become, as a labor reporter of the *New York Times* has appraised it, "as commonplace as the furniture and as useful."[14]

For any type of intervention to be successful, it must be properly timed as well as adroitly executed. Preventive mediation is too often only premature mediation. The parties are notified of third-party interest and, in effect, encouraged to save a little for the mediator. By the time the crisis stage of the dispute is reached, the mediator has likely lost both his novelty and his usefulness. The result is likely to be to set the stage for more intervention rather than to strengthen collective bargaining. Moreover, if the purpose of public policy should be to strengthen collective bargaining, not to set the stage for more intervention, then it follows that mediation can best serve as a remedial function rather than as a preventive function, which in many instances serves to hinder rather than to help collective bargaining.

Evaluation of Mediation

Expert mediation has been described by a famous mediator as acting as "a lubricant, perhaps a catalyst." The essential function of the mediator "is to keep the parties in intelligent discussion with each other."

How the mediator accomplishes his purpose is another matter. Techniques which work in one case will not necessarily work in another. Things proposed by one mediator will be emphatically rejected if proposed by another. The effectiveness of the mediator depends mainly on the confidence he can inspire and on certain indefinable qualities he possesses. Among the latter is his intuitive ability to do what will arouse favorable response and to know when to make his moves. He must be able to anticipate unfavorable reactions and to help temper them so they do not divide the parties further in the search for agreement.

Basically, the mediator proceeds on the theory that a strike is undesirable and that there exists a community or public interest as well as a private interest in avoiding or shortening a strike. This fortifies him; he speaks to the embattled parties as the voice of the community. He has the delicate task of preserving for the parties their resort to economic force while not allowing the economic threat to destroy their ability to reason with each other.[15]

Reflecting on his activity as a mediator while Secretary of Labor, Ambassador Arthur Goldberg, then an Associate Justice of the Supreme Court, was more blunt:

The Secretary [of Labor], as a mediator inevitably is driven to seek peace at any price—for him a settlement without any strike, or at least, without a prolonged strike is the goal. . . . The Secretary's objective is peace—peace almost at any price.[16]

These quotations point up the problem of mediation. By far the least onerous form of intervention, and often an asset in preserving industrial peace, mediation is necessarily also an instrument which can become a tactic of labor, management, or the government to force peace at an untoward price, to upset the power balance, or to provide intervention for the sake of intervention.

The emphasis in this chapter has been on the problems of mediation because this book is concerned with the problems of government intervention and mediation is a form of government intervention. The basic problem is that mediation is like medicine —helpful when it is needed, dangerous in overdose. The interests of the federal and state bureaucracies and of politicians is too often in enhancing their jobs. This results in an overdose of mediation, causes collective bargaining to be inhibited, and produces settlements which reflect "peace at any price." The result too often is not in the public interest.

NOTES

1. For a more complete discussion of the subject contained herein, see Herbert R. Northrup and Gordon F. Bloom, *Government and Labor* (Homewood: Richard D. Irwin, Inc., 1963), Chapters 10 and 11.

2. David L. Cole, "Government in the Bargaining Process: The Role of Mediation," *The Annals*, Vol. CCCXXXIII (January 1961), p. 43.

3. See, for example, Howard S. Kaltenborn, *Governmental Adjustment of Labor Disputes* (Chicago: Foundation Press, 1943).

4. See William E. Simkin, "Code of Professional Conduct for Labor Mediators," *Labor Law Journal*, Vol. XV (October 1964), pp. 627-633.

5. Interview, May 1962.

6. State of Minnesota, Division of Conciliation, *Biennial Report*, July 1, 1958-June 30, 1960 (St. Paul, 1960), p. 25.

7. Arthur Stark, "Are There Too Many Mediators?" *Labor Law Journal*, Vol. VI (January 1955), p. 33.

8. Robert L. Stutz, "Troikas, Duets and Prima Donnas in Labor Mediation," *Labor Law Journal*, Vol. XIII (October 1962), pp. 845-852.

9. J. J. Manson, "The Sunset of Mediation: Prima Donnas, Duets and Troikas," *Labor Law Journal*, Vol. XIII (October 1962), pp. 841-845.

10. Interview, March 1962.

11. Committee for Economic Development, *The Public Interest in National Labor Policy* (New York, 1961), pp. 92-93.

12. Federal Mediation and Conciliation Service, *Tenth Annual Report*, p. 48.

13. From Eisenhower's speech to the AFL Convention in 1952, allegedly written by M. S. Pitzele, later Chairman of the New York State Board of Mediation.

14. Quoted by Allan Weisenfeld, "Labor Dispute Settlement—Local or Federal Function?" *Labor Law Journal*, Vol. X (October 1959), p. 704.

Weisenfeld, Secretary of the New Jersey State Board of Mediation, opposes preventive mediation, among other reasons, because he believes that FMCS activity of such nature tends to reduce still further state mediation activity.

15. David L. Cole, "Government and the Bargaining Process: The Role of Mediation," *The Annals*, Vol. CCCXXXIII (January 1961), pp. 50-51.

16. Arthur Goldberg, "Reflections of the Newest Justice," speech before the Section of Judicial Administration, American Bar Association, Chicago, August 12, 1963.

CHAPTER

10 Regulating Grievance or "Rights" Disputes

THIS BOOK is concerned primarily with governmental machinery designed to prevent or to reduce the number of strikes over the terms and conditions of collective agreements. But there is another kind of dispute machinery into which the government has been injected—that is, disputes over the interpretation of contracts. In Chapter 5, we noted that the National Railroad Adjustment Board was established for the compulsory arbitration of such disputes arising under railway labor agreements. In Sweden, a labor court has been established for this purpose (see Appendix H). In Australia, the arbitration machinery does not distinguish between grievance disputes (disputes over "rights") and disputes over the terms of new contracts ("interests" disputes).[1]

In the United States, public policy is becoming more concerned with grievance or rights disputes, which are the subject of this chapter. Once the agreement is negotiated, a procedure is required to settle such disputes, which may arise over honest disagreements as to what contract language shall mean, particularly when applied to particular situations, or whether a discipline meted out by a supervisor was based on evidence, or followed proper procedure as set forth in the contract, or was based on "just cause;" or whether attempts by union or management officials to "stretch" the contract to suit their purposes will succeed.

Grievance Arbitration

Collective bargaining does not end when the agreement is signed. It simply takes a different form. Union officials are just as alert to the possibility of obtaining additional benefits for their membership after a contract is signed as before. If, for example, the union can induce management to make an exception on vacation policy for one worker, that exception can be made the basis of a demand for liberalization of vacations in the next contract negotiations, either with this company or with other companies with which the union deals. Various groups in the shop may try to gain by direct action or pressure what they failed to achieve in bargaining over the new contract. If a rival for the union leadership can make gains in this manner, he might insure his election to the top union job next time.

Management may also do more than rest upon the contractual *status quo*. Plant managers and supervisors, anxious to maintain their control and profit positions, sometimes attempt to water down the agreement in practice. The contract is, in a real sense, only a temporary resting place.[2]

In most instances, bargaining during the life of the contract is different than bargaining over a new contract. That is true because the bargaining after the contract has been signed is basically over the interpretation and administration of the agreement, whereas before the agreement is signed, it is the content of the agreement which is in dispute. Thus, some observers liken the negotiation of the agreement to the legislative function of writing laws, and the interpretation and administration bargaining which goes on after the agreement is signed to the judicial function of interpreting laws which the legislature has enacted. Like judges, the parties can substantially alter meaning and intent by interpretation.

Nevertheless, the attitude of unions and managements toward interpretation and toward bargaining over new contracts is in many ways quite different. Because the parameters seemed to be limited by the contract, because business, production, profit, income and employment could not be continually interrupted by strikes over relatively small, sometimes trivial (but sometimes significant, too) matters, the unions and management in over 90 percent of the cases in the United States have been willing to provide for the arbitration of grievance disputes—that is disputes over contract interpretation—whereas only about two percent provide for the arbitration of disputes over new or reopened agreements. In other words, unions and managements are willing to allow a third party to settle a dispute over an interpretation of an agreement when they cannot agree on the interpretation; but when it comes to the actual negotiation of the agreement, they want no outsider to do it for them.

Now, this is sensible, because no one is as qualified to write a contract as the parties who have to live with it. On the other hand, if the company is going to get out production, and if the workers are to receive steady pay, then the parties have to agree on a practical method which insures that production will not be interrupted by disputes over contract interpretation and administration. Then, if either party is too dissatisfied with the results of the decision of the outside arbitrator who interprets the disputed clause in the agreement, that party can attempt to have the contract altered at the next negotiation.

Moreover, not all companies and unions permit arbitrators to rule on all grievance disputes. For example, the contracts in the automobile industry exempt production standards and wage setting from any arbitration rulings. This means that if a grievance dispute arises over such matters, and is not resolved, the union, after following certain procedures, may authorize a legal strike during the life of the contract. The General Motors Corporation, for example, regards the control of production standards as so significant that it prefers to permit unions to strike over production standards in order to exempt such disputes from arbitration. General Motors management believes that this results in better production standards from the company point of view, not only because it leaves production standard determination in the hands of management but, equally important, because the importance of standards setting is emphasized by this procedure. If the standards are set too loose, the cost and competitive position of the plant or operation are jeopardized; if they are set unfairly, a costly strike can occur. Plant management is thus under exacting pressure to set proper standards at all times.

It should be stressed here that most grievance disputes in industry generally are settled without recourse to outside help. The typical one is handled by the foreman or supervisor and the union shop steward or committeeman; or if not by these lower eschelons, on appeal by the plant manager or personnel director and local or national union officials.

The disputes which do go to arbitration, however, are likely to be important ones, or ones in which both parties feel they have too important a stake to compromise. That is why the provisions of the contract which concern the arbitration machinery are so important. And that is why sudden changes in the parameters of arbitration authority by the courts and the additional injection of National Labor Relations Board authority are so significant to national labor policy.

The New Law of Grievance Arbitration

Section 301 (a) of the Taft-Hartley Act provides: "Suits for violation of contracts between an employer and a labor organization representing employees in an industry affecting commerce as defined in this Act, or between any such labor organizations, may be brought in any district court of the United States having jurisdiction of the parties, without respect to the amount in controversy or without regard to the citizenship of the parties."

This innocuous-appearing provision, which on its face seems only to provide a new forum for trying cases involving disputes over labor contracts, promises to have far-reaching effects upon a vital area of union-management relations—contract administration. As a matter of fact, some labor experts believe that this provision may well be one of the most important in the entire Act. As Professor Archibald Cox (later United States Solicitor-General) states: "Until the Taft-Hartley Act was enacted, collective agreements were negotiated without much regard to whether they were enforceable contracts or merely treaties resting upon mutual interdependence backed by moral force and fear of economic reprisals. . . . History will mark the Taft-Hartley Act as

the turning point at which law began to play a large role in contract administration."[3] No longer was it to be true as it was prior
to 1947, that unions and management could generally take the
position that the courts should be kept out of contract administration.

Arbitration of disputes over contract administration has become so common on the American labor scene that literally
thousands of decisions are handed down by arbitrators every year
interpreting various clauses in collective bargaining agreements
under a variety of factual circumstances. These decisions are for
the most part rendered by men who are economists or labor lawyers, or who have some special familiarity with the customs and
practices in the particular industry. The hearings before the
arbitrators are less formal than in a court of law, and the rules
of evidence which are controlling in court cases do not apply.
Some arbitration decisions are compiled and printed,[4] and are
consulted by arbitrators who wish to see how other arbitrators
have dealt with similar factual situations. Thus, there has developed outside the courtroom a "law of contract administration"
which has no legal force as such but which serves as a body of
technical precedents in the field of arbitration.

Since Section 301 (a) of the Taft-Hartley Act purports to
apply to suits for violation of collective bargaining agreements,
it obviously applies to disputes involving the applicability of the
grievance machinery terminating in arbitration. For example, the
union may claim that a dispute on a certain issue should go to
arbitration, because the business agent does not want to "stick his
neck out" to make an unpopular decision. The employer, on the
other hand, may not want to go to arbitration on a matter because of a conviction that it is solely a matter of managerial
prerogative and was not intended to be covered by the grievance
machinery.

Suppose an employer refuses to refer such a dispute to arbitration and the union brings suit in federal court to require the
employer to do so. Section 301 (a) might have been construed
simply as a procedural provision permitting such suits for enforcement of an agreement to arbitrate to be brought in federal
court. But the United States Supreme Court has read into the
statutory language much more than that. In the famous Lincoln

Mills case and its companion cases,[5] the United States Supreme Court established that an arbitration agreement in a collective bargaining contract in an industry affecting interstate commerce was enforceable in federal court, and *that the law to be applied in determining the intent of the parties and in interpreting the contract provisions was federal law.* The Court stated unequivocally that a *whole new body of substantive federal law* now has to be devised applicable to the arbitration process in collective bargaining.

This decision has aroused grave misgivings on the part of some labor experts and labor arbitrators. The fear has been expressed that litigation over contract administration will increase and that judges, who are generally unfamiliar with labor practices in industry, will tend to construe collective bargaining agreements literally without sufficient attention to practice and custom. It has been pointed out that collective bargaining agreements are unlike most contracts—they are the basis of a continuing relationship and typically are not complete instruments. As a consequence, arbitrators, after investigating practices and customs in an industry, frequently read things into contracts which are not there. What does "discharge for just cause" mean? This is the kind of cryptic phrase that arbitrators must wrestle with. Are courts equipped to deal with the shorthand phraseology of collective bargaining agreements? The late Justice Frankfurter, who dissented in the Lincoln Mills case, voiced the opinion that "judicial intervention is ill-suited to the special characteristics of the arbitration process in labor disputes."

Arbitrability and Management Rights

The dangers of judicial intervention in collective bargaining contract administration are well illustrated by two important decisions rendered by the Supreme Court in June 1960, involving arbitration under collective bargaining agreements.[6] These decisions concern the basic authority of the arbitrator to arbitrate —a technical issue which on its surface appears to affect only the phraseology of the arbitration clause. The implications of these decisions, however, are much more profound and may well affect the entire area of managerial control in industrial relations.

Let us suppose that management in a particular company makes a decision that it is more profitable to contract out certain maintenance work than to perform the work with its own employees. It therefore lays off 19 men and subcontracts to an outside company the work previously done by the laid-off employees. The union claims that this action violates the collective bargaining agreement and demands that management submit the matter to arbitration. The contract contains a no-strike agreement by the union and an arbitration clause calling for the arbitration of disputes "as to the meaning and application of the provisions of this agreement." Another clause provides that "matters which are strictly a function of management shall not be subject to arbitration." While the matter of subcontracting work is not specifically mentioned in the contract, the company takes the position that this is strictly a management decision. The company emphasizes that for 19 years the union has attempted to make changes in the contract which would have limited this right, and the company has always defeated such attempts as an invasion of managerial prerogative. Should the company now have to go to arbitration on this issue?

It should be noted that the issue is initially only a procedural one: Is this an arbitrable issue? Even if the issue is found to be arbitrable, the company might still be sustained by the arbitrator in its action in laying off the men. But a corollary result would be that management could no longer act freely in this sphere and would have to be prepared to justify its action to an arbitrator whenever it made similar decisions. Thus, procedural decisions tend to affect the substance of employer-union relations and the extent of third party intervention.

The facts set forth above were involved in the case of *United Steelworkers of America v. Warrior and Gulf Navigation Company*. The union brought suit under Section 301 of the Taft-Hartley Act to compel the Company to go to arbitration on the issue of subcontracting out work. The lower courts sustained the management's position that the issue was not arbitrable, but on appeal the United States Supreme Court reversed and sided with the union. The High Court set forth at length its theory of the nature of a collective bargaining agreement: "It is a generalized code to govern a myriad of cases which the draftsmen cannot wholly anticipate," and the parties utilize arbitration as a means of filling in the gaps and taking care of unforeseen circumstances. The Court reasoned that in selecting the system of arbitration for the resolution of differences over contract interpretation and administration, management and labor intend that *every* dispute or grievance be arbitrated unless they have *specifically* included it from the arbitration provisions. The Court emphasized that federal policy is to promote industrial stability through collective bargaining agreements and that giving arbitration clauses the broadest possible coverage furthers this policy.

In dissenting, Justice Whittaker stated:

I understand the Court thus to hold that the arbitrators are not confined to the express provisions of the contract, that arbitration is to be ordered unless it may be said with positive assurance that arbitration of a particular dispute is excluded by the contract, that doubts of arbitrability are to be resolved in favor of arbitration, and that when, as here, the contract contains a no-strike clause, everything that management does is subject to arbitration.

This is an entirely new and strange doctrine to me. I suggest with deference, that it departs from both the contract of the parties and the controlling decisions of this Court.

In a companion case, decided the same day, *United Steelworkers of America v. American Manufacturing Company*, the Supreme Court further amplified its doctrine favoring broad coverage of arbitration in contract administration. In this case the union sought to compel the company to arbitrate the question of whether an employee who had been injured should be reinstated to his job by virtue of the seniority provisions of the collective bargaining agreement. The employee had already obtained a permanent workmen's compensation award based upon 25 percent permanent partial disability which clearly established that he was unable to perform his previous work. The arbitration clause stated that all disputes "as to the meaning, interpretation and application of this agreement" should go to arbitration. The Company's refusal to arbitrate was upheld by the lower courts, which found the union's claim to be a "frivolous, patently baseless one, not subject to arbitration under the collective bargaining agreement."

The Supreme Court reversed and held that the issue was arbitrable. In so holding, it again emphasized that it was attempting to implement the federal policy in favor of settlement of grievances, as expressed in Section 203 (d) of the Taft-Hartley Act. That section states: "Final adjustment by a method agreed upon by the parties is hereby declared to be the desirable method of settlement of grievance disputes arising over the application or interpretation of any existing collective bargaining agreement. . . ." The Court felt that this policy could best be effectuated by giving the arbitration clause "full play." In the words of Justice Douglas: "There is no exception in the 'no strike' clause and none therefore should be read into the grievance clause, since one is the quid pro quo for the other." Furthermore, the Court indicated that the processing of even frivolous claims may have a therapeutic value in labor relations. One writer has commented that as a result of these two decisions, an employee who wants to compel management to let him hang a collection of butterflies in the main lobby to promote employee morale has probably raised an arbitrable issue![7]

Where do these decisions leave the delicate issue of managerial prerogative? The Supreme Court apparently takes a very narrow view of this area and would require a specific exclusion in a written agreement, or "the most forceful evidence" indicating that the parties intended the arbitration clause not to be applicable. Practical labor practitioners will recognize the difficulty in a collective bargaining agreement of enumerating specific subjects which are to be solely the prerogative of management. As a matter of fact, most companies have preferred to rely on a general management clause and would prefer not even to discuss what it encompasses for fear that this will give the union an opportunity to whittle away at managerial authority. Some companies do not even have management rights provisions in their labor contracts and preferred to rely on the so-called "residual rights" theory. Under this theory, management is presumed to have retained all rights governing the conduct of its business that are not limited by the labor agreement. It is doubtful that the Supreme Court would subscribe to this view, for it has defined management rights as only those over which the contract gives management "complete control and unfettered discretion."

What began in the Lincoln Mills case as a simple test of the application of Section 301 of the Taft-Hartley Act opened a vista for unions of a major assault on managerial prerogatives. Union claims which were previously held not arbitrable are now pressed again, and courts following the guidelines set down by the Supreme Court usually consider them arbitrable. The result has been a gradual extension of union control over areas previously reserved for exclusive managerial determination. Coming at a time when the National Labor Relations Board has been instituting a general assault to limit management rights, the Court interpretations have greatly expanded union codetermination of company decision making.

The basic problem is that the Supreme Court enunciated a theory of contract administration which is at variance with what many company and union negotiators have believed was meant by a labor agreement. Suddenly the perimeters of grievance arbitration was unbelievably widened by judicial fiat. Some companies, notably General Electric, were able to rewrite their contracts in negotiations to limit expressly what could be arbitrated.[8] But thousands of companies with less bargaining power found that they had agreed to limited arbitration and were now left with a provision opening up a hornet's nest of union rights for codetermination.

Obviously, the only remedy is for Congress to rewrite the formerly understood judicial rule into law. Nowhere can evidence be found that the framers of the Taft-Hartley Act intended the law of arbitration to be altered or stretched. Nor can it be claimed that industrial peace is furthered by enhancing union codetermination, for managerial resistance to such pressures is certain to increase, particularly where attempted restrictions on efficient and effective operation of the business is concerned. The Supreme Court's romantic and novel interpretation of arbitration is thus of serious consequence.

The Incursion of the NLRB into Arbitration

If an employee is discriminated against because of union activity, he could presumably file a complaint with the National Labor Relations Board. Here individual rights are involved for which the NLRB was established to provide redress. Presumably also, if a union was already bargaining agent, a grievance under the contract could be filed. But if the employee were not acting in concert with the union leadership, the NLRB might well be his only effective remedy.[9]

On the other hand, it is also quite possibly technically correct to cite violations of collective agreements as unfair practices, especially if such violations could be conceived of as deliberate. But such violations are also subject to contractual grievance machinery, and usually arbitration, the scope of which has been greatly expanded by the already noted judicial interpretations. Since the intent of Congress was not to displace the arbitration process, the NLRB at an early date announced it would "not embark on a course of policy of enforcing trade agreements."[10]

Recently, however, the NLRB has adopted a quite different policy, even processing as unfair labor practices cases which are pending in grievance machineries or which the parties clearly intended so to process.[11] The result has been a choice of forums, an expansion of government intrusion into the bargaining process, a greatly increased case load of the Board, and even in some cases, appeal to the NLRB by parties whose positions were not sustained by arbitrators.[12]

Moreover, the NLRB has expanded the Supreme Court's view that where a union fails to win a demand for the inclusion of a provision limiting a management action—for example, the subcontracting of work—it may still force management to arbitrate a dispute arising over the exercise of this mamagement action. The NLRB has carried this a step further by ruling that where a matter was not discussed in bargaining, it can be brought up during the life of an agreement; and again, the employer must bargain. Thus, if a pension plan was not discussed in negotiations, presumably the union could demand that such a plan be inaugurated during the life of the contract. This type of ruling adds more evidence to the need to deprive the NLRB of its authority to determine whether parties "bargained in good faith" by repealing Section 8a (5) and b (3) of the Taft-Hartley Act, as discussed in Chapter 6.

NOTES

1. Material for both Gordon F. Bloom and Herbert R. Northrup, *Economics of Labor Relations*, 5th ed. (Homewood: Richard D. Irwin, Inc.,

1965), and Herbert R. Northrup and Gordon F. Bloom, *Government and Labor* (Homewood: Richard D. Irwin, Inc., 1963), is utilized herein by permission of publisher and co-author.

2. For an excellent analysis of bargaining and group pressures through the grievance procedure, see James W. Kuhn, *Bargaining in Grievance Settlement: The Power in Industrial Work Groups* (New York: Columbia University Press, 1962).

3. Archibald Cox, *Law and the National Labor Policy*, Institute of Industrial Relations Monograph Series, No. 5 (Los Angeles: University of California, 1960), p. 17.

4. See, for example, *Labor Arbitration Reports*, published by the Bureau of National Affairs, Inc., Washington, D. C.

5. *Textile Workers' Union v. Lincoln Mills of Alabama*, 353 U. S. 448, 77 S.Ct. 912 (1957); *General Electric Co. v. Local 205, United Electrical Workers*, 353 U. S. 547, 77 S.Ct. 921 (1957); *Goodall-Sanford, Inc. v. United Textile Workers*, 353 U. S. 550, 77 S.Ct. 923 (1957).

6. *United Steelworkers of America v. American Manufacturing Co.*, 363 U. S. 564, 80 S.Ct. 1343 (1950); *United Steelworkers of America v. Warrior and Gulf Navigation Co.*, 363 U. S. 574, 80 S.Ct. 1347 (1960). A third case, decided the same day, *United Steelworkers of America v. Enterprise Wheel and Car Corp.*, 363 U. S. 593, 80 S.Ct. 1358 (1960), involved the question of whether an arbitrator had exceeded his authority in making an arbitration award after a voluntary submission to arbitration by both parties to the contract.

7. Franklin B. Snyder, "What Has the Supreme Court Done to Arbitration?" *Labor Law Journal*, Vol. XII (February 1961), p. 97.

8. For an analysis of the General Electric Arbitration policy, see Herbert R. Northrup, *Boulwarsim: The Labor Policies of the General Electric Co.* (Ann Arbor: Bureau of Industrial Relations, University of Michigan, 1964), Chapter 13.

9. *Spielberg Manufacturing Co.*, 112 NLRB 1080 (1955).

10. *Carroll Transfer Co.*, 56 NLRB 935 (1944).

11. See T. O. Kammholz, "The Impact of NLRB Decisions on Arbitration," *Labor Law Journal*, Vol. XXV (September 1964), pp. 620-622.

12. Donald H. Wollett, "The Agreement and the National Labor Relations Act: Courts, Arbitrators and the NLRB—Who Decides What?", *Labor Law Journal*, Vol. XXIV (December 1963), pp. 1041-1051.

PART IV

EVALUATION

CHAPTER

11 Collective
Bargaining vs.
Intervention:
*A General
Analysis*

THE DISCUSSION in the previous chapters has indicated that intervention by government in labor disputes inhibits collective bargaining, enhances union power, frequently works at cross purposes with other national economic or social objectives, and, above all, has at best a questionable record in furthering industrial peace. There remain, however, some key questions of public policy for analysis: Is collective bargaining of sufficient importance to protect? Is strike control or emergency strike legislation necessary? Can a form of emergency strike legislation be devised which does not inhibit collective bargaining? What are some of the key administrative, practical, and legal problems which have emerged from the workings of federal and state strike control legislation—other than the effects on the bargaining process?[1]

Why Protect Collective Bargaining?

No institution or method of determining conditions of work is, or can be, perfectly satisfactory to everyone. But few things are more important to both the individual and society than the methods of determining the conditions under which individuals buy and sell each other's and their own labor. In the United States the Civil War was fought essentially over this question. Before and since then, numerous controversies have arisen as to what is the best or fairest method of deciding basic industrial relations questions.

Economics and Equities

If any answer has emerged, it is that no objective criterion is, or can be, developed to determine the employment relationship to the satisfaction of everyone. The employment relationship is, and must remain, an economic one. What is economically desirable or even necessary for the good of the business and therefore for the continued employment of the work force may be quite different from what would be personally pleasant or satisfactory to workers or, in the case of unions, helpful to the union as an institution or to the intraunion political fortunes of the union leadership. Likewise, the very existence of the union as force may make it economically unsound for the employer or corporate manager to operate as he deems most desirable. If the uneconomic is insisted upon by union strength or permitted by employer mismanagement, or furthered by governmental intervention, the net result can well be a decline in the competitive position of the company and a loss of employment to the union members.

When a whole industry embarks upon such an uneconomic course, the results are no different. Competition from other industries—domestic and foreign—makes itself felt. The substitution of oil and gas for coal is a case in point. So is the increasing use of aluminum, prestressed concrete, plastics, and foreign steel, all in place of domestic steel.

Economic conditions change, and economic science is not exact. No one can promise without fear of error that a certain wage will be "proper" to balance income and employment, or wages and profits in a given industry. Moreover, what is "fair" for one is "unfair" for another. There is no objective, exact answer to disputes over wages, working conditions, and other terms of employment, either on the basis of economics or on the basis of equity. "Too high" wages do accelerate or cause unemployment; "too low" ones impede living standards and purchasing power—but between extremes in any given situation, there is likely to be a wide latitude of possibilities and probabilities.

Freedom and Balance .

The facts of economics which make it well-nigh impossible to determine a "proper" wage, and the facts of equity which make it equally difficult to determine what is "fair" to all concerned, give added weight to the general premise upon which our society is built—that is, that the freedom to work or withdraw labor, either singly or in concert, is not to be curtailed lightly. Such freedom has never been considered a totally unrestricted one. Nor does it mean a return to eighteenth-century society. It requires balance and, above all, more governmental restraint than interference.

Balancing Liberties—and Strength

The rise of great combinations of capital in this and other countries through the corporate form spurred demands for curbing business freedom. In effect, the unrestricted freedom of business was felt to impinge upon the freedom of others. From this developed such regulation as the Sherman Antitrust Act, the Securities Exchange Act, and numerous other federal and state enactments. To protect the individual laborer in his dealing with corporate combinations, social welfare legislation was also passed— minimum wage, protective female and child labor laws, and various social insurances.

Then, in the 1930's, came the enactment of countervailing legislation—laws designed to spur the growth of labor combinations in an attempt to build up the power of labor through unions so that bargaining power in the market place would be equated and reasonably "fair" wages and conditions of work would result. The net effect was also to create a whole set of new problems, and more and more governmental regulation of labor combinations. As in the case of freedom for business combinations, freedom for labor combinations was found to impinge on the freedom of others. The Wagner Act was followed by the Taft-Hartley and Landrum-Griffin laws.

Although these laws regulated union and employer tactics, and

certain strikes relating to these tactics, they sought to preserve
the basic right to strike. The main exception was the emergency
procedures of the Taft-Hartley Act, and this moved into the arena
of strike control most gingerly, only as a postponement technique,
like its Railway Labor Act counterpart. The laws regulating
tactics and the weapons of conflict continue to stress the philosophy that "great reatraint should be exercised in interfering with
the freedom of the seller and the buyer of labor to participate
in determining the conditions of sale. These freedoms can be
preserved only under conditions of equitable joint determination
of the terms of sale, namely through bona fide collective bargaining. Otherwise they are shrunken or lost to the degree that
the terms are fixed unilaterally or imposed from the outside."[2]

Again, it is well to emphasize how this philosophical basis of our
society rests on basic economic grounds. Unions and managements have to live with the results of their wage determinations,
a fact which is a restraint on both. Such determinations affect the
public also—through price movements and distributions of
wealth, to name examples. But to permit general wage fixing by
government fiat is also to surrender consumer sovereignty. For
if wages are fixed, so must prices be determined and resources
allocated by the price fixers, not by consumer dictates. That such
arrangements are not likely to be compatible with a free society
is amply demonstrated by contemporary events in other countries.[3]

Therefore, it is difficult to disagree with the succinct summary of Professor John Perry Horlacher:

Essentially economic disagreements between labor and management
are best resolved by the arbitrament of economic facts and forces. To
the extent that the disagreements are noneconomic and involve the
parties' rights, prerogatives, status, emotions and fetishes—the whole
complex of imponderables in their relationship—they are best settled
by mutual accommodation. Management and labor ought not to be
forced by political pressures or political action to relinquish their
sovereignty, their right and power to decide themselves how mutual
concerns shall be adjusted between them.[4]

Collective Bargaining and the Function of the Strike

Granted that "free collective bargaining is the best solution
we have been able to devise to the employer-employee relation-

ship,"[5] does that mean that any interference with the right to strike means the end of collective bargaining? Assuredly not. But if the strike or lockout are removed from the scene, they cannot perform their essential function. For strikes and lockouts serve "as the motive power which induces a modification of extreme positions and then a meeting of minds. The acceptability of certain terms of employment is determined in relation to the losses of a work stoppage that can be avoided by an agreement. In collective bargaining, economic power provides the final arbitrament."[6]

When the right to strike or to lock out is withdrawn, as though strike control or emergency legislation, the inducement to agree declines sharply. *If the parties are not faced with the consequences of refusing to settle, their desire, determination, or even ability to settle dwindles. This has occurred under each and every law or procedure, federal and state, legal and extralegal, which has been in existence.* No strike control law or extralegal method has succeeded in avoiding this pitfall. And this is true of every other democratic country as it is of the United States.

The result is not strike control, but settlement avoidance. Fearing that to settle will mean a less attractive "package," that it will be a sign of weakness, or that it will involve criticism from rivals or fellow officers or managers, union and companies soon prepare for the emergency procedure instead of for collective bargaining and settlement. The aim is to force intervention—to create the emergency. The more adamant, obdurate, and intransigent the parties, the higher is likely to be the return from public intervenors who see as their principal job the task of ending the strike—or avoiding the emergency. With headlines screaming and merchants complaining about business effects, the payoff is likely to be greatest to those most willing to fight for more, and most willing to create more and greater emergencies.

Emergency dispute laws thus create their own rationale. Behavior becomes tailored to the laws. The more laws enacted, the more "emergencies" are created, and the more "necessary" become the laws. Even laws which provide no direct settlement procedure—for example, the Virginia Public Utility Labor Relations Act, or a sophisticated statute like the Massachusetts choice-of-procedures (Slichter) law—have followed this pattern. This raises the question whether such laws are more harmful than helpful—indeed, whether emergency legislation is necessary or even useful.

Are Emergency Strike Laws Necessary?—An Economic View

During wartime, there is little if any disagreement with the proposition that national needs, both physical and political, require a ban on strikes or lockouts. Therefore, a strike of any size during a war period is considered an emergency situation to be stopped as quickly as possible, and not to be permitted to play its collective bargaining role.

It has been suggested that public emergency disputes in peacetime are of a similar nature and that in such disputes the strike cannot "perform its collective bargaining function." Such a stoppage "does not exert pressure primarily upon the disputants to come to terms. The parties can hold out longer than the public or the government. In consequence, a strike which creates a public emergency exerts primary pressure upon the government to intervene and also to specify the terms upon which production is to be resumed."[7]

This analysis is, of course, quite correct. But it does not answer the underlying question: To what extent have emergency situations arisen? An analysis of events in key industries sheds light on this question.

Railroads

The closest approximation to a national emergency strike was probably the railroad operating strike of 1946. Although it lasted only two days, it caused severe passenger and freight dislocations throughout the country, as well as threatening the shutdown of numerous industries and the loss of agricultural crops. If the threat of drastic legislation had not ended this strike so quickly, a very grave emergency might have resulted.[8]

Since 1946 the importance of railroads in passenger and freight transportation has declined precipitously. It is quite probable that a nationwide railroad strike today would have a considerably smaller impact, for railroads carry about 40 percent of the nation's freight today as compared with 75 percent in 1946.

Bituminous Coal

Nationwide bituminous coal strikes, for a decade a thing of the past, were widely publicized as emergencies. But because of the critical oversupply of coal, a strike was usually "an inescapable layoff by another name."[9] Except for the second strike in 1946, coming after an earlier one occurred, most of these strikes did not involve hardship for many communities.[10] The continued decline of coal as both an industrial and a household fuel, plus the large stockpiles kept by utilities, the major customer of coal, make it unlikely that coal strikes will assume emergency proportions soon again.

Steel.

The late Professor Sumner H. Slichter, writing in 1947, believed strongly that "a general steel strike of 100 days would be disastrous."[11] Yet the 1959 steel strike lasted 116 days, "and the brink of disaster was not even then clearly in sight. A critical examination of the evidence and arguments before the courts on whether the national health and safety would be imperiled by continuance of the 1959 strike by no means compels the finding that in another 10 days, or 20 days, or even 50 or 100 days, we would certainly have been over the brink."[12] It will also be recalled that a 55-day strike shutting down the steel industry in 1952 caused neither a civilian catastrophe nor an impediment in the Korean War effort. It was allowed to continue without invocation of the Taft-Hartley Act because of political considerations, although the evidence does indicate that its economic effects were more severe than any steel strike before or since, including the longer one in 1959.[13]

A very careful study of the impact of steel strikes made after the 1959 stoppage reinforces previous conclusions that the economic impacts of steel strikes

on the economy are usually seriously exaggerated. Too often the losses of production, employment and wages are evaluated in a context which assumes that there would have been continuous high-level operation had there been no strike. Such losses . . . must be weighed over a time span that encompasses a period prior to the strike, the period of the strike, and a period long enough following the strike to permit restoration of inventory. The secondary effects of strikes must be evaluated in a context which recognizes the extent to which industry is subject to seasonal and cyclical forces, the fact that American industry generally operates well below capacity and the fact of inventory accumulation at several stages beyond basic steel itself. Viewed in this perspective most strikes can last much longer (even in an industry as basic as steel) than is generally believed before the economy will be seriously hurt.[14]

The intervention of President Johnson to achieve a settlement in steel in 1965 cannot therefore be considered to have thwarted an emergency. Again, political considerations which allowed a strike to last 55 days during the Korean War seemed to have been paramount in the prevention of one in the name of the emergency caused by the Vietnam War.

Maritime and Longshore

The main effect of the 1961 strike by the National Maritime Union and others, according to a survey by the *New York Times*, was to have "the minor role of the United States Merchant Marine in the nation's commerce . . . pointed up. The strike . . . had a negligible effect on export and import traffic. . . ."[15] Yet the national emergency provisions of the Taft-Hartley Act were invoked.

Longshore strikes have a greater effect, but increasing mechanization, and lack of skill in the work and therefore ease of strikebreaking, weakens the potential of longshore strikes for damage. A number of such strikes have occurred with no catastrophe or emergency in sight. The existence of separate unions on the East and West coasts also reduces the potential for emergency. There is no evidence that a real emergency was in sight in 1963 after a one-month strike, despite the claims of the parties and of government officials.

Trucking

Trucking strikes have resulted in the invocation of emergency laws in Massachusetts and Nebraska, but not on the national scene. The increased importance of this industry as a freight carrier and the success of James R. Hoffa, President of the Teamsters' Union, in obtaining a nationwide over-the-road contract, could result in a serious situation, perhaps in time even comparable to the 1946 railroad strike if local truckers also shut down with their over-the-road counterparts.

Utilities

State strike control legislation has been concerned primarily with strikes in utilities supplying electric light and power, gas, water, telephone, and urban or interurban transportation. A few serious strikes have occurred in these industries, but they are becoming less likely. Automation, plus the use of supervisory help, has about insured the ineffectiveness of telephone strikes, and the same is virtually the case in electric light and power, gas, and water. Strikes in urban transit usually add to already intolerable automobile congestion in our cities and make people later than usual for work (or provide an excuse therefor!), but people seem to get to work without a breakdown of business.

Strikes occurred in public utilities in states which did not have strike control laws during the period 1947-1951 while these laws were being most actively invoked in comparable states; and strikes have occurred in utilities since 1951 in a number of states which have laws but which, for constitutional or other reasons, have not invoked them. The impact in both cases has usually been negligible in the case of all utilities except urban transit—and merely troublesome in the case of the latter.[16]

Strikes in General

In terms of strikes in general, the case for intervention is also very weak. In countries throughout the democratic world, strike incidence has been declining.[17] Table 5 shows that this is true in the United States, as well. The case for government interference cannot be made on the basis of widespread stoppages regularly occurring. The rise in strike incidence in 1959 was wholly due to one stoppage—the steel strike, a fact which indicates the current rarity of long strikes.

Economic Basis Not Evident

The conclusion appears inescapable that the economic basis in peacetime for emergency strike control legislation does not ap-

TABLE 5

STRIKES AND LOCKOUTS IN THE UNITED STATES, SELECTED YEARS, 1917–64

Year	Number of Stoppages	Number of Workers Involved (Thousands)	Man-Days Idle (Millions of Days)	Percentage of Working Time Lost
1917........	4,450	1,227	*	*
1919........	3,630	4,160	*	*
1921........	2,385	1,099	*	*
1925........	1,301	428	*	*
1929........	921	289	5.4	0.07
1933........	1,695	1,168	16.9	0.36
1937........	4,740	1,860	28.4	0.43
1941........	4,288	2,363	23.0	0.32
1944........	4,956	2,116	8.7	0.09
1946........	4,985	4,600	116.0	1.43
1947........	3,693	2,170	34.6	0.41
1950........	4,843	2,410	38.8	0.44
1952........	5,117	3,540	59.1	0.57
1956........	3,825	1,900	33.1	0.29
1958........	3,694	2,060	23.9	0.22
1959........	3,900	1,850	69.0	0.61
1961........	3,367	1,450	16.3	0.14
1963........	3,362	941	16.1	0.13
1964........	3,655	1,640	22.9	0.18

* Data unavailable.
SOURCE: U.S. Department of Labor, Bureau of Labor Statistics.

pear to rest upon substantial evidence. This conclusion is reinforced when it is remembered that emergency strike legislation relieves the parties of the incentive to settle. "The freedom to strike is in our society the major deterrent to strikes." As an example, "History in steel indicates that once strikes really begin to be seriously felt over wide segments of the economy, pressure from those affected will in most instances bring about a settlement."[18]

This, however, is not the whole story. Emergency strike control legislation also has a political aspect. And it has also a national defense aspect.

The Politics of Emergency Strike Laws

Actually, emergency strike laws do not derive from economic fact, but rather from an emotional and political context. Most such legislation dates from the World War II period and its immediate postwar era. During World War II, strikes were not only a potential interference with the war effort; they were also unpatriotic. This feeling carried over during the postwar era, and was furthered by the great strikes of 1945 and 1946.

The fact that strikes have been at a very low level since the late 1940's (Table 5) does not seem to have eased the public feeling that strikes are a wrong and harmful thing. The closer such strikes come to industries which either touch the public or are reputed to be "essential," the more they seem undesirable, and the more public opinion frowns upon them. Newspaper headlines screaming that a port is "crippled" because longshoremen or seamen strike (even if the seamen man only a small percentage of the ships) add to the uneasiness and fear, and in some cases aggravate the inconvenience. The fact that the health and safety of the community are in no way involved is not remembered until sober afterthought occurs when the strike has long since past and is no longer food for newspaper sales or television drama.

What happens, therefore, is that a dispute between labor and industry becomes a political issue. To those in power, it seems bad politics to let the parties reach a juncture when the pressures force a settlement. Instead, it seems more heroic (and politically wise) to "save" the public. The appropriate official, with or without appropriate legislation, intervenes and produces a political settlement, which is usually what one or more of the parties want, and which almost always involves a higher economic cost to the public. Again the intervention of President Johnson in the 1965 steel strike is a case in point. I. W. Abel, who had just been elected president of the steelworkers union after a bitter fight with the incumbent, David McDonald, apparently desired presidential intervention so that he would not have to be responsible for the settlement. The industry apparently believed that opportunities for price relief would be greater if intervention occurred. Thus the emergency apparently was created and the President "saved" the republic.

The sources of public opinion creating emotional and political headlines are many and diverse. They include, first of all, one or more of the parties. In past coal industry disputes, for example, John L. Lewis has found great benefits in pushing for emergencies; the coal industry employers tried equally hard to improve their bargaining power by having Lewis encounter court orders head on. In steel, the industry has been accused of failing to bargain in order to justify major price increases; the union has been accused of declining to settle when the White House was in friendly hands and sympathetic intervention was assured.[19] In "the summer of 1961, the government urged subsidized shipowners to give their unions an exceptionally generous settlement. . . . The government's plea amounted to a commitment that bigger subsidies would be forthcoming to cover the increased labor costs. . . . Clearly, the labor-management harmony embodied in the maritime industry is paid for by persistent raids on the public treasury."[20] A dispute involving a fraction of the maritime industry for which the Taft-Hartley emergency procedure was invoked[21] was thus "satisfactorily" settled.

In creating the political emergency, the parties themselves receive powerful assistance. There are, first of all, the indiscriminate news media, more anxious for sensation than fact, blaring out news of grave consequences of things to come, with no note that past promises of disaster in like circumstances were not factual, nor did they actually occur. Businessmen who officially abhor all governmental "interference" deluge a governor or secretary of labor with telegrams "demanding" that this probably all-too-willing official "take action" to stop this "calamity"— which is usually momentary interference with receipt of a product or a part, or other interference with an opportunity for profit. Wives of union members thrown out of work by a strike of their "brother" unionists add their voices to the chorus for action. Other sources creating the climate of public emergency include "the merchant in the strike-bound community who is dissatisfied with his declining trade and his mounting credit transactions as well as the cabinet member who recognizes intervention as an opportunity to increase his political stature and to improve his political fortunes, although he may rationalize his motivation in terms of statesmanship to save the country from the calamity that everybody foresees."[22]

Thus are labor disputes transformed from their economic character into political emergencies "when the disputants themselves seem to want it that way; when public opinion furnishes the appropriate matrix . . . when those who are hurt resort with customary appeals; and when politicians are anxious to make political hay while the emergency sun is bright."[23]

Emergency Dispute Criteria and Proposals

The pressures for intervention, which are so formidable, are thus primarily political, not economic. Therefore, if public policy is committed to the maintenance of collective bargaining—as this author believes is soundly in the public interest—then public policy should be directed toward curbing, not furthering, political intervention. This means that a sound public policy toward labor disputes must penalize the parties for not settling the dispute themselves and must avoid inviting the politicians to intercede. No law discussed in this book, or known by the author to exist, meets this criterion.

If disputes machinery is to be successful it must prevent strikes and therefore supply the need for peace which the proponents of intervention believe exists (but we believe is at best debatable). Moreover, such legislation must also be capable of coping with emergencies should a real one occur. This certainly disqualifies fact finding which, whenever it is extensively used, has tended to promote political intervention, and therefore political emergencies, but which at the same time creates no substitute method of either maintaining work or providing a settlement once the fact finding machinery has run its course and the real emergency, if any, has arisen.

The record of compulsory arbitration is also questionable in this regard. Given the strike record of Australia, one could hardly recommend this experience to the United States. Moreover, our own experiences during World War II and under the state experiments do not augur for any success for a program of compulsory arbitration in achieving either labor peace or non-political settlement of labor disputes.

It has been argued rather cogently that since much of the industrial relations system in the United States is now under some form of compulsion that the addition of compulsory arbitration would involve only a minor step to a point almost arrived at. Therefore, it is maintained that "if the point is reached where certain classes or individual cases of work stoppages are judged to carry too high a social cost to be tolerated, experimentation with some type of compulsory arbitration is a logical extension of past experience."[24]

Certainly, much more of our industrial relations system is subject to directive than most people realize. But because this is so is no reason to go the whole way—*especially if we analyze the problem in the light of experience and in the light of criteria developed out of experience*. For to re-emphasize what has been said: compulsory arbitration does not eliminate strikes but it does destroy the process of collective bargaining so that the parties lose the ability to settle for themselves. The settlement process under compulsory arbitration becomes embroiled in a bureaucratic maze of delay, confusion, and backlog, with resultant unrest, illegal stoppages, disrespect for law, and contrived political solutions usually in favor of the party which can bring the most political weight to bear. To change our system of not completely free collective bargaining for such a system is to move to an entirely new system—but one which has already been found wanting and less desirable.

Protection vs. Settlement

Not only compulsory arbitration and fact findings, but even such innovative laws as the Virginia seizure law and the Massachusetts choice of procedures act have failed in practice to serve their stated purpose because political pressures resulted in their use in trivial disputes. They became enmeshed in the tactics of the parties instead of being administered aloof from the desires of labor and management to use them for their immediate purposes.

If it be granted for argument that emergencies can exist, and do in a political sense, how can the public be protected *and* collective bargaining preserved. It would appear that the only way to accomplish this would be to divorce the settlement process from the protection of the public. There have been several suggestions to attain this objective, such as "statutory strikes" where the parties are penalized without a work stoppage; breaking up unions to prevent industry-wide bargaining; and the partial injunction technique. Of these, the last appears the most promising, for statutory strike proponents have not been able to demonstrate that a simulated strike situation can induce settlement,[25] and the breaking up of unions or bargaining patterns could well create chaos and strife among small employers and bring demands for a concurrent breakup of large industrial companies with resulting ill effects on industrial efficiency.

The Partial Injunction

The partial injunction[26] would require that the government prove to the satisfaction of the judiciary explicitly what the emergency was, and therefore what service would have to be restored. For example, a partial resumption of steel production might be ordered for a period necessary to fulfill certain objectives; when these objectives had been met, then the injunction would be lifted. The partial resumption might involve part of the industry only, leaving the other part on strike. The object would be to force the government to pinpoint with some degree of precision what the emergency was, and what would be needed to dissolve it.

This is a difficult and formidable task.

A vague concept will not do as a basis for saying what steel production is necessary to prevent the threatened emergency from developing. The very necessity, however, for applying a more exact and rigorous concept of national emergency would in itself be a great virtue. That injunctions can now be sustained on the basis of a fairly general and imprecise judgment that an emergency exists has been one of the great shortcomings in the way this problem has been handled.[27]

There are very serious obstacles to be overcome in learning to use such a technique as the partial injunction, but the technique shows enough promise to warrant the most careful study—which should not wait till a problem exists, but should be done in an atmosphere conducive to unemotional responses.

It is possible that the partial injunction could be used as a tactic by either labor or management. For example, under it a union might sustain an "off and on again" strike as a harassment. To prevent this, penalties might be added, such as forcing unions and management to share the government's litigation costs wherever an injunction is granted, plus a sizable assessment of union dues during the period worked under the injunction. To prevent management from encouraging work under the injunction, a substantial tax on earnings during that period would be in order.

The partial injunction is no panacea. It does, however, seem to contain the seeds of a program designed to preserve collective bargaining and to protect the national welfare. It seems sufficiently unpleasant to discourage inducement; if rigorous standards can be developed, emergencies will have to approach reality before the injunction can be invoked; and if no settlement procedure is provided, the ability to substitute the injunction for collective bargaining is very limited. If penalties are added, the propensity to maintain the injunction period is also reduced.

There remains the question of whether employees would work under an injunction. They do now under Taft-Hartley, and the penalties for defiance of a court order can be severe, but the conditions of work under an injunction would not be onerous. Any strike control law must rely on compliance. If a group struck in defiance of an injunction, heavy penalties against its union would soon make the strike intolerable. Laws in our society are generally obeyed. Otherwise, our society, not just our economy, is in danger as a result of an emergency dispute. But a real problem of compliance arises if a law is unpopular or too easily or regularly invoked. The injunction, as we shall note later in this chapter, is the easiest method of enforcement for labor legislation.

The Problem of National Defense

The partial injunction would also be useful in handling national defense issues. Production needed for defense could be resumed under an injunction formula; and at the same time, precise information could be required in court as to what exactly is needed for defense from what plant—not just an assertion by an armed forces spokesman that defense is affected.

The use of the partial injunction, and its rigorous requirement for establishing that an emergency exists, would again be salutary in requiring officials to show factually that a strike is actually a serious deterrent to defense production. Remembering what President Truman stated *would* happen if a steel strike occurred during the Korean War, as compared with what *did* happen when the strike lasted fifty-five days, can demonstrate why a real showing of serious interference with defense requirements is in order.

If production is partially restored in an industry such as steel, it could not be only defense production. Thus, Professor Livernash reports: "In an analysis . . . by the Department of Commerce, the conclusion was reached that it is technically and economically feasible to meet defense needs through partial operation provided the plants which are kept open are permitted to produce their normal output and are not confined in their operations to producing defense items only."[28]

In most cases, it would also undoubtedly be true that operations restored under a partial injunction technique for defense purposes would also require the complete operation of the plant involved.

The use of the partial injunction technique would surely eliminate any need for such an extralegal function as the Atomic Energy Labor-Management Relations Panel. It would also have been of assistance in curbing work stoppages at missile bases.

The missile base problem could probably also have been aided by a rigorous insistence on the part of the government that existing laws be enforced. According to studies of the Missile Sites Labor Commission, most missile strikes involved jurisdictional or interunion disputes.[29] Such strikes are clear violations of the Taft-Hartley Act, Section 8 (b) (4) (D).

Also, according to a careful study by Professor John R. Van de Water:

There was also an extensive violation of Section 8 (b) (4) (A) during the Taft-Hartley era and violation of Section 8 (b) (4) (B) during the Landrum-Griffin Act era, through secondary labor boycotting. There was repeated coercion of employees who wished to exercise their right under Section 7 of that statute to refrain from unionism, through violation of Section 8 (b) (1). And employers violated Section 8 (a) (1) and 8 (a) (3) in discriminating against employees in their terms and conditions of employment because of their employees' favoring a particular union or no union—often such an employer violation being the result of union pressures engaged in inviolation of Section 8 (b) (2).[30]

For such strikes, remedies are available.

In many instances mandatory, temporary restraining orders are available to the injured parties against such conduct, and in all instances permanent injunctions can be gained through Section 10 (j) (1) of the amended National Labor Relations Act; there is a work-jurisdiction settlement procedure available, where the parties do not establish their own means of settlement, through Section 10 (k); and for the most prominent types of illegal strikes at the missile bases, suits for damages have been available to injured parties all along, through Section 303 of the Labor-Management Relations Act of 1947.[31]

These remedies are not taken advantage of because the Defense Department follows a policy of "neutrality." It will not move to punish violators of the Taft-Hartley Act as a matter of policy.[32] Yet, vital defense setbacks occurred, and hundreds of millions of dollars were lost to the taxpayers because of strikes and slow-downs until the McClellan Committee hearings exposed the situation and the Missile Sites Labor Commission was set up. It does seem that when laws are violated and damages occur, and when injunctive relief and damage suits are available, the government has a duty to enforce the law and to collect damages. The present policy of "neutrality" on the part of the Defense Department actually favors unlawful conduct. Professor Van de Water presents convincing evidence that enforcement of the Taft-Hartley and Landrum-Griffin picketing, boycott, and jurisdictional strike provisions, plus a damage suit or two, would have substantially ended the missile sites labor problem without resort to the extra-legal procedures of the Missile Sites Labor Commission.

Need for Experimentation

The partial injunction is suggested here as a likely tool, but not as a final answer, because the author is conscious that in these difficult human and social relationships, final answers may not exist. It is quite possible that scholarly and practical exploration of the issues will uncover either better tools or sufficient flaws in the partial injunction approach so as to reduce its considered potential.

Experience with existing legislation has indicated its basic short-comings, as discussed in this and the preceding chapters. Such experience has, however, been of great value in permitting a test of the applicability of ideas to factual situations.

In the remainder of this chapter, some practical administrative problems are discussed, particularly as uncovered by the richly varied experiences in the states. Use is also made of foreign experience.

Administrative Problems

Laws which substitute a procedure for the right to strike have, as has been noted, a profound effect on the willingness and ability of the parties to bargain and to settle. The administration of such laws also involves other problems of which the student and practitioner should be aware. The most significant are (1) effect on rate control in regulated utilities; (2) application of standards; (3) effectiveness of sanctions; and (4) legal and constitutional problems.

Strike Controls and Rate Controls

The Railway Labor Act and most state strike control laws cover transportation industries and electric light and power, gas, and water utilities which also are under rate regulation by state or federal administrative bodies. There is considerable feeling in these industries that regulatory bodies are more inclined to grant rate adjustments if emergency procedure is invoked and results in an increase in labor costs, than if such labor costs were freely bargained. Obviously, to the extent that this feeling is warranted by the facts, it will insure that emergency procedure will be invoked whenever the employers desire a compensating rate increase for any wage increase granted.

The same problem complicates labor relations under some defense contracts. The Atomic Energy Commission must pass upon whether it will reimburse construction and operations contractors for increased labor costs in disputes settled by recommendations of the extralegal Atomic Energy Labor-Management Relations Panel. The fact that AEC is apparently committed to support the existence of the atomic panel rather than to allow collective bargaining to function uninhibited adds emphasis to this view. And the willingness of the Defense Department to assume added, and often unwarranted, additional construction costs, instead of insisting on the protections afforded by the Taft-Hartley Act against jurisdictional and interunion disputes and boycotts, undoubtedly furthered the use of tactics designed to promote such costs in missile sites construction.

Likewise, in foreign countries where compulsory arbitration has been tried, the interest in peaceful settlement causes governments to approve settlements more generous than economic realities would indicate is appropriate. But price increases can be "justified" because of the ruling of a government tribunal—even when, as in Australia, the arbitration court often ignores government economic policy.[33]

Thus, strike control legislation may be both self-defeating and expensive to the consumer if it provides an easy or more certain way of passing on increased costs.

Application of Standards

Earlier in this chapter, it was stressed that reasonable men tend to disagree on what is fair and what is right. Therefore, management and labor risk a great deal when they turn this task over to a person who is unfamiliar with their problems, and who is not required to live with his decision. The arbitrator or fact finder may apply, in the absence of specific instructions, any one of many standards in determining a wage dispute: Cost of living, ability to pay, wages in comparable industry plants, wages in the area, and correction of intraplant inequities are among the most popular. Whether any of these standards will favor labor or management depends upon the particular circumstances at the time. But an arbitrator who so desires can pick the formula to rationalize a decision which has already been arrived at.

In order to reduce the arbitrator's discretion, to limit the application of his "social philosophy," and at the same time reduce the hazards in arbitration, particularly to management, the drafters of the state arbitration and seizure laws included standards in their laws. But as pointed out in detail in Appendices A, B, and C, arbitrators and seizure administrators found these standards either unworkable, or too confining, or interpreted them in a variety of ways. Definitions of such issues as scope of labor markets, evaluation of fringe benefits, meaning of "fair," etc., all meant different things to different arbitrators and administrators. Standards may have restrained the discretion of decision makers, but they did not destroy it.

This is also the case in foreign systems. Reference to the "public interest" is a frequent criterion for a decision under the Australian system. "It is a broad, changing concept which never has been precisely defined and probably never will be. There is no indication that either Parliament or the industrial tribunals [arbitration courts] ever attempted to define the term. . . . The concept is indefinite rather than precise."[34] Obviously, such a concept permits the arbitrators wide latitude to decide cases on the bases of their social lines and personal predilections.

In New Zealand, compulsory arbitration has been a significant factor in the leveling of wages and the narrowing of both interplant and intraplant wage differentials, reflecting, as one scholar noted, "a deep-seated equalitarian sentiment in New Zealand society . . . under a less regulated system in New Zealand . . . even if the general pattern of wages were the same, the hills would be higher and the valleys deeper. The disparity between the actual rates paid to different classes of workers in different areas and industries would be greater than it is and more of the increased standard of living available from increasing resources would go to better organized workers in the form of wages."[35]

Actually, whether standards are written into law, or adopted by arbitrators or administrators, they are likely to be utilized to rationalize results. Decision makers must justify actions. Reference to standards is one method of so doing—but standards cannot be precise and soon mean what the decision makers desire. The person is the master, not the written or unwritten standard by the very nature of industrial relations. As a keen Australian observor notes, "arbitral bias is not only inevitable, it is also essential. . . . The task of arbitrators making guiding decisions is not one of simply applying predetermined and unequivocal rules in standard situations. It is instead the 'creative' task of resolving problems arising in an area of social and economic policy whose change is a constant factor . . . the industrial arbitrator . . . is obliged to make a decision which he can ultimately justify only in terms of what is essentially a statement of faith—or the same thing, a statement of bias."[36]

Violations and Sanctions

Emergency strike control legislation, like all laws regulating conduct in a democracy, depends largely upon public support, or at least acquiescence, for its successful operation. If the public were completely antagonistic, the law might fail, as did the Volstead Act and prohibition.

But public support is not enough. Fact finding legislation depends upon the support of public opinion to secure compliance with the recommendations of fact finders, and the results, as already noted, have not been encouraging. Methods of enforcement and penalties for violations are, therefore, written into arbitration and seizure statutes in order to deter persons from violating laws and to penalize if they do violate such laws.

These penalties are of three types: criminal, civil, and economic. Criminal penalties are undoubtedly an important influence in restraining possible violations. Once a violation has occurred, however, the effectiveness of criminal penalties may be lessened. Possible political repercussions, the desire to avoid making martyrs out of those who flout the law, and the need to end a stoppage rather than to punish the instigators, may all combine to induce a reluctance on the part of public officials to invoke criminal penalties.

Even when public officials are willing to prosecute, the outcome cannot be easily predicted. All strike control legislation specifically safeguards the right of workers to quit as individuals. To secure a conviction, the prosecution must prove willful intent to violate the law—which usually means that workers quit in concert on the instructions of some person. There is no guarantee that individuals may not quit more or less simultaneously "as individuals" and safeguard themselves from prosecution under the law, especially if their leaders ostensibly order them back and they ignore the instructions.

No case was discovered in which the criminal penalties of a strike control law had been successfully invoked in the United States—although eight states included such penalties in their legislation.

Some idea of how difficult it may be to enforce criminal penalties may be obtained from the experience of the Railway Labor Act. Since 1934, this statute has provided criminal penalties for unfair labor practices on the part of management. In the years in which this provision has been in effect, only one case has been brought to trial, and in that instance the jury declined to convict.

On the other hand, the provisions for injunctive relief are usually more effective. The injunctive process is more easily initiated. There is no jury to convince or no time-consuming process. Moreover, the courts will hold parties in contempt of court if these restraining orders are not observed. To be sure, an "injunction cannot mine coal" or operate a business. It can, however, make it very costly and unpleasant for those responsible for illegal work stoppages. This was discovered by John L. Lewis and the United Mine Workers in 1948 when they declined to obey a Taft-Hartley order requiring a temporary end to a strike and were heavily fined. An order of a court is thus held in high respect, and rarely is it lightly flouted. Like the Taft-Hartley Act, most strike control laws depend primarily upon this method of enforcement.

The economic sanctions found in the Missouri law are about the most drastic for employees (see Appendix B). Being rehired only as a new employee means loss of seniority, pension credits, and all the other perquisites that go with length of service. This penalty was invoked in a case in Missouri in which one union struck a plant in an attempt to upset an order of the National Labor Relations Board. The strike was quickly broken with the assistance of a rival union. Many employees who stayed on strike were forced to rehire as new employees, with the resultant loss of length-of-service benefits, or to seek employment elsewhere.

The other Missouri economic sanction—the threat of loss of a certificate of convenience and necessity for a public utility—is likely to be effective only if the state is able and willing to take over the properties and sell them to a new operator, or to force their sale directly. Otherwise, it could take up to several years to put a new utility into operation—a not very practical sanction when the need for continuous operation is the point of the law.

Can Sanctions Prevent Strikes?

Sanctions are designed as both a deterrent and a curative. Certainly, one would think that the prospect of severe fines would prevent rash acts. And even if the rash act be taken, the cumulative effect of sanctions should result in a speedy reconsideration of the desirability of continued defiance of the law. Yet the most drastic sanctions can often fail where more moderate ones can succeed.

For example, Missouri's drastic economic sanctions on individual strikers and equally harsh fines on unions appear capable of breaking any strike in violation of the Missouri law and of discouraging most of them before they commence. If, however, the employees remain on strike and do not break ranks, the public is likely to clamor for resumption of service rather than punishment of strikers. This can induce officials to agree to waive or compromise the law as a condition of settlement. Once this begins, it can "steam-roller," and both the sanctions and the prohibition on strikes can lose their effectiveness.

It is, moreover, very difficult for public officials to enforce sanctions. In the one Missouri case labor was split, and the strikers were clearly in the wrong in their attempt to upset by force a legal ruling of the National Labor Relations Board. If, however, the strike had been a popular one and labor had been united, the problem of enforcement would have been less easy. Statesmen and politicians do not find it easy to invoke sanctions against large numbers of voters or against influential persons or groups. In New York, for example, a law forbidding strikes by public employees and inflicting severe penalties if they do strike, has been regularly flouted by groups as different as garbage collectors and school teachers. In almost every case, government officials have ignored the violations.

On the other hand, public clamor against an unpopular strike can force politicians to invoke the sanctions of law. The injunction, with its penalties for contempt of court, appears both the easiest to enforce, the most effective, and the least punitive.

Australia, and to a lesser extent, New Zealand, have had considerable experience with sanctions of various types. In Appendix F an article detailing the Australian experience is reproduced. It is clear from the record that penalties are difficult to enforce as strikes are generally outlawed, instead of only emergency disputes. One writer concludes that "It is clear, therefore, that most strikes go unpunished despite the severe penalties which the law provides . . . the threat of severe penalties does not seem to have improved the prospect of eliminating work stoppages."[37]

In a similar view, an observer of the New Zealand scene notes:

The strike is expressly made illegal, though naturally this has not prevented strikes. A scheme of penalties and fines against workers, union officers, and unions for taking part in or instigating strikes is provided in the statute, but these penal provisions are almost never invoked.[38]

Nevertheless, both Australia and New Zealand have inflicted severe penalties against unions and workers for striking. These penalties have included fines, breaking up of a union and deregistering it, and in effect turning over its membership to other unions. Strikes nevertheless do occur, and in Australia exceed those of most countries, year after year.

Legal and Constitutional Problems

Emergency strike control legislation raises many legal problems, but the courts are usually either instructed by the legislation not to, or are loath to, substitute their judgment for the executive. For example, under the Taft-Hartley Act the law provides that "whenever in the opinion of the President of the United States" an emergency situation exists, he may act in accordance with a prescribed procedure. Despite cogent arguments that no emergency exists, courts will not substitute their opinion for that of the President[39] or, in state situations, a governor. When the United States Supreme Court upheld the constitutionality of the 1963 railroad arbitration law, any doubt about the right of Congress to enact such legislation vanished.[40]

Under compulsory arbitration statutes, appeals to the courts from the decisions of arbitrators are usually limited to consideration of whether due process was observed, whether the decision was based upon the evidence, and whether the arbitration board acted within the scope of its authority. Again, even though a judge may believe that a case should have been decided differently, he cannot overturn an award on that basis.

Seizure legislation usually provides that an owner may petition the courts to secure the return of his property if there is reason to believe that the state is holding the property beyond the duration of the emergency. Owners of property may also sue for "just compensation" for the use of their property during seizure if the law provides no direct means of redress.[41]

Fact finding legislation generally contains no provisions for court appeals, because there is no legal compulsion to abide by recommendations of fact finding boards, and hence no grievance of which courts generally take cognizance.

The right of the federal government to limit strikes which it deems emergencies is well established, but litigation over state strike control legislation has had a long history and has resulted in a severe limit on such laws. Except for a right of state mediation agencies to intervene in cases, which is specifically provided in the Taft-Hartley Act, state legislation is effectively barred in interstate commerce covered by the Taft-Hartley Act. The courts have ruled that state fact finding, seizure, and arbitration laws conflict with the Taft-Hartley Act and that the later law preempted the jurisdiction which it covers. The articles in Appendices A, B, and C contain an analysis of the cases which now preclude the interesting experimentation described therein.

NOTES

1. This chapter has used freely material from Herbert R. Northrup and Gordon F. Bloom, *Government and Labor* (Homewood: Richard D. Irwin, Inc., 1963), Chapter 15.

2. John Perry Horlacher, "A Political Science View of National Emergency Disputes," *The Annals,* Vol. CCCXXXIII (January 1961), p. 86.

3. For an illuminating study of how the combination of economic *and* political power in the single hand of government destroys freedom, see Calvin B. Hoover, *The Economy Liberty and the State* (New York: Anchor Books, Doubleday & Co., 1961).

4. Horlacher, *loc. cit.*

5. *Ibid.*

6. George W. Taylor, "Is Compulsory Arbitration Inevitable?" *Proceedings of the First Annual Meeting, Industrial Relations Research Association,* 1948, p. 64. Of course, if the company involved has had its business for the strike period made up by stockpiling, as in steel, or if the union pays heavy strike benefits, the strike may not serve this purpose unless it lasts a long time.

7. Taylor, *op. cit.,* p. 65.

8. Irving Bernstein, "The Economic Impact of Strikes," in Bernstein *et al.* (eds.), *Emergency Disputes and National Policy* (New York: Harper & Bros., 1955), pp. 42-44. See also N. W. Chamberlain and J. M. Schilling, *The Impact of Strikes* (New York: Harper & Bros., 1954), pp. 149-159.

9. Bernstein, *op. cit.,* p. 32.

10. *Ibid.,* pp. 31-33; Irving Bernstein and H. G. Lovell, "Are Coal Strikes National Emergencies?" *Industiral and Labor Relations Review,* Vol. VI (April 1953), pp. 352-367; and C. L. Christenson, "The Theory of the Offset Factor: The Impact of Labor Disputes upon Coal Production," *American Economic Review,* Vol. XLIII (September 1953), pp. 513-547.

11. *New York Times Magazine,* April 27, 1947.

12. Horlacher, *op. cit.,* p. 85.

13. H. L. Enarson, "The Politics of an Emergency Dispute: Steel, 1952," in Bernstein *et al.* (eds.), *op. cit.,* pp. 46-74. See also Bernstein, *op. cit.,* pp. 33-42.

14. E. Robert Livernash, *Collective Bargaining in the Basic Steel Industry* (Washington, D. C.: U. S. Department of Labor, 1961), pp. 48-49.

15. *New York Times*, June 28, 1961, p. 15.

16. As a case in point, prior to the 1963 Philadelphia transit strike, newspapers and radio and television commentators referred to the threatened walkout as one which would "paralyze the city." Federal, state, and local mediators, the chairman of the state public utility commission, an extralegal three-judge fact finding board, and various others all interposed or were interposed as third-party interveners. On the day after the strike began, the *Wall Street Journal* (January 16, 1963) reported that the strike "is putting a heavy burden on other commuter facilities and has slowed downtown store sales, but is having surprisingly little effect on the operations of major companies in the city. The companies in general said they had very few absentees." Reports in Philadelphia papers confirmed this, but as soon as the strike was over, these same Philadelphia papers referred to the "paralyzing" strike, a term never dropped by radio and television commentators despite the clear evidence to the contrary.

17. See Arthur M. Ross and Paul T. Hartman, *Changing Patterns of Industrial Conflict* (New York: John Wiley & Sons, Inc., 1960).

18. Livernash, *op. cit.*, p. 49.

19. Horlacher, *op. cit.*, p. 89.

20. Bernard Rossiter, "Some Hidden Costs of Industrial Peace," *The Annals*, Vol. CCCXLIII (September 1962), p. 106.

21. See Case No. 18, Table 3, p. 119.

22. Horlacher, *op. cit.*, p. 89.

23. *Ibid.*

24. O. W. Phelps, "Compulsory Arbitration: Some Perspectives," *Industrial and Labor Relations Review*, Vol. XVIII (October 1964), p. 91.

25. For a favorable analysis of statutory strikes, see David B. McCalmont, "The Semi-Strike," *Industrial and Labor Relations Review*, Vol. XV (January 1962), pp. 191-208, and his n. 3, p. 191, for a list of citations on this subject. Such arrangements have been tried a few times, once in Miami, Florida, in the urban transit industry. It broke down when the bus drivers were charged with accepting "tips" from riders—a difficult thing to police, indeed! An agreement in the upholstery industry also calls for such an arrangement.

26. The partial injunction is one of the recommendations of the Independent Study Group established by the Committee on Economic Development. See *The Public Interest in National Labor Policy* (New York: Committee for Economic Development, 1961), pp. 101-103. It has also been proposed by Horlacher, *op. cit.*, pp. 94-95; and by Livernash, *op. cit.*, pp. 48-49, among others.

27. Horlacher, *op. cit.*, p. 95.

28. Livernash, *op. cit.*, p. 48.

29. Missile Sites Labor Commission, *Analysis of Work Stoppages on U. S. Missile Sites, June 1961-May 1962* (Washington, D. C.: U. S. Government Printing Office, 1962).

30. John R. Van de Water, "Labor Law and National Defense," *Labor Law Journal*, Vol. XIII (August 1962), p. 615.

31. *Ibid.*

32. *Ibid.*, pp. 613-615.

33. For cases in point, see R. M. Martin, "Governments, Industrial Tribunals and the Rule of Law," *The Journal of Industrial Relations*, Vol. VI (March 1964), pp. 36-50.

34. Paul L. Kleinsorge, "Public Interest as a Criterion in Settling Labor Disputes: The Australian Experiences," *The Journal of Industrial Relations*, Vol. VI (July 1964), p. 12.

35. G. H. Sorrell, "The Determination of Wages in New Zealand," *The Journal of Industrial Relations*, Vol. V (October 1963), pp. 132-133.

36. Martin, *op. cit.*, pp. 45-47.

37. Charles P. Mills, "The Enforcement of Penalties Against Strikes," *The Journal of Industrial Relations*, Vol. II (April 1960), pp. 40-41.

38. G. H. Sorrell, "Industrial Relations in New Zealand," *The Journal of Industrial Relations*, Vol. III (October 1961), p. 127.

39. *United Steelworkers v. United States*, 361 U. S. 39 (1959).

40. *Brotherhood of Locomotive Firemen and Enginemen v. Certain Carriers, et al.*, *331 b(2d)* 1020 (1964); certiorari denied, 84 S.Ct. 1181 (1964).

41. *United States v. Peewee Coal Co.*, 71 S.Ct. 670 (1951).

CHAPTER

12 Conclusions
and
Recommen-
dations

THE EXPERIENCE analyzed in this book confirms beyond a suggestion of doubt that compulsory arbitration:

1. Does not insure industrial peace, but rather can breed strikes, especially short ones.

2. Does not necessarily further the economic or social policies of government, but in fact may work against such policies.

3. Enhances union power and growth, especially through political action.

4. Discourages collective bargaining.

We have also found that other forms of intervention by government tend to have a like effect. And we have noted a number of tendencies in the American industrial relations scene which could propel this country toward a system of governmental fixing of wages and working conditions. For these reasons, a number of recommendations have been made or are in order. In summary, they include:

1. Revision of the Taft-Hartley's national emergency provisions, with a substitution therefor of a technique of the partial injunction, after careful study is made of the means by which discretion for the injunction's use can be controlled by law. In addition, the new law should include penalties for unions and companies during the injunction period—for example, expropriation of union dues and taxes on company profits. The law should include no settlement process—merely penalties levied on the parties for not settling so that it would be decidedly unpleasant and unrewarding to bring the government into the situation.

2. Sections 8 a (5) and b (3) of the Taft-Hartley Act—the "good faith" bargaining sections of the law—should be abolished in order to halt the drive of the National Labor Relations Board toward union co-determination of managerial decisions and toward arbitration.[1]

3. Section 10 (k) of the Taft-Hartley Act which requires the NLRB to determine jurisdictional disputes should be revised to require merely that any strike over a jurisdictional dispute is illegal and to permit such strikes to be enjoined by any affected party. This would force unions and companies involved to settle these disputes themselves and not involve the NLRB in an area where it obviously has no expertise.

4. The representation dispute procedure of the NLRB should be amended by Congress to provide that no certifications of exclusive bargaining agents may be made without an election in which "no union" is a choice on the ballot; and no election may be set aside because of any speech which is not inconsistent with Section 8 (c)—which guarantees free speech where there is no actual threat of reprisal or force or promise of specific benefit. This would halt attempts of the NLRB to install unions as bargaining agents where their majority representation status is in doubt, or where arguments against unionism have been barred so that only one side of the story is heard.

5. The Railway Labor Act should be either abolished or thoroughly revised. The partial injunction technique would eliminate any need for this Act's proved unsatisfactory dispute procedure. The representation procedure under the Railway Labor Act lacks due process by denying the employer the right to be heard and by not placing "no union" on the ballot. As a result, a minority

supported union can be certified to represent the majority. If the NLRB is forced to permit free speech and to cease certifying unions on card checks, it can handle this function on the railroads also. The mediation activities could continue as a division of the Federal Mediation and Conciliation Service. The National Railroad Adjustment Board might continue, but it should receive no tax support, and should be encouraged to decentralize by railroad or by regions.

6. Extra-legal agencies like the Atomic Labor-Management Relations Panel and the Missile Sites Labor Commission have no right or reason to exist and should be abolished.

7. The attempt of the Federal Mediation and Conciliation Service to further its intrusion into the settlement process by so-called preventive mediation should be halted by Congress simply not voting the appropriation for such activity.

8. Congress should act to overrule the novel court decisions by which every issue is arbitrable under a union contract which is not specifically exempted.

The purpose of these proposals is simple and direct: (1) to promote industrial peace; (2) to encourage collective bargaining; and (3) to cease governmental enhancement of union power without withdrawing governmental protection of the right to unionize.

It is noteworthy that the strike is waning as a technique in most democratic countries because neither labor nor management have found it a useful tool for repeated dependence.[2] Yet in Australia, the incidence of the strike has tended to increase, for there it is a tool of the rank and file to use to get attention, or to protest against union and government bureaucracies, or to indicate annoyance with the red tape, delays and legalisms of the compulsory arbitration system. Certainly, this is the time to call a halt to government intrusion and to save collective bargaining —not to continue its slow strangulation.

That bona fide collective bargaining is well worth saving should not require excessive reflection. This country will not return to unilateral employer determination of wages and conditions of employment; nor will—we trust—the Great Society involve such unilateral determination by employees or unions. Therefore if we are to abandon collective bargaining by permitting its underpinnings to be clipped away, the only alternative is the red tape, short-strike-stimulating Australian-type arbitration, or even greater government wage fixing with its concomitant price fixing and loss of consumer sovereignty.

But for collective bargaining to work, two conditions have to be met: the parties must be forced to suffer the consequences of their actions and they must be permitted to develop techniques, concepts, and systems which are based upon the essential economic realities of the enterprise involved.

The first condition means that the right to strike must not be impaired to any significant degree. We have recognized this in most of our laws by confirming regulation largely to tactics and to certain strikes relating to these tactics. But we have failed in that we have established disputes machinery which invites government intervention and destroys the capacity of the parties to act for themselves; and we have permitted the National Labor Relations Board to invade the collective bargaining process far beyond the intent of Congress. The recommendations made herein would, it is believed, remedy these defects.

One cannot, of course, fault citizens for desiring a superior system of wage determination. Collective bargaining is not, even at best, either a pretty spectacle, or essentially a very efficient method of accomplishing the desired end. But because there is no such objective fact as a "fair wage" or "proper working conditions," there can be no objective standards for impartial judicial or third party determination of wages and working conditions—indeed there can be no really impartial judges or arbitrators—just people with ideas, learnings, and prejudices. It is noteworthy that Australia, which more than any democratic country has substituted compulsory arbitration for free collective bargaining, has undoubtedly the worst strike record of any major western nation. Judgments from the arbitration court are no substitute for the basic agreement that is necessary for people to live and to work together.

Collective bargaining must also be permitted to develop to suit its economic environment. To place a growing air line industry under a system designed (and not too well!) for an aging railroad industry was a tragic mistake. To advocate, or to promote "human relations committees," "continuous bargaining,"[3] or preventive mediation which seems to work in one industry, for another, is naive at best for conditions, history, and economic structure vary too widely. The capacity to meet problems is inherent in our system. When industry and union do not measure up, they do not prosper. Government should neither enforce a particular method or approach, nor bail out incompetent management nor recalcitrant union leadership. The first rule of labor policy in a democracy must be to recognize that government regulation in no panacea. A little moderation instead of a lot of intervention would seem to be the rule for maximizing industrial peace and equitable and economically sound labor relations in the years ahead.

NOTES

1. An attempt to support the retention of Sections 8 a (5) and b (3) is made by Professor Philip Ross, *The Government as a Source of Union Power* (Providence: Brown University Press, 1965). But Professor Ross does not deal with the manner in which the NLRB has expanded its function. His book, which was supported by a grant from the NLRB, rather deals with cases where unions have won a contract after a NLRB order. He creates a straw man, but does not deal with the issues as presented by the critics of 8 a (5) and b (3).

2. For details of the meaning of strikes, cf., Arthur M. Ross and Paul T. Hartman, *Changing Patterns of Industrial Conflict* (New York: John Wiley & Sons, Inc., 1960) and annual statistical summaries of the International Labor Office.

3. For a naive attempt to further the practice of "continuous bargaining" as a key to industrial peace and success, see James J. Healy (ed.), *Creative Collective Bargaining* (Englewood Cliffs: Prentice-Hall, 1964).

APPENDICES

A Arbitration and
Collective Bargaining:
*An Analysis of
State Experience**
BY
HERBERT R. NORTHRUP
AND
RICHARD L. ROWAN**

T HE EMPHASIS placed by the
Kennedy Administration on peaceful settlement of disputes raises
once again the question of the use of methods to compel such
settlement. No procedure has been suggested which is new. And
if peaceful settlement without strikes is demanded, factfinding will
not suffice, for as the railway and air transport experience makes
very clear, once the factfinding procedure is complete, strikes are
likely to occur if either part is unhappy about the results.

Nor can seizure be the answer if peaceful *settlement* is the
goal, for seizure in itself is designed merely to block the strike.
It settles nothing. In the final analysis, therefore, the issues must
be determined by someone if compulsory settlement is the

* Reprinted by permission from the Labor Law Journal, Vol. XIV, No.
2, February 1963.
** Assistant Professor of Industry, Wharton School of Finance and Commerce, University of Pennsylvania.

goal—and this means compulsory arbitration. What this would mean to American industry and unions, and particularly to the institution of collective bargaining, can be quite clearly determined by an analysis of state experience with compulsory arbitration after World War II.

State Compulsory Arbitration Laws

American states have experimented with compulsory arbitration for short periods after both World Wars. In each period, state laws banning strikes and providing for compulsory arbitration were enacted following bitter strikes which affected key industries. The post-World War I experiment occurred in Kansas, where a general compulsory arbitration law was enacted in 1920, and rendered inoperative by court decisions in 1923 and 1925,[1] after an interesting, controversial career.[2]

The year 1946, following World War II, set the record for man days lost because of strikes. Among the industries affected were a number of public utilities, including electric light and power and gas operations. As a result, 11 states enacted emergency legislation in 1947. Eight of the laws provided for compulsory arbitration.[3] A majority of these laws became inoperative as a result of a 1951 Supreme Court decision involving the Wisconsin law, but meanwhile, valuable experience was accumulated.

The Indiana Law

A majority of these laws were modeled on the Indiana statute. This law covered privately owned companies supplying electric, power, gas, water, telephone, and transportation (exclusive of railroad and air) services to the public. It exhorted parties to settle their disputes by collective bargaining. In the event a strike was threatened, and the Governor believed severe hardship to the public would occur, he was required to appoint a conciliator who attempted to mediate the dispute. If mediation proved unsuccessful within a thirty-day period, the dispute was referred to a board of arbitration. No strikes, lockouts, or other use of force was permitted once a conciliator was appointed. The Governor could, however, decline to appoint a conciliator if he believed no hardship would endure, and then no prohibition on strikes or lockouts was in force.

The Indiana law featured great care in outlining the duties, functions, and limitations of the Board of Arbitration. It was a public board, selected from a panel chosen by the Governor, and had the power of subpoena, and of administering oaths. It was directed where rates of pay and other conditions of work were in dispute, to establish same comparable to those established by other public utility employers for workers of the same skills in the area where the dispute existed, or if no comparable public utility employer or employees existed in the area, to make the same comparisons with adjoining labor market areas within the state.

Arbitration boards were further required to avoid company-wide determinations but to decide cases by establishing separate labor market areas for each plant, office, or operation of a utility, and in setting wages to take into account fringe benefits and the stability of work of public utility employees.

The standards feature of the Indiana law attracted considerable attention, and was the basis for the adoption of similar laws in Florida, Wisconsin, Michigan, Pennsylvania and Nebraska. As in Indiana, these laws had considerable employer and conservative support, and were opposed by pro-union groups.

Although the laws in these other states closely followed the Indiana format, there were differences. For example, Wisconsin vested chief administrative control in its already existing Employment Relations Board instead of the Governor. Nebraska established a full-time Court of Industrial Relations which acts in place of arbitration panels and *ad hoc* boards chosen from the panels. Nebraska, a public power state, also provided for jurisdiction by its Court of Industrial Relations over disputes involving government owned utilities. Pennsylvania excluded communications and transportation from its law and provided for arbitration only after the employees rejected the employer's "last offer" in a vote conducted by the State Labor Relations Board. And Michigan gave control over its law to the judiciary, which the Michigan courts soon found contrary to the state constitution, and therefore voided all sections of the law pertaining to arbitration.[4]

New Jersey did not go the "Indiana route." As originally enacted in 1946, the New Jersey law provided for a combination of factfinding and seizure. The statute declared that heat, light, power, sanitation, transportation, communication and water were essential and that an interruption of these services was a threat to public health and welfare. To avoid such interruption, a panel was set up by labor and industry representatives through the State Board of Mediation. If the parties did not settle their disputes, members of the panel were appointed to hold hearings and make recommendations for settlement to the Governor. If a strike still threatened, the Governor was empowered to seize the facilities. No penalties before or after seizure were provided.

When this procedure did not stave off a threatened strike of telephone employees, the New Jersey legislature added a compulsory arbitration provision after seizure with severe fines and jail terms for violations. Later the jail terms were eliminated and the fines reduced. Standards were added to the New Jersey law after a court decision requiring such guides as a condition of constitutionality, and the provisions for factfinding before seizure were later eliminated by the legislature as unnecessary. The constitutionality of the New Jersey law was not passed on by the courts after the Wisconsin case was decided by the Supreme Court. The law, however, has not since been invoked.[5]

Minnesota Hospital Act

Minnesota had enacted a comprehensive factfinding law in 1939, which applies to public utilities among other industries. Then in 1947, the state enacted amendments providing for compulsory arbitration for wage and hour issues in charitable hospitals only. Only hospitals in Minnesota are thus subject to arbitration.

Effects on Bargaining

All compulsory arbitration statutes contain pronouncements favoring the settlement of disputes by collective bargaining. Most such laws also provide for attempts at settlement by conciliation or mediation, with the express hope that compulsory arbitration will not need to be utilized except rarely and then only for cases in which the disputed issues are exceptionally difficult to resolve.

Does it work out this way, or does compulsory arbitration

compete with, instead of supplement, the bargaining process? The experience of compulsory arbitration in Florida, Wisconsin, Indiana, New Jersey and Pennsylvania, as set forth in Table I, provides part of the answer by showing certain state and industry differences in the application of arbitration.

In Wisconsin, Indiana, and New Jersey, for example, the administrators of the laws did not hesitate to use them in disputes in which covered industries were involved even though the prospective disputes would not have been of major proportion. Disputes sent to arbitration involved small Rural Electrification Administration cooperatives, accounting employees of telephone companies, and bus operators in small cities. Compulsory arbitration was used, as the Supreme Court stated in the decision invalidating the Wisconsin law, not as "emergency" legislation but as "a comprehensive code for the settlement of labor disputes between public utility employers and employees."

TABLE 1

ARBITRATION CASES BY STATE AND INDUSTRY, 1947[a]-1962

State	Total Cases	Urban Transit	Communi- cation	Electric Light and Power[b]	Gas	Water Works
Florida............	4	3			1	
Indiana............	29	14	8	6		1
New Jersey........	25	3	9	3	9	1
Pennsylvania......	9	([c])	([c])	3	6	
Wisconsin.........	40	2	10	24	4	
Total cases	107	22	27	36	20	2

[a] All laws enacted in 1947; all statistics from dates of enactment.
[b] Includes gas utilities operated in conjunction with electric light and power.
[c] Jurisdiction of Pennsylvania law does not include these industries.

Data on usage follows those set forth in New Jersey Governor's Committee on Legislation, *Report to Governor B. Meyner*, pp. 33–40, except for Pennsylvania, where records of the State Labor Relations Board show two additional cases.

Moreover, the willingness of these states to invoke compulsory arbitration encouraged its use. The belief of some unions and employers that they can do better under arbitration than they could under collective bargaining resulted in perfunctory negotiations and hasty applications for the invocation of arbitration. And the unwillingness of the state administrators to oppose this tide encouraged it.

Wisconsin REA

Special conditions in the electrical industry in Wisconsin and in the gas industry in New Jersey brought increased case loads in those states. By and large, unions and management in the two industries have compiled an excellent record of peaceful settlement without recourse to outside agencies. In Wisconsin, however, a basic dispute over whether Rural Electrification Administration cooperatives should pay rates comparable to private electric utilities accounted for most of the disputes in the electric industry there. And in New Jersey disputes in the gas industry involving competitive rival AFL, CIO and independent unions resulted in nine out of the 25 arbitration board appointments.

Urban Transit

If a union asks a ten-cent increase and a company offers eight cents, the union can refuse the compromise, go to arbitration and point out that the company has already offered eight cents. Then the arbitrators are under great pressure to give, instead of eight cents, a few cents more—in other words, to compromise the company's offer upwards. If this happens once, it is most unlikely that the company the following year will make any offer for fear of seeing that offer used as a springboard for further concessions in an arbitration proceeding. The situation may then snowball; neither party is willing to bargain for fear that any bargaining will be used against it in later arbitration procedure. Such an impasse appears to typify present-day industrial relations in the urban transportation industry in the states surveyed.

The Amalgamated Association of Street, Electric and Motor Coach Employees, the dominant union in urban transportation, has from its inception stated that one of its objectives is "to encourage the settlement of all disputes between employees and employers by arbitration." For more than 50 years, this union has "made it obligatory for local divisions to offer arbitration to the employer where other means of settlement failed. . . . The International (union) has exercised strict control over the making of collective agreements and has attempted to have incorporated in them all a clause that would provide arbitration not only in case of disputes arising out of the agreement but also in the event that a new agreement could not be negotiated to replace an expiring one. By 1905 . . . arbitration was provided in the majority of . . . agreements then in existence."[6]

Post-World War II strike-control legislation, therefore, found this union thoroughly favorable to arbitration as a means of settlement, and, in addition, extremely competent and well staffed to win arbitrations.

Not that the Amalgamated Association welcomed strike-control legislation, in 1919, it had emphatically opposed the Kansas compulsory arbitration law,[7] and since 1947, it has led the fight to invalidate state strike-control laws. Local divisions of the Amalgamated attempted to secure management agreement for voluntary arbitration in those states in which compulsory arbitration existed. In some instances, this occurred, but often management representatives declined on the grounds that management's interests were better protected by arbitrating under state laws which included standards that arbitrators must follow, and which also provide, at least in the minds of managements, preferable methods for selecting arbitrators.[8]

Whether engaged in voluntary or compulsory arbitration, however, it has become fairly common for the parties in the urban transportation industry to prepare for arbitration rather than for collective bargaining. As a result, it is not unusual for the parties in this industry to certify for arbitration, whether voluntary or compulsory, 20 to 40 issues, some of which have obviously been left in by either the Amalgamated Association or the employer in order to improve their chances of winning their really basic demands.

For this industry, it appears that voluntary arbitration has been used as a substitute for collective bargaining. And for a short period compulsory arbitration replaced voluntary arbitration.

Telephone Industry

Although the history and present situation of labor relations in the telephone industry have been quite different from those in urban transportation, the policies of the Communication Workers of America (CIO), the dominant union in the telephone industry, also contributed to the use of governmental strike-control machinery. Perhaps because it was a relatively new organization which did not attain the bargaining power enjoyed by some other large unions, CWA apparently determined that it could secure more favorable results through factfinding and arbitration than through collective bargaining. Thus, although CWA maintained official opposition to compulsory arbitration, it actually indicated a preference to such means of settlement.[9]

In recent years, however, technological developments have rendered the telephone industry largely immune from effective strike action. Dialing for both local and long distance and other automatic mechanisms and controls permits supervisors to operate struck facilities with little or no loss of service. It is doubtful it, today, a strike of telephone workers could cause an emergency or even significant inconvenience to the public.

The Pennsylvania Situation

The Pennsylvania arbitration law is similar to that of Indiana and Wisconsin, except for (1) a last-offer strike vote provision and (2) its narrow coverage which excludes transportation and communication. The last-offer strike vote provision was modeled on the provision in the Taft-Hartley Act and has had similar results. Of the nine votes, eight resulted in rejections of company last offers. The ninth occurred just before the Korean War wage freeze went into effect, and the employees feared that to reject it would deprive them of a wage increase throughout the emergency period.

Under the Pennsylvania law, employees send a case to arbitration by refusing the employer's last offer. In theory, this was a tailor-made provision to encourage arbitration because it invited an arbitration award above the rejected employer's last offer. Actually, Pennsylvania had fewer arbitrations than Indiana, Wisconsin and New Jersey. There are several reasons for this:

(1) One study found that bargaining relations in most Pennsylvania utilities were sufficiently satisfactory to both labor and management that neither desired to force invocation of the law.[10] The fact that three of the nine cases involved one gas utility gives some support to this viewpoint.

(2) Another reason is that the Pennsylvania act was apparently administered with a conscious effort to discourage the use of arbitration. As one industrialist put it: "You have to go to

Harrisburg and camp on the Governor's doorstep for about two weeks and even then he probably won't invoke the law. By that time, the parties usually get so disgusted that they settle the thing themselves."[11]

Probably most important in reducing the number of arbitrations in Pennsylvania is the limited coverage of the statute. For the industries which are covered in Indiana, New Jersey and Wisconsin (but excluded in Pennsylvania) include urban transit and telephone. These industries have been involved in almost one-half the state arbitrations. Moreover, in Pennsylvania, there was no problem of rural electrification wage rates as existed in Wisconsin nor interunion competition in gas plants as existed in New Jersey. Hence the industrial and union factors in Pennsylvania weighed against utilizing the law instead of collective bargaining.

The Florida Situation

Florida did not utilize its law very much, apparently because the opportunity did not arise as for any other reason. The degree of unionism was then lower in Florida, and most disputes which did occur in covered industries did not involve the law. The bitterest, that pertaining to the Miami transit industry, occurred after the *Wisconsin* decision, and caused the Florida law to be struck down by the courts.[12]

The Nebraska Situation

Table II summarizes the experience under the Nebraska law. This act is similar to the Indiana type legislation, but it is administered by a permanent three-man Court of Industrial Relations, and it covers all local transportation and public owned utilities in addition to the coverage of the Indiana type law. The willingness of Nebraska's court to invoke its law when local truckers and taxicab drivers are involved is difficult to justify on the basis of emergency dispute legislation, although a cessation of local truckers in a food industry could well have serious consequences.

Nebraska's power industry is entirely public-owned. The coverage of these government installations by an arbitration law is both unique and interesting in its attempt to provide a means of

Table II

Arbitration in Nebraska by Industry,
1947-1962

Total cases	15
Taxicab companies	5
Power districts	5
Urban transit	3
Motor freight companies	2

Source: Letter dated March 14, 1962 from Court of Industrial Relations, State of Nebraska.

settlement where employees clearly have no protected right to strike.

Hospital Arbitration in Minnesota

As already noted, the arbitration law of Minnesota applies only to charitable hospitals and not those operating for profit. In addition, only "any unsettled issue of maximum hours of work and minimum hourly wage rates" is subject to arbitration, although strikes or lockouts over any issue are forbidden. This latter feature has been strongly criticized by employee groups, who claim that wages won in arbitration can be balanced by unilateral hospital withdrawal of benefits, but this fear has apparently not been realized.

Despite their criticism of the Minnesota arbitration law, hospital employees have not hesitated to use it. The law has been invoked by both professional and nonprofessional hospital workers in Minnesota in recent years in a number of cases. The American Nurses' Association (a professional society which has established a collective bargaining program for its members),[13] as well as unions of nonprofessional hospital workers, realize that they can do better through arbitration than through the use of their limited economic strength. It is noteworthy that surveys have found hospital employees in Minnesota to be more completely unionized than those in most other areas.[14] Organization in Minnesota hospitals is thus being built upon arbitration without collective bargaining over new agreements, having previously existed to a significant degree.

Responsibility and Arbitration

A final factor which affects the relationship of bargaining and arbitration in all the states studied is that the arbitration process at least partially removes from union leaders and management officials the adverse consequences of yielding to an unpopular settlement. This may be especially important to union leaders who are faced with strong internal union opposition or whose position is menaced by a rival union. A settlement reached in collective bargaining can provide fertile propaganda for both the internal and external opposition of union leaders. By going to arbitration, the leadership can blame the arbitrators for an unpopular decision and yet claim credit for a popular one.

A similar situation may occur on management's side if its bargaining representatives are either insecure in their jobs or if the company feels that an arbitration order requiring a wage increase will carry more weight than a negotiated wage settlement when and if application is made to a state public utility commission for a rate adjustment. A public utility commission which even hints at the possibility of considering negotiated settlements and arbitration awards in a different light insofar as rate changes are concerned is inviting the use of arbitration as a substitute for collective bargaining.

Arbitration thus presents a temptation to forego collective bargaining, and therefore, arbitration may erode the collective bargaining process. It is significant, however, that the state compulsory arbitration legislation studied seems to have had an inhibiting effect on collective bargaining to the greatest extent where the bargaining process was the weakest; for example, in the urban transportation industry where voluntary arbitration by pre-existing agreement had already conditioned the parties to prepare for arbitration instead of for bargaining and in the telephone industry where relatively new organization sought to achieve through governmental intervention what it appeared unable to do through bargaining.

It is also noteworthy that state compulsory arbitration appeared to interfere least in the collective bargaining process in industries in which a strike would have the most serious effects on the public health and safety—electric light and power, gas and water. In these industries, the parties have long been aware of the disastrous effects of a stoppage and their responsibility for continuous operation. Hence strikes in these industries have always been relatively rare.

The emphasis on the effects of these settlement procedures on collective bargaining in this study should not be construed as meaning that a settlement by a method other than collective bargaining is *per se* unwholesome. The essential point however, is that legislation aimed at preventing strikes may in itself either cause disputes, or cause machinery designed to prevent stoppages in essential industries to become enmeshed in the settlement of labor-management disputes that the parties could and should settle by themselves.

RELATED PROBLEMS AND ISSUES
Relation to Rate Control

Public utility companies which have been subject to regulations under strike-control legislation usually also have their rates regulated by state public utility commissions.

Thus an electric company which has had its labor costs increased by an order of a state arbitration board cannot raise its charges to customers without permission of the state public utility agency. The relationship—or the lack of it in many instances —between state arbitration and state public utility rate-regulation agencies has caused many problems.

In most arbitration legislation, no mention is made of the problem of rates. The Wisconsin law provides that a copy of the arbitration report be sent to the state public utility commission. No strike-control law, however, specifically directs the state public utility agency to adopt a particular procedure in the event of an increase in labor costs in a public utility which has been brought about by a proceeding pursuant to a state strike-control law.

Some persons have even advocated control of wages by public utility commissions. The basic difficulty, however, is that there is no easy answer as to what this relationship should be. For example, if the law required that a public utility commission automatically compensate a utility for increases in labor costs which resulted from a state labor board proceeding, the utility would have little incentive to oppose increases in labor costs and unions would have equally little incentive to moderate their demands. Moreover, once legislative policy of tying rate adjustments to wage adjustments has been set, arbitration boards would be under great pressure to make their decisions rest on that relationship and give scant attention to the effects of their decisions on the public at large.

Such a legislative policy would also probably end any collective bargaining that exists in industries covered by the strike-control legislation. For if increases in wages and labor costs were automatically offset by rate increases both utility management and labor would be under great temptation to cease attempting to settle their differences and instead to go to arbitration.

Likewise, a legislative policy which unduly restricts rate adjustments resulting from wage increases granted by a state labor agency is likely to prove unsatisfactory. Some adjustments are often needed to maintain wages and labor conditions in line with those in the industry or area, and to permit utilities to obtain a fair share of the cream of the labor market.

The extremes in relationships between state strike-control machinery and state public utility commissions have generally been avoided. Nevertheless, there are a multitude of unsolved problems. In the first place, there is usually a time lag between the decision of a labor board and that of a public utility agency. A state arbitration board may hand down a decision not only increasing wages, but in addition doing so retroactively for several months. If a utility decides that the resulting cost increases require some increases in rates, it then must initiate a proceeding before the state public utility commission acts favorably on the rate adjustment. It cannot include a retroactive adjustment in its decision since it is impractical or impossible to attempt to collect additional rates for services performed and paid for in the past.

Administrative Time Lag Overcome

In some instances, this administrative time lag has been overcome through granting temporary or emergency rate increases which remain in effect pending the outcome of a rate case. On other occasions, utilities have had cases pending before a public utility agency when an arbitration board granted employees increased wages. Then the utility has been able to amend its application before the public utility agency so as to include the cost effects of the wage decision. By and large, however, utilities which request relief by higher rates after being ordered by a state agency to increase wages have found that they have a long wait before that relief is forthcoming.

There is also a question of whether a state public utility commission will view an application for rate relief more favorably if it is based on increased labor costs resulting from the action of a state agency than if those increased labor costs resulted from negotiation and collective bargaining. A majority of the public officials and utility executives questioned felt that both types of cases would receive equal consideration.

A few officials and a sizeable minority of utility executives were, however, of the contrary opinion. In support of this view was cited the following comment of the president of the New Jersey Public Utility Commission made after a rate-increase petition was denied: "If the state should seize the properties under the utility anti-strike law and the state should then ask this board [the Utility Commission] to act, that would create a different situation than the present one in which we cannot act."[15]

The fact that rate-increase petitions may thus receive more favorable treatment after state intervention is signficant. For under such circumstances, the utility would be wary of settling for an increase in wages under collective bargaining, and would tend to force the matter to arbitration in order to strengthen its rate case. The effects on collective bargaining would then be the same as when either labor or management believes it can secure a better deal on labor matters through arbitration than through collective bargaining settlement; collective bargaining would cease to be an important factor in the settlement process.

Standards

Determining terms and conditions of employment is a difficult task at best. Management and labor risk a great deal when they turn this task over to a person who is unfamiliar with their problems, and who is not required to live with his decision. The arbitrator may apply, in the absence of specific instructions, any one of many standards in determining a wage dispute: cost of living, ability to pay, wages in comparable industry plants, wages in the area, and correction of intraplant inequities are among the most popular. Whether any of these standards will favor labor or management depends upon the particular circumstances at the time. But an arbitrator who so desires can pick the formula to rationalize a decision which has already been arrived at.

In order to avoid the hazard of what might be termed the arbitrator's "social philosophy," unions and companies sometimes carefully stipulate in the agreement to arbitrate not only what issues the arbitrator shall decide, but, in addition, the standards which shall be considered in arriving at the decision. Unfortunately, an agreement on a stipulation as to standards is often not easy since the criteria or standards used may determine which party wins a case. In order to reduce the arbitrator's discretion and at the same time reduce the hazards in arbitration, particularly to management, the drafters of the pioneer Indiana arbitration law wrote standards into the legislation.

Standards are also found in the Massachusetts law, and they were added to the New Jersey legislation after the courts of that state declared them a prerequisite to meet the requirements of the New Jersey Constitution.

Standards (Table 3) are designed to reduce the discretion of arbitrators and to produce awards based upon identical or like criteria. Certainly they mark an improvement in the arbitration process, for without agreement upon criteria of some sort, the parties write a blank check for the arbitrator to fill in.

Standards do not, however, insure uniformity of criteria. There is, first of all, the job of determining what a labor market is. Economists and practical industrial relations men alike are not in agreement on a definition of this term. In the Pittsburgh area, for example, there are several electric and gas utilities. One electric utility serves the heart of the city. Another serves the suburbs and the outlying areas, and, in addition, services counties some distance away. Wage rates in the center of Pittsburgh are likely to be higher than those in the less populated neighboring areas. Where one labor market begins and the other ends is a difficult, complicated question upon which reasonable men could easily disagree, but a decision on this question could be decisive in a wage dispute.

Then there is the question of how to evaluate fringe items and perquisites. Should people with steady employment have lower

TABLE 3

STANDARDS FOR ARBITRATORS IN STATE ARBITRATION LAWS

Criterion	Indiana-Type[1]	New Jersey
Public interest		1. The interests and welfare of the public.
Comparative Wage Rate and Conditions of Employment	1. Wages paid and conditions of employment maintained for similar work and skills under similar conditions by like public utility employees in some or adjoining labor market areas. 2. Relationship to wages and employment conditions maintained by all other employers in same labor market areas. 3. Labor market and adjoining labor market areas to be defined by boards of arbitration upon evidence presented. 4. If an employer has different plants in different labor market areas separate rates and conditions shall be established for each labor market area.	2. Comparison of wages, hours and employment conditions in same or comparable work, with due consideration to factors peculiar to industry. 3. Comparison of wages, hours, and conditions of employment as reflected in industries generally and in public utilities throughout nation and in New Jersey.
Fringes and Employment Security	5. In setting wage rates, over-all compensation, including all fringe benefits, and employment security measures shall be considered.	4. Security and tenure of employment with due effect of technological development on such security and of any unique skills and attributes developed in industry.
Other Factors		5. Other factors which are traditionally taken into consideration in collective bargaining and arbitration.

[1] Indiana, Florida, Pennsylvania, Nebraska and Wisconsin.

wages? In other words, what price security? Basically, there is a subjective matter for which no objective criteria have been developed. One could perhaps figure the dollar value of extra vacation and extra holidays, but how about the dollar value of a lenient policy as to absences versus a strict policy?

Perhaps the most difficult question would involve a comparison of pensions. For example, one company might provide a very liberal but nonfounded plan which was rather loosely financed, while another company established a firm pension trust under the most careful financing procedures but with somewhat lower benefits. If the union in the second company demanded equal benefits to those in the first, how would standards help solve this?

The experience with standards in "Indiana-type" states indicates quite clearly that the arbitrators overlooked the restrictive standards and decided cases on broad comparisons with relevant companies in other areas of the state or adjoining states.[16] This administrative departure from the narrow confines of these laws illustrates the difficulties of writing standards into law. Standards restrain the discreation of arbitration; they do not destroy it.

Present Status
of State Arbitration Laws

When the Supreme Court ruled that the Wisconsin Public Utility Arbitration Act was inoperative in interstate commerce because the Taft-Hartley Act had pre-empted the field,[17] most state laws ceased to function. Indiana and Florida courts soon thereafter applied the Supreme Court's standards and enjoyed the application of their state arbitration acts.[18] Pennsylvania, the other state with an arbitration law very similar to that of Wisconsin, avoided final litigation by allowing its law to become dormant, and New Jersey did likewise.

Nebraska has continued to invoke its arbitration law, but, although the law is similar to those in four other states, the coverage is not. Nebraska is a public power state without private electric or gas utilities. Since Nebraska's law is primarily concerned with the public-owned power companies, and since public employment is specifically excluded from the coverage of the Taft-Hartley Act, there is no question of federal pre-emption in this sphere. Nebraska has also invoked its law in the taxicab, urban transit and trucking industries. The first appears so local as to not involve Taft-Hartley jurisdiction. The latter two may well be prohibited to state regulation under the Wisconsin Act decision.

The situation in regard to the Minesota Hospital Arbitration Act is similar to that in Nebraska. Most hospitals—except a few operated in conjunction with businesses—are specifically excluded from Taft-Hartley Act coverage, or excluded by the National Labor Relations Board jurisdictional rules. Hence, the Minnesota courts have concluded that there is no pre-emption bar to the application of this statute.[19]

Should State Arbitration Legislation Be Permitted?

Because state arbitration legislation has been ruled invalid on the pre-emption issue, Congress could, by enacting enabling legislation, permit the states to legislate in this field.

Those who oppose this base their argument on two points: (1) that most so-called emergencies do not actually exist; and (2) that if they should exist, they transcend state lines.

The first point is especially strong. It would be difficult indeed to find a single instance in which a state arbitration law has been invoked where great peril actually was threatening a community. Most of the cases were not even potential threats, although some involving gas or electric power could have possibly been if allowed to continue.

Technological developments give added impetus to this view. Unlike the situation immediately after World War II, when most of the laws were enacted, a strike today in most utilities—electric power, gas or telephone—does not involve a shutdown. Automatic equipment, plus use of nonstriking supervisors permits service to be continued with little or no change to the customer. Only a very long strike in such cases, with a breakdown of maintenance, could involve the type of catastrophe which blacked out Pittsburgh when power employees struck in 1946.

As for urban transit, repeated strikes have served only to prove that people can get to work without public commuter facilities— more harassed, and later than usual—but from experience, we know they get there, and that there is little reason to invoke emergency legislation in most transit strikes.

One area—which only Nebraska and Massachuetts cover— local trucking may create more real emergencies than the traditional critical areas. Milk and food deliveries are involved here. Again, however, most people shop in supermarkets, and most others can. Hospitals are a problem here, and indeed one can make a good case for a law like that of Minnesota which remains operative in this field.

The second point against emergency legislation is that many

of the covered industries are interstate in character. Utilities extend over state lines. Bargaining units are not necesarily geographically oriented. To permit state legislation is often to duplicate, or to subject companies and unions to dual and conflicting regulation. Certainly, if state strike control legislation is validated, Congress must spell out carefully proper areas of state regulation and then leave that jurisdiction solely to the states.

Those who favor permitting state regulation in the strike control areas point out first of all that state officials are closest to a situation and know best the needs of communities beset by labor problems. This is undoubtedly correct, but of course the corollary is that state officials can be more readily pressured into premature action precisely because they are so close to a situation. The indiscriminate use of the Wisconsin and Indiana arbitration laws between 1947 and 1951 is a case in point.

The best—and we think possibly decisive—factor for those who favor permitting state laws to govern strikes deemed to create emergency situations is that the states have been, and we believe, should be experimental laboratories of all forms of social legislation and regulation. The ingenuity and variety of laws in just this one area testify to this. Our federal system is based upon the recognition that in this great country, problems of states vary, and solutions to such problems can be met in a variety of ways. Federal pre-emption is often required. Excessive federal pre-emption, however, rules out experimentation, new solutions and rich experience. We believe that the states should be permitted to determine within reasonable limits whether strikes in certain industries should be permitted. We do not think that such strikes are likely to cause emergencies, and we prefer reliance on the ingenuity of the public and its officials to curb emergencies if they arise. But we also know that others disagree and we would like them to have the right, acting through their state legislatures, to experiment reasonably with legislation such as has been discussed in this study.

NOTES

1. *Wolff Packing Co. v. Court of Industrial Relations*, 262 U. S. 522 (1923); 267 U. S. 552 (1925).
2. For a careful history of the Kansas law, see D. Gagliardo, *The Kansas Industrial Court*, University of Kansas Publications, Lawrence, Kansas, 1941.

3. New Jersey, Indiana, Florida, Wisconsin, Pennsylvania, Michigan, Nebraska and Minnesota.

4. Legal issues are discussed on pp. 231-232.

5. A good review of the New Jersey law and its history is found in Governor's Committee on Legislation Relating to Public Utility Disputes, *Report to Governor Robert B. Meyner*, 1954, pp. 22-25.

6. E. P. Schmidt, *Industrial Relations in Urban Transportation*, University of Minnesota Press, Minneapolis, 1937, p. 194.

7. Cited at footnote 6 at p. 195.

8. See below, pp. 228-231.

9. See the report of CWA Vice-President A. T. Jones to the 1950 CWA Convention, as summarized in "Daily Labor Report," No. 124, June 27, 1950, pp. A-6, A-7. Another indication of the desire of CWA officials to use strike-control machinery was their unsuccessful attempts to bring Western Electric workers within these laws in Florida and Wisconsin.

10. Robert R. France and Richard A. Lester, *Compulsory Arbitration of Utility Disputes in New Jersey and Pennsylvania*, Princeton University (Department of Economics), Princeton, N. J., 1951, pp. 73-74.

11. *Interview*, 1951.

12. See below, p. 231.

13. D. H. Kruger, "Bargaining and the Nursing Profession," *Monthly Labor Review*, LXXXIV, July, 1961, pp. 699-705.

14. Cited in H. Parker, "The Laws Governing Labor-Management Relations in Michigan Hospitales," 12 LABOR LAW JOURNAL 973, October, 1961, footnote 9.

15. *Newark Evening News*, January 31, 1951, p. 2.

16 See, for example, Arthur R. Porter, "Compulsory Arbitration in Indiana," 5 LABOR LAW JOURNAL 776, November, 1954.

17. *Amalgamated Association v. Wisconsin Employment Relations Board*, 340 U. S. 383 (1951).

18. *Marshall v. Schricker*, Cir. Ct., Vandenburgh Co., Ind., (1951), 20 LC ¶66,372; *Henderson v. Florida, ex rel. Lee*, 65 So. 2d 22 (1953) 23 LC ¶67,584.

19. *Fairview Hospital Association v. Public Board*, 241 Minn. 523 (1954), 25 LC ¶68,285.

B State Seizure in Public
Interest Disputes*

HERBERT R. NORTHRUP
AND
RICHARD L. ROWAN**

I NCREASING INTERVENTION in la-
bor disputes by the federal government in so-called public interest
situations has overshadowed the fact that such intervention by the
state is not uncommon. Yet little information on state activity is
available, particularly to industry. The purpose of this article is to
focus attention on seizure as a form of state intervention. Experience in five states—Virginia, Missouri, Maryland, New Jersey, and
Massachusetts—with various forms of seizure laws is analyzed in
terms of the problems and issues that can arise when the government becomes involved in public interest disputes.

Reprinted by permission from the *Journal of Business of the University
of Chicago*, Vol. XXXVI, No. 2, April 1963.
* This study was financed by the Committee on Faculty Projects, Wharton School of Finance and Commerce, University of Pennsylvania, with
funds provided by the Ford Foundation.
** Assistant Professor of Industry, Wharton School of Finance and
Commerce, University of Pennsylvania.

Seizure involves the invocation of state control of a business that is, or threatens to be, shut down by a work stoppage. Strikes or lockouts are forbidden during the period of seizure, which usually lasts until the threat of work stoppage is abated, or for a designated period. Most of our discussion is concerned with temporary seizure wherein the firm reverts back to private hands after the threat of a stoppage is eased.

SEIZURE WITH NO INVOLVEMENT: THE VIRGINIA EXPERIENCE

Virgina enacted three seizure statutes in the post-World War II period as a technique to control strikes in essential industries. The Virginia seizure statutes are unique in that they do not include provisions for any other form of intervention such as arbitration or fact-finding as does such legislation in other states.

The Virginia Ferry Seizure Act.—The Ferry Seizure Act of 1946 was the first attempt by the Commonwealth of Virginia to regulate an industry considered essential to the public welfare. Passage of the act represented almost six years of effort by the state to take over the Chesapeake Ferry Company in order to provide continuous service to people traveling in Tidewater Virginia. During the drafting of the act, the governor stated:

> The proposed action is not to be construed as placing upon either management or labor any blame for the present obstruction of our highways, nor is it intended to in any manner affect the dispute. The sole purpose is to prevent the people of Virginia from being made the unwilling and unfortunate victims of a controversy in which their interests seem to be totally ignored.[1]

The Ferry Seizure Act has been invoked twice: (1) the properties of the Chesapeake Ferry Company were seized on February 25, 1946, and eventually made a part of state ownership in 1948, and (2) the Virginia Ferry Corporation was seized on June 26, 1951, and released to private ownership on September 30, 1951 (Table 1).

The seizure of the Chesapeake Ferry Company resulted from a failure to provide uninterrupted service to the people over a long period of time. The state had made numerous efforts to purchase the company but only succeeded when it seized the company and did not return it to private ownership.[2] When seizure occurred, employees of the company continued to work and preseizure wages and hours were maintained. Because of the willingness of employees to work under seizure, and because permanent state ownership and control were imminent, the seizure method was robbed of its effectiveness as a means of forcing the parties to come to an agreement.

In contrast to the above situation, the Virginia Ferry Corporation was seized on June 26, 1951, and returned to private ownership on September 30, 1951. There was no previous intent on the part of the state to seize the company for permanent holding, the workers were not quite as willing to work under seizure as they had been in the Chesapeake case, and the company desired an early settlement in order to take advantage of rate increases that could not be put into effect until a settlement was reached.

The state found it difficult to recruit workers to run the ferries at the outset of the seizure. Employees initially refused to work and the burden of finding workers rested with the state. After a great deal of solicitous effort, including advertising in newspapers, radio, and other media, failed to provide a sufficient staff to run the four ferries, the state insisted that the employees return to work. The employees responded to the state's wishes and returned to work after a two-week delay.

Pursuant to Section 33-207 of the Ferry Seizure Act, the owners of the Virginia Ferry Corporation were entitled to "reasonable, proper and lawful compensation" for the use of their facilities. This, by implication, entitled the Commonwealth to retain an amount to cover its expenses and to share in the profits. As noted in Table 1, the Commonwealth did this, in this case by agreement with the ferry company. If no agreement had been

TABLE 1

Seizures Under Virginia Ferry Seizure Act to March, 1962

Company	Period of Seizure	State Share of Net Profit
Chesapeake Ferry Co.......	2/25/46–2/25/48	*
Virginia Ferry Corp........	6/26/51–9/30/51	$7,353.39†

* The Chesapeake Ferry Company was not returned to private ownership. The state purchased the company under condemnation proceedings at $3,100,070. This figure included payment of $2,622,930 for the property of the company exclusive of spare parts, materials, and supplies carried on the vessels assessed at $50,000. Rental value in the amount of $427,070 was agreed upon for the period of seizure.
† In addition to this figure, the state retained $3,038.30 to cover certain administrative expenses incurred during the operation.
Source: Curry, op. cit., pp. 16–17.

reached, the law provides for settlement by the Commonwealth courts.

The Public Utility Labor Relations Act.—The Ferry Seizure Act set the stage for the passage of the Virginia Public Utility Labor Relations Act, which was passed in 1947 and amended in 1952. Like the other Virginia seizure laws, it does not combine seizure with either fact-finding or arbitration. It was enacted following a threatened strike in an electric utility. Besides electric light and power, however, the law covers water, heat, gas, communication, and transportation not subject to the federal Railway Labor Act. Of the eleven seizures that have occurred as of April, 1962, nine have involved urban transit units and the other two have involved telephone companies (Table 2).

TABLE 2

SEIZURES UNDER VIRGINIA PUBLIC UTILITIES LABOR RELATIONS
ACT TO JANUARY 1, 1962

Company	Industry	Period of Seizure	State Share of Net Profit (15 Per Cent)*
Chesapeake & Potomac Telephone Co..........	Telephone	5/20/47– 5/23/47	$ 62.76
Citizens Rapid Transit Co..	Urban transit	7/ 3/48– 3/28/49	245.40
Virginia Transit Co. and Portsmouth Transit Co...	Urban transit	2/ 3/49– 3/ 2/49	1,067.16
Alexandria, Barcroft & Washington Transit Co..	Urban transit	7/21/49– 5/19/50	No profit†
Clifton Forge-Waynesboro Telephone Co...........	Telephone	8/10/49– 6/ 7/50	4,071.33
Washington, Virginia & Maryland Coach Co.....	Urban transit	11/ 2/49– 7/31/50	No profit†
Virginia Transit Co. and Portsmouth Transit Co...	Urban transit	2/11/50– 6/20/50	18,052.80
Citizens Rapid Transit Co..	Urban transit	6/25/51– 6/28/51‡	203.11§
Virginia Transit Co. and Portsmouth Transit Co...	Urban transit	1/24/52– 1/25/52	12,925.06§
Washington, Virginia and Maryland Coach Co.....	Urban transit	12/10/52– 2/ 8/53	5,374.92§
Alexander, Barcroft & Washington Transit Co..	Urban transit	11/ 1/52–11/ 9/52	848.72§

* The expenses incurred in the operations by the state and its agents are charged to the companies as a part of their operating expenses, and are paid the state in addition to the 15 per cent (see n. §).
† If, in normal operations, the utility does not earn a profit, the state neither furnishes money to provide a profit nor assumes any percentage of the loss as its obligation.
‡ After two and one-half days of preparation by the State Corporation Commission to take over the company, the strike was called off.
§ This figure represents the cost to the company as its part of expenses of the operation. Sec. 12 of the Virginia law pertaining to the sharing of profits was changed slightly in 1952. The state still turns over 85 per cent of net income to the utility, however; the law provides that this "shall in no wise control the amount of just compensation to be allowed to the utility."
Source: Virginia State Corporation Commission.

Although the original 1947 law made some attempt at promoting dispute settlement by the parties with the governor's aid available, the amended law of 1952 makes no mention of the collective-bargaining process except as it may affect the parties themselves. The law is not a dispute-settling device. Its only intent, as indicated earlier in the Ferry Seizure Act, is to provide service to the people while the parties attempt to settle their differences.

When there is a threat of a work stoppage in a public utility that would cause serious inconvenience and harm to the public, the governor is given authority to take immediate possession of the utility. If seizure occurs, the governor ascertains which jobs are necessary to operate the utility, and present jobholders are given the opportunity to state their willingness or lack of willingness to work during government operation. Any employee who is willing to work during state operation must declare that fact and then is entitled to do so; those who do not wish to do so may remain away from their jobs during state operation without penalty. The law states that "the status of no person as an employee of the utility shall be affected by either his acceptance of employment by the State or by his refusal of such employment.

If a stoppage occurs and the governor takes possession, strikes, lockouts, picketing, etc., are forbidden and subject to severe penalties. Wages and conditions of employment must be maintained at the levels existing when negotiations were commenced. Seizure remains in effect until the governor is satisfied that the utility is capable of "normal" operation and "the public interest so requires."

The Virginia law contains a punitive device that has been effective in bringing the parties to an agreement. Any profit made by the company under seizure is shared by the government. The law provides that "after payment of proper operating expenses and reimbursement of the State for all expenses incurred in preparing to operate same . . . eighty-five percentum of . . . net income shall be paid to the utility as compensation for the temporary use of its business, facilities and properties." Net income, as defined in the Public Utility Labor Relations Act, is construed to mean the gross revenues derived from such operation after deducting these from:

(1) the costs of operation and maintenance of the utility;
(2) the amount of depreciation during the time of such operation based on the amount allowed in the utility's federal income tax return;
(3) Federal, State, and local taxes which would be payable by the utility, if the properties were operated by it;
(4) interest on the indebtedness of the utility; and
(5) payments for the cost of insurance.

All of such items shall be prorated on annual basis in proportion to the time the plant is operated by the State.

The state retains 15 per cent of net income as compensation for its services in operating the utility (see Table 2, n. §). In addition to the compensation paid to the state, costs incidental to the operation of the utility incurred by the state are charged to the company as part of its operating expenses. In case of a loss, the state takes nothing. It neither provides funds for a profit nor assumes any part of the loss as its obligation. The Virginia law differs in the foregoing respects with the laws of Missouri and New Jersey, which do not carry financial penalties.

The Mine Seizure Act.—As a result of industry-wide strikes in coal mining during 1949 and 1950, Virginia passed a Mine Seizure Act similar to its previous legislation dealing with public utilities and ferries. There was no mention made of labor disputes, work stoppages, or the events occurring in the mining industry that led to the enactment of the act. The spirit of the earlier laws was carried forth in the act with emphasis, once again, on the maintenance of service to the public rather than entering into the actual dispute-settling arena.

The three experiences under the Mine Seizure Act, summar-

TABLE 3

SEIZURES UNDER THE VIRGINIA MINE SEIZURE ACT

Company	Period of Seizure
Universal Construction Corp.........	11/4/49–3/16/50*
Raven Red Ash Coal Corp..........	3/2/50–3/ 6/50
Consumer Mining Corp............	3/3/50–3/ 6/50

* The Universal Construction Corporation was taken over by the state before the Mine Seizure Act was passed; however, it continued to be operated under the Act from the day of its passage, February 17, 1950, until March 3, 1950.

Source: Curry, *op. cit.*, pp. 483–543

ized in Table 3, give some added insight into the effectiveness of seizure as a means of providing for the public welfare in times of work stoppages in essential industries. If the parties involved in a strike co-operate to the fullest with the provisions of the act, it can serve a useful purpose. On the other hand, if employees elect not to work for the state during the period of seizure, serious difficulties may arise. Even though there was difficulty in getting the employees to work during the mine seizures, the strikes did not last long enough to cause a great deal of concern. The absence of nationwide coal strikes since the early 1950's ended Virginia's highly publicized efforts to prevent strikes in its few coal mines along its western border.

There is no information available to indicate how much the companies were compensated by the state as a percentage of profits during seizure. The act did not contain the same provisions for compensation as were contained in the 1947 Public Utility Labor Relations Act and the 1946 Ferry Seizure Act. A stipulation was made that any owner whose properties were acquired by the state was entitled to receive "reasonable, proper, and lawful compensation for the use of the properties so acquired by the State and paid the same out of the State treasury."

Special aspects of the Virginia laws.—A problem under the Virginia laws concerns the role during seizure of the State Corporation Commission, the state public utility regulating body. In one case, the commission was placed in the anomalous position of having before it an application for a rate increase from a utility that had been seized and was being operated by the commission. The utility maintained that the increase was needed to pay a wage increase so as to settle the dispute and repossess its properties. The commission managed to postpone action until after seizure was terminated.[3] Since, however, the Public Utility Act does not require that seized utilities be operated by the commission, this problem is easily avoided.

Another problem that might arise under the Virginia public utility law is the reaction of a union to a wage-cut request by management during a period of economic depression. A union could refuse to take the cut or to arbitrate the dispute, and threaten to strike. This would involve state seizure with its statutory ban on changes in wages and conditions of work. Utility employees, "as the law now stands . . . could remain employed by the Commission indefinitely. Their wages might be greatly out of line, the utility might be shoved into the bankruptcy by the distorted costs of labor, but as long as the workers remained adamant the law could not touch them."[4]

A principal criticism of the administration of the Virginia Public Utility Labor Relations Act is that it has been invoked in relatively minor disputes. In a real sense none of these disputes were actual emergencies. The fact that the law has not been invoked since 1952 may indicate a realization that such minor disputes do not deserve state intervention. Or it may merely be that Virginia desires to avoid litigation over the constitutionality of its law.[5]

Another aspect of the Virginia utility law is that it could guarantee a minimum increase to employees. If seizure is to cost a public utility 15 per cent of profits, why not give that amount to employees in the form of wages and avoid the problems of a state takeover? Certainly it would seem that a union which felt seizure was a possibility would not consider settling for less. Of course, the reluctance of the state to invoke the act in recent years has no doubt curbed any union policy based on this theory.

Strikes, moreover, are more likely to be concerned with so-called non-economic issues, the basic factors involved in control of the shop that are really very economic in effect, and that often mean more to the parties than a few cents in wages. Where such issues are at stake, or where the company is operating at a loss, as some of the urban transit concerns seized in Virginia were, the 15 per cent cost of seizure would not be a deterrent to management action or a spur to union policy.

Despite these problems, the Virginia seizure laws appear to be well-considered legislation. They aim to afford the public protection but, at the same time, attempt minimum interference with collective bargaining by making the parties settle a dispute themselves and by penalizing them during a seizure period. In a true sense, Virginia's laws are not "dispute-settlement" statutes but rather threats to parties who do not settle. Certainly they are not a substitute for collective bargaining, nor are they designed as such.

FACT-FINDING AND THE THREAT OF
SEIZURE: THE MISSOURI
EXPERIENCE

Missouri's Public Utility Seizure Act, referred to as the King-Thompson Act, was passed in 1947. The preamble to the act declares it "to be the policy of the State that heat, light, power, sanitation, transportation, communication, and water are life essentials of the people; . . . and the State's regulation of the labor relations affecting such public utilities is necessary to the public interest."[6] In contrast to the Virginia laws, the Missouri act does not automatically invoke seizure when the parties are not able to resolve a dispute.

A public hearing panel or fact-finding board is formed when the parties are unable to agree on contract changes or to submit a dispute to arbitration. If either party does not accept the recommendations of the panel or engages in a strike or lockout, the governor is authorized at his discretion to seize the company when he finds that the public interest, health, and welfare may be jeopardized. Since 1947, there have been nine seizure cases in Missouri public utilities and approximately twenty other cases in which fact-finding was invoked, but in which no seizure occurred despite strikes. All the seizure cases (summarized in Table 4) were settled by the parties with the exception of the latest case, which remains in the courts, with the state still in technical possession of the property.

TABLE 4

SEIZURES UNDER THE KING-THOMPSON ACT OF MISSOURI*

Company	Industry	Period of Seizure
Kansas City Public Service Co............	Transit	4/29/50–12/11/50
St. Louis Public Service Co..............	Transit	8/10/50–10/19/50
St. Louis Public Service Co..............	Transit	8/11/55–12/23/55
Laclede Gas Co.........................	Gas	7/ 5/56–10/31/56
Kansas City Power & Light Co...........	Electricity	7/ 6/56– 7/17/56
Kansas City Power & Light Co...........	Electricity	8/31/57– 6/25/58
Kansas City Public Service Co............	Transit	11/ 6/57– 3/ 6/58
Kansas City Power & Light Co...........	Electricity	8/ 5/60– 5/31/61
Kansas City Transit Co.................	Transit	11/13/61– 6/10/63†

* Since Missouri enacted the King-Thompson Act, about twenty strikes in public utilities have occurred in which seizure was not invoked. The governor did not find that these strikes jeopardized the public interest, health, and welfare.
† The Kansas City Transit Co. was under seizure when the U. S. Supreme Court found that the King-Thompson law was inapplicable in interstate commerce. See last section of article.

Source: Missouri State Board of Mediation.

The seizure procedure under the act has three steps: (1) the governor issues a proclamation that an existing or threatened strike jeopardizes the public interest, health, and welfare; (2) Executive Order No. 1 is issued constituting the official act of seizing the utility; and (3) Executive Order No. 2 establishes the governor's agent and gives him authority to take possession of the utility.

As in Virginia, seizure in Missouri does not serve as a dispute-settling device.[7] But unlike Virginia, when the state has taken over, it has been pretty much "business as usual." No penalty accompanies the seizure, except the limitations on the right of unions to strike and on employers to lock out. Since the law is silent on the subject, the company is presumably entitled to "just compensation" for the taking of its plant according to a Supreme Court decision.[8]

Penalties are provided in the act for unlawful conduct by either party. If a labor union, a labor officer, or a public utility calls a strike or work stoppage in violation of the seizure provisions of the act, a fine of $10,000 per day may be levied against the union or utility and $1,000 against the union offiical. The penalty was used in the Laclede Gas Company strike of 1956. Since the employees refused to return to work until a Circuit Court injunction was issued eight days after seizure, the union and union leaders were subjected to these penalties. Another penalty action that is now under court review involves the union in the St. Louis Public Service Company seizure of 1955. Here the union continued the strike three days after seizure.[9]

Seizure laws provide generally that the state may bring action to restrain violations, and the violation of court orders is punishable by contempt of court. The economic sanctions found in the Missouri law, however, are about the most drastic for employees. Being rehired only as a new employee means loss of seniority, pension credits, and all the other prerequisites that go with length of service. In the Laclede Gas case, the penalty was invoked when one union struck a plant in an attempt to upset an order of the National Labor Relations Board. The strike was quickly broken with the assistance of a rival union. Many employees who stayed on strike were forced to be rehired as new employees, with the resulting loss of length-of-service benefits, or to seek employment elsewhere.

The other Missouri economic sanction—the threat of loss of certificate of convenience and necessity for a public utility—is likely to be effective only if the state is able and willing to take over the properties and sell them to a new operator, or to force their sale direct. Otherwise, it could take up to several years to put a new utility into operation—a not very practical sanction when the need for continuous operation is the point of the law.

MEDIATION AND ARBITRATION AFTER
SEIZURE: THE MARYLAND
EXPERIENCE

The State of Maryland passed a public Utilities Disputes Act in 1956. The law was written in order to deal with a thirty-seven-day-old strike of the Baltimore Transit Company. It has not since been invoked. The Maryland Act, although depending upon seizure as its ultimate device, provides for various means of dispute settlement including voluntary arbitration, seizure, compulsory arbitration, and compulsory mediation. And before the state enacted the seizure law in 1956, almost every means of voluntary settlement had been pursued by various city, state, and federal government officials.

A review of the incidents leading to state intervention in this case sheds light on the usefulness of many conventional forms of dispute settlement.[10] The issues in the strike were typical, that is, wages, hours, and fringe benefits, but the parties were widely separated in their thinking concerning equitable amelioration of differences. During the early period of the strike, the Mayor of Baltimore, Maryland's Commissioner of Labor and Industry, and a federal mediator met with the negotiators in an attempt to bring about a settlement. When their efforts seemed to be of no avail, the governor advised that "the full power of the state would be exerted to terminate the dispute." Although the active interest of those involved in the dispute may have been commendable, the results were of questionable effectiveness in resolving the issues. Too many interveners proved a handicap by giving the parties excuses not to settle, as the final settlement of the dispute proved.

Three days after the strike began, the governor proposed a fact-finding board composed of prominent civic leaders who would "arbitrate" but whose findings would have no binding qualities. Since the union was already committed to binding arbitration, it rejected the plan even though the company was eager to accept. The plan was abandoned and the issues further complicated when the company offered a wage increase tied to fare increases. This action was opposed by the mayor, who threatened to fight fare increases before the State Public Service Commission.

Rejection of the governor's fact-finding plan and new difficulties arising over company proposals and union counter-proposals brought pressure on Baltimore delegates to the General Assembly to get a broader and more forcible approach to settlement. An inquest, the strongest inquisitorial device available to the Maryland legislature, was asked in order "to determine causes of the strike and facilitate legislation to restore service and prevent future disputes."[11]

The prospects of an inquest motivated both parties to increase their meetings with the mayor, and at this time, a federal mediator was introduced "whose expertise in collective bargaining technicalities would aid the cause of agreement, it was hoped."[12] Little was accomplished at these sessions, with the mayor's influence once again unable to bring the parties together. At this point, the governor called for seizure legislation and criticized both parties for displaying "intolerable arrogance and utter lack of concern for the public interest."[13]

As the inquest date became imminent, the federal mediator and regional director of the Federal Mediation and Conciliation Service agreed to meet with the mayor and the parties. Hearings began in this inquest and complaints were heard. Other groups submitted their own plans to end the dispute including the Baltimore Association of Commerce, the Greater Baltimore Committee, and the Baltimore Retail Merchants Association. These groups suggested that the parties submit the issues to a three-man arbitration committee and stop the strike. Both the union and the company rejected the proposal but for different reasons. The company felt that it could not adjust fares to the arbitration awards and maintain service. The union made it clear that since so many officials and agencies were already involved in the dispute that it had lost interest in all outside proposals for settlement.

After ten days of hearings, the inquest ended on February 23, 1956, and the company made a "last offer" proposal to the union which was promptly rejected. Seizure was now much in the news, and the governor made it clear that he would sign any seizure bill that came across his desk; a bill was approved, and the governor chose March 5 to put it into effect. Final agreement could not be reached by the parties, and the transit company was seized with services to be resumed on March 9, 1956.

Under provisions of the act, state seizure is immediately followed by a fifteen-day period of mediation that may be extended to sixty days if the parties so elect. If mediation fails, a three-member board of arbitration is empowered to reach a final decision. With the seizure in effect, the state commissioner of labor took up the duties of state administrator of the transit system and mediation talks began.

The fifteen-day period of mediation came to an end with little progress being made as a result of the hearings. When the parties indicated that they did not wish to extend the mediation period to sixty days, the governor established machinery for compulsory arbitration and asked each party to name one member to a three-man panel. The union agree to name an arbitrator, but the company refused in order to gain ground to test the constitutionality of the seizure law. Action was brought in the federal court with the Baltimore Transit Company claiming that the law violated the right to due process. In the meantime, the state amended the law to empower the governor to name representatives of the arbitration board if one of the parties refused to comply, as the Baltimore Transit Company had done.

The company then asked the federal judge for a temporary restraining order to prevent the governor from appointing the company arbitrator until the question of constitutionality had been resolved. The restraining order was issued, with the company being sustained in its contention that "(1) if the seizure law were to be invalidated, expenditures on arbitration would prove futile for all concerned, and (2) if the law was invalid, free collective bargaining would be hampered because 'any findings of the arbitration board would affect bargaining later on by indicating a basis for settlement.' "[14]

Strangely enough the day after the restraining order went into effect, the union announced a settlement with the company. The settlement had been reached in a series of closed sessions and with no outside parties except the federal mediator present.

When the transit facilities were returned to private ownership, the Baltimore Transit Company suit was dismissed by the Federal court, and the constitutional question has never been clearly defined. One may assume that the threat of seizure forced the parties to make a settlement, but, with the constitutional issue still in abeyance, it is merely conjectural as to how effective it may be if used again. Certainly, the mediation period after seizure proved of little value, as one would expect in a case where mediation before seizure was both extensive and unsuccessful. Perhaps, however, in this case, the threat of arbitration was useful in inducing agreement.

SEIZURE AS A PRELUDE TO ARBITRATION: THE NEW JERSEY EXPERIENCE

As originally enacted in 1946 the New Jersey statute provided for a combination of fact-finding and seizure. The statute declared that heat, light, power, sanitation, transportation, communication, and water were essential and that an interruption of these services was a threat to public health and welfare. To avoid such interruption, a panel was set up with labor and industry representatives through the State Board of Mediation. If the parties did not settle their disputes, members of the panel were appointed to hold hearings and make recommendations for settlement to the governor. If a strike still threatened, the governor was empowered to seize the facilities. No penalties before or after seizure were provided.

When this procedure did not stave off a threatened strike of telephone employees, the New Jersey legislature added a compulsory arbitration provision after seizure with severe fines and jail terms for violations. Later the jail terms were eliminated and the fines reduced. Standards were added to the New Jersey law after a court decision requiring such guides as a condition of constitutionality,[15] and the provisions for fact-finding before seizure were later eliminated by the legislature as unnecessary.[16]

Under the New Jersey law, the governor is empowered to seize plants or businesses when he finds that an emergency occurs or impends. After seizure, the dispute is sent to arbitration. Although the state is in nominal possession of the plant, the arbitration is between labor and management as if the latter were in complete control of the plant. When the arbitration has been completed and the threat of a work stoppage abated, the plant is returned to its management.

According to Professor Lois MacDonald, neither labor nor management in New Jersey was happy about seizure:

> The attitudes of the parties were most emphatic on the subject of seizure, both attacking it as bad policy. The company representatives were not concerned as long as seizure continued to be token in character, but were apprehensive lest it should assume a different aspect in the future. The opnion of the unionists was that seizure without exertion of real control was nothing short of strike breaking by the state. Both groups pointed out that seizure had not prevented strikes.[17]

In view of this reported dislike of seizure in New Jersey, it should be noted that it would have been entirely feasible to dispense with it altogether. The law is primarily a compulsory arbitration statute that has no real need to use token seizure to maintain the status quo during the arbitration process.

Table 5 summarizes the experience in New Jersey with arbitration cases. Over half the cases have occurred in communications and gas companies with the remainder in urban transit, electric power and light, and water works.

TABLE 5

SEIZURE-ARBITRATION CASES IN NEW JERSEY, 1947–52

Utility	No. of Cases
Urban transit	3
Communication	9
Electric light and power	3
Gas	9
Water works	1
Total	25

Source: New Jersey Governor's Committee on Public Utility Disputes Legislation, *op. cit.*, and records of the New Jersey State Board of Mediation. No cases have occurred since 1952.

SEIZURE AS A CHOICE OF PROCEDURE:
THE MASSACHUSETTS EXPERIENCE

Because emergency laws may tend to become substitutes for collective bargaining, one school of thought advocates giving the chief executive a "choice of procedures" to utilize so that those who are pushing an interruption of a vital service may not be able to compare settlement by collective bargaining with settlement under governmental direction.[18]

The choice of procedures theory has been written into law in Massachusetts, as a result of a unanimous report by a tripartite committee, appointed in 1947, by the then Governor Robert Bradford, to survey the labor legislation of the state. The "Slichter Law," as it is known, applies to the "production and distribution of food, fuel, water, electric light and power, gas, or hospital or medical services." It provides that in the event of a threatened stoppage in those industries which the governor finds would endanger the health or safety of any community, he may:

1. Require the parties to appear before a governor-appointed moderator, who must be "an impartial person skilled in industrial relations," and show cause why the dispute should not be submitted to voluntary arbitration. The moderator's job is to induce the parties to arbitrate, or to make public the reasons for their refusal to do so.

2. Or, the governor may request the parties to submit the dispute to a tripartite arbitration board. This board is required not only to decide the issues but also to "fix in its recommendations the date, prospective or retroactive, as of which its recommendations shall be made effective and in so doing shall consider evidence as to the responsibility of either party for delaying the settlement or rejecting arbitration."

If neither of these methods is successful in avoiding a stoppage, or if the dispute "is of such a nature that these procedures cannot be applied thereto," the governor is required to declare the existence of an emergency during which he may either:

a) "Enter into arrangements with either or both parties" to continue to produce or to distribute sufficient essential services, "to safeguard the public health and safety"; or

b) Seize the business and operate it "for the account of the person operating it immediately prior to the seizure"; or, if such person elects within ten days after seizure, he may waive the proceeds during seizure and receive instead "fair and reasonable" compensation for the appropriation and use of his property for which he may sue the state. But in determining this compensation, the courts are directed to take into account the fact that a labor dispute existed which interrupted, or threatened to interrupt, private operation of the plant "and the effect of such . . . upon the value to the petitioner of the use" of the facility.

During the emergency seizure, all federal and state labor legislation remains in effect. Conditions of employment, however, may be altered by the governor upon recommendation of a tripartite arbitration board appointed by him. "Such recommendations will be based on the conditions in existence in the industry affected." Strikes, lockouts, or supporting activities to such are forbidden during the emergency period.[19]

An interesting and novel concept in the law is the show-cause procedure before the moderator as to why the dispute should not be submitted to arbitration. This procedure was designed to encourage voluntary arbitration by the parties themselves, with the idea that no union or company would like to face a charge that it would rather endanger the community than arbitrate. Moreover, if arbitration is refused, a penalty may be imposed by compulsory arbitration in the form of prospective or retroactive application of the award.

The show-cause procedure may have another and, paradoxically, contrary merit. A demand, for example, may, in the eyes of the other party, be so extreme or so lacking in conformity with existing practices that he feels arbitration involves an impossible risk. But the party refusing to arbitrate has a forum to which he can explain and attempt to justify what the public might otherwise regard as pure disregard of its interest.

The Slichter Law attempted to meet all contingencies arising under seizure. Profits and losses go to the private owners unless they elect compensation for use instead. In the latter event, they risk a lesser figure, since their compensation must consider losses that might have occurred if a stoppage were effective. Labor legislation remains in effect. And, unlike the Virginia legislation, wages can be raised or lowered by an arbitration board if the governor so desires.

On the other hand, altering conditions of work during seizure has its dangers. Permanent and costly concessions can be made to a union that an employer must accept in order to secure the return of his property. The fact that any contractual changes must be in accord with existing industry conditions does afford protection against startling innovations; but the danger of costly changes is not completely removed.

Another provision in the Slichter Law may prove troublesome—that calling for three-man tripartite arbitration boards. This could result in three-way, no-decision splits in cases where a decision is imperative to maintain peace. Or it could result in the public member being forced to modify his judgment drastically in order to secure a majority report.

Experience with the Slichter Law.—As Table 6 indicates, the Slichter Law has been invoked six times but not since 1953. How has it worked in practice?

TABLE 6

CASES INVOLVING THE SLICHTER LAW

Company	Union	Dates of Initial Proclamation and Final Settlement	Procedures Used	Method of Final Settlement
Truckers Association	Teamsters Local 25 (AFL)	January 1, 1948 February 4, 1948	Moderator Mutual agreement for partial operation	Collective bargaining
Eastern Gas and Fuel Associates (gas manufacturing plant that serves Boston area and is part of large utility organization)..........	Gas, Coke and Chemical Workers (CIO)	January 30, 1948 February 17, 1948	Moderator Seizure	Collective bargaining
N. E. Electric System (gas-distribution facilities).........	United Mine Workers District No. 50	February 17, 1953 March 3, 1953	Moderator	Collective bargaining
Worcester Gas Light Co. (subsidiary of New England Gas and Electric Association)..........	United Mine Workers District No. 50	March 1, 1953 May 11, 1953	Moderator Seizure	Collective bargaining

TABLE 6—Continued

CASES INVOLVING THE SLICHTER LAW

Comapny	Union	Dates of Initial Proclamation and Final Settlement	Procedures Used	Method of Final Settlement
Montaup Electric Co. (electric-power generating and transmitting subsidiary of Eastern Utilities Associates)........	Utility Workers of America (CIO)	June 25, 1953 September 9, 1953	Moderator Emergency Arbitration Board (held no hearings on merits of dispute)	Voluntary arbitration outside procedures of Slichter Law (same arbitration board as appointed by governor but accepted by union only after it became private board)
Association of Milk Dealers (supplying less than half of Greater Boston's needs)...........	Teamsters, Milk Wagon Drivers Local (AFL)	April 9, 1953 December 23, 1953	Moderator Emergency Arbitration Board Seizure Special Commission for Recommendations (never issued recommendations)	Unanimous decision of tripartite voluntary board (same personnel as Special Commission)

Source: Shultz, *op. cit.*, 364.

A careful study of the law found that the health and safety of any community in Massachusetts had not been imperiled since the passage of the law, but neither had such peril occurred in neighboring states that do not have any emergency legislation.[20] This same study also found indications that the final settlement in four of the cases was about the same as would have occurred under collective bargaining. In two of the cases, however, it noted that the final settlement was probably higher, being more than the unions had been willing to accept for settlement at one point.[21]

There seems to be general agreement that the Slichter Law has not disrupted collective bargaining. This has been attributed by one author to restraint in administration.[22] *Fortune* magazine noted that the unions were beginning to utilize the law to gain greater benefits when the then governor, Christian Herter, was advised by the authors of the law to choose not to invoke the law[23] in situations where it previously had been utilized. This seems to have stabilized the situation.

A more practical reason for withholding use of the law has been the political situation in Massachusetts. The Slichter Law was enacted by a Republican Administration and has been invoked by Republican governors. Although the labor members of the Slichter Committee supported it, the law did not have union support and was opposed by the Democratic party in the state. Professor Slichter told one of the authors several years before he died that the law could always be more successful under governors who were opposed to it, because they would invoke it only reluctantly. The fact that Massachusetts has had few governors favorable to the Slichter Law may indeed be a factor in its limited encroachment on collective bargaining.

It should also be noted that technical factors have contributed to restraint under this and other emergency dispute laws. Thus, because of automation, supervisors could operate a utility in 1957 that perhaps they could not have four years earlier.

The law's coverage, which excluded urban transportation and communication, appears to be wise, although the worst strikes since the passage of the Slichter Law have been in transportation industries. In 1954, the coverage of the Slichter Law was extended to the ferry that operates between the mainland and the islands of Martha's Vineyard and Nantucket. Nevertheless, a long strike in 1960 involving this ferry did not result in the invocation of the law. Likewise, other transportation strikes have been long and hard in the state. In 1962, however, a special statute was enacted when a strike occurred on the transit system servicing metropolitan Boston. Seizure under this statute occurred and lasted one month, although the Slichter Law could have as easily been extended.

Whether choice of procedures in fact creates the uncertainty that in theory it is supposed to, so as to discourage it being substituted for collective bargaining, remains a question. Certainly, as administered by Governor Herter in 1953—at least until he stopped invoking the law—it did not. To be sure, the threat that seizure authorities will disburse company cash has given management considerable pause and acts as a spur for management to settle. No such incentive to unions has been demonstrated.

SOME ISSUES AND PROBLEMS

Like all innovating legislation, seizure laws have raised some problems. Among them are willingness of employees to work, effect on collective bargaining, rate increases, standards, sanctions, and constitutional issues.

Willingness to work.—The Virginia experience with seizure laws, as discussed above, indicates the kind of problems that may arise when employees are not willing to work under seizure. It is conceivable that in time of high employment it would not be possible to replace personnel who exercised their right not to work for the state during the seizure period. In the eleven seizures to date under the Virginia Public Utility Labor Relations Act, this problem has not arisen; however, in cases arising under the Ferry Seizure Act and the Mine Seizure Act, some difficulty has been incurred in getting employees to work under seizure.

In judging the merits of seizure as a method of dealing with work stoppages that affect the public interest, it is worthwhile to consider what might have happened if the workers had not returned to work. It may be concluded that the adverse effects of a strike can be averted by state seizure only if the employees are willing to accept employment under seizure.

Effect on collective bargaining.—The success of seizure laws, like other strike-control legislation, may depend on its effect on collective bargaining. The Massachusetts experience under Governor Herter shows how emergencies may be created if one or both parties feel that it is to their advantage to have the law invoked. The New Jersey and the Virginia Public Utility laws were invoked in numerous minor urban transit and telephone cases that at most caused some public inconvenience. In many of these cases, the will to create an emergency exceeded the will to settle. Since 1952, when the laws were last invoked, collective bargaining has been normalized in these areas without any public outcry or major inconvenience.

Likewise, the Chesapeake Ferry case shows how the threat of permanent seizure kills the incentive to settle. Just as in some cases, the idea of "Why settle? We may get more from state seizure," hinders settlement, so does the idea that seizure will be permanent.

Given the tendency of parties to take advantage of emergency legislation, seizure standing alone, as it does in Virginia, without settlement procedures, and with penalties, may well be the best choice if collective bargaining is to survive emergency procedures. Certainly, it appears from this review that seizure provides ample public protection without the supplement of an easy substitute for labor-management decision making.

Rate increases.—There is the question of whether a state public utility commission will view an application for rate relief more favorably if it is based on increased labor costs resulting from the action of a state agency than if those increased labor costs resulted from negotiation and collective bargaining. Most public officials and utility executives questioned thought that both types of cases would receive equal consideration, but some held the contrary opinion.[24] In support of the latter view was cited the following comment of the president of the New Jersey Public Utility Commission made after a rate-increase petition was denied: "If the state should seize the properties under the utility anti-strike law and the state should then ask this board (the Utility Commission) to act, that would create a different situation than the present one in which we cannot act."[25]

The fact that rate-increase petitions may thus receive more favorable treatment after state intervention is significant. For under such circumstances, the utility would be wary of settling for an increase in wages under collective bargaining, and would tend to force the matter to seizure in order to strengthen its rate case. The effects on collective bargaining would then be the same as when either labor or management believes it can secure a better deal on labor matters through seizure or arbitration than by collective bargaining settlement: collective bargaining would cease to be an important factor in the settlement process.

Standards.—If a state seizes the property of a company what rules should govern it?

Maryland, Massachusetts, and Virginia provide definite legislative guides for the administration of seized properties (Table 7). New Jersey and Missouri merely empower the governor to make the necessary rules and regulations.

Seizures in New Jersey and Missouri have not resulted in any

TABLE 7

STANDARDS GOVERNING PLANT OPERATION DURING SEIZURE BY STATES

State	Wages and Conditions of Employment	Disposition of Business Profits	Applicability of Labor and Social Legislation During Period of Seizure
Maryland.....	Seizure authorities shall put into effect recommendations of Board of Arbitration appointed pursuant to statute, and retroactive to date of last agreement where possible, provided that if a valid agreement exists no action inconsistent with that agreement may be taken	Plant operated for account of owner; or if owner elects, he may waive same and sue for just compensation, but courts must consider effect on compensation of fact that a labor dispute threatened to cut off production	No state or federal law affecting health, safety, security, and employment standards shall be affected. All such laws must be complied with during state operation
Massachusetts.	Governor may alter upon recommendation of a tripartite board. All changes must be based on going industry practice and must be consistent with any existing agreements of parties	Plant operated for account of owner; or if owner elects, he may waive same and sue for just compensation, but courts must consider effect on compensation of fact that a labor dispute threatened to cut off production	No state or federal law affecting health, safety, security and employment standards shall be affected. All such laws must be complied with during state operation
Virginia.......	No changes permitted	Cost to state of operation and 15 per cent of net profit paid to state; rest of profit to owner	Nothing specific in law
Missouri.......	"The Governor is authorized to prescribe the necessary rules and regulations ..."	"The Governor is authorized to prescribe the necessary rules and regulations ..."	Nothing specific in law
New Jersey....	"The Governor is authorized to prescribe the necessary rules and regulations ..."	"The Governor is authorized to prescribe the necessary rules and regulations ..."	Nothing specific in law

legal tangles over the disposition of profits or whether wages should be maintained or altered during the seizure period. Under a Supreme Court decision, an employer whose property was seized in these three states presumably could sue the states for "just compensation" for the use of his property.[26]

It would also appear that if New Jersey or Missouri would alter wages or conditions of employment the state would be liable for any additional costs resulting therefrom during the period of seizure.[27]

Seizure legislation usually provides that an owner may petition the courts to secure the return of his property if there is reason to believe that the state is holding the property beyond the duration of the emergency. As noted, owners of property may sue for "just compensation" for the use of their property during seizure.

In Virginia, the law would seem to preclude such suits—since just compensation is declared to be 85 per cent of net income during the period of seizure. In Massachusetts and Maryland, the owner may elect to waive any suit and permit the state to operate a business for his account, or he may elect to sue for just compensation, but the courts are instructed to take into account in determining just compensation for the seizure period the fact that a strike might have occurred if such strike were not prevented by the seizure.

Sanctions.—Can sanctions prevent strikes? Sanctions are designed as both a deterrent and a curative. Certainly one would think that the prospect of severe fines would prevent rash acts. And even if the rash act be taken, the cumulative effect of sanctions should result in a speedy reconsideration of the desirability of continued defiance of law. Yet the most severe sanctions can fail.

For example, Missouri's economic sanctions on individual strikers and equally harsh fines on unions appear capable of breaking any strike in violation of the Missouri law and of discouraging most of them before they commence. If, however, the employees remain on strike and do not break ranks, the public is likely to clamor for resumption of service rather than punishment of strikers. This can induce officials to agree to waive or compromise the law as a condition of settlement. Once this begins, it can steam-roller and both the sanctions and the prohibition on strikes can lose their effectiveness.

It is, moreover, very difficult for public officials to enforce sanctions. In the one Missouri case, labor was split and the strikers were clearly in the wrong in their attempt to upset by force a legal ruling of the National Labor Relations Board. If, however, the strike had been a popular one and labor had been united, the problem of enforcement would have been less easy. Statesmen and politicians do not find it easy to invoke sanctions against large numbers of voters or against influential persons or groups.

Constitutional issues.—In 1951 the United States Supreme Court declared the Wisconsin Public Utilities Arbitration Act inoperative in interstate commerce on the grounds that it conflicted with the Taft-Hartley Act, which had pre-empted the field.[28] Since then the constitutionality of seizure laws has not been finally determined.

The Massachusetts and Maryland legislation have no court record. The Virginia courts have ruled that state's law a valid exercise of police power,[29] and the United States Supreme Court denied a hearing but the case involved was moot at the time.[30]

* * *

Since the publication of this article, the Supreme Court of the United States has reversed a decision of the Missouri Supreme Court which upheld an injunction issued under the King-Thompson Act (Missouri's seizure law). In making a ruling which invalidates the State's seizure law, the U. S. Supreme Court made two interesting points:

(1) "None of the distinctions drawn by the Missouri court between the King-Thompson Act and the legislation involved in Wisconsin Board seem to us to be opposite. First, whatever the status of the title to the properties of Kansas City Transit, Inc., acquired by the State as a result of the Governor's executive order, the record shows that the State's involvement fell far short of creating a state-owned and operated utility whose labor relations are by definition excluded from the coverage of the National Labor Relations Act. The employees of the company did not become employees of Missouri. Missouri did not pay their wages, and did not direct or supervise their duties. No property of the company was actually conveyed, transferred, or otherwise turned over to the State. Missouri did not participate in any way in the actual management of the company, and there was no change of any kind in the conduct of the company's business."

(2) "The Wisconsin Board case decisively rejected the proposition

that a state enactment affecting a public utility operating in interstate commerce could be saved from a challenge based upon a demonstrated conflict with the standards embodied in federal law simply by designating it as 'emergency legislation.' There the Court said that where 'the state seeks to deny entirely a federally guaranteed right which Congress itself restricted only to a limited extent in case of national emergencies, however, serious, it is manifest that the state legislation is in conflict with federal law.'[31]

The Court stated further:

"The short of the matter is that Missouri, through the fiction of 'seizure' by the State, has made a peaceful strike against a public utility unlawful, in direct conflict with federal legislation which guarantees the right to strike against a public utility, as against any employer engaged in interstate commerce. In forbidding a strike against an employer covered by the National Labor Relations Act, Missouri has forbidden the exercise of rights explicity protected by par. 7 of that Act. Collective bargaining, with the right to strike at its core, is the essence of the federal scheme. As in Wisconsin Board, a state law which denies that right cannot stand under the Supremacy Clause of the Constitution."

In light of these recent events, one may ponder just what the future may hold for the laws of Massachusetts and Virginia if and when they are challenged on similar constitutional grounds. This is particularly true in the case of Virginia where employees of a transit company have been made employees of the State under the seizure law.

NOTES

1. Ben F. Curry, "Strikes and Seizure Laws in Virginia" (unpublished Ph.D. dissertation, University of North Carolina, 1956), p. 21.

2. See Table 1, n. *.

3. D. W. Gray, "It's the Law—No Utilities Strikes in Virginia," *Bus Transportation*, December, 1949, p. 63.

4. Editorial, *Richmond News-Leader*, August 26, 1949.

5. See the concluding section of this article for a discussion of this issue.

6. Missouri State Board of Mediation, *Twelve Years under the King-Thompson Act, 1947-1959* (Jefferson City: State Board of Mediation, 1959), p. 3.

7. For an early account of the Missouri experience see Vance Julian, "Mediation of Labor Disputes in Missouri Public Utilities," *IRRA Proceedings, Missouri Law Review*, XXIV (November, 1959), 445-55.

8. *United States v. Pewee Coal Co.*, 71 Sup. Ct., 670 (1951).

9. Constitutional issues are discussed in the concluding sections of this article.

10. See Seymour H. Lehrer, "The Maryland Public Utilities Disputes Act," *Labor Law Journal*, VII (October, 1956), 607-17, for an excellent account of the Baltimore transit situation and the enactment of the Maryland law.

11. *Ibid.*, p. 609.

12. *Ibid.*

13. *Baltimore Sun*, February 10, 1956.

14. Lehrer, *op. cit.*, p. 611.

15. *New Jersey Bell Telephone Company v. CWA*, 75A (2d) 284, 1950.

16. A good review of the New Jersey law and its history is found in Governor's Committee on Public Utility Labor Disputes Legislation, *Report to Governor Meyner* (Trenton, N. J., 1954), pp. 22-25.

17. Lois MacDonald, "Compulsory Arbitration in New Jersey," *Proceedings of Second Annual Conference on Labor* (New York: Matthew Bender & Co., Inc., 1949), p. 65.

18. Mr. W. W. Wirtz, Secretary of Labor in the Kennedy Administration, has long been an advocate of this approach. See his article in I. Bernstein (ed.), *Emergency Disputes and National Policy* (New York: Harper & Bros., 1955), pp. 149-65.

19. The report on which the Slichter Law is based is "Report of the Governor's Labor-Management Committee" (Commonwealth of Massachusetts, House Document No. 1875, 1947).

20. George P. Shultz, "The Massachusetts Choice-of-Procedures Approach to Emergency Disputes," *Industrial and Labor Relations Review*, X (April, 1957), 363.

21. *Ibid.*, pp. 364-65.

22. *Ibid.*, pp. 365-70.

23. "Boston Roulette," *Fortune*, February, 1961, pp. 190, 193.

24. These officials of utilities were interviewed in two periods: 1950-51, and 1962.

25. *Newark Evening News*, January 31, 1951, p. 2.

26. *United States v. Pewee Coal Co.*, 71 Sup. Ct. 670 (1951).

27. *Ibid.*

28. *Amalgamated Association v. Wisconsin Employment Relations Board*, 340 U. S. 383 (1951).

29. *Harris v. Battle*, Chancery B-1708, Va. Cir. Ct., City of Richmond, January 2, 1953, and June 12, 1953.

30. *Harris v. Stanley*, 99 Sup. Ct. 80 (1954).

31. *Division 1287, Amalgamated Association v. State of Missouri*, 374 U. S. 74 (1963).

C Fact-Finding in Labor
Disputes: *The States'*
*Experience**

HERBERT R. NORTHRUP**

A PERSISTENT PROPOSAL to avoid costly strikes would have unions and management submit their disputes to impartial "fact-finding" by responsible third parties; if the disputants do not agree, the fact-finding may become compulsory, or be converted into an "investigation." In either case, the idea is that when the facts are known, agreement will be induced on the basis of the facts made apparent to unions and management, or if either or both remain obtuse to the facts, by public opinion forcing them to see the light.

Fact-finding has had its most complete exposure under the Railway Labor Act. Most observers agree that it has not worked in either the railroad or airline industry as the theory dictates.[1]

* Reprinted by permission from the *Industrial and Labor Relations Review*, Vol. XVII, No. 1, October 1963.

** This study was financed by the Committee on Faculty Projects of the Wharton School with funds provided by the Ford Foundation. Dr. Richard L. Rowan assisted in the data gathering for parts of this article.

In the first place, the facts are rarely in doubt—the interpretation thereof, however, is usually not only in doubt, but also in controversy, and not subject to objective determination (What is a fair wage? What pertinence is a contract provision in another industry?). In the second place, public opinion has not risen to enforce fact-finding recommendations. Rather, they have been ignored with impunity. And finally, instead of strengthening or supplementing collective bargaining, fact-finding has tended to supplant it in the railway and airline industries. The parties no longer prepare to bargain; rather, they prepare for a fact-finding proceeding. Bargaining, if it occurs, is more likely after the fact finders report. Then if no agreement is reached, the fact-finding procedure is not available—it has been used up as part of the tactics of the parties.

Is this experience indigenous to the Railway Labor Act, or the railway or airline industries, or is it inevitable under fact-finding procedure? The question is significant because fact-finding remains a popular political remedy. Greater use of it in so-called emergency strikes has been suggested recently by the President's Advisory Committee on Labor-Management Policies, and by the Governor of Oregon, among others. Opponents regularly refer to the Railway Labor Act experience.

Besides the Railway Labor Act, considerable experience exists with fact-finding at the state level. The variety of state laws and diverse conditions provides good additional bases for determining how fact-finding might work under different conditions, and what pitfalls may develop in its administration.

DEFINITION

Fact-finding involves an investigation by a public body aimed primarily at discovering the issues, and usually making recommendations for their settlement. Finding areas of agreement is a primary duty of the fact finders.

Usually under fact-finding procedure, strikes and lockouts are forbidden, and the status quo is maintained until a period of ten to thirty days, after a report is made. Then the parties are freed of legal restraint.

A SUMMARY OF STATE LEGISLATION

The laws of twenty-eight states (Table 1) provide for some form of official investigation or fact-finding or both, where labor

TABLE 1

Fact-finding and Investigation by States

State	Summary of Statute	Character of Intervention	Comment
Alabama......	Governor may appoint a tripartite board of mediation	Fact-finding to gather facts and make report and recommendation	Inactive
Arkansas......	Commissioner of Labor may conduct investigations and hearings, publish reports, advertisements, etc.	Investigation and report	Inactive
California.....	Department of Industrial Relations may investigate and mediate labor disputes	Investigation	California relies almost exclusively upon mediation. Investigation is used only to develop nature and possible effect of dispute prior to intervention
Colorado......	Industrial Commissioner may conduct investigation and hearings, publish reports and advertisements, etc.	Original compulsory investigation law passed in 1915, provided for notices, cooling-off period, and compulsory investigation and report	The investigation functions have been infrequently utilized and more recently have rarely been invoked
Georgia.......	Commissioner of Labor may conduct investigations and hearings, publish reports and advertisements	Investigation and report	Inactive
Hawaii........	Where Governor finds mediation has failed, he may appoint an emergency board to investigate and report on controversy	Fact-finding, with recommendations	Active (special fact-finding provision for public utilities was ruled inoperative by the United States Attorney General while Hawaii was a territory)
Illinois........	Department of Labor may investigate dispute and make findings and recommendations public if public utility, food, fuel, or other inconvenience to public is involved	Investigation and fact-finding of emergency disputes	Inactive. State Mediation Service advised writer it had no knowledge of law

TABLE 1—Continued
FACT-FINDING AND INVESTIGATION BY STATES

State	Summary of Statute	Character of Intervention	Comment
Indiana	Commissioner of Labor may investigate disputes, publish reports, and do other necessary things	Investigation and report	Inactive (note: Indiana also has a compulsory arbitration law which is inactive and inapplicable to utilities in interstate commerce, *Marshall* v. *Shricker*, 20 CCH Labor Cases, 66, 372, 1951)
Iowa	Either party to a dispute or persons affected may apply to the Governor for appointment of a board of conciliation and arbitration	Fact-finding. Board of Conciliation and Arbitration's report is not binding unless parties so agree beforehand	Inactive
Kentucky	Commissioner of Industrial Relations may hold hearings to determine the reason for the labor dispute and make public findings of fact	Investigation and report	Inactive
Louisiana	A tripartite Labor mediation board may mediate unsettled dispute, and render unenforceable decision and make it public if mediation fails	Fact-finding with recommendations	Relatively inactive
Maine	Board of inquiry may be set up if mediation is declined and if one of parties or interested persons affected request. Report can be made public	Fact-finding and report	Inactive
Maryland	Commission of Labor may investigate dispute, determine which party is mainly blameworthy or responsible, and publish report in some daily newspaper assigning responsibility or blame	Investigation and assignment of responsibility	Inactive (note: Maryland also has a seizure law affecting utilities which has been invoked only once)

TABLE 1—Continued
FACT-FINDING AND INVESTIGATION BY STATES

State	Summary of Statute	Character of Intervention	Comment
Massachusetts.	Tripartite Board of Conciliation and Arbitration, where no settlement is agreeable and parties will not arbitrate, shall investigate dispute and publish a report	Investigation and assignment of responsibility	Active until found inapplicable to interstate commerce in *General Electric* v. *Callahan*, 294 F. 2d 60 (1962) (note: Massachusetts also has a "choice of procedures" law affecting utilities)
Michigan......	Fact-finding by board composed of three disinterested persons and two nonvoting members, one from labor and one from industry. Findings not binding, but made public. Law applies to public utilities, hospitals, and government employees	Fact-finding with recommendations	Law extensively used for hospital and government employees. Found inapplicable to utilities in interstate commerce in *Grand Rapids City Coach Lines* v. *Howlett*, 137 F. Supp. 667 (1955)
Minnesota.....	Fact-finding by three-man, tripartite commission where public interest, life, safety, or health involved	Fact-finding with recommendations	Most active of state fact-finding agencies (note: Minnesota also has a compulsory arbitration statute applicable to hospitals only)
Missouri......	Tripartite fact-finding panels may be appointed by parties and State Mediation Board	Fact-finding with recommendations *but* if parties refuse to accept recommendations and strike threatens public interest, health, and welfare, Governor may seize utility— and then strikes are forbidden	Active.* Seizure aspects found inapplicable to utilities in interstate commerce in *Division 1287 Amalgamated Association* v. *State of Missouri*, 374 U. S. 74 (1963)
New Hampshire	If parties refuse to arbitrate, Commissioner may investigate and issue a report assigning responsibility	Investigation with assignment of responsibility	Fairly active, but future in doubt as a result of Massachusetts case

TABLE 1—Continued

FACT-FINDING AND INVESTIGATION BY STATES

State	Summary of Statute	Character of Intervention	Comment
New York.....	If Board of Mediation certified that it cannot settle a dispute by mediation, Industrial Commissioner may appoint a board of inquiry to make report and recommendations	Fact-finding with recommendations	Active
North Dakota.	Head of Labor Division of state may request Governor to appoint a mediation board which may issue report and recommendations	Fact-finding with recommendations	Active. Applies to both private and public employees
Ohio..........	Industrial Commission may investigate dispute, ascertain which party is responsible, and make that fact public. At request of one or both parties, it may make recommendations for settlement, and if not accepted, publish same	Investigation, with assignment of responsibility; fact-finding with recommendations	Relatively inactive
Oklahoma.....	Where a strike or lockout exists which causes injury or inconvenience to the public, the Board of Arbitration and Conciliation may investigate and publish findings and recommendations which will contribute to an equitable settlement	Fact-finding with recommendations	Inactive. Tenth court of Appeals ruled fact findings inapplicable to disputes in interstate commerce, May 28, 1964, *Oil, Chemical & Atomic Workers* v. *Arkansas-Louisiana Gas Co.*, 320 F(2d) 62 (1964)
Oregon........	Facilities of Labor Conciliator available to public employees and government agencies for "fact-finding purposes only"	Mediation and fact-finding	Public employees and licensed nurses in health care institutions only

TABLE 1—Continued

FACT-FINDING AND INVESTIGATION BY STATES

State	Summary of Statute	Character of Intervention	Comment
Rhode Island..	Director of Department of Labor, with approval of Governor, may appoint Boards of Conciliation and Mediation to investigate and report on disputes	Fact-finding with recommendations	Law invoked only twice in forty years, and in neither case was a board actually appointed
South Carolina.	Commissioner of Labor may appoint tripartite committee with himself as chairman to make findings of fact designed to induce agreement	Fact-finding with recommendations	Inactive
South Dakota..	Deputy Commissioner of Labor may investigate a dispute, make a report of the issues involved, and make recommendations public. He may do this alone or as chairman of a tripartite panel	Fact-finding with recommendations	Inactive
Texas.........	Governor may appoint a five-man tripartite commission to investigate dispute and make report and public recommendations	Fact-finding with recommendations	Relatively inactive
Washington...	If the parties to a dispute refuse to arbitrate, Director of Labor and Industries endeavors to have each put in writing his position and why he refused to arbitrate	Investigation by indirection	Relatively inactive

Source: State statutes, and field work relating thereto (including interviews with government officials, union officials, and employers).
* Discussed as a seizure statute in Appendix B.

disputes remain unsettled or threaten to upset, inconvenience, or imperial a community; or where one party to the dispute simply requests "investigation." Under these laws, fact-finding has a variety of interpretations, some narrow, some broad. California, for example, with its well-developed and manned mediation staff, follows

a narrowly restricted definition of "investigation" . . . an assignment to develop information as to the nature of a dispute and the possible consequences of a work stoppage. This investigation is made preliminary to a decision to proffer or not to proffer the facilities of the [State Conciliation] Service in a labor dispute.[2]

On the other hand, statutes in Massachusetts and New Hampshire require their state mediation agencies to investigate a dispute and to issue a public report assigning responsibility for its continuance *after* mediation has not settled the dispute and one or both of the parties have refused the agency's proposal that the case be arbitrated.

In Michigan, Minnesota, and New York, fact-finding involves the traditional concept of holding hearings, and writing a report and recommendations. In other states, fact-finding is largely mediation in another form, with the "fact finders" actually a mediation panel.

The procedure, the method, and the experiences vary from state to state even where laws are written in similar language. The coverage of the laws also varies. In some states, the laws may be involved in any dispute. In others, only public utilities are within the jurisdiction of the fact finders. And in still others, the jurisdiction covers utilities plus "industries affected with a public interest." Wherever the covered industry lies within the jurisdiction of the Labor-Management Relations (Taft-Hartley) Act, the constitutionality of state fact-finding or investigation is in doubt.[3]

Besides the fact-finding provisions of state laws, there are many cases where state governors or mayors of large cities have appointed fact-finding commissions as a means of trying to resolve diputes which have seemed of serious consequence to the local citizenry. Such ad hoc fact-finding usually has no legal basis, but depends for its success upon the prestige of the public official and the willingness of the parties to cooperate. For example, a citizen's panel appointed by the Mayor of Philadelphia in early 1962 resulted, with considerable pressure from both the Mayor and the Governor of Pennsylvania, in a settlement of the six months' strike between Yale and Towne Manufacturing Company and the International Association of Machinists. Here, mediation had clearly failed and no end to the dispute appeared in sight before the special panel led to settlement. On the other hand, those ad hoc interventions too often appear either politically inspired to bail out a faltering union strike or they are bumbling efforts on the part of well-meaning but ineffectual citizens who do not understand the issues and whose efforts may actually prolong, rather than help to solve, the dispute.

Many of the state fact-finding laws are virtually unused in practice and represent little more than a chance idea which was enacted by the state legislature without consideration of the law's role in dispute settlement and which is all but forgotten by the state administrator. For example, in Texas, one of the few states which has no mediation law or agency, the Governor is authorized, when a labor dispute arises, to appoint an "Industrial Commission" to hold hearings and to make a public report on the dispute. In Alabama, where the state does virtually no mediation, the Governor is authorized to appoint, or even to sit upon, a tripartite fact-finding agency. In neither of these states do we have any record of such provisions being utilized. In Rhode Island, the Director of the Department of Labor may, subject to the approval of the Governor, appoint a board "for the consideration and settlement" of disputes not terminated by mediation. This law which was enacted in 1919, has been invoked only twice, but in neither case was a board actually appointed.

COMPULSORY INVESTIGATION IN COLORADO

The pioneer state fact-finding law passed in the United States was the Colorado Compulsory Investigation Act of 1915, which was modeled on a prior Canadian law.* Under the Colorado act, employers and employees are required to give each other and a tripartite Industrial Commission thirty-days' written notice of any desired change in the terms and conditions of employment,

[*See Appendix L, below.]

and all such changes are prohibited until after the Industrial Commission has investigated, held a hearing, or by consent of the parties, arbitrated the dispute. After that the parties are free to strike, or to lock out, or to alter terms of employment. In 1943, Colorado enacted its Labor Peace Act, a comprehensive labor relations law, but the essential features of the compulsory investigation law were not changed.

Under the Colorado law, the Industrial Commission has jurisdiction over all labor disputes within the state. In addition, the commission administers all other state labor, social insurance, and welfare programs. Its reports cover a wide variety of functions, but do not provide much detail for most years on its activities in the labor relations field.

A study of the first eleven years of the Colorado act's history questioned the commission's effectiveness in major controversies and found that it was most successful where unions were weak and afraid to test their economic strength—the usual situation of the weaker party seeking government help. The authors of this study found the commission's records confused and incomplete, and doubted that the commission's claim of handling 1,157 cases between 1915 and 1924, with only 73 strikes or lockouts occurring, was an accurate reflection of its work. Very little fact-finding was done, and no effort was made to inform the public. Most investigations were perfunctory and mediation rather than fact-finding was usually attempted, if the investigation went beyond the initial stage.[4]

Later studies largely agree, concluding that the Industrial Commission actually did little fact-finding. Most of the cases were docketed pro forma, being in effect merely acknowledgment of notices of an impending desire to change an agreement or a notation that a dispute was no longer pending. Mediation was actually the principal dispute activity of the commission between two World Wars.[5]

Following World War II, the Industrial Commission's labor relations activity increased markedly with the temper of the times and the growth of industry in the state. But although the commission received over 4,000 notices of impending contract changes between 1946 and 1952—almost triple both the previous and the following six years—its fact-finding activity remained negligible. Some typical Colorado reports are found in the exhibit.

Exhibit

Case Reports—Colorado Industrial Commission.

Case 4343. Amalgamated Association of Street, Electric Railway and Motor Coach Employees No. 1142 vs. Continental Bus System. Negotiations in this case were carried on outside of Colorado. The file consists of information designed to comply with Colorado laws.

Case 4344. Produce Drivers, Warehousemen and Helpers Local Union No. 452 vs. General Outdoor Advertising Co., Inc. Notice was received in this case but further information regarding the situation was not procured. We, therefore, closed our file at the end of the statutory period.

Case 4345. Amalgamated Meat Cutters and Butcher Workmen No. 634 vs. Safeway Stores, Inc., Cut-a-Corner Market, Colorado Springs Food Store and Piggly Wiggly Stores (Colorado Springs). Negotiations in this case resulted in a mutually satisfactory agreement.

Case 4346. Drivers vs. Zone Cab Company. A wildcat strike of short duration occurred. No notices were given but the file contains information concerning the situation.

Case 4347. Painters, Paperhangers and Decorators Local Union No. 284 vs. Boulder Contractors. Notice under the Industrial Commission law was received in this case. Subsequent information was not forthcoming. We, therefore, closed our file in the case when the laws had been observed.

Case 4348. Hod Carriers, Building and Construction Laborers Local Union No. 354 vs. Pueblo Contractors. This case turned out to be the same matter discussed in Case No. 4339.

Case 4349. Bakery Drivers and Salesmen's Union No. 219 vs. Merchants Biscuit Company. Negotiations in this case effected an agreement which is on file here. There was no dispute involved which could not be settled by the parties concerned.

Case 4350. International Ass'n of Machinists Lodge No. 86 vs. Illinois-California Express Company. This case was settled by representatives of the union and the company. No notice was served on the commission except by the Employers' Council.

Case 4351. Teamsters Union No. 17 vs. West Coast Fast Freight. Notices under the Industrial Commission law and the Colorado Labor Peace Act were regularly filed in this case. There being no request for a hearing or for mediation services, the case was closed at the end of the statutory period.

Source: Industrial Commission of Colorado, 1946-1948 Biennial Report.

The clerical nature of the Industrial Commission's activity, the insignificant cases which come to its attention, and its lack of concern as to whether the provisions of the compulsory investigation law are flouted are all clear from these cases. Apparently, it has not been the policy of the commission to concern itself with the last point unless a complaint is made.

Between 1915 and 1937, when a complaint of violation was made, the Industrial Commission had authority to request an injunction from a state district court in order to restrain illegal strikes, boycotts, picketing, or lockouts. A few of the commission's orders were concerned with such prohibitions. Then in 1937, the state courts ruled that the Colorado "Little Norris–La Guardia Act," passed in 1933, withdrew this authority from the commission.[6] Ten years later, this authority was revived by the passage of the Colorado Labor Peace Act.

The Colorado Labor Peace Act also charged the Industrial Commission with preventing unfair labor practices of both unions and employers, and with conducting representation and union-shop elections. Since then, the commission's principal labor relations activity has been the holding of elections. In fact, there has been no indication of any fact-finding in the biennial reports since 1950. It appears that Colorado's pioneer law is quite inactive in its most widely heralded sphere.[7]

FACT-FINDING IN MINNESOTA

The late 1930's saw young Republican leadership in Minnesota under Harold Stassen come to power, ousting an avowedly pro-labor, farmer-labor administration. Among the factors which aided the Stassen candidacy were a series of violent trucking strikes in Minneapolis and St. Paul, and the feeling of many independent voters that the state government was unduly sensitive to union desires. Mr. Stassen's program, therefore, included "a better method" of handling labor disputes. In practice, this meant the enactment of the Minnesota Labor Relations Act of 1939—a law designed to eliminate antisocial activities of labor and management, and to provide an orderly settlement of labor disputes.

The Minnesota law, as amended several times, includes guarantees of free organization by employees and employers, unfair labor practice prevention aimed at both employers and unions, prohibitions against boycotts and jurisdictional strikes, a special compulsory arbitration procedure covering charitable hospitals,[8] an apparently never used law to insure democratic unionism, and the subject of this article, a procedure for mediation and fact-finding of labor disputes.

THE MINNESOTA FACT-FINDING PROCEDURE

The Minnesota Act established a Division of Conciliation supervised by a Labor Conciliator who, with his staff, is charged with mediating labor disputes. Until the law was changed in 1955 as a result of an adverse court decision,[9] the parties were required to notify the Conciliator if a strike or lockout impended and to maintain the status quo for ten days thereafter. At present the parties may merely petition for conciliation. If the Conciliator is unable to settle the dispute by mediation, he suggests arbitration. If this suggestion is not accepted and if the dispute is in an industry "affected with the public interest,"

which includes, but is not restricted to, any industry, business or institution engaged in supplying the necessities of life, safety, or health, so that a temporary suspension of its operation would endanger the life, safety, health or well being of a substantial number of people of any community,

the Conciliator must notify the Governor who may appoint a tripartite commission "to conduct a hearing and make a report on the issues involved and the merits of the respective contentions of the parties to the dispute."

The commission's report must be submitted to the Governor after twenty-five days and may be publicized by him. Strikes and lockouts are prohibited for thirty days after the Governor is notified of the existence of a "public interest" dispute, in order to give the commission time to report. If the Governor does not appoint a commission, strikes and lockouts are permitted five days after he is notified, instead of thirty.

This procedure is, of course, very similar to that of the Railway Labor Act, which was enjoying its unearned reputation as a "model law" when the Minnesota legislation was first enacted.

An examination of the Minnesota experience indicates some of the same ills which befell its prototype on the railroads—overutilization, inhibition of collective bargaining, lack of the parties' respect for fact-finding recommendations, and lack of public interest in supporting those recommendations.

The Minnesota law began at a difficult time because, soon after its enactment, came the defense program, and then World War II. Early in this emergency period the Conciliator adopted a policy of considering any industry "affected with the public interest" where the employer was materially engaged in the production of defense items. Between 1940 and 1945, 167 commissions were appointed—70 between July 1, 1941 and June 30, 1942. If the commission's recommendations were not accepted, the case might be referred to the National War Labor Board. In any case, the war period provides no real guides to the act's effects.[10]

After World War II, an overeagerness to permit Minnesota's unions and employers to utilize the act persisted for several years. Table 2 shows that an annual average of 43 commissions were appointed between 1946 and 1949. Hotels and restaurants, manufacturing of every description, laundries, optical firms were found to be "affected with the public interest." After analyzing the first decade of the Minnesota law (including the war years), Professor Stieber found "considerable evidence . . . to indicate that factfinding procedure, as practiced in Minnesota, has hindered free collective bargaining." He found a tendency for the same unions and employers to appear before fact-finding commissions each year; for a high percentage of rejection of fact-finding commission reports; and for the Conciliator or the Governor, or both, then to step in and usually effectuate a settlement by compromise between what the commissions recommended and what the party holding out would take.[11]

Stieber's analysis, of course, is quite consistent with the findings, already noted, of most observers who have carefully studied the Railway Labor Act. If the parties learn to expect that a fact-finding board or commission will be appointed, they soon toss everything into the commission's lap rather than settle anything in collective bargaining. The fear is that anything conceded in bargaining or mediation will be used as a spring board for further concessions before the commission. If, however, the commission poorly gauges the relative strength of the parties, or otherwise turns in a report which is rejected by either or both parties, the real emergency occurs. For then, both collective bargaining and the emergency procedure have been exhausted and nothing has been settled.

If, at this stage, a Conciliator or Governor or other public official is available to seek a settlement by putting pressure on one party to make further concessions, the tendency of the party seeking additional concessions to reject a recommendation of a fact-finding commission is further encouraged. Between 1946 and 1949 (Table 2), 45 percent of the cases for which fact-finding commissions were appointed pursuant to the Minnesota law, were settled on the basis of "modification by further conciliation," whereas only 23 percent were settled on the basis of the commissions' reports.

By 1950, the administrators of the Minnesota law were determined to improve the effectiveness of the fact-finding commission procedure by giving "a more strict interpretation of the legislative intent."[12] The following year the Conciliator pointed with pride to the fact that "there has been a continued decrease in the number of disputes referred to fact-finding commissions. This section of the law has been given a more strict interpretation in an attempt to make it more effective."[13]

Table 2 shows that since 1950, there has been a steady decline in the use of fact-finding commissions. There are several reasons for this; one is the new policy of the law's administrators. Certainly, they are correct in stating that the more commissions appointed, the weaker their effectiveness. During the first ten years of the act, public opinion did not rise to support commission recommendations nor did strikes decrease as compared with other areas or states.[14] If the fact-finding commission is to be of even limited service, it must be used most sparingly.

Another reason for the declining use of fact-finding commissions in Minnesota since 1950 has been the general lack of serious strike situations. The most important stoppages in Minnesota since then have been steel or mine strikes under national bargaining, in which the state has been helpless to intervene. The 1950's were a decade of relative labor peace in Minnesota as in the rest of the United States.

TABLE 2

Fact-finding in Minnesota, 1946–1962

Year	Number of Commissions Appointed	Number of Reports	Dispute Settled on Basis of Commission Recommendation	Dispute Settled by Conciliation or Other Modification of Commission Recommendation	Strike Occurred	No Record of Result
1960–1962....	2	2	2			
1958–1960....	1	1*	1*			
1956–1958....	5	5	2†	1†	2	
1954–1956....	2					2
1952–1954....	10					10
1951–1952....	8	8	6	1	1	
1950–1951....	10	9	3	5	1	
1949–1950....	15	13	7	4	2	
1948–1949....	44	29	7	10	12	
1947–1948....	52	33	6	16	1	10
1946–1947....	37	34	8	17	1	

Source: State of Minnesota, Division of Conciliation, Annual and Biennial *Reports*.
Notes: 1939–1940 data not clearly distinguished. 1941–1946 data not comparable because of war situation and activities of War Labor Board.
* Listed in reports as 13 disputes—actually one multiemployer dispute.
† Statistics not clearly categorized, distinguished by estimate.

Finally, like most states with strike control laws which have not been ultimately tested in the courts, Minnesota is loath to bring about a final test of constitutionality by forcing the issue through the appointment of fact-finding commissions which are unacceptable to the parties. Most appointments in recent years have not been opposed by the parties. In such instances, of course, with compulsion lacking, fact-finding has its greatest opportunity to achieve—actually through a sort of intensified mediation—an acceptable settlement. This is a far cry from the traditional theory of fact-finding which assumes that an impartial commission can, by discovering the facts and publicizing them, induce the parties to agree to a rational settlement.[15]

FACT-FINDING IN NEW YORK

Fact-finding in New York State dates back to 1887 under a law providing for mediation, arbitration, and "investigation" of labor disputes. This authority was later placed in the hands of the State Industrial Commissioner, who is empowered to "inquire into and report on the causes of all strikes, lockouts, and other industrial controversies and labor disputes, and may appoint boards of inquiry for that purpose." In 1941, the law was amended to provide that boards of inquiry may be appointed by the Industrial Commissioner only after the State Board of Mediation certifies "that its efforts to effect a voluntary settlement of the dispute have been unsuccessful."[16]

New York has generally made restrained use of fact-finding. In most cases boards have been appointed because of strikes heavily affecting a particular community, or because a strike involved a problem which was especially difficult to resolve (see Table 3). By contrast, Minnesota has appointed more fact-finding commissions in some months than New York has appointed in twenty-five years.

New York has not had the same experience in having the recommendations of fact finders rejected, which has been a recurring problem in Minnesota over the years. There are several reasons for this. In the first place, because New York has appointed so few boards of inquiry, they have not become commonplace; therefore, when they are appointed, their importance and the consequences of rejecting their recommendations have been dramatized quite vividly. An additional result of such infrequent use has been that the parties have been unable to feel sufficiently assured that a fact-finding board will be appointed, so they have not tended to substitute the fact-finding procedure for collective bargaining.

Another reason why New York boards of inquiry have been relatively successful, at least in terms of achieving settlement on the basis of the fact finders' recommendations, is that they have usually been appointed at that period of time in a dispute when the parties themselves were looking for a way out. Fact-finding in New York has actually been used more as a final mediation procedure than as a formal method of investigating and reporting the facts.

With this interesting record, it is unfortunate that New York State chose to interfere in the Long Island Railroad case in the summer of 1960, for this intervention raised the question of jurisdiction in a manner which may imperil the future usefulness of the New York procedure. Under long-standing federal law, all railroads are within the sole jurisdiction of the Railway Labor

TABLE 3
FACT-FINDING IN NEW YORK, 1937–1962

Company	Union	Year	Issues	Settlement
Brooklyn Daily Eagle	Newspaper Guild, CIO	1937	Wages and Conditions	Member of Board of Mediation designated as chairman of panel but acted as mediator and settled case
Ludwig Bauman & Co. Furniture retailers	Teamsters, AFL Building Service Employees and Furniture Workers, CIO	1937	Jurisdictional and/or representation disputes	Furniture workers backed down after strike over validity of arbitration award which fact-finding board sustained.
F. W. Woolworth & Co. (124 stores)	United Retail and Wholesale Workers, CIO	1938	Wages and benefits	Fact finders mediated dispute and helped to provide data for settlement.
Woodlawn Cemetery	United Cemetery Workers, CIO	1938	Validity of contract	First case in which a tripartite board was appointed; labor member mediated case by getting union to recognize validity of contract.
Bell Aircraft Corp.	United Automobile Workers	1949	Long strike. Back to work movement. Contract renewal.	First board of inquiry under 1941 law mediated agreement which called for arbitration of some issues, negotiation of others.
Realty Advisory Board	Building Service Employees Union	1950	Wages and conditions	Parties agreed to a voluntary fact-finding panel to end strike. Report of panel accepted.
Yonkers Bus Co.	Transport Workers Union	1950	Wages and conditions	Tripartite fact-finding board set up on urging of chairman of State Mediation Board. Board report not unanimous. Strike continued and was settled by mediation later on somewhat different terms than proposed by fact finders.

TABLE 3 (Continued)

FACT-FINDING IN NEW YORK, 1937–1962

Company	Union	Year	Issues	Settlement
New York Shipping Association	International Longshoremen's Ass'n.	1951	Rejection of new contract by some locals who staged wildcat strike	ILA wanted President to set up emergency board but was refused. Then New York State intervened and a board of inquiry was appointed. Board mediated between factions to get strike over. Then heard case and issued long report on longshore conditions.
Rochester Transportation Co.	Amalgamated Ass'n. Street Electric & Motor Coach Employees	1952	Wages and conditions	Dispute settled on basis of board report.
Milk Companies	Teamsters	1957	Wages and conditions	Dispute settled same day board of inquiry appointed.
Long Island Railroad Co.	Brotherhood of Railroad Trainmen	1960	Hours	Board of inquiry appointed after emergency board under Railway Labor Act had reported and union struck rather than accept recommendations. Strike finally settled in Governor's office after many officials "got into act" over one month period.

Source: Arthur Stark, "Fact Finding in Labor Disputes," *Labor Law Journal*, Vol. III, December 1952, pp. 859–868; and files of New York State Board of Mediation.

Act. An emergency board had reported on this dispute, after which the Brotherhood of Railroad Trainmen had rejected the report and had instituted a strike which closed the railroad. The strike had been in effect for several weeks with resulting inconvenience but with surprisingly little serious difficulty for the thousands of commuters who seemed somehow to reach their jobs by other means of transportation.

As a tactic, the National Mediation Board announced it was discontinuing its efforts to try to settle the strike, undoubtedly in the hope that this would help bring the parties to agreement. Instead, New York State leaped into the fray; the Board of Mediation entered the case and, on the same day, certified that it could not settle the dispute by mediation. The State Industrial Commissioner then appointed a board of inquiry.

Quite likely, either the railroad or the union could have obtained an injunction precluding the state from proceeding with its inquiry.[17] Instead, they both attempted to cooperate with the state as well as with the federal government. The latter promptly reentered the dispute, in which it had never really released, and actually could not release, jurisdiction. The state fact finders issued a quick report and recommendation which was promptly turned down by the union membership.

As A. H. Raskin of the *New York Times* pointed out in a cogent analysis that this competitive fact-finding served to hinder rather than help settle the dispute:

In the eight months since the controversy over a shorter workweek began, everyone from President Eisenhower to the Supervisor of the Town of Babylon has tried his hand at settling it. The overlapping peace efforts are suspected of having been a major factor in fortifying the "all-for-nothing" position taken by the two Long Island lodges of the Brotherhood of Railroad Trainmen.

The union based its strategy on an expectation that one politician or another among those who moved into the picture would put sufficient heat on the railroad to force a quick capitulation. However, the relative ease with which subways, buses and car pools swallowed up the displaced commuters was credited with causing a falling-off in the anxiety felt by state, city, and county officials. . . .

The lack of liaison among the would-be peacemakers proved particularly costly in the make-or-break developments of the last two weeks. And the man both sides considered best qualified to effect an accord [the Chairman of the National Mediation Board] found himself repeatedly pushed off-stage by Governor Rockefeller and other officials.[18]

INVESTIGATION AND ASSIGNMENT OF RESPONSBILITY IN MASSACHUSETTS

Massachusetts typifies a special type of fact-finding. When mediation fails and the parties cannot agree on other means of settlement, the mediation agency may make an investigation and may publish a report assigning the blame or the responsibility for the existence or the continuance of the controversy. The theory is that either the threat of such public censure or such censure itself by a governmental agency will have the effect of inducing a recalcitrant party to move toward settlement. The results do not seem to bear out the theory.

Public opinion to influence a settlement is difficult to mold. Experience under the Railway Labor Act, the Taft-Hartley Act, and various state laws would seem to indicate that unless the public is made to feel directly and dramatically involved, appeals to "public opinion" are not likely to produce results. Moreover, frequent use, or use for minor disputes, soon causes the public to lose interest and to regard the whole procedure as commonplace even when a major dispute does occur.

The following is a typical Massachusetts assignment of responsibility notice:

> After a thorough investigation, followed by a public hearing at the Town Hall in Clinton . . . for the purpose of determining which party is to blame for the continuance of the strike at the Colonial Press, Inc., and after listening for three hours to testimony from all persons desiring to be heard, and carefully weighing every bit of evidence that could be deduced from that testimony together with the facts established by our investigation, the Board is forced to place the blame on the Colonial Press, Inc.[19]

It would seem too much to expect the public to become excited over a pronouncement of this character, which tells nothing of the history, the issues, or even the parties involved. As an opinion mobilizer, such an investigation notice is not likely to have much effect.

In addition to its failure to mobilize public opinion effectively in favor of dispute settlement, the administration of the Massachusetts law has raised considerable question as to the general appropriateness of an investigation provision. For by its very nature, such investigation demands a very high measure of *expertise* and impartiality. To assess responsibility for the continuance of a strike demands that one make a value judgment on a very great number of issues where there is no question of right or wrong, but rather the question of whose views shall prevail.

For example, if the union desires to limit the employer's right to subcontract work and the employer feels that to yield would threaten the profit margin he regards as necessary to operate the business, the fact that other labor agreements in the area may or may not have a provision on this subject is a bench mark but no criterion on which one can "blame" either party for not yielding. There are hundreds of such issues involved in labor negotiations. And neither the Massachusetts Board of Arbitration and Conciliation nor any other agency or person has ever defined a "fair wage" satisfactorily to a party who desired to disagree.

The fact of the matter is that investigation and assignment of responsibility open the door to all sorts of partiality and political pressure and chicanery. To avoid such abuse, appointments to an agency of the highest caliber and professionalism are obviously required. Whether Massachusetts meets this qualification is debatable. As a tripartite agency, the Massachusetts Board is composed of a majority of partisans, each of whom is very unlikely to blame the group he represents for the continuance of a dispute. Consequently, assignment of responsibility has become a matter of pressure on the chairman, with the merits of the case subordinated to union, management, and political pressures. Moreover, the appointment of a number of political personages, not necessarily skilled in industrial relations, to the Massachusetts Board in recent years has not generated confidence in its decisions. In any case, a recent court decision will probably have the effect of doing away with the use of the investigation function of the Massachusetts and similar state laws, except in purely local situations.[20]

MEDIATION PANELS IN NORTH DAKOTA— PRIVATE AND PUBLIC

In 1953, North Dakota adopted a law providing for investigation of labor disputes by the Head of the Labor Division of the Department of Agriculture and Labor. Such investigation usually involves an attempt to mediate the dispute. If mediation fails, the Head of the Labor Division may certify the cases to the Governor for the appointment of a panel to mediate such disputes, or otherwise attempt to resolve them.

The Governor's mediation panels handled approximately fifteen disputes between 1953 and 1960, most of which involved small intrastate situations.[21] In such situations, fact-finding is actually an adjunct of mediation. The mediation panels supplement the Labor Division Head who is the one-man state mediation staff. They perform further mediation work when he feels unable to effectuate a settlement. Whether parties will "save something" for panel mediators and thus render ordinary mediation ineffective remains to be seen.

North Dakota's law also applies to all public employment under state jurisdiction, including municipal employment. It provides for the appointment of tripartite "mediation boards," whose job it is to find facts and make recommendations for the settlement of such disputes. The law also contains a strong prohibition against public administrators' interfering with the right of employees to organize and to bargain collectively. This portion of the law does not appear to have been invoked much, if at all.

FACT-FINDING IN MICHIGAN:
HOSPITALS AND PUBLIC EMPLOYMENT

In both the hospital and the public employment fields, Michigan has had the most extensive fact-finding experience. Procedures to handle disputes in both these areas have been largely ignored by both the federal and state governments until recently. Hospital employee relations have been especially unattended. Section (2) of the Taft-Hartley Act specifically excludes from its jurisdiction non-profit hospitals. In its decisions, the National Labor Relations Board has declined jurisdiction over proprietary hospitals unless they are vital to national defense, located in the District of Columbia where the NLRB acts as a local agency, or operated in connection with an interstate business.[22] And, of course, government-owned hospitals are excluded from NLRB coverage by the general exclusion of all government employment from the act.

Michigan is one of the four states[23] to step actively into this vacuum, which with the growth of hospital care has become a significant part of our economy, with 6,786 hospitals controlling $15 billion in assets and employing 1,460,000 persons.[24] Under the Michigan statute, non-governmental controlled hospitals are handled under one procedure; state-or municipal-owned hospitals under another. Federally operated hospitals are, of course, outside the pale of the Michigan law.

Insofar as non-governmental hospitals are concerned, the Michigan law establishes a Railway Labor Act—like procedure which requires prior notice of proposed contract changes or threatened strikes, urges the parties to settle disputes by bargaining, provides for mediation by the Michigan Labor Mediation Board or its staff where bargaining does not succeed, and directs that the mediators must urge arbitration if the dispute is not settled by mediation. If either party refuses arbitration, the Michigan Board so reports to the Governor who is required to set up a fact-finding commission composed of three public representatives and the parties may each add a non-voting member. No strikes or lockouts are permitted until thirty days after the report and recommendations of the commission.

Table 4 shows that the number of Michigan fact-finding com-

TABLE 4

FACT-FINDING IN MICHIGAN, 1956–1961

Year	Public Employees Fact-finding Reports	Hospital Employee, Governor's Commission Reports and Recommendations
1956.........	4	
1957.........	0	
1958.........	3	1
1959.........	3	2
1960.........	11	3
1961.........	17	6
1962.........	10	5

Source: Michigan Labor Mediation Board.

missions appointed in hospital cases has risen since 1958. This trend may well continue because hospital employees remain one of the largest and lowest paid groups in the country among which union organization is slight.[25] Moreover, Michigan fact-finding commissions for hospital cases are likely to increase in number because, if the hospital does not consent to a representation election, the only way a union of hospital employees in Michigan may achieve legal recognition as bargaining agent is to threaten to strike, achieve through this means the appointment of a fact-finding commission, and then if the hospital refuses a representation election, again threaten to strike. At this point, the Michigan Board must take a strike vote which the Michigan courts have construed as a representation election also because the issue on the ballot is stated in terms of desiring a strike because of the hospital's refusal to recognize the union.[26]

Where state or municipally owned hospitals are concerned, the procedure in Michigan follows the one generally applicable to state employee relations. The Hutchinson Act of Michigan of 1947 strictly forbids work stoppages for employees of the state or its subdivisions, but provides a means whereby such employees may secure mediation or fact-finding of their disputes. Moreover, if the majority of the groups of state government employees petition the Michigan Labor Mediation Board to mediate their grievances, the public employer must attend the mediation hearing and must discuss the issues with the employees or their representative. The employee representative is, of course, usually a union. The public body, as the employer, need not sign a union contract, although some have done so. Typically, the public body issues a statement embodying the results of the discussion with the union and/or employees.[27]

In 1954, the Michigan Labor Mediation Act was amended to provide a fact-finding procedure for government employees. When mediation fails to resolve a dispute, either the public body or the employees may petition the Labor Mediation Board for fact-finding. The Board may then require the parties to present their case to one of its hearing officers in a formal hearing. The hearing officer's report goes to the parties and to the Labor Mediation Board. The parties then have ten days to file written comments with the Board, which reviews the entire record and issues findings of fact and recommendations. Although such recommendations are not binding, and although the union cannot strike, the employer is usually a municipal public body advised by a state agency as to what it should do to settle its labor problem. The experience has been that such recommendations are persuasive.

Since 1956 an amendment provides that public-employee disputes may go to tripartite mediation panels instead of to the more formal hearing officer system. This procedure, however, requires prior agreement of the public employer and this has not been usual.

Table 4 shows a marked increase in Michigan fact-finding reports involving public employees commencing in 1960. The financial crisis in Michigan has perhaps made the settlement of such disputes difficult, but by providing a reasonable method of settlement Michigan has undoubtedly eased a difficult period. It remains to be seen whether fact-finding in Michigan will assist hospitals, public bodies, and their employees to settle disputes, or whether it will become the method of settlement. If the latter turns out to be the case, would the finality of arbitration be preferable?

CONSTITUTIONAL ISSUES

In 1951 the United States Supreme Court ruled that the Wisconsin Public Utility Arbitration Act was inoperative in interstate commerce because the Congress, through the Taft-Hartley Act, had preempted the field.[28] In two significant judicial decisions, as well as in an opinion of the Attorney General of the United States, this same reasoning has been applied to state fact-finding legislation.

On the basis of the Wisconsin decision, the Attorney General of the United States ruled in 1952 that Hawaii, then a territory, could not apply its public utility fact-finding law in industries covered by the Taft-Hartley Act.

Then, in a significant case, the Michigan Labor Mediation Board was enjoined from asserting fact-finding jurisdiction over state public utility businesses which are within the jurisdiction of the Taft-Hartley Act. A federal district court ruled that the fact-finding function of the Michigan Board was the same as the Wisconsin arbitration procedure except that the results were not binding; that a utility would be subject to considerable pressure to settle on the basis of a fact-finding report, but that under federal law, it was entitled to a settlement after "free and unfettered collective bargaining." Hence the conflict between state and federal provisions ruled out jurisdiction of the state.[29] The case was not appealed, and henceforth Michigan confined its fact-finding activities to areas outside the purview of Taft-Hartley, that is in hospitals and state and municipal employment.

A similar federal-state conflict caused the Massachusetts investigation law to be enjoined from applying to activity in interstate commerce. This case involved an action in 1960 by the then Governor of Massachusetts, who at the request of the American Federation of Technical Employees, asked the Massachusetts Board of Conciliation and Arbitration to investigate a dispute between this union and the General Electric Company's Lynn, Mass., plant and to assess responsibility for its continuance. General Electric appealed to the courts, which found a clear federal-state conflict. Said the court of appeals, first circuit:

> The obvious statutory purpose is to coerce agreement by invoking official action to mold public opinion with respect to a labor dispute to the end of bringing the pressure of public opinion to bear to force a settlement. This is quite contrary to the national policy not to compel agreement but instead only to encourage voluntary agreements, freely arrived at after "good faith" bargaining between the parties. The conflict between state and federal policy is obvious.[30]

On June 10, 1963, the Supreme Court invalidated Missouri's "King-Thompson Act," which, as noted in Table 1, provides for a fact-finding procedure involving public utilities, and then permits the state to seize the utility if the Governor believes that the dispute will tend to create an emergency. The court found that the seizure was merely of token variety and that the net effect was to deprive public utilities employees of the right to strike which was guaranteed by the Taft-Hartley Act.

The net effect of the decision is to narrow once more the area of allowable state action in public interest disputes. This would seem to indicate that the already cited lower court decisions invalidating state fact-finding legislation in jurisdictions covered by the Taft-Hartley Act would probably find a favorable reception in the United States Supreme Court.[31]

It would thus appear that unless Congress enacts enabling legislation, or unless the above cases are reversed, state experimentation in fact-finding must be confined to local disputes or to special areas such as hospital or government employment. This appears unfortunate.

CONCLUDING EVALUATION

State experience in fact-finding legislation adds considerably to our knowledge of this technique. The value, first of all, appears greatest where its use is most limited. When it becomes commonplace, as it was at first used in Minnesota, it is more crisis-creating than crisis-solving, for the knowledge that a fact-finding board will be named is an invitation to refuse to settle, or even to bargain, until after the fact-finding report has been made. It is so much easier to refuse to settle if the result of such refusal is not a strike but only the appointment of a fact-finding board. Then a dissatisfied or aggressive party can use the fact finder's report as a springboard for more. Fact-finding, under such circumstances, may actually be of negative value, for it can induce crises, instead of avoiding them.

On the other hand, if the administrators use restraint, fact-finding can be a useful tool when parties are looking for a means of restoring their relationships. Usually this is where a strike has occurred and the will to settle is present, but mediation has been unable to find the mechanism for settlement. Here, fact-finding, adroitly handled, can provide the means, the face saving, or the persuasion to end a dispute. But here again, too much use can perpetuate strikes by calling for fact-finding when its utility is questionable. With headlines screaming and inconveniences irritating the public, such calls are difficult to resist. Yet, diminishing returns set in fast. A governor or administrator who automatically pushes the panic button or who yields to every pressure to appoint fact finders is likely to find that he has created a monster which in time will bring him more headaches than glory.

Where fact-finding is used, as in North Dakota, merely as additional mediation, it has merit because it provides staff help to situations where mediation facilities are in relatively short supply. On the other hand, too great a dependence on panels of this sort for mediation can make the regular mediator's job pro forma, with the parties holding back for settlement until the final mediators have an opportunity to hold their sessions. As in more traditional fact-finding situations, this type of fact-finding, if overutilized, may induce one party to refuse to reduce its demands in the hope of obtaining more—and without fear of losing anything—and another to refuse to grant minor concessions in order to save something for the final mediators or fact finders. The cumulative effects of these attitudes can soon make a mockery of collective bargaining.

Perhaps a cardinal weakness of fact-finding is that the facts are rarely in doubt. The parties are usually reasonably aware of the issues, but their interpretations and their ideas concerning the effects of these facts on the future are not only likely to be divergent but also not subject to a factual test. To assume that the facts of a case, if known, will settle a dispute is quite naïve. Pressure and mediation are more likely the ingredients for obtaining settlement, especially if used at the right time and place, by the right person in the right way. This is why mediation by fact finders is often the most effective use of the fact-finding technique.

It would seem that the shortcomings of competitive fact-finding boards and of investigating in order to cast blame are too obvious to require additional comment. Constitutional restrictions have apparently solved these problems where administrative overeagerness, glory hunting, or political manipulation replaced reasonable restraint and concern. On the other hand, constitutional restrictions now limit valuable experimentation to a degree which appears undesirable.

The activity of the Michigan Labor Mediation Board in the hospital and public employee field is likely to increase because unions in these areas either are too weak or are under such legal restraint as to render them dependent upon government machinery for growth or even existence. To what extent the government should foster union growth in these areas remains an unanswered question, which, in turn, begs the question of the extent to which fact-finding in Michigan does aid union growth. Certainly, it does seem that if strikes are banned, as they are by Michigan's Hutchinson Act for public employees, or if at least emotionally they are almost intolerable, as they are in hospitals, a substitute method of settling disputes is appropriate. In these situations, collective bargaining may become, as it often does, seriously inhibited by the existence of the governmental fact-finding machinery. In such instances, however, there is no reason why we should expect the parties, who in practical terms do not have the rights of private parties, to act as we expect labor and management in private industry to behave. In short, the differences of public and hospital employment from private employment may be such that collective bargaining, as we know it in private industry, cannot work in the hospital and public field, anyway. Therefore, the Michigan experience is likely to prove both interesting and helpful.

NOTES

1. See, e.g., H. R. Northrup and G. F. Bloom, *Government and Labor* (Homewood: Richard D. Irwin, 1963), Chap. 12; David Levinson, "The Railway Labor Act—The Record of a Decade," *Labor Law Journal*, Vol. 3, January 1952, pp. 13-29; J. J. Kaufman, "Emergency Boards under the Railway Labor Act," *Labor Law Journal*, Vol. 9, December 1958, pp. 910-920, 949; and Herbert R. Northrup, "The Railway Labor Act and Railway Labor Disputes in Wartime," *American Economic Review*, Vol. 36, June 1946, pp. 324-343.

2. California, Department of Industrial Relations, *Third Annual Report of the Conciliation Service*, 1950, p. 5.

3. See below, pp. 288-289 for a discussion of the problem of constitutionality.

4. C. E. Warne and M. E. Gaddis, "Eleven Years of Compulsory Investigation of Industrial Disputes in Colorado," *Journal of Political Economy*, Vol. 35, October 1927, pp. 657-683.

5. See H. S. Kaltenborn, *Governmental Adjustment of Labor Disputes* (Chicago: The Foundation Press, 1943), pp. 193-196; and B. M. Stewart and W. J. Couper, *Fact Finding in Industrial Disputes* (New York: Industrial Relations Counselors, Inc., 1946), pp. 21-23.

6. *Sixteenth Report of the Industrial Commission of Colorado*, 1938-1940, p. 13.

7. These statements are based on a careful analysis of the biennial reports of the Colorado Industrial Commission between 1936 and 1960. This analysis is also confirmed by H. Seligson and G. Bardwell, *Labor-Management Relations in Colorado* (Denver: Alan Swallow, 1961) who report "one of the functions of the Commission is to engage in preventive investigation and mediation; little of this has been done, although the 1915 law creating the Commission emphasized this function," p. 151. My analysis of the commission's records does, however, find support for more mediation and unfair labor practice activity on the part of the commission than did these authors.

8. For a discussion of this arbitration law, see H. R. Northrup and Richard L. Rowan, "Arbitration and Collective Bargaining: An Analysis of State Experience," *Labor Law Journal*, Vol. 14, February 1963, pp. 184, 189. [Appendix A]

9. *Automobile Workers v. Finklenburg*, 53 N. W. 2d 128 (1952).

10. J. W. Stieber, *Ten Years of the Minnesota Labor Relations Act* (Minneapolis: University of Minnesota Press, 1949), p. 23.

11. *Ibid.*, pp. 22-23.

12. State of Minnesota, Division of Conciliation, *Annual Report, 1949-1950*, p. 9.

13. *Ibid.*, 1950-1951, p. 27.

14. Stieber, *op. cit.*, pp. 17-23.

15. For a different view of the Minnesota law and its alleged effectiveness, see Joseph Lazar, "Tripartitism in Minnesota," *Industrial Relations*, February 1963, pp. 119-126; and for a criticism of Professor Lazar's view, see this writer's comment, *ibid.*, October 1963.

16. For a good discussion of fact-finding in New York State, see Arthur Stark, "Fact-finding in Labor Disputes," *Labor Law Journal*, Vol. 3, December 1952, pp. 859-871. Acknowledgment should also be made to Mr. Eric Schmertz, former member of the New York State Board of Mediation, for helpful information.

17. For a discussion of this constitutional question, see below.

18. *New York Times*, July 19, 1960.

19. Quoted by Kaltenborn, *op. cit.*, p. 191.

20. See below, for a discussion of this decision.

21. North Dakota State Department of Agriculture and Labor, *Biennial Reports of the Deputy (Labor) Commissioner*, 1952-1960. Since 1962, the Labor Division has been made a separate department, and the fact-finding provisions are administered by a Labor Department Commissioner.

22. A discussion of the jurisdiction question is found in the excellent article by Hyman Parker, "The Laws Governing Labor-Management Relations in Michigan Hospitals," *Labor Law Journal*, Vol. 12, October 1961, pp. 974-975.

23. Minnesota, as noted, provides for a compulsory arbitration procedure for hospitals. In 1963 New York adopted compulsory arbitration for hospitals located in New York City only. In 1961 Oregon established a mediation and fact-finding procedure applying to "licensed professional and practical nurses employed in health care facilities." Recently several states have enacted such laws.

24. Parker, *op. cit.*, pp. 972-973.

25. Probably less than 5 percent of the hospitals have union contracts according to a 1960 survey of the American Hospital Association. Parker, *op. cit.*, p. 973.

26. *SCME, Local 1644 v. Oakwood Hospital*, Wayne County Circuit Court, Michigan 1960, Cited in Parker, *op. cit.*, pp. 982-986. Parker's article contains a good account of this case and others involving hospitals under the Michigan law.

27. See Hyman Parker, "The Role of the Michigan Labor Mediation Board in Public Employee Labor Disputes," *Labor Law Journal*, Vol. 10, September 1959, pp. 633-642.

28. *Amalgamated Association v. Wisconsin Employment Relations Board*, 340 U. S. 383 (1951).

29. *Grand Rapids City Coach Lines v. Howlett*, 137 F. Supp. 667 (1956).

30. *General Electric Company v. Callahan*, 294 F. 2d 60 (1962). [See also *Oil, Chemical and Atomic Workers v. Arkansas Louisiana Gas Co.*, 320 b (2d) 62 (1964) for a similar case involving the Oklahoma law.]

31. *Division 1287 of the Amalgamated Association of Street, Electric Railway and Motor Coach Employees of America v. State of Missouri*, 374 U. S. 74 (1963), reversing Missouri Supreme Court 361 S.W. 2d 33 (1963).

D Strike Notice and
Strike Vote Legislation*

HERBERT R. NORTHRUP
AND GORDON F. BLOOM

Strike Notices and Votes

A NUMBER OF STATES have laws
on their books which require notice of an intent to strike in industry generally or in specific industries, such as those "affected
with a public interest" or those which would affect the survival of
an agricultural crop.[1] The objective is to permit the parties to
"cool off" before overt action is taken. The theory is that if a
notice is given, ample opportunity for collective bargaining or
government intervention will occur, and therefore strikes will be
prevented.

In practice, however, things have not worked out this way.
The most important reason is that the strike notice, like the Taft-
Hartley notice of failure to reach agreement, becomes either a
perfunctory gesture or an integral part of the bargaining proc-

* From Herbert R. Northrup and Gordon F. Bloom, *Government and
Labor* (Homewood: Richard D. Irwin, Inc., 1963), Chapter 14, by permission of the publisher and courtesy of the co-author.

ess. The notice is usually given automatically by the unions so as to insure the legality of any action if a strike does occur and, in addition, to increase the union's bargaining power. The union then enters negotiations with the legal technicalities cleared, and with the threat hanging over the employer's head that a strike will take place if a satisfactory agreement is not reached. Failure to give that notice before negotiations would, most union leaders believe, be looked upon as a sign of weakness. There seems to be no relation between the number of strikes and the existence, or lack thereof, of strike notice provisions.[2]

These laws were never strictly enforced, except possibly in Wisconsin, where failure to give notice is an unfair labor practice.[3] Since the passage of the Taft-Hartley Act in 1947, notices required by it, which must also be sent to state mediation services, have supplanted state requirement, except in purely intrastate commerce; but in any case, such notices also satisfy state requirements, so that state laws are largely dormant.

Strike Votes

Florida, Kansas, Michigan, Minnesota, Missouri, Utah, and Wisconsin,[4] as well as the federal government during the latter part of World War II, have enacted legislation requiring a vote of the membership before a legal strike could occur. The Minnesota law, for example, required the union to take the vote by secret ballot at a meeting after reasonable notice of time and place had been given to affected employees. The Michigan and Missouri laws were more stringent. Both required an affirmative majority of those in the bargaining unit to authorize a strike—which means that those not voting were counted against striking. Michigan modified its law in 1949 to permit strikes if a majority of those voting approved. Both Michigan and Missouri required state agencies to conduct the strike votes.

Whether a government agency or the union itself has conducted the strike votes, the results appear to be the same—an overwhelming vote in favor of a strike. The reason is that the vote becomes one of confidence in the union and of support for the pressure which the union may apply to the employer, who now sees evidence that employees are ready and willing to back up the union demands by walking out. The fact that few actual strikes occur despite the great number of votes in favor of strikes is further proof that these strike vote laws become bargaining tactics, not strike controls.

In Minnesota the law never had a significant effect. The strike vote was usually the most perfunctory procedure conducted by the union and was challenged by the employers only rarely.[5] Likewise, in Florida and Kansas the law does not seem to have been of much significance.[6]

Table 1 shows the experience under the Missouri law from its enactment in 1947 till its repeal two years later; Table 2 summarizes the Michigan experience; and Table 3 describes the wartime experience of the federal government in taking strike votes. Even in wartime, employees voted "to interrupt war production" in more than 80 percent of the cases, knowing full well that the chances of an actual strike occurring were very limited, but that to vote against it would lessen their opportunities for economic gain.[7]

TABLE 1

EXPERIENCE UNDER THE MISSOURI STRIKE VOTE LAW,
APRIL 12, 1948—OCTOBER 14, 1949

Strike Votes		Strikes Authorized				Actual Work Stoppages	
				Employees Voting to Strike			
Number of Elections	Number of Employees Voting	Number	Per Cent	Number	Per Cent	Number	Percentage of Authorized Strikes
475.......	49,680	407	85.7	44,144	88.9	20	4.9

SOURCE: National Industrial Conference Board.

In 1950 the United States Supreme Court ruled that state strike vote laws were inoperative in interstate commerce because they conflicted with the notice requirements of the Taft-Hartley Act.[8] The confinement of Michigan votes to intrastate commerce accounts for the sharp drop in votes and voters after 1950, as noted in Table 2.

The Wisconsin and Utah laws remain on the books because they do not forbid strikes, but prohibit picketing, boycotts, and similar secondary support of strikers where the strike is not authorized by a majority of employees in the bargaining unit voting by secret ballot. This restriction has been used to enjoin

TABLE 2

RESULTS OF STRIKE VOTES CONDUCTED BY MICHIGAN LABOR
MEDIATION BOARD, 1947–54*

	November, 1947–June, 1950	July, 1950–June, 1954	Total, November, 1947–June, 1954
Number of Elections:	409	138	547
For strike............	358	89	447
Against strike........	47	49	96
Tie.................	4	0	4
Percentage of Elections:			
For strike............	87.5	64.5	81.7
Against strike........	11.5	35.5	17.6
Tie.................	1.0	...	0.7
Number of Workers:			
Eligible to vote.......	275,225	6,557	281,782
Voting...............	226,389	5,734	232,123
For strike..........	189,906	3,181	193,087
Against strike......	34,730	2,337	37,067
Spoiled or challenged ballots...........	1,753	216	1,969
Percentage of:			
Eligible workers voting	82.3	87.4	82.4
Voters favoring strike..	83.9	55.5	83.2
Eligible workers voting strike.............	69.0	48.5	68.5

* Between July, 1954, and June, 1961, 244 strike votes were held in Michigan, in 133 of which the employees voted to strike. The Michigan Labor Mediation Board, which supplied these data, advised that it does not have readily available the number of employees involved.

SOURCE: Adapted from data provided by the Michigan Labor Mediation Board by Herbert S. Parnes, *Union Strike Votes: Current Practice and Proposed Controls* (Princeton: Princeton University, Industrial Relations Section, 1956), p. 125.

TABLE 3

RESULTS OF POLLS UNDER THE WAR LABOR DISPUTES ACT, 1943–45

	Number	Per Cent
Total number of polls*..................	2,168	100
Voted in favor of interruption of work....	1,850	85.3
Voted against interruption of work†......	318	14.7
Total number eligible to vote..............	2,923,655	...
Total valid votes cast....................	1,926,811	100
Votes in favor of interruption of work....	1,593,937	82.7
Votes against interruption of work.......	332,874	17.3
Number of employers involved............	26,630	...

* Polls were conducted in 1,571 separate cases, but involving 2,168 separate voting units.
† Includes 59 polls in which no votes were cast and 28 polls which resulted in a tie vote.
SOURCE: National Labor Relations Board, *Eleventh Annual Report* (Washington, D. C.: U.S. Government Printing Office, 1946), p. 91.

"quickie" stoppages by a majority, as well as picketing in support of strikes not authorized by a majority.[9]

In the main, however, strike vote laws remain inoperative. How to require that so serious a matter as a strike be passed upon by the majority of those affected in a democratic manner without having the process degenerate into a perfunctory bargaining tactic remains an unsolved problem of public policy.

NOTES

1. Colorado, Georgia, Hawaii, Michigan, Minnesota, and Wisconsin.

2. See, for example, the comparison of the Minnesota and Michigan records, and discussion relating thereto, in B. M. Stewart and W. J. Couper, *Fact Finding in Industrial Disputes* (New York: Industrial Relations Counselors, Inc., 1946), pp. 33-35.

3. But apparently no case has been adjudicated under this provision. See Justin C. Smith, "Unfair Labor Practices in Wisconsin," *Marquette Law Review*, Vol. XLV (Fall, 1961), p. 247.

4. Alabama, Colorado, Delaware, Hawaii, North Dakota, and Oregon also enacted such laws, but they were either repealed or declared invalid before becoming effectively operative.

5. Herbert S. Parnes, *Union Strike Votes: Current Practice and Proposed Controls* (Princeton: Princeton University, Industrial Relations Section, 1956), pp. 126-129.

6. *Ibid.*, pp. 129-133.

7. Almost the only occasion where employees have failed to give their union a "bargaining club" by voting to strike has been where the employer has a reputation for sticking closely to his position, even if a strike occurs, and where in addition the employer vigorously communicates his position to the employees. This, of course, is the situation in the General Electric Company.

8. *International Union v. O'Brien*, 339 U. S. 454 (1950). Minnesota's courts similarly restricted the Minnesota Act (*Automobile Workers v. Finklenburg*, 53 N.W. [2d] 128 [1952]), and it was then repealed.

9. *International Union v. Wisconsin Employment Relations Board*, 27 N.W. (2d) 875 (1947); affirmed, 336 U. S. 245 (1947). For a discussion of this approach, see Parnes, *op. cit.*, pp. 113-121, 129-130; and Smith, *op. cit.*, pp. 245-248.

E Grievance Machinery
and
Strikes in Australia*

JAMES W. KUHN**

IN THIS *Review* three years ago,
Arthur Ross and Donald Irwin presented an analysis in interpretation of twenty-one years of strike experience in five countries.[1] The
statistics with which they had to work were aggregates which
averaged together strikes of varying duration and extent and of
different industries and unions. Such aggregate figures can hide
important differences in the kinds of strikes that occur and mask
secular changes in the type of strikes conducted by unions.

American and Australian data covering twelve years, 1941–
1952, have become available and allow more detailed and revealing analysis. We can compare the relative importance in the
two countries of strikes of one day, one week and longer than
one day, and of those longer than a week.

* Reprinted by permission from the *Industrial and Labor Relations Review*, Vol. VIII, No. 2, January 1955.
** Associate Professor, Graduate School of Business, Columbia University.

As measures of the relative importance of the strikes, we use the number of workers engaged in the strikes of different duration as a percentage of the nonagricultural employees and also of union membership. These two measures provide a common relative basis for comparing strikes in the two nations whose labor force and union membership differ so greatly in size. Two measures are presented because neither of the bases is strictly comparable between the two countries.

Between the two countries, there is a considerable difference in the degree of union organization. Among the nonagricultural employees, it is nearly 57 percent in Australia and only about 33 percent in the United States. Australia also has relatively a somewhat larger number of workers in coal mining, the railway services, maritime transportation, and wharf employment. In spite of the differences in the two labor forces and union organization, a comparison of the strike data does give some indication of the outstanding characteristics of strikes in the two countries.

During the period of analysis both countries enjoyed substantially full employment and a considerable measure of inflation in the postwar years. Unions increased their membership in both countries; in Australia by about 50 percent and in the United States by over 60 percent.

STRIKE PARTICIPATION AND DURATION

The most striking feature revealed by our measures of strikes (Tables I and II) is the very much greater participation of Australian workers in short strikes. On the average, over eight times as many Australian workers, as a percentage of union membership, have been involved in strikes of one day or less. On the basis of nonagricultural employees, the Australian participation rate is nearly sixteen times that of the United States. Another noticeable difference between the countries is the greater relative number of American workers who have engaged in the longer strikes, over one week. On the average, the relative number of American workers in the long strikes is two and a half that of the Australian average on the membership base, and not quite one and a half as large on the employee base. The differences in the relative number of workers involved in strikes of over one day but not greater than one week are not as great, but the

Australian average on either base is larger. The short strikes of one day and less include so large a proportion of Australian workers that the ratios of all strikers to union membership or nonagricultural employees are greater than those of the United States, even though a larger share of American workers are involved in strikes longer than one week.

The aggregate data of both countries suggest that for many years strikes in Australia have been short in duration, but that worker participation has been more widespread or more frequent than in the United States. Between 1927 and 1940, nearly twice as large a share of Australian workers engaged in strike activity as in the United States, yet only one-half as many working days were lost per worker involved in strikes.[2]

TABLE 1

WORKERS INVOLVED IN STRIKES,*† AUSTRALIA AND THE UNITED STATES, AS A PERCENTAGE OF NONAGRICULTURAL EMPLOYEES, BY DURATION OF STRIKE,‡ 1941–1952§

Year	One Day and Less Australia	U.S.	Over 1 Day but less than 1 Week Australia	U.S.	Over 1 Week Australia	U.S.	All Strikes‖ Australia	U.S.
1941	7.1%	0.7%	2.9%	2.0%	2.9%	3.8%	12.9%	6.5%
1942	5.8	0.4	2.2	1.1	0.9	0.7	8.8	2.1
1943	8.8	0.7	4.4	2.4	2.3	1.6	15.5	4.7
1944	7.7	0.6	4.6	3.1	2.1	1.5	14.4	5.1
1945	7.9	0.6	4.5	3.2	5.5	3.8	17.9	7.7
1946	9.6	0.6	2.7	2.4	4.3	8.9	16.6	11.9
1947	7.4	0.5	5.7	0.8	1.3	3.7	14.4	5.0
1948	7.9	0.3	3.6	0.8	1.8	3.3	13.3	4.4
1949	7.3	0.4	1.9	1.1	1.6	5.6	10.8	7.0
1950	10.5	0.5	3.6	1.6	2.8	3.3	17.0	5.5
1951	10.0	0.5	—	1.7	5.6**	2.6	15.5	4.8
1952	10.1	0.5	—	1.6	9.4**	4.5	19.5	6.6
Average‖	8.3	0.5	3.6	1.8	2.6	3.6	14.7	6.8

* The number of workers involved in strikes includes duplicate counting where the same workers are involved in more than one strike.

† The basic data may not be strictly comparable because of differences in reporting. "Workers involved" in the American data covers all workers made idle for one or more shifts in establishments directly involved in a stoppage. It does not measure the indirect or secondary effects on other establishments whose employees are made idle as a result of material or service shortages. In the Australian data, "workers involved" covers directly and indirectly involved workers in stoppages of one day or less.

‡ The Bureau of Labor Statistics indicates that prior to 1950 there was underreporting of small strikes amounting to 5 percent in 1950 and 10 percent in 1951. The error in our strike classification "one day and less," due to the underreporting, would probably be less than 2 percent. See *Monthly Labor Review*, Vol. 74, No. 5 (May 1952), p. 512.

§ American data figured from series in the Bureau of Labor Statistics, *Handbook of Labor Statistics*, 1950, Bulletin No. 1016; Bureau of Labor Statistics, *Analysis of Work Stoppages*, 1951, Bulletin 1090, and 1952, Bulletin 1136. Australian data calculated from series in Department of Labor, *Labor Bulletins*, and also in Commonwealth Bureau of Census and Statistics, *Labour Reports*.

‖ Totals and averages from original calculations before rounding.

** Data not available for "over one day but less than one week"; figure is for all workers involved in strikes over one day.

TABLE 2

WORKERS INVOLVED IN STRIKES,*† AUSTRALIA AND THE UNITED STATES,
AS A PERCENTAGE OF UNION MEMBERSHIP BY DURATION
OF STRIKE,‡ 1941–1952§

| | One Day and Less | | Over 1 Day but less than 1 Week | | Over 1 Week | | All Strikes‖ | |
Year	Australia	U. S.	Australia	U. S.	Australia	U. S.	Australia	U. S.
1941	12.7%	2.8%	5.1%	6.9%	5.2%	12.8%	23.0%	22.5%
1942	9.3	1.5	3.5	3.9	1.5	2.4	14.3	7.8
1943	14.0	2.2	6.9	7.4	3.6	4.9	24.5	14.5
1944	12.0	1.6	7.2	8.7	3.4	4.1	22.6	14.5
1945	12.5	1.8	7.2	8.6	8.8	13.0	28.5	23.4
1946	16.0	1.8	4.4	6.5	7.2	22.4	27.6	30.7
1947	12.3	1.5	9.5	2.2	2.1	10.3	23.9	14.0
1948	12.9	0.8	5.8	2.4	3.1	9.4	21.8	12.6
1949	11.7	1.0	3.0	3.0	2.7	15.5	17.4	19.5
1950	16.6	1.6	5.8	4.6	4.5	9.3	26.9	15.5
1951	15.3	1.6	—	5.0	8.6**	7.7	23.9	14.3
1952	19.2	1.6	—	5.6	8.6**	15.1	27.8	22.2
Average‖	13.7	1.7	5.8	5.4	4.2	10.6	23.5	17.6

For footnotes, see Table 1.

INSTITUTIONAL NEEDS AND STRIKE ACTIVITY

The strike experience of Australia as revealed by more detailed analysis, however, does not completely fit Ross and Irwin's hypothesis that strikes must be analyzed in terms of the institutional strivings of unions and the personal motives of union leaders. They maintain that the "frequency of strikes between one country and another can best be explained by differences in the position of the union and the union leader." According to them, the needs and grievances of the workingman play a small part in the occurrence of strikes. Nevertheless, their aggregate strike data presented an anomalous relationship in Australia between a high worker participation in strikes and institutional circumstances that, according to the Ross and Irwin hypothesis, should be conducive to a relatively low degree of strike activity.

If we compare the major, over-all institutional framework within which Australian unions function with that in which American unions operate, it would appear that the Australian unions, as organizations, and the Australian labor leaders have much less need or reason for strike activity.

First, Australian unions have enjoyed greater organizational stability for many years than American unions have yet achieved. In Australia, the law demands employer recognition of unions and forbids hostile actions toward unions. Through the arbitration court, the unions enjoy guaranteed jurisdictional rights. Behind the laws and the courts is the influential political power of the Labor party, ready at all times to ward off attacks upon the unions' legal safeguards.

In the United States, unions have had to conduct prolonged strikes, for employers were often aggressively hostile. Unprotected jurisdictional rights of unions, and even unionism, have promoted intense rivalry between unions and union leaders. The stakes have been high in strikes, and union leaders have not given in easily. Strikes are seldom just demonstrations of dissatisfaction. Rather, they are instruments of coercion, wielded with all the effectiveness possible to win union demands.

Second, the Australian unions do not conduct their major contract negotiations directly with the management of a single company but with representatives of a whole industry through the intermediary of abribration officers. This procedure discourages strikes. A long industry-wide strike is expensive and difficult to organize. Furthermore, a strike that shuts down a whole industry is apt to arouse unfavorable public opinion and provide government sanctions against the unions, since according to law the dispute should be settled in the arbitration courts; all strikes, strictly speaking are illegal.

In the United States, industry-wide bargaining is not as widespread as in Australia, and government intervention in bargaining is less frequent. Intervention, if it does occur, usually comes only after a strike is in progress. In the absence of alternative methods of settlement, the fight is carried on to the limit of the strikers' resources.

Third, most of the Australian unions are either an integral part of the Labor party or staunch supporters of it. Strikes, particularly prolonged ones, may interfere with public services and are apt to alienate the middle class of voters. Embarrassing the party thus would jeopardize its legislative program by which the unions have secured many benefits in the past and expect to secure more in the future. Instead of conducting long, costly strikes, the union leadership fights for its demands in the political

sphere. In contrast, the American unions have many fewer political inhibitions and can expect a good deal less from political
action.

Ross and Irwin noticed that the Australian experience appeared
to contradict their hypothesis, and they suggested several reasons
why the incidence of strikes was higher there than expected.
First, there are few centralized national unions in Australia that
might be expected to exert a restraining influence upon the
local sections. Second, the Communists—who have controlled
many of the leading unions—are interested in stirring up industrial unrest and have provoked strikes that would not have
otherwise occurred. Third, the coal mining and maritime industries engage a very large share of the nation's workers,
and industrial troubles have been especially severe in these
sectors in all countries. Fourth, the Australian arbitration system
has weakened collective bargaining, but it does help to settle
disputes quickly.

Except for the last, we find too many shortcomings in these
explanations to accept them. There are few centralized national
unions in Australia, but the unions are not therefore bereft of any
centralized, responsible authority. Union power is concentrated
in the hands of state officials, most of whom are intimately
a part of the Labor party and extremely responsive to political
pressures. For the most part, they desire neither to offend public
opinion and the arbitration courts, nor to embarrass the party
with strikes.

The Communists have made use of every opportunity to promote strikes since the war, but during the war—from mid-1941
on—they were most anxious to keep production going at almost any cost. Communist union officials tried to keep the
workers from striking, but our data show that, except for 1942
when Australia was threatened by invasion, worker participation in strikes during the war was not significantly different
from that of the postwar period. A reading of the Parliamentary
debates will also show that neither the Labor government nor
the union officials—Communist and non-Communist alike—were
able to keep the incidence of strikes down during the war.

Industries, which in every country appear to be centers of
industrial conflict, are prominent in Australia and do contribute

heavily to that country's strike record. If the unexpectedly large worker participation in strikes is to be explained by the position of the coal and maritime industries in the Australian economy, however, one must further explain why the acute labor problems of these industries should appear in Australia so strikingly in the form of short strikes. Moreover, a breakdown of the working days lost per striker indicates that the predominance of strikes of one day and less exists in all industries. The typical length of strikes during the forties for the major industries is given in Table III.

TABLE 3

TYPICAL LENGTH OF STRIKES, SELECTED INDUSTRIES, AUSTRALIA, 1941–1949*

Industry†	Average Days Lost Per Worker Involved
Engineering, metalworks, etc.........	10.4
Food, drink, etc.....................	5.8
Books, printing, etc..................	5.4
Shipping, wharf labour, etc...........	5.4
Building...........................	4.1
Clothing, textiles, etc...............	3.8
Wood, furniture, etc.................	3.0
Coal mining.......................	2.2
Railway and tramway services........	2.0
All industries......................	4.0

* Data calculated from series in *Labour Reports.*
† Industrial classifications are those of the Australian Bureau of Census and Statistics.

The more detailed strike data reveal that the problem is not simply explaining the high incidence of strikes in circumstances that should reduce it, but rather it is explaining the relatively high worker participation in short strikes and the relatively low worker participation in long strikes.

GRIEVANCE PROCEDURE IN AUSTRALIAN INDUSTRY

The Ross and Irwin hypothesis appears to explain the longer strikes of over a week in duration. These are *union* activities, and probably they are carefully organized and directed by the union leaders. As we would expect, given the Australian conditions, the incidence of the long strikes is considerably less than in the United States.

But does the Ross and Irwin hypothesis explain the short

strikes of one day or less? We believe it does not. The ultimate cause of the high rate of these strikes, we believe, is the arbitration system and the unions' political involvement, both of which have weakened the vital day-to-day, local collective bargaining. A discussion of the effects of these institutional arrangements upon union bargaining is outside the scope of this paper. The proximate cause of the short strikes, however, is the unattended grievances of the rank and file, and the spontaneous outbursts that are the workers' reactions against tensions and frustrations on the job.

An analysis of the union workers' shop organization and local methods of settling disputes will show why the Australian workers should have more unattended grievances and unrelieved tensions at their work than the American workers. In this analysis, the federal and state rules of thirty-two Australian unions, with jurisdiction in the major industries, were examined.[3] The unions are, for the most part, the larger ones and account for approximately two thirds of the total Australian union membership. Almost all of the unions provide for union representatives on the job who go under the various names of delegate, collector, or steward. The only unions that do not mention shop representatives in their rules are the postal workers, the storemen and packers, and the coal miners.[4] The primary and most widely recognized duty of the shop representatives, since it appears in all but one union's rules, is to collect dues. Only four unions, the Boilermakers, the Amalgamated and the Society Engineers, and the Gas Workers, charge their shop representatives with the responsibility of trying to settle worker grievances before notifying higher officials.[5]

Three other unions require only that their representatives report all disputes and complaints to the first level of full-time officers, usually the branch secretary. In four other unions, the representatives are asked no more than to report infringements upon standard working conditions, or more vaguely, "to report on all matters affecting the trade." Thus, in our sample of union rules, the role of the shop representatives in two thirds of the unions is limited to that of a dues collector.

The rules of only the four unions mentioned above outline any kind of shop organization and provide for responsible local activity. In all the remaining unions, according to their rules, shop problems are handled at a higher level, and there are no recognized, formal union activities at the place of employment except at the specific direction of the top officers. The general structure of Australian unions, as presented in the rules of the larger organizations, indicates that the focus of union work and interests is in the branch or higher offices and that the problems of members on the job are not, in the first instance, union concerns.

The formal rules of an organization are not necessarily the procedures followed in practice, but there is good reason to believe that in this case they correctly indicate union practice. Researchers of the Department of Labor and National Service, after a study of 181 representative Australian firms varying in size from 50 to 3,000 workers, reported that in general there was very poor development of shop organization in which the workers could responsibly participate and very few effective means whereby the workers could treat local job problems at the place of employment. That there are plenty of local grievances needing attention has been demonstrated in the experience of some firms where management set up shop committees, usually in the face of union indifference. The workers' representatives brought up "an interminable list of petty grievances" and turned the meetings into "petty grievance sessions" although the committees were organized for other functions.[6]

Twenty-six years ago, Carter Goodrich found little rank-and-file organization in the factories and the unions' use of shop stewards less developed than in the United States.[7] In more recent years, other students of the Australian labor scene have noticed that union officials show an indifference toward their members' shop problems and that shop procedures for settling local disputes are redimentary or completely undeveloped.[8] Prominent Labor party representatives who have held high union offices have complained that minor disputes often led to industrial unrest and strikes simply because the workers have no other way of calling attention to their complaints.[9]

The Australian union organization at the place of work and the union services provided for members contrast markedly with those of the United States. An examination of the rules of American unions and collective bargaining agreements will show that the shop organization and the handling of grievances are given major emphasis. In most instances, the bulk of American union business is made up of grievance handling and local bargaining. The union is constantly demonstrating in an immediate fashion its services to the rank and file, and the union leaders are concerned with their members' job problems. Generally throughout American unions, day-to-day adjustment of local and shop problems is the basic work of unions and the foundation for the other union-management relationships.[10] As a result, small disputes arising at the place of work in the United States probably have a better chance for quick, peaceful settlement than in Australia.

GRIEVANCE HANDLING AND STRIKE DURATION

It is a reasonable assumption that petty grievances and local disputes are most likely to lead to short walkouts when they are otherwise untreated or not settled by immediate shop procedures. If workers cannot secure recognition of their job grievances or make demands for remedy of their complaints through regular, peaceful procedures available at the shop level, they would probably demonstrate their dissatisfaction by work stoppages and strikes that would not need to be of long duration. A short strike would serve as a demonstration of the workers' concern and bring the grievance to the attention of the union or of management. If the grievance had been continuing or long standing, the action would also serve to release the workers' pent-up, irritated feelings. For many of the minor grievances and local problems, a short stoppage would apply sufficient pressure on the employer to gain a satisfactory settlement or, at least, to initiate remedial action.

The Australian unions do not provide for the peaceful, regular handling of their members' job problems. The whole system of industrial relations in Australia is based upon a rudimentary foundation which gives little protection against misunderstanding, hostility, and petty strife at the shop level. The trade unions can contribute little to the alleviation of industrial unrest at the lower levels since they give little attention to their members' shop interests and poor treatment to worker problems. At best, the union members are provided with local union representatives who are given little union responsibility and are often bypassed or ignored; the unions commonly supply paternalistic grievance procedures which are seldom regular, immediate, or continuous. The channels of communications betweeen the union members and their officers are usually inadequate for the maintenance of a free, integrating exchange of ideas and decisions. The lack of regular and full exchange of views among the various levels in the union leads to misunderstandings and conflicts, since the leaders cannot easily explain their work and responsibilities to the members on the job, nor can the members easily bring their opinions and concerns to the leaders.

The Australian unions' shop grievance procedures, which allow only little member responsibility and participation, compound the opportunities for provoking unrest, dissatisfaction, and resentment among the workers. The procedures in use are poor means of securing from the workers voluntary acceptance of their job obligations or of getting peaceful compliance to agreements (or arbitration awards) upon matters of concern to the workers but beyond the scope of the local shop.

The union in the shop thus tends to be an informal, fighting organization that maintains its identity and protects the workers through such actions as short strikes, slowdowns, work stoppages, and overtime bans. The members may indignantly suffer what they believe to be violation after violation of their rights, and they have few means of registering their dissatisfaction except by taking overt action. Only when the workers' protests are dramatized or loudly insistent can they get the attention of management or their union leaders.

CONCLUSION

The more detailed analysis of Australian and American strike experience suggests that there are at least two types of strikes whose causes are quite different. If the causes are different, the remedies for avoiding, alleviating, or settling the strikes may be different, too. The psychological and sociological approach to the strike problem may be more than the mere "verbal magic" that

Ross and Irwin believe it is, in institutional circumstances such as those of Australia.

In the United States, we may have underestimated the success that unions and management have had in developing arrangements at the local level whereby the worker's position is protected and his individual rights safeguarded. We may have failed to recognize the importance of shop organization and grievance procedures. The employers and unions have been able to develop a mutual trust and cooperation in their day-to-day relationships at the job level which help to promote efficient production. Work is seldom interrupted because of minor disputes and changes in production processes are carried out with a minimum of disruption. And the firm foundation of understanding and bargaining at the job level helps to maintain worker-management cooperation in production in spite of the deep fissures that may be caused by major strikes.

NOTES

1. Arthur M. Ross and Donald Irwin, "Strike Experience in Five Countries, 1927-1947: An Interpretation," *Industrial and Labor Relations Review*, Vol. 4, No. 3 (April 1951), pp. 323-342.

2. Ross and Irwin, Tables III, IV, and VII, pp. 329-333.

3. The rules of the Waterside Workers' Federation (longshoremen) were not available and are a major exception in the sample.

4. The miners' union is loosely organized in the pits, and union business is conducted extremely haphazardly. Every petty grievance gives rise to pit-top, stop-work meetings where the men air their views and delay work. After such meetings, the men frequently go home. There is local activity, but it is not responsible and only in a broad sense is it union activity. The central office has very slight day-to-day control upon local sections. For a discussion of the problems, see the *Reports of the Coal Commission Inquiries*, 929 and 1945-1946.

5. It is significant that the average length of strikes by workers in the metal trades covered by these four unions is considerably longer than the strikes of other workers.

6. See "The Personnel Function in Industry," *Bulletin of Industrial Psychology and Personnel Practice*, Vol. 5, No. 2 (June 1949), p. 11; and "A Study in Joint Consultation," *ibid.*, Vol. 5, No. 4 (December 1949); and "Wage Incentives in Operations, Case Study No. Three," *ibid.*, Vol. 6, No. 3 (September 1950).

7. Carter Goodrich, "The Australian and American Labour Movements," *Economic Record*, Vol. 4, No. 7 (November 1928), pp. 193-208.

8. Noel Butlin, *Australian Trade Unionism* (Unpublished Lectures, W.E.A. Library, Sydney University) and Mark Perlman, "A Survey of

Functional and Structural Relationships in the Australian Trade Union
Movement, 1952" (mimeo.), p. 23.

9. *Parliamentary Debates* (Hansard) House of Representatives, Vol. 191,
Thomas Sheehan, pp. 1460-1462, and E. J. Holloway, pp. 1317.

10. See National Planning Association, *Causes of Industrial Peace under
Collective Bargaining*, Case Studies 1-11, and Sumner Slichter, *Union Policies and Industrial Management* (Washington: The Brookings Institution,
1941).

F The Enforcement of
Penalties
Against Strikes*
CHARLES P. MILLS**

Iɴ ᴄᴏɴɴᴇᴄᴛɪᴏɴ with the pres-
ent discussion centering around those provisions of Australian
arbitration laws which penalise strikes it may be useful to examine
the practical application of the law to actual cases. It is proposed
to examine briefly the incidence of fines on unions and the considerations which actuate the tribunals in their decisions imposing
and fixing the penalties. The information on which the discussion
is based is confined to decisions of the New South Wales and
Commonwealth tribunals.

Fines on unions are not the only penalties which may follow
illegal strikes. Deregistration of the union is the ultimate sanction to be applied in extreme cases. Individuals may become
liable to financial penalties or imprisonment. Strike leaders and

* Reprinted by permission from *The Journal of Industrial Relations*, Sydney, Australia, Vol. 2, No. 1, April 1960.
** Reader, University of Sydney.

unions may be liable to employers affected for damages. In Queensland a union may lose its preference clause from its award and the coal miners may lose (for a time, anyway) their long service rights. The fine on the union is, however, the commonest remedy today and examination of its application is likely to be the most fruitful.

Naturally enough the strongest condemnation of the penal clauses in the legislation comes from the unions themselves. A statement issued by the interstate executive of the Australian Council of Trade Unions recently[1] urged the repeal of the penal clauses of both State and Federal laws because:

1. They suppress the natural and justifiable reaction of workers to industrial injustice.
2. They enable organisations to be destroyed by deregistration and repeated heavy fines and costs.
3. They are being used in the first instance by employers without recourse to conciliation in an effort to settle the dispute.
4. They are used capriciously by employer organisations and in a manner that results in the highest possible costs against the unions.
5. Orders are made and fines imposed by industrial courts without regard to merits of the dispute.
6. The proceedings arise from disputes which are usually beyond the adjudicating powers of the industrial tribunals.

Academic writers[2] consider that the arbitration system and its prohibition of strikes tend to inhibit the growth of voluntary machinery for the settlement of disputes which would develop a fuller sense of responsibility in both parties to the disputes and which would thus promote better relations in industry. Employers generally see the prohibition of strikes as an integral part of industrial arbitration and they are reluctant to advocate the abandonment of the present system, but sometimes they agree that the system makes it almost certain that the right to strike will be raised as a vital issue.[3]

Paradoxically enough the trade unions have from the beginning of the century strongly supported compulsory arbitration but the sanctions against direct action, as necessary implications of the system, are "not readily accepted even by moderate trade unions and repudiated by the militant ones".[4]

The Legal Sanctions Against Strikes

The (Federal) Conciliation and Arbitration Act itself contains no prohibition of strikes and lock-outs, but an award made under its authority may provide that the unions which are parties to the award shall not take part in any strike or restriction on work in the industry covered by the award; such provisions have come to be known as "bans clauses". If there is reason to believe that a breach of such a provision is about to occur the Commonwealth Industrial Court may make an order requiring the union concerned to refrain from participating in the anticipated breach, and disobedience to such an order will then make the union liable to a penalty.[5]

The New South Wales Industrial Arbitration Act 1940-1958, provided[6] that certain strikes should be illegal, viz.: —

(a) Strikes by employees of the Crown (which for the purpose is given a somewhat extended meaning),

(b) Strikes commenced without the giving of 14 days' notice to the Minister, and

(c) Strikes in an industry subject to a State award or industrial agreement, with the proviso that in certain circumstances a union may render an award no longer binding on its members.

A union whose members are taking part in an illegal strike may be fined but certain defences are open to it.[7] The summons initiating the penal proceedings must be issued while the men are actually on strike.

New South Wales Experience

In the case of both these laws not only is there not complete prohibition of strikes (although the New South Wales law constitutes a more severe limitation than the Federal law), but the very cumbersomeness of the procedures which have to be put in motion limits the use which is made of them. It is left to the employers to commence the proceedings and they will be reluctant to do so unless they consider that the occasion warrants it. Moreover, the form of the proceedings before the tribunals and the attitudes of the tribunals themselves provide some opportunity for unions to avoid the ultimate penalty of the fine. The result, in practice, is quite different from what might be expected from a simple reading of the legal provisions and an examination of strike statistics.

During the period 1939 to 1949 the New South Wales Department of Labour and Industry recorded 10,481 strikes in the State—an average of 953 a year—but there is not one instance of enforcement of the penal provisions in this period. From 1950 to 1958 there were 10,216 strikes recorded—an average of 1,135 a year—and it has been estimated that, of this total, 2,116 strikes were in industries covered by State law. During the same period proceedings were commenced in 182 cases for penalities under the State strike provisions but penalties were imposed in only 41 cases—an average of less than 5 a year. There were 13 unions involved in the 14 cases where penalties were imposed, and the penalties totalled £7,366—an average of £180 per case compared with the maximum penalty of £500.[9]

It is clear that the limited scope provided by the New South Wales law for exercise of the right to strike is enlarged considerably in practice by restraint on the part of the employers and the tribunals. This situation is not peculiar to one State. Professor Sawer has summed up the position thus: "Over a long period no consistent and automatic policy of invoking sanctions against direct action has proved politically or industrially possible. Prosecutions under the South Australian and Western Australian provisions have been extremely few; none has occurred in South Australia for more than twenty years, though that State has on paper the most draconic and elaborate penalty provisions, and there have been many strikes during the period."[10]

Reported decisions of the Industrial Commission of New South Wales usually outline in some detail the circumstances surrounding the incidents which give rise to the penal proceedings and from this we can form some estimate of the weight which the Commission gives to each relevant factor when in deciding, not the legal question of whether an offence has been committed, but the more difficult question of whether a penalty is to be imposed and, if so, the amount. The most significant factor seems to be the earlier conduct of the union. Where fire brigade employees had been on strike for a long period, and two years earlier had been fined £350 for a similar offence, the Industrial Commission imposed the maximum penalty of £500, saying that "what made the case all the more serious is that this is not the first time that the members of this union have broken the law in a similar fashion."[11] The whole industrial history of the union so far as the State law is concerned, previous penalties imposed, and warnings which have been given to the union and to its executive are also very relevant.[12]

Cases decided by the Commission from 1953 to 1957 indicate that the following factors have also had a bearing on the seriousness with which the Commission has regarded particular strikes:—

(1) The effect on the supply of essential goods and services to the public. A strike by employees in electricity generation evoked this comment from the Industrial Commission: "The result of the bans was to reduce the supplies of electricity available both to industry and to homes and . . . the point had been reached when the jobs of thousands of workers were in jeopardy and suffering, inconvenience and hardship were threatened to all persons in the community".[13]

(2) The Strike is in defiance of the Commission's order or amounts to a protest against an award. A strike by fire brigade employees because they were dissatisfied with the refusal of the Industrial Commission to grant them a 40-hour week was said to reveal "a bad case indeed" and resulted in a fine of £350.[14]

(3) The cost to employees indirectly affected by the strike. This is frequently referred to where a small number of men in one key occupation can, by striking, force the employer to stand hundreds, or perhaps even thousands, of his employees down.[15]

(4) The fact that the union entered upon the strike as a result of a misunderstanding or wrong assessment of the situation. For example, where one union became involved in a dispute which had originated with another union and the

employer was inclined to agree that the involvement was the result of a misunderstanding on the part of the first-mentioned union, the Commission agreed to the employer's request for permission to withdraw proceedings against that union.[16] In another case, where a large number of unions were involved, the secretary of one union had come to the conclusion before the strike commenced that the trouble would not in fact lead to a strike; the Commission excused the inactivity of the union and imposed no penalty on it although its members had in fact taken part in the strike.[17]

(5) The importance of the issue. Thus in one case the Commission referred to the "relatively small claim of three men" for payment for one day which had led to some 700 men being out of work and eventually nearly 3,000 men would have been affected.[18]

(6) The significance of participation by one union in a strike involving several unions. In the Bank Holiday Strike Cases the Commission recognized that, because of its small membership, it was unlikely that any efforts on the part of the executive of the Plumbers' Union would have prevented members of that union from taking part in a stoppage which involved members of sixteen other unions and accordingly it did not impose any penalty.[19]

(7) Prompt action by the union to secure a resumption of work immediately on the strike occurring is a consideration in favour of the union;[20] but it is indefensible for a union to negotiate with an employer on a matter, to enter into an industrial agreement on that same matter and then within a few months to make further demands on the same subject while threatening strike action to enforce the new demands.[21]

EXPERIENCE UNDER FEDERAL AWARDS

Under Federal awards also it is obvious that comparatively few strikes lead to penal proceedings. Most work stoppages are dealt with by the ordinary processes of conciliation and arbitration.

In the nine years to 1958 penal proceedings had resulted in

fines totalling £4,157/10/0 being imposed on 11 unions in 42 cases —an average of about five penalties per year, each averaging £220.[22] These figures are not very different from those relating to the State proceedings in New South Wales, although there is one important difference in the principles applied to these cases by the two tribunals—under the State Act a union may be fined only once in respect of any one strike, whereas a strike in defiance of an order to the Commonwealth Industrial Court may attract a separate penalty for each day of the strike. In one case in 1958 a union was fined £50 for each of 10 consecutive days in the one strike. In another case the union was fined £500 for each of four separate breaches of the Court's order although each incident complained of would appear to have been part of one strike.

Applications for the insertion of "bans" clauses in awards are usually concerned with major instances of industrial unrest. Individual members of the Conciliation and Arbitration Commission may have differed in their treatment of these applications, but such differences as have existed are ones of degree rather than of principle. Where an arbitrator acting under the Conciliation and Arbitration Act is asked to enact in an award a bans clause, and he thinks that the situation may not call for a remedy quite so drastic but the circumstances indicate some possibility of further unrest, he may adjourn the hearing without reaching a final determination. In this way the application is kept alive in the event of a situation developing where the award of a bans clause is likely.[23] The Commission is always reluctant to insert a bans clause in an award, and Foster J. has shown himself to be perhaps more reluctant in this respect than any other member of the Federal arbitration tribunals. He has explained his attitude in these words: "The essence of conciliation and arbitration is goodwill; 'bans' clauses are the antithesis; not only do they jeopardise good relations but they impede my work as arbitrator. The present separation of the judicial from the arbitral function makes me, if possible, more reluctant than ever to accede to the applicant's plea for this variation. I as the arbitrator have now lost control of the consequences which follow the insertion of 'bans' clauses".[24] Later in the same decision he said: "One ground upon which in the present state of the arbitration system I would be prepared to put one in an award would be a direct flouting of the Commission or a repudiation of conciliation and arbitration in favour of direct action". In the previous year the same Judge had spoken of a refusal of duty by shipping masters as "a rebellion by men entrusted with authority", and he told them that he regarded certain resolutions which they had passed as "a complete affront to the Court and the law". He granted the employers' claim in that case for the insertion of a bans clause.[25]

While it is more usual for decisions in matters of this kind to be very briefly expressed, the occasional longer decision seems to stress the importance in the mind of the tribunal of the threat to its authority. Chief Conciliation Commissioner Galvin explained that he had first inserted a bans clause in the Metal Trades Award in 1951 only "after being convinced that the authority of the tribunal was involved" and he did it "against the instincts of a lifetime".[26]

Conciliation Commissioner Austin presented a somewhat different point of view when he pointed out that a union had been involved in some 38 disputes in about four years and it had notified only one of these to him. He referred to the resulting serious disruption of vital production affecting the public interest and the standing down of other employees. He made it clear, however, that not all strikes had his disapproval: "I accept the right of a union and its members to engage in a strike when vital industrial principles are involved, but not on ordinary 'day to day' problems, nor to enforce job decisions or union policy on issues such as requiring an employer to seek permision from a union delegate before he arranged 'manning' to suit his requirements".[27]

While in most cases the decisions do not disclose the influences which motivate the tribunal in reaching those decisions, the published reasons seem to stress, more than anything else, the threat which strikes present to the arbitration system and to the tribunals themselves. It is, however, unlikely that the threat to production, to the employers' business, to the workers' livelihoods and to the general public interest is ignored.

The second step is the making of the order by the Industrial Court enjoining breaches by the union concerned of the bans clause in the award. This step is in two parts—an order nisi, followed closely by the hearing and, in an appropriate case, by the order absolute. Where the application for this order flows from the dispute which gave rise to the bans clause being inserted in the award, the application for the order will follow almost immediately upon the award variation. In the normal course of events this will allow a short delay during which the union can attempt to achieve some peaceful settlement of the dispute. This period of time will, of course, be shorter where there is a permanent bans clause, but again it will provide some opportunity for the union to attempt a settlement.

The Court's usual order restrains the union from "committing or continuing" a breach of the relevant clause, and it is not necessary for the applicant to show that there has been an actual breach of this clause. It is sufficient to found an order that evidence should show a reasonable apprension of such breach.[28] The whole conduct of the union is relevant—perhaps as early as the time before the insertion of the bans clause, up to the conclusion of the hearing of the case before the Industrial Court.[29] If the Court is satisfied before the hearing concludes that the dispute has been settled, or if the union undertakes sincerely to observe the award, the proceedings may be discharged or at least adjourned.[30] If, however, the strike is still in progress when the hearing concludes, or if the union will not give the appropriate undertaking, the order will be made as a matter of course.[31]

At this stage of the proceedings it is rare to find in any of the Court's decisions any application of any other form of discretion; if a strike is in progress or appears likely the order will be made.

The final step—in imposition of the penalty—is again the function of the Industrial Court in proceedings initiated by the employer, and the chief consideration is whether the evidence shows beyond reasonable doubt that the union has been guilty of wilful default of the Court's order. In one case less than twenty-four hours had passed between the making of the order and the union's actions which gave rise to the penalty proceedings. Nevertheless the Court pointed out that the ban by the union of the work in question had been in existence for two months; the secretary of the union knew of the terms of the order at the time it was made; the union had not communicated to the employers any notice that the ban had been lifted or that members of the union would be available for work as required, and the union had called no evidence at all in the proceedings. In these circumstances the court found that the union's failure to obey the order had been wilful.[32] "One aggravating factor arises out of the nature of the proceedings that Parliament has prescribed for this sort of offence. These are not summary proceedings; they are proceedings which are preceded by a warning, unlike proceedings ordinarily taken for breaches of the law. A safety valve is provided by Parliament to allow an association involved in these difficulties to escape from this trouble".[33] The offence accordingly will always be regarded by the Court as a serious one and while its chief ingredient will be contempt of the Court, the effects of the strike on the employer's business, on the community in general and on the employees affected directly and indirectly, will also affect the seriousness with which the offence is regarded and hence the amount of the penalty finally imposed.[34]

The gravity of the contempt itself may be affected by the efforts made by the defendant union to remedy the situation out of which the proceedings arose. The Court "is not unsympathetic towards an organisation which finds itself in difficulties owing to the intractibility of some of its members",[35] and, where a union has made genuine though unsuccessful efforts to get strikers back to work, the Court has on occasions recorded a conviction while imposing no fine, but the costs against the union, even in these circumstances, may constitute a substantial penalty. The maximum penalty is likely to be imposed where the offence amounts to a deliberate refusal to obey the Court's direction.[36]

Some of the above points are well illustrated in proceedings which arose out of a strike at Mort's Dock in Sydney in 1955. The issue was the appropriate award rate to be paid to riggers' assistants and eighteen employees had stopped work on 15th February. The Conciliation Commissioner, before whom the matter came on 23rd February, considered that an interpretation of the award was involved. Since this was out of his jurisdiction, he suggested that the union apply to the Court for an interpretation and in the meantime instruct its members to return to work.[37]

On 14th March the employers' association applied to the Arbitration Court for an order enjoining the union from committing a breach of the award in connection with the work at Mort's Dock. The hearing before the Court took place on 22nd and 23rd March and on the second day the order was made as for, the union to pay the applicant's costs.

On 13th April the association issued a summons asking that a penalty be imposed for breach of the order of 23rd March. At the hearing on 28th April the Arbitration Court was told that other employees had joined the strike and on 15th April an overtime ban had been imposed in part on the works. The union had suspended the original strikers from membership and had told those who had joined the strike later that they would have until 2nd May to resume work or face the risk of a similar suspension. On 29th April the Court announced that it would defer its decision unil 6th May so that the union would have a further opportunity for action, particularly in relation to the overtime ban.[38]

On 6th May the Court was told that the overtime ban had been lifted on 29th April, meetings had been held and another meeting was planned for 9th May. To encourage the efforts of the union the Court then adjourned the matter until 17th May.

When the hearing was resumed on that day the Court learned that the meeting of 9th May had decided to continue the strike but a further attempt would be made on the next day by the union towards the settlement and the Court once more adjourned the hearing until 20th May. On that day the Court was told that, despite a direction by union officials to resume work, the men had voted to continue the strike. The Court immediately decided that the union had been guilty of contempt as charged. Although it had made genuine efforts to obey the Court's order, its earlier attitude towards the strikers had contributed to the failure of those efforts. In all the circumstances no fine was imposed but the union had to pay the employers' association costs of 150 guineas. These had been assessed having regard to the numerous adjournments given for the benefit of the union and to the fact that the hearing on the last two days had had to be held in Melbourne. The Court remarked that if the union had been judged by the conduct of its few members on strike rather than by the recent action of its leaders it would have been heavily fined.[39]

The strike still continued and on 2nd June the employers' association issued another summons for a penalty on the union. The strike was still in progress on 14th June when the Court sat to hear the case. The union was fined £500 and ordered to pay the employers' association's costs; it was told that the leniency shown earlier by the Court had not led to any effective action on its part to end the contempt. The union was guilty, not merely of a first contempt, but of a serious and continuing one.

On 28th and 29th June the Court sat to hear yet another summons for contempt issued against the union. The union said that it had directed the strikers to return to work and when this was not obeyed it had expelled one member and fined a number of others £10 each. In the light of this and the stated intention of the union to grapple firmly with the question of its members collecting, and contributing to, the strike pay which was being paid to the strikers, the Court, although finding that the union was still concerned in the strike and was therefore guilty of contempt, imposed no fine. Again, however, the union had to pay the association's costs, which were assessed at 50 guineas. This, the Court said, was not by way of punishment but simply to reimburse the association for the expense it had necessarily incurred.[40]

About the same time another union was fined £500 for breach of a Court order which had directed it to cease being a party to or concerned in any ban on the performance of work at Mort's Dock. Members of this union had been contributing to a strike fund set up for the benefit of the strikers, but the union had claimed that it had taken the view that it should not direct its members to contribute, or for that matter not to contribute, to this fund. The Court held that in permitting these contributions by its members the union was actively—through its contributing members—subsidising the strike and prolonging it.[41]

Finally the Commission may rescind the bans clause in the award when the circumstances which gave rise to its insertion have disappeared, even though it is "asked to retain it on the ground of the history of frequent stoppages".[42] The Industrial

Court is even more reluctant to make an order of indefinite duration enjoining breaches of the bans clauses thereby turning the Commission's award prohibiting strikes into a perpetual injunction made by the Industrial Court.[43]

Thus the Federal arbitration system applies, as the principal test of guilt and of the amount of the penalty to be imposed, the extent of the union's submissiveness to the tribunal. All other issues are merely of secondary importance.

EFFECTS OF THE MANNER OF APPLICATION OF PENAL CLAUSES

It is clear, therefore, that most strikes go unpunished despite the severe penalties which the law provides. This was also the experience in England under war-time compulsory arbitration.[44] This is not to say that the legal sanctions have little practical effect. In many cases proceedings are withdrawn or, at least, discontinued on work being resumed or as part of the terms of settlement of the dispute. In such cases the penal provisions seem to be used, not simply as an instrument of punishment for a breach of the law, but rather as the employer's new weapon (replacing the lock-out) to counter the continued use of the union's economic weapon, the strike. Nevertheless, the threat of severe penalties does not seen to have improved the prospect of eliminating work stoppages.[45]

J. H. Portus has expressed the view[46] that in the public opinion—

(a) when a strike has ended, the enforcement of penalties is an unnecessary irritant;

(b) when a strike has failed, the failure and the loss of wages are sufficient penalty; and

(c) when a strike has succeeded, the public find it difficult to appreciate why persons should be punished for obtaining a remedy for what they consider was a legitimate grievance.

It is not intended in this article to come to any conclusion as to the desirability of a law which forbids unions to participate in strikes. Any answer to such a question would need to include many qualifications. However, one clear inference may be drawn from the foregoing discussion—neither the New South Wales law nor the Federal law on this subject is enforced, nor expected to be enforced, in the great majority of cases to which they apply. One result of this is that a union which meets two or three substantial fines in a year and sees hundreds of other strikes go unpunished feels that it is being unfairly attacked. The ideal law is one in which the rights and obligations it establishes are set out clearly and distinctly. Of necessity, the very wide terms of the penal provisions as they apply to trade unions have been restricted greatly by the practice of employers and the manner of application by the Courts. There is at least some ground for an attempt to cast the statutory provisions in a form which approaches more clearly to current practice.

NOTES

1. *Sydney Morning Herald*, August 26, 1958.

2. K. Laffer, "Problems of Compulsory Arbitration," in *International Labour Review*, Geneva, May, 1958, pp. 417-433; E. I. Sykes, "The Rôle of Law in Industrial Relations," in *Australian Quarterly*, Syd., June, 1957, pp. 21-28; J. E. Isaac, "The Prospects for Collective Bargaining in Australia," in *Economic Record*, Melb., Dec., 1958, pp. 347-361.

3. R. G. Fry, "Systems of Arbitration: Some Observations and Conclusions," in *Metal Trades Journal*, Syd., May 15, 1953, pp. 177-9.

4. G. Sawyer, "Industrial Law," in G. W. Paton (Ed.), *The Commonwealth of Australia, the Development of its Laws and Constitution*, Lond., Stevens, 1952, p. 313.

5. Conciliation and Arbitration Act 1904-1959, ss. 109, 111.

6. The New South Wales Act has been amended by the Industrial Arbitration (Amendment) Act, 1959, which is dealt with elsewhere in this issue (in D. C. Thomson, "Recent Developments in the Australian Industrial Scene"). The provisions described in this article are those which were in force in the period discussed.

7. Industrial Arbitration Act, 1940-1958, ss. 99, 100.

8. *N.S.W. Industrial Gazette*, March, 1959, vol. 132, p. 489.

9. These details were given by the Hon. J. J. Maloney, M.L.C., in his second reading speech on the Industrial Arbitration (Amendment) Bill 1959. See N.S.W. *Hansard*, November 26, 1959, p. 2361.

10. G. W. Paton (Ed.), *op. cit.*, p. 312.

11. *Board of Fire Commissioners of N.S.W. v. N.S.W. Fire Brigade Employees' Union*, 1955 Arbitration Reports (N.S.W.) 819 at p. 828.

12. *Electricity Commission of N.S.W. v. Federated Engine Drivers and Firemen's Assn. of A'sia (Coast District)*, 1956 A. R. 629 at p. 648.

13. *Electricity Commission of N.S.W. v .Amalgamated Engineering Union (Australian Section)*, 1954 A.R. 349 at p. 358.

14. *Board of Fire Commissioners of N.S.W. v. N.S.W. Fire Brigade Employees' Union*, 1953 A.R. 622 at p. 638.

15. E.g. *MacDonald v. Federated Engine Drivers and Firemen's Association of Australasia (Coast District)*, 1954 A.R. 283.

16. *Garnham v. South Maitland Railways Employees' Association, Wages Division*, 1953 A.R. 466 at p. 469.

17. *Electricity Commission of N.S.W. v. Federated Engine Drivers and Firemen's Assn. of A'sia (Coast District)*, 1956 A.R. 629 at pp. 654-5.

18. *MacDonald v. Federated Engine Drivers and Firemen's Assn. of A'sia (Coast District)*, 1954 A.R. 283.

19. *Electricity Commission of N.S.W. v. Federated Engine Drivers and Firemen's Assn. of A'sia (Coast District)*, 1956 A.R. 629 at p. 658.

20. *Gallery v. Printing Industry Employees' Union of Australia, N.S.W. Branch*, 1954 A.R. 115 at p. 119.

21. *Electricity Commission of N.S.W. v. Federated Engine Drivers and Firemen's Assn. of A'sia (Coast District)*, 1956 A.R. 629 at pp. 639-640.

22. Commonwealth *Hansard*, May 5, 1959 (Senate), p. 1177. See also Commonwealth *Hansard*, August 27, 1959 (House of Representatives), p. 717.

23. For examples of this see *Re Australian Workers' Union Construction and Maintenance Award* (1958), 13 Industrial Information Bulletin (Commonwealth Dept. of Labour and National Service) 925, Commissioner Donovan; *Re Marine Cooks Award and Marine Stewards (C.S.O.A.) Agreement* (1957), 12 I.I.B. 394.

24. *Re Marine Cooks Award* (29th June, 1957), Serial No. A5838.

25. *Commonwealth Steamship Owners' Association v. Merchant Service Guild* (1956), 84 Commonwealth Arbitration Reports 91.

26. *Re Metal Trades Award* (1955), 82 C.A.R. 270.

27. *Re Engine Drivers and Firemen's (General) Award* (1954), 80 C.A.R. 339.

28. *Re Marine Stewards and Pantrymen's Award* (30th October, 1957), Ser. No. A 5987.

29. *Commonwealth Steamship Owners' Association v. Waterside Worker's Federation of Australia* (1958), 13 I.I.B. 647; *Re Marine Stewards and Pantrymen's Award* (30th October, 1957), Ser. No. A 5987.

30. For examples of this see *Re Ship Painters and Dockers' Award* (1958), 13 I.I.B. 280; *Monsanto Chemicals (Aust.) Limited v. Amalgamated Engineering Union (Australian Section)* (1958), 13 I.I.B. 359.

31. *Re Seamen's Award* (1st October, 1957), Ser. No. A5882; *Ansett Airways Pty. Ltd. v. Aust. Air Pilots' Association* (16th April, 1957), Ser No. A 5747.

32. *Matthews v. Seamen's Union of Australia* (24th May, 1957), Ser. No. A 5566.

33. Per Dunphy J. in *Caterson v. Aust. Air Pilots' Association* (1958), 13 I.I.B. 907.

34. *Metal Trades Employers' Association v. Boilermakers' Society of Australia* (1955), 81 C.A.R. 231.

35. *Ford Motor Co. of Aust. Pty. Ltd. v. Amalgamated Engineering Union (Australian Section)* (1954), 80 C.A.R. 230.

36. *Caterson v. Australian Air Pilots' Association* (1958), 13 I.I.B. 907; *Metal Trades Employers' Association v. Federated Ironworkers' Association of Australia* (1955), 81 C.A.R. 122.

37. 10 I.I.B. 169.

38. 10 I.I.B. 279.

39. 10 I.I.B. 435.

40. 10 I.I.B. 567.

41. 10 I.I.B. 566.

42. *Commonwealth Steamship Owners' Association v. Merchant Service Guild* (1956), 84 C.A.R. 91: *Commonwealth Steamship Owners' Association v. Waterside Workers' Federation of Australia* (1956), 84 C.A.R. 31.

43. *Commonwealth Steamship Owners' Association of Australia v. Waterside Workers' Federation of Australia* (1958), 13 I.I.B. 647.

44. K. G. J. C. Knowles, *Strikes*, O.U.P., 1952, p. 118.

45. K. F. Walker, *Industrial Relations in Australia*, Harvard U.P., 1956, p. 355.

46. J. H. Portus, *The Development of Australian Trade Union Law*, Melb. U.P., 1958, p. 224.

G Industrial Relations in
New Zealand*

G. H. SORRELL**

I

INDUSTRIAL RELATIONS in New
Zealand means industrial conciliation and arbitration, the system that
has grown up under the Industrial Conciliation and Arbitration Act
during the past 67 years. It is "hardly too much to assert that the
structure of industrial relations in New Zealand, and to some extent the structure of society itself, has developed within the framework of the Act."[1] This article deals with the institutions and some
of the problems of conciliation and arbitration that help to give
some insight into the system of industrial relations in New Zealand.

In 1900 Demarest Lloyd, extolling compulsory arbitration,
called New Zealand "a country without strikes," a statement
probably no more dishonest than any other piece of special
pleading. Unionists, still smarting from the defeat of the Mari-

* Reprinted by permission from *The Journal of Industrial Relations*
(Australia), Vol. III, No. 2, October 1961.
** New Zealand Department of Labour, Wellington, N. Z.

time Strike, could not do other than accept and work with the order of industrial relations imposed by the Industrial Conciliation and Arbitration Act 1894; and there were some ready advantages to be got from doing so. It is likely that the sort of facts that have made the strike less prominent in New Zealand are a primitive economy, an uncomplicated social structure, and a small and fairly homogeneous population. This is not to deny the statute some mitigating effect; but that it could not remove whatever social and economic disequilibria make for open industrial warfare must always have been clear to the disinterested observer and has been made apparent by history.

The Act of 1894 has been re-enacted many times, the last consolidation being made in 1954. In summary, it provides for a Court of Arbitration, the registration and regulation of unions of employers and workers, and for compulsory reference of disputes to conciliation and to the Court of Arbitration. It also provides for enforcement of its provisions and of awards of the Court, and for such peripheral matters as audit of union accounts, compulsory membership of unions, inquiries into elections in unions, and strikes and lockouts. It forms an almost complete code, regulations made under it being procedural only.

Compulsory conciliation and arbitration have not been immune from criticism; but the only successful attack came from employers, in the early years of the depression of the 'thirties, culminating in the 1932 Amendment to the Act which made reference to the Court voluntary. Compulsory arbitration, then a disrupter of the economy, holding wages at uneconomic levels, has since acquired from the pens of publicists a certain divinity. It represents the "rule of law" in industrial relations, and legislative direction to the Court is described as "improper interference." So much difference has twenty years of rising prices made to the outlook of the critics who were most vocal in the years 1930 to 1932.

Industrial Disputes

The central elements of the Act relate to industrial disputes. The Act does not say what a dispute is, or when it arises, but the typical dispute with which Conciliation Councils and the Court are concerned arises on the expiry of an award of the Court. In practice it is created when one party serves claims on another and the respondent party rejects the claims, or makes a counter-claim (usually) or even preserves a studied silence.[2] The creation of a dispute is essential to the jurisdiction of a Council or of the Court.[3] Since a dispute may not go directly to the Court,[4] the first step in settling it is application by an association,[5] a union, or an employer for the dispute to be heard by a Council of Con-ciliation.

CONCILIATION

A Council consists of a Conciliation Commissioner and assessors representing employers and workers. Assessors must be persons who are or have been engaged in the industry, though there is pro-vision, often used, to include a union official among the assessors, for appointment of a person not so qualified. The Act absolutely prohibits appearance of a barrister or solicitor before a Council, and the prohibition has been held at different times to cover the cases of a solicitor who had not practised for twenty years and the President of a union who was a solicitor.[6]

The Act allows for the appointment of four Commissioners, though at present there are three only. The Commissioners, usu-ally former employees of the Department of Labour having long experience of the administration of the Industrial Conciliation and Arbitration Act, enjoy a high standing in industrial circles because of the calibre of the men appointed, the considerable powers vested in them by the Act, the fact that they are an in-tegral part of the scheme of the Act and not merely adventitious thereto, and also, perhaps, because of a tendency discernible in the cases for the Court to lend support to them.

Out of 318 disputes finalised by Councils of Conciliation dur-ing the two years ended 31 March, 1960, 242 (76%) resulted in complete agreement in conciliation.[7] On the face of it concilia-tion works; but this merely illustrates the measure of agreement achieved, and simplifies without explaining. Conciliation is only part of a process which, if agreement is not reached, is completed by reference to the Court of Arbitration, and unquestionably prospective factors, as well as the standing and character of Con-ciliation Councils, influence the willingness of parties to agree. Foremost among these prospective factors is the known policy of the Court as evidenced by awards already made and other indications given from time to time. Other factors include the power which can be exercised by the Court under section 141 of the Act to refer a dispute back to Conciliation, if it believes that a greater measure of agreement could be reached by this means or that the parties have not seriously attempted to reach agreement; and, perhaps, the short term of awards (often no more than twelve or fifteen months), making immediate agreement less liable to be vitiated by drastic change in circumstances, whether economic or other, and reducing the urgency of insuring against the future.

THE COURT OF ARBITRATION

The institution that attracts most public attention is the Court of Arbitration. However important conciliation may be, it is the decisions of the Court that are effective and it is in the Court that wage policy, affecting ultimately almost all wage and salary earners in the country, whether or not covered by awards of the Court, is crystallised. The Court consists of a Judge and two members nominated by unions of workers and employers. In the past the Judge has usually been the junior puisne Judge of the Supreme Court. The present Judge, Sir Arthur Tyndall, though a solicitor, is not and presumably was not appointed as a jurist.[8] His appointment in 1940 evoked at the time a great deal of criticism which served no better purpose than to show the lack of comprehension of the critics. Arbitration, the principal function of the Court, is a somewhat different kind of activity from a judgment between parties, and many lawyers fail to see the dynamic and non-rational element or, perhaps, the greater area of free choice, involved in the former. The present high regard in which the Court is held by those most closely concerned is undoubtedly due in some degree to the ability of the present Judge as an arbitrator. Judge Stilwell, the additional Judge of the Court and a former Stipendiary Magistrate, may well be a better lawyer, but, when presided over by him during the absence from the country of Sir Arthur Tyndall in 1952-1953, the Court was subject to strong criticism, and at least a partial boycott, by unions of workers.

The Court's procedure has been criticised by practitioners

used to the solemnities of the Supreme Court; and it is true that proceedings are often more inquisitorial than adversary, the Judge and Members entering into them in a spirit that would make a Judge of the Supreme Court blanch. The criticism misses the point; effective arbitration often calls for more information than the parties will willingly lead in evidence, and an inquisitorial procedure is almost inevitable if the Court is to get a full factual background. The Court is not a lawyers' court, a fact which may condition the attitude of lawyers. In arbitration proceedings a party may be represented by a barrister or solicitor with the consent of all the parties, but the consent is seldom if ever forthcoming. It is doubtful that legal representation at this stage would cure the bad drafting that makes many awards difficult to interpret; it is certain that its absence reduces the technicality and length of proceedings; and the absence of such intermediaries permits the affected parties to come together without hindrance in what is, after all, a legislative and not a judicial context. Parties may be represented as of right in proceedings for enforcement or interpretation of awards.

The Court has been judicially criticised[9] for failure to give reasons for an award, but appears, wisely, to have ignored the criticism. The Court combines the legislative function of making awards and the judicial function of interpreting and enforcing those awards (a combination which may baffle constitutional purists but has, in New Zealand, produced no practical difficulty). In the latter case reasons are usually given. In the former case it is only occasionally that reasons for a decision are given in a memorandum appended to the award. But precisely because the making of an award is a legislative process, containing a dynamic and non-rational element, and also because the decision must frequently take into account a speculative future, it is difficult to see how the Court could in many instances give clear reasons that will not create more disharmony than is warranted by adherence to a reputable, but largely irrelevant, form.

The Court is a creature of the statute and its jurisdiction is strictly limited by the terms of the statute. Some limits have already been indicated, but the central limitation, pervading the Act, is that which confines conciliation and arbitration to "industrial matters," an expression that has been judicially interpreted in terms similar to its interpretation in Australian Courts and often with reference to Australian cases.[10] There is no appeal from decisions of the Court, and section 47 of the Act purports to preclude removal of proceedings into any Court by certiorari or otherwise. Nevertheless the jurisdiction of the Court will be reviewed by the Supreme Court on application for certiorari or prohibition[11] and mandamus.[12] But showing its failure, proper in New Zealand, to be influenced by dogma about separation of powers, the Supreme Court has affirmed the power of the Court alone to interpret its own awards[13] and has consistently refused to allow such procedures to be used as oblique means of appealing decisions of the Court.[14] Within its own jurisdiction, therefore, the Court is the ultimate arbiter of disputes between employers and workers, and the ultimate interpreter of its own decisions, a fact that has significant effects, particularly in conciliation.

AWARD OF THE COURT

The effect of an award of the Court was stated as long ago as 1900.[15]

"All contracts regarding labour are controlled and may be modified or abrogated. The Court can make the contract or agreement that is to exist between the workmen and the employer. It abrogates the right of workmen and employers to make their own contracts. It in effect abolishes 'contract' and restores 'status.' "

Despite its element of truth, in the present economic context the statement goes too far. Technically, application of an award to a worker requires the existence of a contract of service; at a practical level that contract will frequently provide conditions significantly better than the minima prescribed by the award. But apart from this an award is usually a reasonably comprehensive document with few interstices to be filled by the common law and governing with some adequacy the relations of employer and worker, though in a less detailed way than most Australian awards.

It is not possible, here, to deal with the subject matter and problems of awards, e.g., hours, disputes committees, welfare provisions, overtime and penal rates, interpretation, and the innumerable other matters which form the substance of relations in the workplace, but one major element in rendering the Act effective must be dealt with, that is, the application of an award.

Before 1937 an award applied only to employers cited as parties and those entering the industry after the making of the award. By a rather strained interpretation of the predecessor of the present section 145 the Court decided in 1904[16] that an award did not apply to employers engaged in the industry when the award was made but who were not cited in proceedings for the award. Consequently, full coverage for an award often required the citation of hundreds of employers, as in the case of Federal awards in Australia.

This difficulty was removed by provision for a representative citation (section 112 (5) of the Act). The substance of the rule is now that if a union of employers is cited as respondent in the application of a union of workers all employers in the area to which the dispute relates who are not members are also deemed to be cited. If an employers' organisation is not named it is enough that a number of representative employers are named. Roughly, the representative citation may be achieved by naming an employer of each class to be covered in each industrial district.[17] This, in effect, aids in fixing the area in which the award applies and the Court usually includes in the award a "blanket clause" giving it the force of a common rule in that locality. The blanket clause,[18] as will be seen later, is also an essential element in a weapon by which the Minister of Labour can discipline a recalcitrant union.

WAGES

These notes are chiefly concerned with the framework within which decisions are reached, but something should be said of the role of the Court as the principal wage-fixing body in the country.

Traditional economic thought may not support the idea that decisions of the Court have any material influence on the level of wages, and the constancy of the percentage of national income going to salary and wages is sometimes given as evidence against it. On the other hand there is a widespread popular belief that the Court has some decisive effect, and such a belief, whether or not initially well grounded, has a way of generating its own kind of truth. Certainly the wages structure of the Dominion would be different if there were no Court, and probably the general level of wages (if so vague a concept has any validity) would be quite other than it is.

The Court's wage-fixing power derives from two sources, viz. section 148 (3) of the Act which empowers the Court to prescribe a minimum rate of wages when making awards, and the Economic Stabilisation Regulations 1953 under which general wage orders are made.

The normal process of wage fixation goes hand in hand with the making of awards. In almost 70% of cases where agreement is not reached in conciliation the disagreement involves rate of wages so that wage fixation for particular industries and occupations is a major part of the business of the Court. On some occasions the Court has expressly stated its policy in making awards, by this means facilitating conciliation. At the present time it is not difficult to discern in most cases, from summaries of changes in award provisions prepared by the Department of Labour, what is the policy of the Court.

Superimposed on this process is the making from time to time of general wage orders, corresponding, somewhat, in significance to decisions of the Commonwealth Arbitration Commission on the basic wage and margins. The factors which the Court is required to take into account are set forth in regulations[19] as being:

(a) Changes in retail prices;
(b) Economic conditions affecting finance, trade, and industry;
(c) Changes in productivity and production;
(d) Relative movements in incomes of different sections of the community.

Since the effect of a general wage order pervades the whole economy these requirements are not unrealistic; but they do help to make of each hearing a massive general inquiry into the state of the nation. The last hearing commenced 26 May, 1959, and continued, with interruptions, for three months. Witnesses included the Government Statistician, the Secretary to the Treasury, the Governor of the Reserve Bank, and a miscellany of company directors and others. The case for the applicant union was taken by the President of the Federation of Labour, Mr. F. P. Walsh.

The general order takes the form of a percentage increase of most rates of remuneration fixed by awards with a portion of weekly remuneration excluded from the scope of the order (at present the amounts in excess of £13 for adult male workers, and smaller weekly amounts for female and junior workers are excluded).

II

* * *

There are only a few New Zealand unions which can seriously be thought of as having an independent existence and an "organic" relationship with the workplace. These are mainly, though not exclusively, the "militant" unions (the militancy is relative)—freezing workers, watersiders, seamen, and miners. The unions tend to be small in size and restricted in area. Though the fragmentary and politically impotent Communist Party has had some power at some times unions have been and are substantially identified, politically, with the Labour Party.[20] Finally, the activities of unions in New Zealand are for the most part rather narrowly circumscibed.

SIZE OF UNIONS

At 31 December, 1959, there were 399 unions registered under the Act, having over 327,000 members. The size of these unions in terms of membership is indicated by the facts that 58%, with only 6% of all membership, had 250 members or fewer; 26% of unions with 16% of all members had 250-1000 members. The remaining 16% of unions, with membership ranging from 1000-25,000 (Engineering) embraced 78% of all membership. In terms of area covered, 85% of unions with 60% of all membership covered one, or a part only of one industrial district (this is, admittedly, an unsatisfactory measure since the districts vary enormously in size). The bulk of the remaining 15% of unions cover New Zealand or seven of the eight districts.[21]

* * *

The Act now permits national and combined district unions; but unionism in New Zealand grew up under a system of single district unions and since then such factors as regional and occupational jealousies, the inapplicability of certain general awards to particular occupations, and, possibly, the system of voting in the Conference of the Federation of Labour[22] have helped to maintain the predominance of small unions.[23]

COMPULSORY UNION MEMBERSHIP

Since 1936[24] it has been compulsory for every worker covered by an award or industrial agreement[25] to be a member of a union bound by the award or agreement. The National Party in its election programme announced its intention to abolish compulsory membership and since taking office has reaffirmed that policy.[26] The official attitude of the trade union movement has, ostensibly, been modified by the Government's resolve and the last conference of the New Zealand Federation of Labour[27] decided to take "industrial action" if needed, and agreed, in the light of that policy, not to reaffirm the principle of compulsory conciliation and arbitration.[28] Since then the Federation's President has gone on record[29] with an exaggerated forecast of "bloody revolution" if the proposal is adhered to.[29a]

It is not possible to isolate the effects of compulsory membership of unions. It is not central to the Act (it may even be regarded as a corollary of, or rider to the more basic compulsions), and it has been accompanied by a great many other changes in the Act and external to the Act. It is neither the dragon painted by its opponents, nor the moral imperative seen by its beneficiaries.

It is unlikely that compulsory membership has made any difference to the character and governance of basic industrial unions in which, before 1936, such compulsion was a discipline imposed by members; and it is unlikely that abolition will make any difference. It has not created apathy among union members; but, by making members of people who would not otherwise belong it has given some prominence to that universal problem of the trade union movement. It is not clear that it has created a trade union hierarchy, as is alleged by some critics: men seeking, and seeking to retain, power in them exist wherever there are trade unions. It is not even clear that it has changed the character and functions of the leadership of unions: in this respect much more might be attributed to twenty years of rising prices and a good employment market.

On the other hand it has given financial stability to a great many unions in existence before 1936, which, if compulsory unionism is abolished, will probably continue to get awards covering the industries in which they function without being able to induce a great many workers in those industries to join them. The 1936 amendment has also had, marginally, a creative effect, and there is now a small number of unions that would probably not exist without it.[30] Creation by some means of such paper unions is a legitimate function of a modern system of industrial relations if it means that protection is given to workers which they would otherwise lack; and abolition, without account taken of this, will be retrograde.[30a]

In sum, twenty-five years of compulsory union membership has brought some advantages to wage-earners in New Zealand, within the context of compulsory conciliation and arbitration, by providing a more stable structure for negotiation and enforcement of awards. It has changed the face, but not altered materially the basic structure of unionism, which continues as the product of the needs of wage and salary earners and of the Act; and it has proved an important factor in the disciplining of unions by de-registration.[31] The only serious argument advanced for abolition is that it is a denial of the freedom of the individual,[32] and reference is made to the Declaration of Human Rights. This is a dangerous argument really not to be maintained by those who applaud other sanctions, e.g., against the strike, contained in the Act.

REGULATION OF UNIONS

Registration under the Act offers real advantages to most unions, making irrelevant the problem of recognition of the union by employers, providing a medium of negotiation which cannot readily be by-passed, and culminating in an award enforceable by the union as a party. But a high price has been paid in the extent of regulation by the State of the activities of unions. The functions of unions tend to be confined to a rather narrow range. This is perhaps inherent in a system which makes an award of the Court the chief aim of organisation; but even where the activities of unions go beyond the collection of dues and "getting the extra ha'penny" their scope is limited by the decisions of the Courts.

The Act allows registration as an industrial union of "any society consisting of not less than fifteen persons lawfully associated for the purpose of protecting or furthering the interests of workers engaged in any specified industry. . . ." This would seem to leave no room for the restrictive interpretation of powers of trade unions given in *Amalgamated Soc'y of Railway Servants v. Osborne;*[33] but the Supreme Court in *McDougall v. Wellington Typographical Union*[34] did just that. *Osborne's* case is now firmly embedded in New Zealand law. It made necessary section 4 of the Political Disabilities Removal Act 1936, enabling unions to apply funds for political purposes; and it has prevented unions from providing benefits for members.[35] More recently it was held[36] that affiliation to the Trade Union Congress (a national organisation, now deceased, of unions leaving the Federation of Labour) was invalid, and legislation had hastily to be passed (see now s. 88) negativing the effect of the decision so that the Federation of Labour might not, itself, disappear.

The content of rules of unions is determined to a considerable extent by the Act and they may be amended by the Registrar of Industrial Unions to bring them into conformity with the Act. The Registrar has also a limited power to refuse to register a rule which is in his opinion unreasonable or oppressive. Elections of officers must be by secret ballot; there is provision for audit of accounts of unions and supply of audit certificates to the Registrar; and restrictions are imposed as to subscriptions and levies payable by members. The registration of unions is closely regulated and in some cases, to avoid multiplicity of unions in the one district, a union may be registered only with the consent of the Minister of Labour.

It has been an article of faith with the publicists that Communists always get office in unions by rigging ballots, and, in 1951, Government introduced legislation[37] empowering the Court on the application of members of the union to inquire into irregularities alleged in connection with elections. Since then there have been six such inquiries in only one of which it can certainly be said a Communist was involved—as an applicant;

but, of course, it is impossible to assess the negative effect of such legislation. Applications have tended, like the action for defamation in the Supreme Court, to become in New Zealand a weapon in factional disputes in unions.

Many of the controls are integral to and inseparable from the total process envisaged by the Act, but others are adventitious, external regulators of that process. The justification often given in the past for these is that, with union membership compulsory, workers need and are entitled to the protection given by such limitations upon the powers of unions and their officers. Inevitably, the question has been raised whether Government will see fit to relax the measure of control if it carries out its promise to withdraw the benefit of compulsory union membership.

The Strike

The strike is expressly made illegal, though, naturally, this has not prevented strikes.[38] A scheme of penalties and fines against workers, union officers and unions for taking part in or instigating strikes is provided in the statute, but these penal provisions are almost never invoked. Thus the report of the Department of Labour for 1960 records that of 26 stoppages in the meat freezing industry 19 were settled by the parties themselves and "In the remaining seven stoppages the Department took prompt measures . . . by means of ad hoc committees, etc.", which indicates accurately the pattern evolved in New Zealand for the settlement of strikes.

But sometimes the pattern fades; and in this case, apart from such an extreme measure as invoking the Public Safety Conservation Act 1932,[39] the most effective weapon against a recalcitrant union is the power given to the Minister of Labour by section 198 of the Act to deregister a union. The scheme, as it worked out in practice at the time of the Auckland carpenters' dispute in 1948-49, is as follows. The union is deregistered and a new union, formed by "free" labour, is called into being and registered with the consent of the Minister. The free union seeks an award from the Court, and the award, when made, becomes binding on all employers in the industry in that locality by reason of the "blanket clause" referred to above. By section 153 of the Act the award also binds every worker employed by any such employer.

Compulsory membership of the new union plays a material part in strengthening its hand and in weakening the position of the deregistered union, and it has been recognised by the Minister of Labour that abolition of such compulsion may weaken the effect of deregistration.[40] While the weapon is clumsy and indirect and liable to create at least as much industrial ill-will as it cures, deregistration remains, potentially, a serious threat to a union.

. . . . . .

New Zealand's system of industrial relations has at present a rather uncritical popular acceptance. The Act has become a sort of godhead, with the Court as its shrine, though there does exist an important and valuable minority view which on a complex of grounds questions the system at its roots. The highly centralised control of the institutions involved and the consequential weaknesses of structure and operation give grounds for such criticism. But in its way the system works, probably dispensing adequate social justice; and while it has almost total acceptance in a democratic community the first task is to look at the thing as it is rather than enter into a kind of criticism which has too often become speculative and divorced from the day-by-day world in which people work together in industry.

NOTES

1. Keith Sinclair, *A History of New Zealand* (*Penguin Books*, 1959), p. 181.

2. See 12 B.A. (Book of Awards) 918.

3. *Cromwell and Bannockburn Colliery Co.* case (1906), 25 N.Z.L.R. (New Zealand Law Reports) 986. Cooper J. also discusses in this case the meaning of "dispute."

4. *Hikurangi Coal-Miners*, 4 B.A. 117.

5. An Industrial Association is a "council or other body . . . representing not less than two unions connected with one industry or related industries of employers or workers" and registered in the same manner as a union (Industrial Conciliation and Arbitration Act 1954, s. 87).

6. *Nelson General Labourers' Union*, 4 B.A. 117. The value of, indeed the need for, this prohibition has been illustrated by the unduly protracted and technical proceedings in the Court on an arbitration under the Agricultural Workers Act 1936 (which contains no such prohibition) commencing on 13/6/1961.

7. Report of the Department of Labour for the year ended 31 March, 1960 (Appendix to Journals: H. 11), p. 20.

8. Hon. Sir Arthur Tyndall: Judge, Court of Arbitration (1940); Solicitor of Supreme Court; 1909, Cadet, Public Works Dept.; 1913, Asst. Eng., Dunedin City Corp.; 1920, in charge P.W.D., Western Samoa; 1925, Engineer, Main Highways Board; 1934, Under-Sec. of Mines; 1936, also Director of Housing Construction.

9. *Attorney-General v. Butler*, (1953) N.Z.L.R. 944 S.C.

10. *Magner v. Gohns*, (1916) N.Z.L.R. 529, for example.

11. See *N.Z. Waterside Workers Federation v. Frazer*, (1924) N.Z.L.R. 689, especially the judgment of Salmond J.

12. *Wellington Foremen Stevedores, etc., Union v. Tyndall*, (1944) N.Z.L.R. 52.

13. *Wgtn Municipal Officers Ass'n v. Wgtn City Corpn.*, (1951) N.Z.L.R. 786.

14. *N.Z. Harbour Boards Union of Employers v. Tyndall*, (1944) N.Z.L.R. 584.

15. *Taylor & Oakley v. Mr. Justice Edwards* (1900), 18 N.Z.L.R. 876, per Stout C.J. at 885.

16. *Auckland Builders' Union v. Clark* (1904), 6 G.L.R. (Gazette Law Reports) 538.

17. An employer's application still needs full citation to make all employers respondents.

18. This is the usual colloquial description of the clause in New Zealand where the expression "common rule" is not used.

19. The Economic Stabilisation Regulations 1953, Reg. 3 (2) as amended. These regulations are the successor to the wartime Stabilisation Emergency Regulations.

20. The strike of 1951 is commonly and incorrectly described as "Communist," but if a political label must be stuck on, it would more properly be "Syndicalist," and the leadership of the strike came preponderantly from members of the Labour Party or of no party.

21. See for details Report on the Department of Labour for the year ended 31 March, 1960, Appendix II.

22. Affiliations having members:

Up to 250	1 vote
Over 250 and up to 500	2 votes
Over 500 and up to 1000	3 votes
Over 1000 to 2000	4 votes
. . . . . .	
Over 7000 to 8000	10 votes

One extra vote for each complete 1250 members.
No affiliation to exercise more than 20 votes.

23. The effects of the preponderance of small unions are somewhat mitigated by the formation of industrial associations consisting of two unions or more. At 31/12/1959 there were 41 such associations registered under the Act comprising 219 unions.

24. Industrial Conciliation and Arbitration Amendment Act 1936, s. 18: Compulsory membership had been held in 1916 to be not an industrial matter: *Magner v. Gohns* (supra, note 10).

25. An industrial agreement under the Act is an agreement between the parties filed with the Clerk of Awards and having the force of an award

between the parties making the agreement and any others concurring in it.

26. A National Government's attempt, in 1950-51, to abolish compulsion was abandoned in the face of opposition from both unions and employers; see R. M. Martin, "Twenty Years of Compulsory Unionism," *Political Science*, Vol. 8, No. 2, Sept., 1956, pp. 107ff. But this experience did not deter the National Party from including in its 1960 platform a plank which could have brought the party few votes and may prove intensely embarrassing.

27. Analogous to the A.C.T.U.

28. *Evening Post* (Wellington), 4/5/1961 and 5/5/1961.

29. *Dominion* (Wellington), 3/6/1961.

29a. Since this was written, the Employers' Federation has also announced its opposition to the Government's proposals, thus reaffirming its position of a decade earlier and, possibly, foreshadowing a similar outcome: see n. 26 above.

30. For an indication of the character of and the measure of apathy in such unions see the Court's decision on an inquiry held into an election held in the Wgtn, Taranaki and M'borough Clerical Workers' Union (60 B.A. 532).

30a. Since this was written, Government has announced, in broad terms, its proposals. They provide for "unqualified preference" or "union shop" by agreement in Conciliation or if the union shows the Court that a majority in the industry wants it. In other cases the Court will provide such lesser preference as seems appropriate. Consideration is being given to a limited right for employers to apply for exemption from "union shop" provisions if a majority of employees wants it (*Dominion*, 12/6/61).

31. See "The Strike," infra.

32. A bow is made in the Act toward this principle by provision for exempting conscientious objectors from membership. The worker must pay the union subscription to the Social Security fund.

33. (1910) A.C. 87 (H.L.); based on the meaning of "trade union" in the Trade Union Act 1871 (U.K.).

34. (1913), 16 G.L.R. 309.

35. *Ohinemuri Mines & Batteries Employees*, (1917) N.Z.L.R. 829.

36. *The Auckland Freezing Works Union v. The N.Z. Freezing Works Association*, (1951) N.Z.L.R. 341 (S.C.).

37. Now ss. 89-102 of the Act. The legislation is modelled upon corresponding Australian provisions: (Commonwealth) Conciliation and Arbitration Act, ss. 159-69; (N.S.W.) Industrial Arbitration Act, ss. 111A-111M. The Court has recently held, on a case stated by the Registrar of Industrial Unions (unreported yet) that these sections do not apply to associations.

38. Reports of the Department of Labour show that in the five years ended 31/3/1960, there were 44 stoppages of 3-10 days and 13 stoppages of over 10 days.

39. As was done at the time of the 1951 waterfront strike.

40. *Evening Post*, 13/6/61.

H Sweden's System of Industrial Relations*

ARTHUR DONNER

Introduction

THE SWEDISH SYSTEM of industrial relations reflects very closely the social and economic development of that country. Sweden is a small, export-dominated country, with a high standard of living and a high degree of labor organization; however, interest in the Swedish system of industrial relations exists far out of relation to either the size or importance of that country. Part of the explanation of this unusual interest may be traced to a discreet use of government pressures to bring about the development of harmonious labor-management relations. This unorthodox blend of government pressures and peaceful industrial relations has helped in raising Sweden's living standards to one of the highest in the world.

* Compiled by Arthur W. Donner, research assistant, Industry Department, Wharton School of Finance and Commerce, University of Pennsylvania, from T. L. Johnston, *Collective Bargaining in Sweden*, and other sources cited in the footnotes.

The two most important organizations in the Swedish labor market are the LO, the Confederation of Swedish Trade Unions, and the SAF, the Swedish Employers' Confederation. Forty-four national unions, with 7,930 local branches are affiliated with the LO. In 1960 these unions had approximately 25,000 contracts in force, of which 334 were national in scope.[1] The other major labor organization in the market is the TCO, the Central Organization of Salaried Employees. The TCO membership embraces approximately three-fourths of all salaried employees, while the LO membership comprises nearly all of Sweden's wage earners.

In Sweden collective bargaining occurs at three levels, central, national, and local. The two major confederations, the LO and the SAF, negotiate the general or framework agreement, which is normally used as a guide line for negotiations at other levels. National unions and employer associations, both of which represent an entire industry or all wage earners within an industry, undertake negotiations of national agreements. Finally, local level negotiations are engaged in between local unions and local employers or small employer associations.

A logical outgrowth of central bargaining has been the development of a "national incomes policy" since the mid 1950's. This is understandable when one considers that the leading agreement between the LO and the SAF covers about 900,000 workers out of an approximate total of 3,000,000 Swedish employees.

"It contains a clause to the effect that the SAF and LO agree to see that all other groups of wage and salary earners, including government employees, follow the guiding principle in the SAF-LO agreements. By special agreements, the incomes of farmers have been linked to the incomes of industrial workers. Thus, the agricultural sector may be said to be included in this partial national incomes policy."[2]

These agreements do not extend beyond the memberships of the associations involved. For example, the incomes of small businessmen, professionals, and management personnel, as well as the profits of limited companies, are not part of these agreements, and are left to be determined by market forces.[3]

The objective of a controlled wage policy has been somewhat hampered in the post-war period by the existence of the phenomenon of wage drift. Wage drift refers to the difference between the planned wage increase stipulated in an agreement and the actual wage increases earned by the workers.

"Under normal conditions, the wage drift usually stays within the range of 2 to 3 percent per year, though it went up as high as 8 percent in 1951 and 5 percent in 1955. It has added to the difficulties of collective bargaining and tends to counteract the central employer and employee organizations' influence on wages."[4]

Although government mandatory or voluntary mediation is a part of the Swedish collective bargaining system, the role of government has been relegated in the most part to the codification of practices previously agreed to by the two major parties, the SAF and the LO. In some cases the use of impartial mediators appointed by the government has facilitated the reaching of an agreement. In these cases the only obligation the parties are under is to accept a mediator's call to negotiate. The mediator presents no legal restraint on their freedom of action.

The Principal Organizations in the Labor Market

A major element accounting for industrial peace in many West European countries has been the strength and stability of the union movement. Among the factors which contribute to this situation in the Swedish case are the high degree of union organization, the loyalty of the union membership, and the existence of a strong, centralized labor confederation. Probably one of the key elements in the Swedish case is the strategic control the LO has over its member unions.

"The Swedish national trade union center exhibits a significant degree of centralized power and control. Proposed strikes involving more than three percent of the workers in an industry must have the approval of the General Council of the LO before LO strike benefits can be paid. The LO officials have the right to supervise bargaining if two or more unions are affected. LO leaders and representatives participate in negotiations and may submit proposals of their own. Above and beyond these formal provisions, control of the central federation is strengthened by the long tradition of solidarity within the labor movement."[5]

The tripartite structure of the LO, viz. the congress, the representative assembly and the secretariat, has been in existence since the founding of the organization in 1898. The congress is the supreme decision making authority of the LO and it meets every five years. Between congresses, authority is vested in a representative assembly which consists of a secretariat and representatives of affiliated unions. The assembly normally meets only twice a year and hence continuity is provided by the secretariat, which consists of thirteen members of affiliated unions, three of whom are full time salaried officers. The four main areas in which the secretariat is involved are interpretation of organization matters, wage policy and negotiations, financial support to unions, and an active role in any decisions concerning industrial disputes.[6]

The other major institution in the labor market, the SAF, has been much more active in the trend towards centralization of control. The difference in emphasis may be traced to the fact that the trade union movement evolved more slowly than its employers' counterpart, while the SAF, almost from the period of its inception, was a highly centralized body.

The SAF was organized in 1902, and like the LO its structure is tripartite. The SAF originally consisted of a General Meeting as a supreme authority, a General Council, and an Executive Board. This structure is still in existence, but the Executive Board, followed by the General Council, have replaced the General Meeting as centres of power.

From its very beginning the SAF has been an active and effective organization. As early as 1900 it employed the use of the lock-out as an offensive weapon.

"Offensively, SAF used the lock-out in the early days to try to adjust the wage level to the state of the industry, obtain uniform agreements, and develop a settled procedure for negotiations, whereas the LO had to overcome the parochial and democratic ideals of the national unions. In 1908 and 1909 SAF, by contrast to LO, was able to roll a series of small disputes into the gigantic clash of the Great Strike of 1909, which left LO very feeble, and SAF triumphant. In later years aggressive use of lock-outs has given way to moderation. . . ."[7]

Johnston mentions that the threat of a large scale lock-out, as recently as 1955, indicates that the effective use of this weapon is not outdated.[8]

In addition to the LO and SAF, other organizations wield considerable strength in the labor market. Paralleling a rapid growth in the number of salaried employees, was the growth of the rival employee organization, the TCO, which was originally created in 1944. In 1960 the TCO consisted of 36 affiliated unions, covering 394,000 employees primarily in the banking, insurance, government, and retail trade industries.[9] The TCO bargains with employer associations and other employers not affiliated with the SAF. In many ways it is similar to the LO, although it does not have the latter's financial strength and its members bargain solely on a company to company basis.

While the function and purposes of the TCO are much the same as those of the LO, there is some difference in the area of politics. The TCO is politically independent, while most of its members probably vote Liberal or Conservative. The LO, though not formally affiliated with the Social Democratic Party, which has been in government alone or in coalition since 1933, does support the party at elections. Furthermore, the LO has been operating on the egalitarian principle of raising the wage rates of the lowest-paid workers, even though this has necessarily resulted in the narrowing of wage differentials among all categories of labor.

Other smaller employee organizations bargaining in the labor market are the Swedish Confederation of Professional Associations, consisting of about 57,000 members, and the National Federation of Civil Servants, having an approximate membership of 16,000.[10]

The Negotiation Process

Since most large agreements in Sweden terminate approximately at the end of the calendar year the "collective bargaining season" usually begins in the fall and may last through until the following spring. An element in any final settlement is the government's announcement, early in January, of its economic plans for the following fiscal year.

On its part, the LO representative assembly hears a report from the Wage Policy Council and discusses the policy to be pursued in the forthcoming negotiations with respect to wages. In those years when a central framework agreement is negotiated, the national unions await the results of the SAF-LO negotiations. These results constitute a guide line for the magnitude of over-all wage increases, but negotiations at the lower levels determine the distribution of increases among the different categories of labor. Central agreements are not universally popular, and the typical criticisms levied against them have to do with their lack of flexibility and the fact that they do not take into consideration the developments within specific industries. Even with these drawbacks the likelihood is that central agreements will continue to form the pattern for future determination of general wage levels.

In the past when a central agreement was not negotiated, the length and character of negotiations varied among unions. Generally, the workers in the fabricated metal products industry, with a labor force of about 150,000 employees, would settle their agreement first and set a wage pattern for the rest of the country.[11]

Government involvement in collective bargaining negotiations occurs generally when a state mediator, a mediation commission, or both, are requested.

"In 1953, for example, the negotiation of fifty-five agreements, covering about two hundred thousand workers, required the appointment of special mediators without a subsequent mediation commission, and mediation commissions were appointed at one stage or another in the negotiation of twenty-six agreements, covering about six hundred thousand employees."[12]

To the negotiators, mediation has several advantages. It allows for time to see how negotiations in the other industries are going, it partly shifts responsibility for settlement on to the mediators, and it helps prove to the rank and file that a union is presenting very firm proposals on their behalf.[13]

Government Regulations

In Sweden industrial disputes are divided into two separate categories, non-justiciable and justiciable.[14] Non-justiciable disputes are those involving disagreements about matters not regulated by contract or statute, while justiciable disputes are those which arise over the provisions of a statute or contract.

The Swedish Mediation Act was set up to deal with the former kinds of dispute and a Labor Court was designed to deal with the latter variety of dispute.

The original Mediation Act of 1920 was predominantly concerned with non-justiciable disputes. A 1935 act provides that parties to a dispute must give seven days' notice of a strike or boycott to the mediator, who has no other purpose than that of bringing about an agreement. The mediators are not able to impose either the government's or their own personal views on the contract provisions.

The Swedish Labor Court was established in 1928 to interpret provisions written into collective agreements. One of its principal powers is the right it has to levy fines for violation of collective agreements.

"Popularly, it has been called a court of arbitration, but that obscures its essential function. It is not at all concerned to adjust differences of opinion, to compromise or conciliate, but to adjudicate on what collective contracts mean in the light of the Act when disputes about them arise. It does not have complete jurisdiction over justiciable disputes, since the parties are free to arrive at alternative peaceful methods of settling disputes about collective agreements. . . . But no direct action can be taken over justiciable disputes, and the Labor Court is a final court of judgement. No appeals can be made against decisions."[15]

The Basic Agreements

A mutual desire to avoid government regulation, plus the minority position of the Social Democratic government at that time, were motivating factors in influencing the LO and the SAF into agreeing to a basic code of behavior in the labor market in 1938. Formal discussion on this subject had been going on since 1926, but it required a favorable combination of circumstances and people to bring about a final agreement in 1938.[16]

The Basic Agreement of that year, composed of five chapters, sets out a procedure for the negotiation of grievances and a machinery for dealing with disputes where the public's interest is involved. Moreover, the Basic Agreement contains a number of regulations intended to prevent injury to neutral third parties in a labor dispute.

The Basic Agreement allows strikes, lock-outs, boycotts, and a wide range of bargaining pressures by either party to a dispute, with some reservations. Following regulations laid down in the Mediation act, it is necessary for parties to completely exhaust the bargaining procedure before resorting to any coercive measures.

Chapter 4 of the Basic Agreement, dealing with the control and limitation of certain types of direct action and protection for neutral third parties, was conceived mainly because of demand made in the 1930's for such labor legislation. In this chapter, the participants employed an interesting approach to the problem of defining neutral third parties.

"The problem of defining and safeguarding third parties arises because it is not always possible to confine a dispute to the direct disputants. . . .
A neutral third party is not defined directly in the Agreement, but primarily by the negative approach of stating the circumstances in which an outside party is non-neutral.
Broadly, where economic sanctions against another party are forbidden third parties are also given at least as much protection."[17]

In Chapter 5 the Basic Agreement is extended to cover conflicts which threaten Swedish public interest. In effect this chapter commits both the LO and SAF to apply their influence towards preventing or bringing to an end such disputes. Johnston points out that from the experience of Chapter 5 and its sparing use, neither parties wish to have their disputes habitually referred to the Labor Market Council.[18]

In 1961 approximately 560,000 LO members of 16 national unions were covered by the terms of the Basic Agreement. This represents approximately 80% of the workers employed by SAF affiliates, but as Johnston specifies these statistics are not a sufficient indication of the impact of this legislation.[19] For one reason as a deterrent factor its quantitative merit cannot be measured. Similarly the Basic Agreement of 1938 established a precedent for other forms of cooperation in the labor market. For example, in 1942 the two organizations established a Joint Committee for Workers' Protection, a 1944 agreement led to the creation of a bipartisan Vocational and Guidance Council, in 1948 a Joint Time-and-Motion Study Board was set up, and in 1951, a joint Labor Market Council for Women's Questions was established to deal with sex differential in wages.[20]

Thus, a precedent was established by the Basic Agreement of

1938 which served to inspire other more comprehensive and detailed forms of cooperation between labor and management.

The Scope of Bargaining in Sweden

In relation to North American practices, the bargaining package in Sweden is far more restricted, and due to the generally sympathetic position of the government in power, the Swedish labor movement has been able to derive many of its benefits through legislation. This situation has served to narrow bargaining, at the national level, primarily to wages. There is also the prevailing view among the two top confederations that all their affiliates must willingly accept any agreements made by the central organizations.

As socialists, many of the Swedish labor leaders maintain that any benefits derived by one group of workers should be universally extended to all workers. Hence, in their view, there is the need for government to maintain equality among the workers. But, as Lester indicates, their ideology is inconsistent since they also maintain with equal vigor "that union administered unemployment compensation, with worker contributions and state subsidy, is an appropriate method for handling that form of social insurance."[21]

In recent years the SAF has come to realize the advantage of negotiation over legislation and has initiated pressures in this direction. As an example of this position may be cited their proposal for a private pension program arrived at through a collective agreement between the two major confederations.[22] The LO, however, has favored government legislation as the proper vehicle for the introduction of a pension program.

A tactic often employed by individual employers to head off LO demands is to provide their own benefit schemes, outside of collective bargaining, as a means of insuring the loyalty of their employees, since the economy has been functioning under conditions of labor scarcity in most of the post-war period.

Concluding Remarks

Ross and Hartman have summarized succinctly the four key elements accounting for the relatively peaceful system of industrial relations in Sweden. These elements are:

1) the high degree of union organization;

2) the fact that employers agreed quite early to recognize the right of workers to organize and strike;

3) the existence of strong organizations on both sides leading to a tightly controlled bargaining situation; and

4) the agreement by both federations to minimize the role of government in their affairs. (The Basic Agreement) [23]

It is interesting to note Galenson's remarks on the fact that grassroots control of bargaining is vanishing and that centralized collective bargaining has proven to be incompatible with the membership referendum. As Galenson indicates, the terms of a collective agreement involving more than one union cannot be blocked by the members of any one of the participating unions; whereas, twenty-five years ago, no collective agreement could be ratified by a union unless it was supported by a majority of its workers. [24]

An analysis of statistics on days lost through industrial stoppages in Sweden ranks her very well on the world scene. But the strike-record alone is not a sufficient indication of whether or not an industrial relations system is operating smoothly. It does not include a measure of output lost to industrial slow-downs prior to stoppages, and as Johnston points out, an industrial stoppage is not always more costly to society than, for example, a wage settlement which may be inflationary. [25]

In Sweden grievance procedure is well organized, both through private arrangement and through the machinery of the Labor Court.

"The law, as we saw, has aimed at developing the collective contracts system as a private system of government in the labor market, even for groups of employees, such as civil servants, who have traditionally been agents of, rather than bargainers with, the government. The absence of legislation, judged at least by international standards, makes it crystal clear what the alternative to agreement are in the event of non-justiciable disputes. This has led the parties, under the threat of law, to work out for themselves a code for industrial peace through the Basic Agreements which control sanctions, protect neutrals, and society, and endeavour to resolve the vexed questions of job security." [26]

Another factor which may be noted as a cause for the disappearance of strike activity in Sweden is the political effectiveness of the labor movement, and its close interaction with the Social Democratic party.

This cannot be overstressed. Sweden's government has been dominated since World War II by the Socialists. When the unions do not obtain their objectives, they have recourse to favorable Government action. Hence strikes are unnecessary. If the Social Democrats fall from power, the peaceful nature of Swedish labor relations could change.

NOTES

1. T. L. Johnston, *Collective Bargaining in Sweden: A Study of the Labor Market and its Institutions* (Cambridge, Mass.: Harvard University Press, 1962), p. 235.
2. K. O. Faxim, "Income Policy In Sweden; Problems And Developments," *British Journal of Industrial Relations*, Vol. II, No. 3 (November, 1964), p. 340.
3. *Ibid.*, p. 340-341.
4. L. Lohse, "Centralization of Bargaining in Sweden Since 1939," *Monthly Labor Review*, Vol. 81 (November, 1958), p. 1235.
5. A. M. Ross and P. T. Hartman, *Changing Patterns of Industrial Conflict* (New York: Harvard University Press, 1962), p. 109.
6. Johnston, *op. cit.*, p. 39.
7. *Ibid.*, p. 77.
8. *Ibid.*
9. *Ibid.*, p. 92.
10. *Ibid.*
11. L. Lohse, "Centralization of Bargaining in Sweden Since 1939," *Monthly Labor Review*, Vol. 81 (November, 1958), p. 1232.
12. R. A. Lester, "Reflections on Collective Bargaining in Britain and Sweden," *Industrial and Labor Relations Review*, Vol. 10, No. 3 (April, 1957), p. 395.
13. *Ibid.*, p. 396.
14. Johnston, *op. cit.*, p. 138.
15. *Ibid.*, p. 154-155.
16. *Ibid.*, p. 173-174.
17. *Ibid.*, p. 178.
18. *Ibid.*, p. 186.
19. *Ibid.*, p. 191.
20. Lester, *op. cit.*, p. 390.
21. *Ibid.*, p. 397.
22. *Ibid.*
23. See Ross and Hartman, *op. cit.*, p. 107-113.
24. W. Galenson (ed.), *Comparative Labor Movements* (New York: Prentice-Hall Inc., 1952), p. 133.
25. Johnston, *op. cit.*, p. 339.
26. *Ibid.*, p. 338-339.

I Incomes Policy: *Norwegian Experience**

HERMOD SKÅNLAND**

* * *

Whēn the Norwegian system of economic planning was first developed in the immediate post-war years, a great number of direct regulations were generally accepted as necessary in the situation of shortages and excess demand which was then prevalent. Interference from the side of the Government in the formation of incomes constituted a part of this system. During the period from 1945 to 1952 practically all labour disputes were referred to a wage board if the parties concerned did not succeed in reaching an agreement between themselves. For a few months in the latter part of 1947 even a wage-stop law was in effect. The wage boards were tripartite in character representing employers, employees and an independent chairman. The chairman, who in general had the decisive vote, would form his opinion mainly on the basis of equity and the Government was given no

* Reprinted by permission from the *British Journal of Industrial Relations*, Vol. II, No. 3, November 1964.
** Head of Economics Department, Norwegian Ministry of Finance.

formal power of instruction. The most important aim of the system was to avoid conflicts in the labour market. The general economic situation was, however, also taken into consideration, and the development of wage incomes during these years was indeed well suited to the formidable task of reconstruction by which the country was confronted.

Other elements of an incomes policy were limitations of dividends and price control. Dividend distribution was gradually liberalized, but was not abolished until 1960. Price control was rather rigid until the beginning of the 1950s and served both as an instrument of price policy and for the purpose of influencing non-wage incomes.

This strong influence upon wages, salaries and other incomes could be tolerated in a period of national emergency. But both the trade unions and the Employers' Federation were in principle opposed to Government control in this field; the trade unions were opposed in spite of the very strong connections with the Labour government which had held the power almost continuously since 1945. The main reasons for this attitude from the side of the trade unions can be summarized as follows:

(a) As a result of the full employment policy pursued by the government and because of the high demand for Norwegian exports, there was a permanent shortage of labour. In this situation the workers felt that wage policy consisted of preventing them from obtaining what the labour market might offer. This objection was certainly justified in terms of nominal wages and to some extent probably also in real wages. High business earnings (and thereby savings) were necessary if investments were to be kept at the high level which rapid reconstruction required.

(b) It was believed that wage control led towards undue standardization of wage rates. Increases were often made in öre per hour, thus levelling out differences in stipulated rates. At the same time wage drift maintained the differences in real earnings, and those who failed to gain by wage drift felt that they were lagging behind because they did not obtain larger improvements in rates than the others.

(c) Thirdly, the possibility of trade union leaders influencing wage earnings was reduced to the same extent as Government influence was increased. A governmental wage policy would therefore tend to weaken the position of trade union leaders and the members' affiliation to their union.

Although it may be assumed that the employers by and large profited from the wage policy pursued during this period, their resistance against the system was as great or even greater than that of the trade unions. Partly their reasons may have corresponded to those mentioned under (b) and (c) above, but a general hostility towards most kinds of government regulation or 'planned economy' may have been just as important.

The system of compulsory arbitration by a wage board was first relaxed in 1949 when disputes arising out of demands approved by the executive bodies of the National Labour Union or the National Federation of Employers were exempted from it. Thereafter, this kind of procedure was finally allowed to expire in December 1952. Since then, wage boards have repeatedly been established by separate laws in order to avoid labour conflicts which would seriously endanger national interests. Like the former permanent wage board, these *ad hoc* boards appear to have been more influenced by considerations of equity than of economic policy. By and large, therefore, it seems correct to say that the responsibility for wage determination during the following ten year period was vested in the organizations of the labour market.

Wage contracts in Norway are in most cases concluded for two years, occasionally for one or three years. In most cases contracts covering about two-thirds of union membership come up for renegotiation during a period concentrated into three or four months. The extent to which these negotiations are centrally conducted may differ, but in most cases some central issues, such as a general wage increase or a reduction of working hours are decided by the central leadership of the unions. General guide lines for the unions may also be issued by a central Council of Agreements.

The greater the group to which the result of the negotiations applies, the greater will also be its effect upon the national economy. The 'national interest' thus tends to be a consideration of higher priority in centralized than in decentralized bargaining. The organizational structure of the Norwegian trade union movement should therefore by itself be a favourable factor for the construction of an incomes policy.

The Instrument of Price Subsidies

The two or three year agreement periods have been considered by most people in Norway as much preferable to those of only one year. Labour conflicts are prevented for a similar period of time and the management of the organizations have avoided some of the pressure and the heavy work-load of general wage negotiations and thus got more time for other organizational activities. The wage-earners, on their side, have made it a condition for accepting such long contract periods that they should be given a certain guarantee of the purchasing power of their earnings. The guarantee has been given in the form of the price escalator clause. This has been included in the standard wage contract during fourteen out of the nineteen years 1945-63. For most of the time these were of a semi-automatic character, giving wage-earners the right to demand negotiations for wage increases when the price index rose above a certain level. That they could also work the other way round has been mainly of theoretical interest. An automatic price escalator operated only during the immediate post-war years and for one short period in the beginning of the 1950s. Out of the four general escalator revisions of wages and salaries, one was the result of the automatic clause; in the three others, the degree of compensation varied between two-thirds and three-quarters. Two of the three cases were decided by a wage board.

Together with the wage increase following these revisions, there would also generally be adjustments of farm prices, thus bringing the total price level up a few points in between the regular termination and renegotiation of wage and farm price agreements. Most of the time the Government has been very anxious to prevent such events taking place and has for this purpose used price control and price subsidization. We will return to the price control later, here we will deal with the instrument of price subsidies.

The policy of price subsidization was initiated during the war. After the liberation it was generally assumed that the level of world market prices would again fall. By maintaining and if necessary increasing the price subsidies and then again abolishing them when the expected price fall occurred, we would be able to 'cut through' the period of high prices, coming out on the other side with reduced subsidies and a stable price level. As everybody knows, the great fall in prices never came about, and after the devaluation price subsidies had to be drastically reduced. The gradual increase in the price level, which other countries had experienced for several years, was then concentrated into a period of little more than two years, from 1950-52, when consumer prices increased by about 30 per cent in Norway.

The Government's intention in 1950 was to gradually abolish the price subsidies. However, the sharp rise in prices and the prospect of a continued price-wage spiral, led the Government to increase again the price subsidies on milk towards the end of 1952 in an attempt to establish a new stabilization line. This attempt was rather successful for some time.

In succeeding years the Government has repeatedly increased price subsidies when there has been a serious danger that the index of consumer prices would break through the established level, thus giving the wage earners the right to demand a wage increase. These subsidies have been given on a few important foodstuffs, such as milk, margarine, flour and sugar. By this intervention the consumer price index has been kept sufficiently low to postpone a regulation of wages and farm prices until the regular termination of agreements. Then a difficult decision had to be made. Should the subsidies be reduced, thereby pushing the price index upwards a few extra points, something which would undoubtedly complicate the negotiations, or should they be maintained with the heavy drain upon Government finances which this would constitute? Increases in price subsidies in order to prevent the price index breaking through the 'ceiling' have regularly been considered as temporary until the forthcoming negotiations, but the Government has nevertheless shrunk back from the steep price increase which a reduction would imply. The price subsidies have, therefore, been continued until the financial burden of them has become intolerable. A very much sharper upwards jump in prices has then been unavoidable.

* * *

Price Regulation

It is generally recognized that any policy on incomes meets with its greatest technical difficulties in attempting to influence incorporated income and income from self-employment. By excluding such forms of incomes, however, it may tend to have unfavourable redistributive effects, and, at any rate, it is unlikely to meet with acceptance by wage and salary earners. In Norway, as in most other countries, these have expressed their opposition against having their own incomes regulated unless measures are taken by Government which can influence other forms of income as well. Some aspects of Government policy with respect to farmers' and fishermen's income, which by and large can be said to be regulated along lines parallel to those of wage incomes, have been mentioned earlier. The wage- and salary-earners' attitude towards a one-sided wage policy is based upon the fear that those earning profits in industry, by trade margins or by the various kinds of income from self-employment, are those who will ultimately benefit from a wage restraint.

The Government has used two measures in order to influence non-wage income outside farm and fishing income; dividend control and price control.

Dividend control was introduced immediately after the war and lasted until 1960. It took the form of approval by the Price Directorate, if dividends above 6 per cent were to be distributed in corporations with share capital above a certain amount. The rational of this control was partly to prevent a sharp increase in personal income from capital and partly to make sure that profits would remain with the company. The control was gradually liberalized during the 1950s. Although the requirement of approval by the Price Directorate was maintained, guide lines laid down for its activity in this field allowed average dividends to increase almost every year.

In 1960 a new law was passed requiring special reserves to be set aside when dividends above 5 per cent of net assets (including share capital) were distributed. Aside from this, dividend distributions have been free. The law has not changed very much the level of dividends, nor the wage earners' confidence in control of non-wage incomes.

Price control has been much more important as an instrument in this field. Regulation may apply to all levels of production or distribution. The techniques can be grouped into three main categories.

(a) Maximum prices, which apply to a number of agricultural commodities, transport, and hospital rates. In towns and built-up areas price regulation also covers rent and real estate prices.

(b) Price stop, which recently has been used for prices and profits fixed by restrictive business associations.

(c) Regulation of profits, which at present applies to a number of foodstuffs and their transformation. Retail profits on basic general foods have in addition been fixed by special agreements between representatives of the trade and the price authorities, covering such items as eggs, cheese, sugar, a number of soft drinks, beer etc.

There is furthermore control of restrictive business practices. Retail price maintenance is, among other things, prohibited. Although considerable progress has been made in this field, we still meet with the well-known difficulties which any anti-monopoly policy is usually faced with.

* * *

Government Intervention in Income Determination

We have so far considered the background and institutional framework of income determination in Norway and the most important instruments at the Government's disposal. It remains to consider the Government's attempts at making the parties concerned use their own instruments in such a way that an intended redistribution of real income could be achieved by a minimum increase in the level of costs of production.

One of the great assets of the Government in its incomes policy has been its close contact with the trade union movement. Traditionally there exists a very close co-operation between the National Union and the Labour Party, and as there has been a Labour Government during the whole post-war period, but for one month, a corresponding contact has existed between the National Union and the Government. The Government has, therefore, had considerable opportunity to influence the unions through persuasion. The Prime Minister, or the Finance Minister, will generally address the Convention of the Union, or the Council of Agreements, when they meet to decide on strategy before new wage negotiations are opened. More important probably are the personal relations between the leaders of the party, the Government and the trade unions.

With the established connection between wage and farm income, which I have already described, it has been a matter of particular importance to find some way of co-ordinating wage increases and increases in farm prices. To the Government the contact with the other parties concerned in the income settlements has been equally as important as the contact with the trade unions.

The first attempt at this kind of co-ordination took place in 1956, when the Finance Minister called the parties together and informed them of the Government's plan to reduce subsidies, and at the same time suggested a standard for average wage increases and increases in farm prices. The settlement by and large followed these lines. The new wage contracts included an index clause and the Government promised to avoid keeping prices just below the ceiling set by this clause. If the Government decided to keep prices stable by means of subsidies, the level of this stability should be at a reasonable distance from the new 'red line' which had been established. The Government did choose to introduce price subsidies in order to avoid an escalator revision of wages, and before the tariff period was out, price subsidies were increased by several steps and by a considerable amount. The success of the settlement of 1956 was, therefore, very much dependent upon the Government's willingness to spend the necessary sums in order to avoid the underlying tendencies for prices to increase to become effective in the cost of living.

The negotiations in 1958 resulted by and large in a prolongation of the existing agreements, but with a reduction of working hours to take place in 1959, and a corresponding increase in time rates of pay. Price subsidies were reduced, an index settlement took place, and a new ceiling was established at a higher level. During the years 1958-61 subsidies were again increased in order to keep the cost of living from rising above the new ceiling.

When the three-year agreement expired in 1961, five years had passed since there had been negotiations by the industrial unions. There was, therefore, a strong need for a general rivision of agreements on this level. The Government again reduced price subsidies and did not interfere in the negotiations. The price agreement between the Government and the farmers followed the general pattern then set by the parties in the labour market. These negotiations took place in an atmosphere where the general demand situation was favourable for most industries, with the result that wage rates were increased on average by about 10 per cent and farm incomes by no less. The increase in consumer prices during the first year after the conclusion of the agreement was about 6.5 per cent, and the strongest supporters of the independence of labour market organizations were, at least for the time being, convinced of the necessity of some kind of Government intervention in income determination.

In good time before the negotiations in 1963 were due to take place, the Prime Minister called upon the trade unions, the Employers' Federation and the farmers' organizations, to take part in the construction of a joint committee to deal with price and wage revisions. This invitation was declined by the Employers' Federation, probably for political reasons. It appears reasonable to assume that they did not want formally to take part in anything that could be interpreted as an acceptance of the Government's economic policy. However, all parties did agree to meet at rather frequent intervals for mutual information on prospects and policies. At these meetings, the organizations have been represented by their presidents and vice-presidents, and the Government by the Prime Minister, the Finance Minister and the Minister of Prices and Wages. These meetings have fulfilled very much the same purpose as that which was intended by the joint committee.

In the National Budget for 1963 the Government presented its general views on price and incomes policy. As a guiding line for national incomes policy it stated that 'the least that can be demanded of the Norwegian price and cost developments is that they be such that Norwegian competitiveness abroad is upheld'. This put the consideration of long term growth and production at the forefront, making price stability an aim secondary to that of growth. Prices must be prevented from rising too fast, not so much because of the unfavourable redistributive effects of a continuous price increase as because of possible detrimental effects upon production.

The National Budget pointed out, with respect to the wage and price negotiations in 1963, that adjustments which were at that time already known would result in an increase in total wages that would lay a heavy claim on improved productivity in the year ahead. 'Any further income increases which may occur must be expected to react on the price level.' This suggested a prolongation of existing wages and farm prices. It very soon became clear, however, that it was impossible to maintain such a restrictive line. Little is known of the discussions which took place in the Prime Minister's office or directly between the parties in the labour market. The result, however, can be summarized as follows:

(a) a general increase of 'leading wage rates' (wages in manufacturing industry, building and construction) of 2.5 per cent,

(b) an increase in prices of agricultural products and fish giving a corresponding percentage increase in income to these groups,

(c) an increase in price subsidies to an upward limit of N. kroner 150 mill. for the rest of the year (corresponding to a reduction in the consumer price index of 1.3–1.4 per cent). The subsidies were to be abolished from the beginning of 1964.

Concurrently, some profit margins in the retail trade were reduced and price supervision in general was intensified.

This income settlement was generally considered as a successful one. The parties were hailed for their moderation and it was considered a great step forward in incomes policy. From a fiscal viewpoint, however, there was reason for some reservation. Although the result was probably the best that under given circumstances could be achieved, it weakened a budget which already was weaker than the Ministry of Finance would have liked to see. On the other hand, the settlement did produce a comparatively stable price level throughout the year and a very moderate increase in labour costs. As prices and costs continued to rise in most other countries, Norway thereby probably obtained a certain improvement in its competitive position.

The agreements of 1963 were concluded for only one year, and in course of last spring we have therefore had another round of income and price revisions. Again, there were joint meetings between the key ministers and representatives of the wage earners, the employers, and the farmers. At the same time regular negotiations took place between the Trade Unions and the Employers' Federation, and between the Government and the farmers' and fishermen's organizations. The parties in the labour market did not, however, succeed in reaching an agreement. The most important reason was probably different opinions concerning how a rather sharp increase in social fees levied upon the employers should be considered in relation to an increase in regular wages. In order to prevent a general work stoppage, a bill was passed referring the whole matter to a wage board. The board's decision was a little bit closer to the last demand of the unions than to the last offer of the employers. The increase, which was stipulated in øre per hour, was higher for the lower paid than for the higher paid workers. While it would give the former an average increase of about 5½ per cent in 1964, and about 3 per cent in 1965, the latter would get 2½ and 1¼ per cent respectively. For the wage earners as a whole, the increase would be about 3⅓ per cent in 1964 and 1⅔ per cent in 1965. In addition the usual semi-automatic escalator clause was included.

This was the first time a wage board had been used in order to decide on a general revision of agreements. In earlier cases it had dealt only with special groups or escalator revisions. Although it was accepted as the only solution at the time, all parties were anxious to make clear that in principle they much preferred agreements which they were able to reach themselves. This year's events do therefore not imply that a decision by a wage board as a general rule will be regarded as an acceptable alternative to a labour conflict.

With respect to the farmers, the Government offered them a calculated percentage increase in their incomes which would roughly correspond to that of the lower paid workers. The farmers, however, demanded a similar increase in öre per hour. As the calculated income per hour on the farms is lower than wages per hour of lower paid workers, this would give the farmers a much higher percentage increase in incomes than the workers. The comparability of the two concepts of income is very doubtful, however, and the farmers' demand was declined by the Government. As no agreement could be reached, another bill was proposed and passed, referring the question of farm incomes to an arbitration board. The board awarded a calculated increase in farm incomes a little closer to the last offer of the Government than to the final demand of the farmers.

Almost the whole income settlement of 1964 has thus taken place by arbitration, and the fear has been expressed that it will be very difficult again to have realistic negotiations between the parties. Only the future can tell whether this fear is justified or not.

Conclusions

The performance of price stability in Norway during the post-war period is poorer than in countries like the United States and Canada, Switzerland and Western Germany. It is clearly better than that of France, Italy, Iceland or Finland, but not markedly different from that of Sweden, Denmark and the United Kingdom. From international comparisons there is thus no evidence either of success or of gross failure of our incomes policy in so far as it aims at stabilization of the price level. But this fact does of course not deny the possibility that we might have been still worse off with less of a policy in this field.

The Norwegian authorities feel that the kind of co-ordination of income revisions which was achieved in 1963 and 1964 has considerable advantages. If this co-ordination were perfect, and if prices and wage rates could be reduced as easily as they can be increased, it would in principle be possible first to reach an agreement on the changes in real earnings which should be attempted, and then calculate the changes in wages and prices this would require while maintaining a stable price level. Even if this is not possible and a certain change in relative incomes can only be brought about by increasing prices and wages, the resulting rise in the general level of prices will be lower if the parties concerned do not have to protect themselves against expected, but unknown increases in incomes of other groups. Similarly, it reduces the need for a group to push up its incomes in order to gain or maintain a certain position relative to other groups. In total, the co-ordination of income settlements puts a brake both on the price-wage and on the wage-wage spiral.

Because it is very difficult to obtain agreement on changes in the relative income position between groups, one will tend to fall back upon maintaining the existing position, giving proportional increases in rates to all groups. This was what happened in 1963, while in 1964 it has been true to a much lesser extent. The wage drift, as well as the drift in non-wage incomes for that matter, continues rather unaffected by the revision of rates. Those groups which have least to gain by wage drift—and the lowest paid belong in general to these—will therefore feel that they are at a loss in these broad income settlements. The experiences of this year may have weakened this impression somewhat, but there is certainly still no general satisfaction among the groups who feel that they have been losing ground. At the present state of imperfection in incomes policy it is therefore necessary to have negotiations on the industry level at not too infrequent intervals. Such settlements will in most cases lead to higher increases in prices and nominal incomes than the co-ordinated ones.

There are not many who are in principle in favour of the policy of price subsidization. To what extent this policy has been an efficient brake on the long term increase in prices and nominal incomes will always be an open question. It has also distorting effects which are not intended. There have, however, been many situations where the danger of an uncontrolled price increase has been considered so great that an increase in price subsidies has appeared as the least evil.

We feel in Norway that although our incomes policy is far from perfect, we have been able to make some progress during recent years. Further progress is not so much dependent upon economic technique as upon a general understanding of the questions involved. [The defeat of the Labour Party in the 1965 elections could end the union-government cooperation and some of the policies herein described.—H. R. N.]

J The Strange
Adventures of
Dutch Wage Policy*
J. PEN**

1. *Dutch Folklore*

IN MANY RESPECTS Dutch wage
policy is an improbable affair. To begin with it is an offence to pay
wages that deviate from the basic wage rates that are fixed by the
Government. This draconic legal interference with collective bargaining seems hardly compatible with the idea of a free economy.
There exist an impressive number of organs which have a say in
wage policy and at first sight it is difficult to distinguish between
them. Wage directives are complicated; they were especially so in
the years 1960 and 1961 when formulas were used and agreements
concluded, which made an almost surrealistic impression on many

* Reprinted by permission from the *British Journal of Industrial Relations*, Vol. I, No. 3, October 1963.
** Professor of Economics, Groningen University, The Netherlands;
formerly Director of General Economic Policy, Ministry of Economic
Affairs, The Hague.

observers. Remarkable, too, is the continuous discussion around these things; a seeming paradox, for instance, is that the employers insist, in theory, on freedom—whatever that may be—but in practice shrink back from it. The results of the wage policy are that some partners in the E.E.C. hold the view that the Dutch are guilty of social dumping, but the Dutch trade union movement co-operates in the scheme and, although there are slight differences of opinion, is content with it. Real wages have continually risen as has labour's share in the national income, and wage inflation has been kept within narrow limits. Some people readily hold up the system as an example to other Western countries, who allegedly can find no solution for their price-wage difficulties ('The biggest unsolved economic problem of our time' according to P. A. Samuelson.) Other voices are heard to say that this special folklore is no more suitable for export than Volendam costumes. Moreover, the system appears to be crumbling.

In the beginning of 1963, fairly radical changes were introduced; the Government's legal powers were cut for the first time since 1945. It might be argued that the basic principle—the all important influence of the Government—has now been deserted, although it has been said *plus ça change, plus ça reste la même chose*. This article seeks to describe the events and considerations that have led to these changes. As yet, not much can be said about the working of the new system, which has been functioning only a few months.

Much was written about Dutch wage policy in the first ten years after liberation[1]; I will only say a few things about it. The stress in this article will be on the period from 1959 until 1963. It is perhaps useful to know that the present writer was not actively engaged in wage policy matters during this period and that consequently his objectivity is not affected by the wish to grind any administrative or political axe. On the other hand he does not feel that he should entirely relinquish viewpoints he took up previously; he has a vested interest in his earlier opinions. Moreover, any views in this field are liable to be controversial and he does not expect that his conclusions will be accepted by everybody.

2. *Legal and Institutional Arrangements*

The law on which the Government's special authority rests,

the 'Buitengewoon Besluit Arbeidsverhoudingen' (Extraordinary Decree concerning Labour Relations) of October 1945, remained unaltered until 1963. The law was passed at a time when one needed a special passport to travel from one part of Holland to another; in this spirit it forbids workers to give notice to quit, and employers to dismiss workers, without previous permission from the authorities, i.e. the regional labour exchanges, which are organs of the Ministry of Social Affairs. This prohibition is still in force, although the economic reasons for it have long since ceased to be valid. It is an illustration of the fact that as a nation we move slowly.

The 'Buitengewoon Besluit Arbeidsverhoudingen' ordains that collective wage agreements need to be approved by a government body, the 'College of Rijksbemiddelaars' (Board of Mediators, henceforth to be referred to as the Board). After approval it is an offence to pay wages that deviate from the levels established by the agreements. In those sectors in which no collective agreements are negotiated, the Board may issue a wage regulation which is also binding.

Some important groups of employees are not covered by this procedure. Formally the civil service, teachers, clergy and domestic servants are excluded from this system of wage regulation. The salaries of executives and staff employees are also not covered; in fact any wages which at the moment exceed £800 p.a. escape from this control.

The problem of enforcement is less serious in the Netherlands than would perhaps be the case in less-disciplined countries. Legal sanctions against 'black wages' are real; prosecutions are instituted regularly, fines are imposed, and there have been employers who have been sent to jail. Yet I would not like to assert that there were no 'black wages' that did not keep out of harm's way.

The Board, which was a real mediating organ before the war, has had an unusual and difficult task since 1945. It is controlled by the Minister of Social Affairs, but it paddles its own canoe. The Minister may give instructions, but at first he did this only in exceptional cases such as general wage rounds; since the 'free' wage policy of 1959 these instructions have, paradoxically, become more frequent. But for the rest the Board operates independently of the Minister, which has the advantage that the latter can shrug his shoulders at too detailed questions concerning wages in Parliament. In another way, too, the Board of Mediators, which still has its old and misleading name, is rather independent. Its members combine authority with incomes from other sources (professors, a mayor etc.) and are not bent upon carving their way in the world any more. They do not worry much about popularity. I shall refer to this factor again in my evaluation of the new arrangement since 1963.

The legal structure could give the impression that from 1945 to 1963 the Board acted as a wage dictator. However, this was not its line of conduct. To a great extent the Board conformed to the wishes of the Foundation of Labour. Until 1963 the Foundation was a private institution without formal authority. It was established in 1945, twelve days after the liberation, as a first attempt to improve relations between employers and workers. The Foundation consists of the three big federations of trade unions, Socialist, Roman Catholic and Protestant, and a number of employers' associations, neutral,[2] Roman Catholic and Protestant; also associations covering agriculture and commerce. The Foundation's ideological aims were elevated; it was a body dedicated to achieve better understanding between the two sides of industry. Later on these aims were also adopted by quite different organizations which will be discussed later.

In practice the Foundation has become especially concerned with wage policy. This body discusses all wage proposals coming from the various branches of industry, and sends them on to the Board with its recommendations. As a rule the Board has followed this advice. Yet it cannot be said that the Foundation has been the source of the Board's policy; for the Board's likely views were taken into account in the recommendations of the Foundation. The interplay between the two was such that the chairman of the Mediators could maintain that he was the Foundation's messenger-boy, while the latter institution could depict itself as a powerless and innocent advisory body. The opposite, too, could be maintained, as circumstances might require. The truth is more subtle and its revelation would demand the space of six volumes, in which events between 1945 and 1963 and the interaction of the daily decisions were scrutinized. It is this kind of inter-play between men and institutions which is so characteristic of Dutch conditions.

A new committee in addition to the Board and the Foundation appeared in 1950: the 'Social Economic Council'. It is the apex of so-called *publiek rechtelijke bedrijfsorganisatie*, an untrans-latable expression really something like 'public organization of business'. The basic idea is that bipartite organs are established in all branches of industry 'schappen' which not only discuss all problems thoroughly (except for prices, for in that case they would assume the character of a cartel!) but which can also issue regulations. Consequently they are legislative bodies; their deci-sions bind the whole industry. The inspiration behind this organ-isation is strongly ideological; generally speaking the Catholics are in favour of it, so are most socialists. The liberals are not so enthusiastic, although some lip-service is paid to the system. The institutional pattern and ideology is reminiscent of the corporate state, although it is not the done thing to remind people of it. The establishment of new 'schappen' has ground to a halt; at the mo-ment the organization is not as comprehensive as its advocates have wanted.

The central organization, the Social Economic Council, flourishes. It is a tripartite committee; apart from employers and workers' representatives it consists of independent members appointed by the Government. Our concern here is not with the responsibility of the Council for the supervision of the working of the system, but with its external function—to advise the Government. In accordance with the law, the Government hears the Council on all questions concerning general social-economic policy and wage policy. In practice, the Council confines its advice to the big problems, such as general wage rounds, which imply a diagnosis of the macro-economic situation, and changes in the institutional system. This is the difference between it and the Foundation, which advised on day-to-day matters. Despite this difference there has been some overlapping, and the relation between Foundation and Board has not always been an easy one.

However, the relationship changed in 1963. Broadly speaking, the situation now is that the Board has receded into the background and the Foundation has come more to the fore. This is called more freedom. The 'Extraordinary Decree concerning Labour Relations' was changed. The Board's signature of approval on collective labour agreements is no longer required; proposals for wage changes are now adopted by the Foundation. Before the Foundation takes this step, so-called 'internal co-ordination', under the supervision of central employers' and employees' associations, has taken place in the different branches of industry. Some people have great expectations of this 'internal co-ordination' and the hope it inspires has an important place in the philosophy of the new system.

Under these new arrangements the Board may still oppose a decision of the Foundation; if it does it must report this to the Minister of Social Affairs, who then has to decide what will happen to the proposed collective agreement. If the Board does not do anything, the agreement comes into effect after its endorsement by the Foundation. The Foundation, while testing proposals, will have to take into account the entire economic situation (balance of payments, prices, productivity etc.). To this end, it is provided with recommendations by the Council, which relies on calculations by the Government's Central Planning Bureau, staffed by the most sophisticated economists produced by the Tinbergen school.

If the Government has the feeling that the Foundation is transgressing the directives of the Council it can order a temporary wage stop, during which the operation of new collective agreements is suspended, the Council is asked for advice and the Board is temporarily restored to its old powers. This, however, is meant for abnormal cases.

Whatever the qualities of the new system may be—I shall return to this—a certain complexity is already evident from this brief description. Foreign observers will, I think, understand the Dutch system less and less. While before 1963 formal authority resided with the Board, with only the Minister of Social Affairs as the supreme authority, we now have the Foundation, the Council, the Board and the Minister, all with some kind of formal authority. The greater amount of freedom which, rightly or wrongly, is attributed to the new system means, in fact, a greater number of controlling bodies.

3. *The Four Stages of Wage Policy*

The institutional machinery described above had been established primarily in order to keep the wage level within feasible limits, and to improve peaceful industrial relations. Over and above this, another objective had come into being, which probably was just as important; namely the achievement of a harmonious wage structure. These fundamental objectives have remained the same throughout, but shifts in methods and criteria have made their appearance. Thus four stages can be distinguished: the first of 1945-1954, the wage stop; the second of 1954-1959, welfare wage rounds; the third of 1959-1963, differentiated wage policy; the fourth, since 1963, the new wage policy.

The wage stop of 1945-1954, which was not a genuine wage stop, was promoted by the idea that the real level of wages in 1945 was higher than the national economy could cope with. With the social minimum an advance had been given on later increases in productivity. Reconstruction and balance of payment requirements made high demands on the strictness of the wage policy. The Board, it is true, did allow special wage increases which improved the wage structure, but the general wage level was increased only if the cost of living had risen. In 1948 there was a wage round amounting to one guilder; in 1950 to 5 per cent. (after the devaluation); in the same year another 5 per cent.; in 1951 again 5 per cent.; in 1952 a compensation of 2 per cent. for increased social charges[3]; in 1954 a round of 5 per cent. in the cities, increasing to 12 per cent. in the country. With this last increase, the principle of uniformity was departed from.

The latter round paved the way to a certain shift in the system. Many had been arguing that uniform wage rounds were unnatural and inflated costs. Differentiated rises would provide a greater possibility of increasing wages wherever profits permitted, so that the wage-price spiral could be avoided.

Employers and confessional trade unions favoured this notion of differentiated wage increases; the socialist unions saw in the differentiation a breaking away from the principle of labour solidarity. The Government showed understanding for this argument, yet looked for an intermediate solution. It was found in the 'non-obligatory wage round'; the second stage in the wage policy

(1954-1959). Real wages were allowed to rise, as the recovery of the Dutch economy had been completed by this time. A general pay rise was no longer made up of a compulsory percentage but of a maximum. In practice, however, this was realized in all industries, so that the difference between the first period and the second lay less in the differentiation than in the greater generosity. This generosity was justified by continued growth of the national income. Every 'welfare round' was supported by the Council's advice, which to this end entered again and again into detailed economic discussions about 'room'; an ambiguous but very popular term, about which much could be written. I shall not do that here.

This much is certain, that thanks to economic expansion welfare rounds were allowed in 1954 (6 per cent.) and in 1956 (9 per cent.). At the same time a great many special wage adjustments took place by means of job evaluation, merit rating, improvement in the wage structure, etc. In this respect the Board showed great liberality. The nominal wage increase amounted to 40 per cent. in this period; that is an average of 8 per cent. a year.

The third stage (1959-1963) produced an effort to achieve further differentiation. A new cabinet with a slant to the right had appeared. Freedom became a new goal. The aim now was to do away with the wage round altogether and to spread wage increases in time as well as in size. Over-all economic policy and planning were to be pushed more into the background. 'Greater responsibility for the separate sectors of industry' was the slogan. Reality, however, proved to be in flat contradiction to the objective proclaimed. Government intervention increased in the period 1959-63, instead of decreasing. Small wonder that at the end of this cabinet's period of office in 1963, everybody wanted something different. The basis had been laid for a 'new policy'. Because this stage was decisive for the next development, I will go into it a little more deeply.

4. The Third Stage: Pseudo-Freedom and Rebellion

The new 'freedom' demanded a new philosophy. This new view focused around the idea of productivity, which has a certain amount of public appeal. It is a popular idea that wages ought to go up with productivity, although people will sometimes forget that labour productivity is determined not so much by the worker's exertion but by the amount of capital and by technology. Economists were pleasantly reminded of J. B. Clark and their textbooks, but in fact the new philosophy was different from marginalist theory.

It was based on the notion that labour's part of the national income should not be allowed to decrease and wage costs not allowed to increase. The role of productivity fitted in nicely with both objectives. Labour's share equals the quotient of real wages and labour productivity[4], so that money wages rise with labour productivity, given a constant share and given stable prices. In this case, wage costs also remain constant, which is a condition for stable prices. This philosophy suited the Minister of Economic Affairs, who is responsible for price policy, and his colleague the Minister of Social Affairs, who has to see to it that everybody gets his share of the cake.

It also suited the trade unions, and the employers could not reasonably object. It looked as if this criterion—wage rises in accordance with increasing productivity—could produce the basis for wage differentiation and institutional decentralization. The rule of the new game became: wage increases, wherever possible, without rising prices. This rule was supplemented by another one. Wages were allowed to diverge, but not too far. This is a typically Dutch restriction. The harmonious wage structure was not to be upset. In those branches of industry that were expanding rapidly, the increase in wages should be moderate, and there would be some room for a price cut. This would come in handy, for in the sectors that were lagging behind pay rises were necessary for the sake of harmony, but since they were not covered by productivity they would consequently lead to rising prices. All this sounds very reasonable. But in practice it caused difficulties, which upset the system.

There were three hitches. The first and most fundamental one was that the productivity of each industry could not be calculated in a sufficiently exact manner. The margin of uncertainty creates plenty of scope for negotiations. Bargaining about wages became bargaining about output and input figures. These discussions sometimes assumed surrealistic proportions. Parties approached the Central Bureau of Statistics for help and so this usually serene government office was implicated in social conflict in a way it was not used to, and which it did not appreciate. The statistical experts were quick to explain that their figures were inapplicable to the end for which people wanted to misuse them. The discovery that, even in statistics, many knots had to be cut deprived the wage policy of its objective basis. It was felt that the lid was off. The strain on the labour market also operated in this direction.

The second hitch was that working hours were reduced from 48 to 45 in these very years. In this respect the Netherlands were clearly lagging behind, as compared to the rest of Europe. The Government had meant this reduction to be an experiment in some branches of industry after which others might perhaps follow—completely in accordance with the philosophy of differentiation and liberty. The idea of slow differentiation never materialized; the 45-hour week swept like a wave through all industries, including those coping with a great shortage of labour. It increased costs and created a conflict with the wage policy. Nobody asked the question which had priority—wages or shorter working hours; people wanted both at the same time.

The third reason for the failure was that the Government, startled at its own generosity, and at the marked wage increases, tried to keep the lid on, by issuing directives to the Board. This was something new. Under the old system, directives had been restricted to general wage rounds—for specific wage proposals the Board, together with Foundation, were given a free hand. But now directives started to pour from the Government. Personal elements also played a part; the Secretary of State for Social Affairs[5], who (under an unusually weak Minister) really determined the wage policy, was an able as well as energetic man. He had come from the Protestant trade union movement and set to work in his new job energetically and pugnaciously. He clearly thought it unnatural to stay aloof from such important business as wage negotiations. This made for some opposition, not only from the industry, but also from the Board. The opposition took the shape of a rebellion. This was met by new instructions, further instructions and supplements to the further instructions. Ministers never went to bed so late, there were never so many nightly meetings on the question of wages.

I will not try to follow closely the strange story of this period. A few of the more important stages are given here. In 1960 a prohibition of short-run pay rises was introduced; parties were told they had to wait until existing collective wage agreements, mostly concluded for several years, had run out. This could mean, in some cases, no wage increase for two or three years. A three year wage stop for an industry is today hardly tenable psychologically; especially if in the meantime productivity has increased substantially. Consequently employers and trade unions did not at all see eye to eye with the Government, and they did not adhere to the regulations.

There was a strike in the building industry in that year; although the employers were willing to concede the union's demands they did not want to guarantee constant prices. The Government, therefore, intervened with a price stop for this industry.

Also in 1960 a wage increase proposed by the sugar refineries, that had come about after a great deal of arithmetical calculation, was halved by the Board following government intervention. The employers made it known to the Government that they were not going to observe this cut. The wages originally proposed were in fact paid and no sanctions followed. All of these revolts against official policy were signs of the dissatisfaction that had grown with the chops and changes; it was apparent that a new approach would have to be found.

In 1961 the Government and the Foundation came to an agreement, in which the policy for 1962 was laid down. This included, among other things, a formula, which raised a good many laughs.

Take the average annual productivity increase in a branch of industry over a previous period of time. Multiply this percentage by three. Add two. Divide by four. The result was the wage increase permitted. This agreement was followed by another formal instruction (March 2nd 1962), in which the Government gave an interpretation of the arrangements, which did not tally with the views of most of the industry. The quarrel ran high; now it was not only a single branch of industry that was involved, but over-all policy. In the course of the discussion it appeared that the system was no longer workable, because the Foundation did not want to co-operate any longer. Faith in the Government had disappeared; the rebellion took the form of a final breach. People wanted something different, that is, employers and workers wanted to be delivered from detailed government intervention. The main reason for this disenchantment undoubtedly lay in the paradox, that since 1959 more freedom had been promised, but what had actually come about was more interference.[6]

5. The Present Stage: Transition

The new institutional set-up, which has been functioning from the beginning of 1963, has already been described. The Board's task was shifted to the Foundation, which receives bi-annual economic recommendations from the Council, based on the econometrics of the Central Planning Bureau; there is also the possibility of the Government bringing the Board of Mediators into play once again if this is deemed necessary.

There was a hot debate about this system in the Council, which had to give its advice. Discussions had been going on since 1960, but they were speeded up by the discord in 1962. There were many differences of opinion, but it was clear that almost nobody wanted to return to a really free system of wage determination. Wage policy continues to be directed and centralized, even if at the moment a central organ of employers and workers has the final say. Neither the industries, which have to submit their proposals to the Foundation, nor the individual employers, who are not allowed to pay 'black wages', have any more 'freedom' through this shift in authority.

The new philosophy gives plenty of room, it is true, for internal negotiation in the trade unions and the employers' associations before the proposals reach the Foundation, but this 'internal co-ordination' is not freedom yet. It is at most a training in responsibility for the 'lower' organizations which can help to prepare for real freedom. It seems probable that this fourth stage will once again be a period of transition. In my opinion it will not stand much longer than its predecessor. The excessive intricacy is already a pointer in this direction. Moreover, there is good reason to expect new difficulties that might be more serious than the old system. Why is this probable?

The basic reason why it is likely that serious difficulties will arise is to be found in the main objective of the policy, that is to prevent wage inflation. Holland has to regulate the wage level in such a way that exports continue to grow in accordance with the demands of a rapidly growing population. This job has to be done under conditions of full or over-full employment. Consequently, the controlling body has to exert a strong downward pressure on wages. It has to object to wage increases which seem reasonable to those sections of industry which think only of their own economic needs. This unpopular task was fulfilled for several years by the Board of Mediators—an independent body, which did not care a straw about adverse criticism. The trade unions and the employers' associations did co-operate in the shaping of wage policy, but they did not have to take responsibility for unpopular decisions. They often did, in fact, accept responsibility but in emergencies, when under pressure from their rank and file, they could always shrug their shoulders and pass the buck. The Board deliberately functioned as a scapegoat and it was well suited for this purpose.

The Foundation of Labour is in a different situation. Now the employers and workers must themselves take this final decision. If tensions arise, they cannot be shifted to somebody else. The parties have the choice between conflict and wage inflation. But this choice is not a real one, because conflicts within the Foundation always lead to pay rises in the long run. And, what is also important, they make people wish for a change in the system.

Wage inflation will mean that the Foundation has exceeded the limits fixed by the Social and Economic Council. The Council can note the fact, but cannot do anything about it. However, it can anticipate inflationary trends in the Foundation. It did so already in the very first advice it tendered under the new system. On October 26th 1962, the Council issued its recommendations for wage policy in 1963. The general economic situation led the Council to declare that there was only 'room' for pay-rises of 1.2 per cent. The reader who might be surprised at this precision should remember that the Dutch have a long tradition of penny-wise calculations. But, said the Council, it is impossible not to exceed this percentage, since there are too many pressures, and too many wage corrections pending in various sections of industry. It was therefore decided to add another 15 per cent., thus making 2.7 per cent. in all. This was the Council's advice for 1963.

The Government, which had been weary of the struggle for a long time, accepted this figure. It was a significant example of political arithmetic, into which a macro-economic analysis and an elastic retreat had been woven.

This outcome augurs little good; the Council in this case gave way in advance. But it is probable that the limit will be exceeded by the Foundation. If this happens the Council is impotent, for it has no vote in the final decisions on wages. The Government may intervene and order a 'temporary wage stop'. But it is clear that this latter measure puts the Government in an awkward position, for some collective agreements will just have been renewed and others will have to be shelved. In a small country with good communications this inequity is bound to produce immediate and widespread reactions. Organized business and trade unions will be angry with the Government, which will find itself in a difficult political situation unless it can soon liquidate the position in which it will be placed.

In the meantime the Council has to advise, according to the rules, on the economic situation. However, the same people who will bring the grudges of organized business to the deliberations of the Foundation are also members of the Council. So we would get some months of bickering, then the temporary wage stop must end since it can only last one or two months. The Government then has to choose. It can either fall back on stage three, that is restore the Board of Mediators to its previous authority; or let the Foundation do as it pleases, which means that the corked-up energy will be translated into inflation.

This strange game gives an impression of instability. It is, of course, possible that there will be no conflicts. In that case the whole complicated system would not have been necessary, and wages could have been left free, in the sense that the industries could have been left to arrange their own affairs. The Foundation can supervise, intercede and co-ordinate, but under a free wage policy it can issue no formal prohibition orders. It is even questionable whether under such a system 'black wages' should remain punishable, for no other Western country knows sanctions on wages that are too high. It seems probable that eventually the present wage system will suggest the idea to the participants that their freedom is in a sad state indeed, and that they will aim at further liberalization.

6. *Perspectives*

In my opinion—but it is a contestable one—two possible systems in the Dutch constellation might prove to be stable. The first is that under which the Board formally controls wages with a subtle interplay between the various sections of industry. The second is a wage policy under which the various sections of industry arrange their own affairs, while central organs without legal power do their best to keep the wage structure in balance and the wage level within bounds. The latter is roughly the state of affairs in a country like Sweden.

I think that the Netherlands will eventually adopt the Swedish approach. The way back to the system of before 1959 is too difficult. The tactical mistakes made in the period of 1959-1963 have spoilt the Government's position. More strange adventures are bound to follow; that they have not occurred yet under the new system is due to the fact that it is hardly working. These events will most probably steer us in the direction of more decentralization.

The question arises whether that is a good or a bad thing. The answer depends on one's ideological frame of mind and on one's evaluation of the force of supply and demand. If one holds, as B. C. Roberts does,[7] that in the long run wage policy cannot run counter to supply and demand, then complicated machinery is superfluous. But to my mind this pessimism is not convincing, because Dutch experience does not confirm the view that wages follow the market. In the first fifteen years after the liberation we succeeded in maintaining a managed wage level lower than that of other countries. The difference in wages and social charges, not taking into account productivity, between Belgium, Western Germany and France on the one hand and Holland on the other, amounted to roughly 25 per cent. In 1959. This is only in part—what part is unknown—compensated for by the difference in productivity. So there was a substantial difference in wage costs; and this despite over-employment in the Netherlands. Since that time this difference has diminished a great deal—probably by more than half—which from the point of view of European integration is an advantage, but which has created a certain internal anxiety. The reason for the increase in labour costs since 1959 lies only partly with the forces of the market; political and institutional circumstances have also played an important role.

The low wage level certainly was one of the causes of the rapid growth of Dutch exports, which account for half of the national income; and so of the satisfactory expansion of the Dutch economy. We need this extra growth in view of the rapid increase in population. In the last resort the reason for our special wage policy lies in the high rate of population growth (1.5 per cent.) and in the Dutch inclination to set up perfect rules. A slight abatement of economic expansion with its repercussions on investments would lead to structural unemployment. Therefore we have to avoid wage inflation or be prepared to devalue. Both evils compel us to be prudent, which explains the unusual character of our wage arrangements. It is for these reasons that I shall be watching the adventures of our wage policy, in days to come, with some concern.

[Bearing out Professor Pen's analysis, the Dutch approved an across the board 15 per cent increase in 1964 because workers were leaving for higher paying jobs in other common market countries. The effect was a substantial price inflation.—H. R. N.]

NOTES

1. A good description (but rather disputable evaluations) is given by B. C. Roberts in his 'National Wages Policy in War and Peace,' London, Allen and Unwin, 1958. I shall come back to this book.

2. This is not the word by which they term themselves. In Dutch terminology they are liberals, but this sounds too leftish in British ears. Perhaps no injustice is done if we call the neutral association conservatives in the English sense of the word.

3. This special round did not compensate for the rise in prices. Consequently real wages suffered a cut. This was necessary owing to the deficit in the balance of payments due to the Korean war. The trade unions agreed with this austerity—a remarkable and praiseworthy sign of macro-economic thinking.

4. I do not claim to be the author of this simple thought, although it can be found in *The Wage Rate under Trade Unions*, by the present author (Dutch edition, 1950; Harvard University Press, Cambridge, 1958) and in previous Dutch articles.

5. Under-Minister.

6. A few figures about the pay rises: from 1959 to 1962 average wages rose by 30 per cent. Labour productivity rose by some 20 per cent., notwithstanding the shorter working week. Wage costs in national currency rose by 10 per cent. Moreover competitive power deteriorated by another 5 per cent., because of the revaluation of the guilder in 1961—a very disputable decision.

7. *Op. cit.*, p. 172.

K New Trends in the Legal Regulation of Collective Bargaining in Italy

GINO GUIGNI

[In Italy government intervention in collective bargaining is not substantial, perhaps as a reaction against the total control of Fascism under Mussolini. The government, however, does regulate collective bargaining. The following excerpt from the recent article by Gino Giugni which appeared in the *International Labour Review*, Vol. 91, April 1965, and is reprinted here by permission of the International Labour Organization, bears on this subject.—H. R. N.]

The major problem that the Constitution of 1948 (article 39) endeavoured to solve was how to make collective agreements "generally" binding—that is, on all employers and workers operating within the scope of the bargaining unit.[1] For this purpose it provided for the registration of the unions, the recognition of their legal personality, and the application of a bargaining procedure involving proportional representation of each union operating within the scope of the bargaining unit.[2]

This standard-setting solution was obviously modelled on the bargaining machinery that was predominant when the Constitution was drafted and which was based almost exclusively on national agreements. For, if there is any interest in plant agreements, which did not attain any great importance until ten years later, being binding on all and sundry, such interest is purely theoretical. In fact, employers never discriminate, when applying a collective agreement, between workers who are members of the union concerned and those who are not. Indeed, under the conditions prevailing in 1948, when industrialisation was still retarded, there was a real need for agreements to be generally binding because of the higher proportion of small- and medium-sized production units not covered by collective agreements and located in areas where the labour force was virtually unorganised.

The constitutional norm briefly described above has remained a dead letter because the legislation required for its implementation was never passed. This is due to a number of reasons, but there is no point in analysing them here and now.[3] It is interesting instead to note that the strong pressure for the implementation of article 39 of the Constitution, at first exerted by certain workers' organisations, has declined greatly in recent years, if it has not virtually disappeared. This is chiefly due to the fact that, under the altered conditions now prevailing, collective agreements have a far wider sphere of application. At the same time the strategy of bargaining at plant level, even if confined within the limits described below, strengthens the position of the union in the undertaking and so naturally pushes the question of general applicability into the background.

In 1959 the Government promulgated a law[4] under which the collective agreements then in force were incorporated in special statutes, thus receiving legal sanction and becoming generally binding. In the years that followed, collective bargaining developed along the lines of "common law"; this means that the agreements were binding only on employers who belonged to the associations that had negotiated them. Nevertheless, nowadays in the majority of industries collective bargaining starts out from an absolute minimum, namely that stipulated in the former collective agreements which received the force of law in 1959 and are considered, by and large, as constituting a minimum legal "standard".

This is a second factor that reduces the pressure for the implementation of the constitutional provision mentioned above. At the same time the unions, realising the strength of their position, have begun to question—at least in theory—the expediency of extending all the benefits obtained by bargaining to non-member workers.[5]

The evolution of collective bargaining in Italy in recent years has two aspects that are specially worthy of note. First, the implementation of the constitutional provision that collective agreements must be generally binding is growing less and less probable. Second, the major feature of the system that is becoming firmly established is the lack of any specific legal provisions for the bargaining procedure and, in general, for the conduct of the parties to the negotiation and application of collective agreements, excepting the provisions of civil law concerning contracts in general. This means that if there is a country where this fundamental element of the system of industrial relations we are considering is subject to little or no legislative interference it is Italy.

This situation, which stems rather from a number of inertia factors than from a conscious choice of principles, has led to consequences of some importance to the bargaining procedure. First, because the latter has been able to adapt to economic and technological conditions, which have radically altered in the last 15 years, without coming up against obstacles in the shape of existing legal structures based on completely different conditions.[6] Second, because the lack of legislation on collective bargaining has fostered the growth of rules of self-discipline dictated by the collective agreements instead of by law. This applies to the bargaining level, which will be discussed below; to the discipline of strikes (the spread of the truce clause); and to the settlement of legal disputes (agreed procedure for dealing with grievances; gradual spread of arbitration). As a result, in a country where the prevalent traditions and ideologies favoured the establishment of trade union autonomy within a well-defined legal framework—this was equally the case in France and the United States—the trend is towards a system of self-discipline in industrial relations which recalls certain aspects of that established in the United Kingdom a great many years ago.

NOTES

1. A few valuable contributions to the study of the trade union movement can be found in the works of economists, sociologists, jurists and historians, but such things as industrial relations reviews or institutes virtually do not exist [in Italy]. Even in the universities "labour law" is the only branch of studies that deals with labour relations. See the documented analysis by GIUGNI and MANCINI: "Per una cultura sindacale in Italia," in *Il Mulino*, 1954.

2. See F. PERGOLESI: "The place of labour in the constitution of the Italian Republic," in *International Labour Review*, Vol. LXI, No. 2, Feb. 1950, pp. 118-142. See also I.L.O.: *Legislative Series*, 1947—It. 5.

3. See L. MENGONI: "Les sources du droit du travail en Italie," in *Les sources du droit du travail* (Luxembourg, European Coal and Steel Community, 1962), p. 148.

4. I.L.O.: *Legislative Series*, 1959—It. 3; see also NEUFELD, op. cit., p. 514.

5. One of the basic principles of the Italian trade union movement—not always explicitly stated but in keeping with the movement's traditional philosophy—has always been that a union represents the interests of a "class" (Marxists) or a "category" (Catholics) and not merely of the affiliated workers. Hence the unpopularity of such policies as the "reservation of benefits to members" (as practised in Belgium) and the intense interest in the general application of collective agreements.

6. Opposition to the implementation of article 39 of the Constitution, based chiefly on these arguments and in open contrast with the prevalent legal opinion, is expressed by MANCINI: "Libertà sindacale e contratti collettivi 'erga omnes'," in *Revista Trimestrale di Diritto e Procedura Civile*, 1963 and *Il Mulino*, 1964.

L Difficulties and
Opportunities in
Canadian
Mediation*
H. D. WOODS**

THE USE OF THE TERM *mediation*
in the title reflects the fact that this paper is written for an audience
largely American rather than Canadian. Since the paper is concerned specifically with Canadian problems a word of explanation
about terminology is necessary. As a general rule, in Canada *conciliation* is the operative term applied to those activities of governmental agencies which intervene in labour disputes with the object
of bringing the parties of interest to an agreement. Whereas in the
United States the agency of intervention appears to be the Federal
(or State) Mediation Service, in Canada the same agency will be
called the Federal[1] (or Provincial) Conciliation Service. I am
assuming no important difference in meaning between mediation

* Reprinted by permission from the *Labor Law Journal*, Vol. XIII, No.
12, October 1962.
** Professor, Industrial Relations Center, McGill University, Montreal,
Canada.

and conciliation. They are taken to be roughly synonymous, as indeed they are used very largely in practice. Henceforth the term used will be conciliation in conformity with Canadian usage, unless the context or a quotation requires the use of the term mediation.

Canadian Approach

Canadian and American public policy in labour relations appears on casual observation to be very similar, yet there are important differences which in some areas become so marked that it is not incorrect to think of two different systems of industrial relations. Conciliation is one of these areas of difference which justify a separate classification for the Canadian and American systems. A short examination of the Canadian approach is therefore in order.

It must first be emphasized that in Canada the authority in labour relations is largely decentralized and rests with the provinces rather than the Dominion. The central government is limited normally in practice to jurisdiction over labour matters involving inland or maritime shipping, railways, canals, telegraphs and other works connecting provinces or extending beyond the border of a province, the air industry including aerodromes, radio and television, and works or undertakings situated wholly within a province but declared by Parliament to be for the general advantage of Canada. Effectively the rest falls within the jurisdiction of the respective provinces.[2] Thus almost the entire industrial, mining, shipping, and service trades areas fall within provincial jurisdiction. Yet these are the very areas in which collective bargaining is most prevalent, and they are also the areas where most growth can be anticipated.

The importance of this allocation of authority, which is so different from that found in the United States is that it opens the door to a multiplicity of systems of conciliation, and indeed of industrial relations in more general terms. Each province is, within its very extensive jurisdiction, free to experiment with whatever forms and varieties of public policies it may desire. And since public policies tend to reflect the political influences of the balance of social forces involved, it is not surprising that there have emerged a variety of public policies regarding intervention in labour disputes across Canada. This is particularly true in the case of intervention in the negotiation area.

Dominion's First Important Steps

It is necessary, in order to gain perspective, that the evolution of Canadian conciliation be traced in outline. While there were some largely ineffective experiments by the provinces in the last two decades of the nineteenth century, the first important steps in conciliation were taken by the Dominion parliament in the first decade of the twentieth. In 1900 a Conciliation Act was passed which provided for voluntary conciliation and established a service to carry out the function. In 1903 the Railway Labour Disputes Act introduced an element of compulsory conciliation for a single industry by establishing agencies before which parties in industrial disputes were required to appear. But the real Canadian experiment began in 1907 when parliament passed the Industrial Disputes Investigation Act,[3] which was applicable to coal mines and public utilities only. The Act was passed following, and as a consequence of, a very serious strike in the Alberta coal fields in the late months of 1906. Both the crisis circumstances and the restricted jurisdiction are important, because in the course of time these two limiting principles were abandoned although the conciliation process was retained and became a part, not only of the Dominion system of intervention but of those of the provinces as well.

Industrial Disputes Investigation Act

Some provisions were borrowed from earlier legislation and some were new. The important features included in the I. D. I. Act, as it has come to be called, were: 1) Resort to the use of either the strike or lockout was forbidden until after a conciliation board established according to the procedures set out in the Act had reported and a statutory waiting period had elapsed; 2) The board of conciliation was composed of one nominated by the employer, one nominated by the employees, and one chosen jointly by the nominees of the parties. If either the employer or employees failed to nominate a representative the Minister of Labour was authorized to nominate in default. In case of a failure of the parties' representatives to agree on a neutral chairman, the Minister was authorized to choose a chairman. This is the three-member board which has become a very familiar instrument in Canadian conciliation procedures; 3) The board so constituted was clothed with powers to compel attendance at meetings, the production of documents and witnesses; it could visit premises and generally possessed the authority necessary to conduct an investigation and prepare a written report for the Minister; 4) The Minister was empowered, at his discretion, to publish the report of the board.

There can be no doubt that a basic purpose of this Act was the prevention of strikes.[4] Indeed the legislation was passed, as noted, because of a serious strike a few months earlier. Yet it also was concerned with promoting negotiation and even a form of recognition.[5] This it did by forcing the parties to come together around the same table to discuss the dispute in circumstances where the conciliation board was present and empowered to require the presentation of data and testimony. It was a far cry from the compulsory recognition and bargaining introduced in the United States in the Wagner Act 28 years later; yet it contained the germ of that famous piece of labour legislation. Nevertheless the Act was focused on the specific dispute. It was based on certain notions or beliefs about the nature of industrial conflict and its settlement. These beliefs are revealed in the nature of the machinery that was created to promote industrial peace. There are at least five of these beliefs implicit in the I. D. I. Act: 1) A cause of industrial conflict is the failure of communication, which is aggravated by the reluctance of employers to meet with representatives of employees. This problem could be partly overcome by forcing the parties to meet together before a board on which both sides had representation; 2) The atmosphere of compromise and concession necessary to bring about agreement between parties in conflict in industrial relations requires freedom from the danger of a resort to the strike or lockout by employees or employers respectively. Statutory prohibition of a resort to such direct economic action would remove the threat of strikes or lockouts during the period of negotiation and create an atmosphere more conducive to reason and concession, and therefore would encourage negotiation and settlement of disputes;

3) The presence of a conciliation board with nominated representatives of the parties and a neutral chairman possessing the confidence of the nominees would act as a catalytic agent and aid in the resolution of the dispute; 4) Industrial conflicts may be resolved if reason is displayed by both sides but where such reason is not forthcoming the intervening body can find a reasonable solution which should be acceptable to both, hence the provision for a board report with recommendations; 5) Stubborn unreasonableness can be weakened or overcome by the pressure of public opinion enlightened by the contents of the report of a conciliation board; hence the provision for publication of the report.

An appraisal of these notions and consideration of their validity may be postponed until after a brief examination of the manner in which the I. D. I. Act system became more or less universal in Canada. If it be recalled that the policy of 1907 applied only to public utilities and coal mines, it will be realized that to become universally applied it would be necessary to enlarge the range of industries, and either to widen the scope of Dominion jurisdiction or to have similar legislation passed in the provinces.

The first step was in fact provided for in the original Act. A provision made it possible for parties not covered by the Act to seek its application. Since this called for an agreement to its use by both sides, it was a voluntary arrangement. An employer included in the public utility or coal mining category could be forced by his employees to become involved in conciliation board proceedings. An employer not within the jurisdiction of the act could not.

A more significant step occurred after 1925 when, because of a Privy Council ruling declaring that the Act was *ultra vires* the Parliament of Canada, the Dominion parliament enacted a modified form which restricted the coverage of the compulsory features of the Act to those areas of industry clearly within Dominion jurisdiction. At the same time, a clause was inserted permitting provinces to pass enabling legislation to make the Dominion law and policy applicable with the specific province. Within a few years most of the provinces passed such legislation and the I. D. I. Act system was by consent retained more or less across the country.

Changes During the 1930's

The decade of the 1930's was the decade of the great depression in both the United States and Canada. It was also a period during which public labour policy in the former country underwent a revolution. There was the ill-fated experiment with Section 7a of the National Industrial Recovery Act, and the permanent change of the Wagner Act of 1935. Collective bargaining became public policy, and was imposed on reluctant employers through the agency of the National Labor Relations Board. It will be recalled that this public labour relations policy was built on the constitutional support of the commerce clause of the constitution. The expansion of interstate commerce was a "good thing;" industrial conflict prevented such expansion; collective bargaining was the road to industrial peace; therefore, collective bargaining was the road to expansion of interstate commerce; hence, public policy supported collective bargaining.

Under the influence of the Wagner Act example, and the demands of organized labour, several of the Canadian provinces passed laws in the last half of the 1930's which contained the Wagner principles of freedom of association, and imposed on employers the responsibility to recognize the representatives of their employees and to bargain with the intention of signing collective agreements. However, none of this legislation contained provision for enforcement and it was therefore ineffective. But it was apparent that Canadian interest was developing in support of compulsion in collective bargaining along American lines.

Privy Council Order 1003 of 1944

When compulsory recognition and bargaining did come it was through the Dominion authorities rather than the provinces.[6] Privy Council Order 1003 of 1944 for the first time established a system of compulsory recognition and bargaining in Canada as a whole. The authority to enact this legislation derived from the emergency powers of war possessed by the Dominion and the War Measures Act of 1917. Such legislation was beyond the scope of parliament in peacetime.

It is important for our purposes to see what this famous order did because it not only introduced compulsory recognition and bargaining on the United States model, it also retained the much older Canadian system of compulsory investigation and conciliation which derived from the I. D. I. Act of 1907. Thus was combined in one system of industrial relations policy a Canadian experiment designed to eliminate disputes, and a United States experiment in promoting union recognition and compelling collective bargaining. It is the interaction of these two streams of experience which gives the Canadian system its unique character. Before examining this, however, it is necessary to complete the brief outline of the history of policy.

For the period of the war and the transitional emergency the Dominion policy continued in force. It involved freedom of association for workers, compulsory recognition of unions certified by the Canada Labour Relations Board, compulsory collective bargaining, the prohibition of strikes and lockouts until after the disputing parties had been subjected to a two-stage compulsory conciliation process including, first, a conciliation officer, and secondly, a conciliation board complete with its report. The first three of these dealing with individual rights and the establishment of collective bargaining, it will be observed, were derived from the Wagner Act, while the remainder dealing with disputes, conciliation and the restraint on strikes and lockouts came from the established Canadian policy.

In the years around the end of the war and thereafter the individual provinces enacted labour relations laws patterned fairly closely on the Dominion wartime policy, and in 1948 the Dominion itself replaced its prewar legislation and its wartime labour relations orders by the Industrial Relations Disputes and Investigation Act. However, the wartime extended coverage of the Dominion was contracted and brought within the peacetime range of Dominion constitutional authority. Both the Dominion and practically all of the provinces retained the two streams derived respectively from Canadian and American experience.

One of the most significant effects of the evolution of policy is the emergence of compulsory conciliation and the temporary suspension of the strike and lockout as regular and universal features of Canadian policy in industrial relations. Yet it will be recalled that at its inception in 1907 in application to public utilities and coal mines alone, there were limited situations which almost always involve a high degree of public interest as distinct from the interest of the parties directly involved. In a rough way these disputes might be classed as emergencies. During the second world war the boundaries of the dispute area which could be classified as emergencies was vastly increased by wartime necessity. It is therefore not surprising that the machinery of compulsory conciliation should have its coverage extended. When most disputes were emergencies, there was justification for applying the emergency technique. What is surprising is that both the Dominion and provinces should, following the end of the emergency period, reconstruct their labour relations laws on the assumption that *all* disputes are public emergencies. The result is that Canada entered the decade of the fifties with a decentralized industrial relations system which is really eleven systems, one for the Dominion and one for each province, the essential features of which were designed to meet critical situations which no longer occur in a very large range of situations in which compulsory conciliation is applied. It is a contention of this paper that the system in operation in Canada has some serious faults and that these faults relate to the two major features of decentralization and universal coverage within the respective political jurisdictions, and to the interaction of the two streams, the American and Canadian, within one system of public intervention.

The Dominion System

A complete analysis of the various legal provisions for conciliation in each of the political jurisdictions is not necessary to illustrate the basic structures of the system. It will be sufficient to examine the main provision of one jurisdiction, and to draw attention to some of the more significant deviations found in others. The Dominion system will serve as a model. The Industrial Relations and Disputes Investigation Act provides[7] that, in a situation when notice to commence collective bargaining has been given, and either collective bargaining has not commenced within the statutory time limits, or having commenced has not been successful, either party may request from the Minister of Labour the services of a conciliation officer. The Minister may grant such request. Indeed, in any case when the Minister deems it advisable he may send in a conciliator with or without a request. If the conciliation officer fails to effect an agreement within four-teen days, the Minister may appoint a conciliation board. There is provision in the law for an extension of the time of the conciliation officer at the discretion of the Minister. If he fails the officer must report to the Minister on the matters agreed upon, the matters still in dispute, and whether or not a conciliation board seems to be indicated.

It will be noted that the primary function of the officer is to get an agreement if possible. A secondary responsibility is to report on the status of the dispute at the time of reporting. The only recommending he has to do is regarding the usefulness of setting up a conciliation board. However, once a board is established the situation changes somewhat. The board is required, like the officer, to "endeavour to bring about agreement between the parties in relation to the matters referred to it."[8] But the board is also required to "report its findings and recommendations to the Minister."[9]

It is this reporting function which has had a most important influence in shaping the character of conciliation and probably of collective bargaining in Canada. While the Dominion law is not specific as to the meaning of the expression "findings and recommendations," the vast majority of conciliation boards established in both the Dominion and provincial jurisdictions have undertaken to include in their recommendations their proposals, for inclusion in the agreements, covering the unsettled issues. Conciliation boards have made specific recommendations regarding wages, hours, shift differentials, holidays, sick-leave benefits, seniority rights, union security provisons, and so on throughout the entire range of issues over which unions and management from time to time negotiate. It is interesting to contrast this wide freedom to recommend in Canadian law and practice with the severe limitation placed by United States federal law where even the board established under the emergency provision is instructed to stick to the facts and the respective positions of the parties, but its report "shall not contain any recommendations."[10]

The other important feature of the Dominion law affecting conciliation is the provision[11] that no strike or lockout shall take place until after the report of the board has reached the Minister and seven days have elapsed. If the Minister rejects the application for a board or fails to act within fifteen days from the application, the restraint on the use of the strike or lockout terminates and the parties are free to continue negotiations or engage in a work stoppage or both.

Differences in British Columbia

Several of the provinces have framed their conciliation provisions very close to those of the Dominion. There is the restraint on the work stoppage until conciliation is completed or has been refused by the Minister, the conciliation officer stage when an attempt is made to work out an accommodation, the conciliation board stage when the same attempt is made again but by the board, followed by a report with recommendations if agreement is not reached through accommodative mediation. But certain noteworthy differences have appeared. Thus in British Columbia the conciliation officer, if he decides to recommend against the establishment of a conciliation board, may himself make recommendations respecting the matters in dispute; and the Minister may substitute this report for the report of the board of conciliation which would otherwise have been established.[12] It should be noted, however, that this procedure is not an inevitable alternative to a conciliation board since the conciliation officer may recommend against a board without making any recommendations on the merits of the dispute.[13] While this set of alternatives is somewhat complicated it at least has the merit that it creates uncertainty in the minds of the parties. The more choices of action there are in the discretion of intervening agencies, the more probable will it be that the parties will negotiate as a means of avoiding the uncertainties. This was the basis of the "Slichter" act in Massachusetts which, however, was limited to emergency public interest disputes. [See Appendix B]

A second unusual feature of the British Columbia system is the requirement for a government supervised strike vote before the union can engage in a strike. This vote may be requested by either party after receipt of either of the above mentioned reports or after the Minister has informed the parties that a conciliation board is not to be established. The vote is a referendum conducted among the members of the bargaining unit, thus making the union officer responsible to a constituency which may take in many who are not members of the union and subject to its constitutional authority.

The Alberta Procedure

The province of Alberta has introduced important modifications. The term "conciliation commissioner" is used to designate the officer performing the functions assigned to conciliation officers in other jurisdictions. To avoid confusion the more common term will be used in this paper. The conciliation officer is required to perform much the same functions in Alberta as in most of the other jurisdictions, including a recommendation on whether or not to set up a conciliation board. But in the case of the conciliation board itself there is an important difference in emphasis. The usual instruction to boards in other jurisdictions is first to try to effect an agreement, and if unsuccessful to render a report with recommendations. However, in Alberta only the latter function is assigned to the conciliation boards. The boards are required to deal with the dispute item by item and make an "award" which "shall state in plain terms . . . what in the opinion of the conciliation board ought or ought not to be done by the respective parties concerned."[14] The Alberta law requires two votes before a strike can take place. The first is on the award of the board, and the second is on the issue of the strike itself. In both cases the constituency is the bargaining unit rather than the membership of the union.

The Alberta procedure represents the most extreme degree of intervention in bargaining disputes in Canada. It may be summarized as follows: the strike and lockout are forbidden until the parties have negotiated, the conciliation officer has attempted to produce an agreement, the board has been established, the board has conducted its investigation, made its award, the award has been voted on and rejected by a majority of the bargaining unit, a strike vote has been held and a majority of the bargaining unit has voted in favor of the strike. Only then may the union engage in direct economic action.

An important step on the opposite side to that of Alberta was taken in Quebec recently when, among other changes, the conciliation boards were forbidden to make any recommendation regarding the issues in dispute. This amendment in 1961 limited the boards to reporting success or failure in their efforts to get the parties to agree.[15]

Ontario Jurisdiction

Most jurisdictions have made provision for the Minister of Labour to bypass or eliminate a stage in the compulsory process, particularly the use of the board, but this is not universal. Another discretion is that prevailing in Ontario where an application for conciliation may be delayed by the Labour Relations Board[16] and the parties instructed to continue negotiation in the interim.[17] Bypassing on the initiative of the parties of interest is also possible in a few situations. Thus in Ontario the parties may agree on their own *mediator* and jointly request that he replace the government conciliator and the conciliation board. A mediator appointed in this way functions in the dual capacities of the officer and the board.[18] British Columbia has a somewhat similar arrangement for a "mediation committee" chosen by the parties to replace the usual conciliation board.[19]

Differences in Saskatchewan Provisions

Finally the province of Saskatchewan differs fundamentally from all other jurisdictions in that there is no formal provision for a conciliation service, although officers of the Labour Department do carry out conciliation functions. Secondly the delay on the strike and lockout is absent although it is possible for the Minister to establish a conciliation board which does impose the suspension. Generally, however, Saskatchewan operates on a voluntary system of conciliation.

Summary of Canadian Approach

We may therefore summarize the Canadian approach to intervention in negotiation disputes somewhat as follows: On the one extreme is Saskatchewan which relies almost entirely on voluntarism and is closest to the American federal approach. On the other end of the spectrum is Alberta with an elaborate complex of intervention terminating in the strike vote. In between and displaying no complete uniformity are the remaining jurisdictions. But in contrast to the United States there is an almost universal reliance on compulsion with regard to procedure, and in all but two jurisdictions, Quebec and Saskatchewan, emphasis on normative awards or recommendations. Three provinces, British Columbia, Alberta, and Manitoba have adopted the strike vote and thereby given referendum control to the members of the bargaining unit over the union officers, and priority over the union's constitution. The whole system involves a considerable effort at staffing the public agencies and much public expense.

National figures on conciliation are not available, partly because statistical reporting has not been standardized. Yet an idea of the extent of the application may be gained by looking at one or two provincial reports. In Ontario for the year 1961 conciliation officers were appointed in 903 disputes involving 103,500 employees directly and 1,078 employers.[20] Agreements were effected in approximately one half the cases, boards were recommended in 372 cases and opposed in 82 cases; 347 conciliation boards operated during the year[21] and 153 agreements were directly effected; 161 were not settled. Ontario is the largest industrial province. The figures for a small province, Nova Scotia, show[22] that 80 cases were processed at the officer level of which 40 were settled; 27 cases were handled by conciliation boards of which 16 were settled.

Value of Compulsory Conciliation

It is very difficult to assess the value of compulsory conciliation in Canada. The figures just quoted superficially seem to indicate that both officers and boards are quite successful in settling large numbers of cases that come before them. But, of course, what we do not know is what would have been the situation if no compulsory conciliation had been applied. Unfortunately there is no completely reliable comparison to be made with other countries because of certain uncontrollable variables. Ross and Hartman[23] do seem to suggest that the strike pattern in Canada, while somewhat different from that of the United States bears a fairly close similarity. Yet the former operates within the compulsory conciliation system and the latter does not. For what they are worth, comparisons between Saskatchewan, which follows voluntarism in conciliations, and those provinces which have compulsion show a record as free from strikes in the former as in the latter. It can be said without too much question that a convincing statistical case in favour of compulsory conciliation has not been made. There is, however, statistical evidence to show that both conciliation officers and boards have most of their apparent success with the smaller of the cases that come before them.[24]

Compulsory conciliation, as practiced in Canada, does not stand up too well on theoretical and analytical grounds. Its weakness rests on certain questionable assumptions. Perhaps the most questionable of these is the notion that the parties need to be removed from the pressure of the strike threat while they negotiate an agreement, or some outside third party, either officer or board, negotiates one for them. Indeed the reverse may very well be true; namely, that the potentiality of the strike threat may be needed to force the parties to strive for agreement. Certainly in practice Canadian disputes have a habit of dragging out over long periods of time.[25] The statistical evidence and the complaints, especially from unions, but also from some management personnel shows that it is normal for conciliation proceedings to exceed by a wide margin the statutory time limits.

A more serious weakness is to be found in the impact the system has on parties of interest and the relationship between them. Particularly in those jurisdictions where the emphasis is placed on conciliation board reports and recommendations, the parties of interest as a practical matter of self-defence will adopt a justifying approach and prepare an elaborate case in which they are trying to convince the board chairman of the objective fairness and justice of their position. The essential ingredient of collective bargaining, the search for compromise, is set aside while the attempt is made to capture the minds of the board with a "case." Only after the board report is in is it safe for the parties to engage in genuine negotiation. Indeed it now at last becomes dangerous not to, since the alternative to negotiation and settlement may be the work-stoppage.

A more subtle impact of the process is to create a reliance on the third party, particularly by the weaker of the two contestants. Small employers or weak unions are inclined to seek the services of conciliation boards as a means of gaining support through a board report more favourable than one which might be bargained. It is perhaps not too much to suggest that this availability of conciliation board support has tended to delay the evolution of collective bargaining institutions in the direction of larger and more viable bargaining units.[26]

Change in Policy in Quebec

This paper has been largely an explanation and criticism of Canadian compulsory conciliation, and it was meant to be. However, there is much to be preserved even if one were in a position to reform it on logical lines. The principal error, it would seem, was in generalizing a system that was designed for emergency situations with a high public interest content. Reform lies in the direction taken by Quebec. There, at least the most unfortunate influences of the conciliation board have been removed. It will take some time for the parties to adjust to the new system, but the net effect should be to strengthen collective bargaining and encourage greater self-reliance and efficiency on both unions and companies, especially small ones. It should be noted, however, that Quebec has taken a large part of the public service emergency dispute area out of collective bargaining by imposing compulsory arbitration.[27] In those provinces where no special provision has been made for such public interest disputes it would be well to retain the conciliation board for these emergency situations, or to replace it with an enquiry commission. But if this is done, the legislation should be clarified to make it apparent that the primary functions are investigation and recommending. For the ordinary case it is hard to defend the suspension of the strike or lockout. This is the principal effective conciliating device. It should be restored to its proper place. It carries its own antidote.

The change in policy in Quebec leads to speculation about the prospects for further changes in the same direction in Quebec and other provinces, and invites discussion of yet another problem which touches on the nature of collective bargaining itself and the whole concept of industrial self-government. The Quebec move to transform the conciliation board from a *normative* role in which the board tried to find proper standards, fair wages, reasonable fringe benefits and so on, and recommend them to the parties and the public, to an *accommodative* role in which it seeks to get the parties to reach agreement, and makes no recommendation in its report, is not merely a reduction of the function, it is a redirection of the role of the board. Since it has aban-

doned the recommending report, it has based the entire conciliation effort including the officer and the board, on the principle
of accommodation. It has also enhanced the responsibility of the
parties and returned to them the matter of decision-making regarding the contents of collective agreements.

It may be that the example of Quebec will not be imitated by
other jurisdictions. If it is, and particularly if the trend goes further and, for all practical purposes eliminates compulsion in
conciliation, a number of difficulties barring the natural evolution of collective bargaining would be removed. There would
be, as already suggested, a transfer of decision-making from
third parties, especially conciliation boards, to the parties of interest, the unions and management. But there would also be a
larger opportunity for the parties to assume more control of their
relationship, even in the area normally under the control of
labour relations boards. This would be so because the restraint on
the parties now imposed by compulsory conciliation and the
suspension of the work stoppage and particularly the time control would be eliminated. At present, it is virtually impossible for
the parties to combine bargaining units covering operations in
more than one province, because of the control over negotiations
through compulsory conciliation procedures. As long as there is
the slightest desire by one of the parties to bargain in small units,
the constitutional allocation of jurisdiction, the built-in bias in
our laws in favour of small units, and the delay on the strike or
lockout, working together can guarantee the *status quo* so far as
the institutional relationships are concerned. Under present circumstances no public authority, except the Dominion in its
very restricted jurisdiction, can authorize a bargaining unit going
beyond provincial boundaries. The parties can, however, negotiate agreements at one time for bargaining units separately certified, even by different labour relations boards. But the will to
do so is seriously frustrated by the legal provisions for conciliation officers and boards, and the restraint on the work stoppage.
In the logic of Canadian constitutional division of jurisdiction and
labour relations law, for the vast bulk of industry there can be no
labour dispute or clash of interests that transcends provincial
boundaries. Nor is there in this logic such a thing as a multi-
province strike.

The sensible way to resolve this problem of the size of the bargaining unit is to reallocate authority among the political jurisdictions, a solution hardly probable in the present temper and climate of Canadian politics. But something approximating a satisfactory solution could be achieved if the influence of compulsory conciliation were removed by legislative changes within the provinces. While the formal determination of bargaining units would still rest with provincial labour relations boards, some important barriers to informal adjustments would be removed. A more natural growth could result.

Canadian Conciliation Unrealistic

In summary it may be said that Canadian legislative bodies have created a system of conciliation which is constructed on a foundation of questionable assumptions regarding the nature of industrial conflict, and which is forced into a constitutional mold which, to say the least, is highly unrealistic in relation to the forces at work in industrial society. The assumptions of dubious validity include: 1) the idea that disputes can best be settled if the influence of the strike threat can be removed for a time during which reasonable men can negotiate reasonably; 2) that stubborn cases can be helped toward resolution by converting the intervening agency into a recommending body which substitutes its judgment for that of the parties; and 3) in three western jurisdictions, Manitoba, Alberta and British Columbia, that more responsible results will emerge if one or more important decision areas are transferred from union executives to rank and file unit members. It has been the contention of this paper that these assumptions have been allowed to creep into policy without due regard to the impact of such policies on the behaviour of the parties of interest toward one another and toward collective bargaining. Finally, the constitutional division of authority has placed some problems in a category of unsolvable issues.

Canadian conciliation needs a thorough re-examination, but the first step is to decide what we expect should be accomplished by collective bargaining; the second is to reach agreement on the nature of industrial conflict and the process of accommodation; the third is to come to agreement as to what, precisely, the public interest in labour relations is; and the last is to remake our procedures in the light of the findings on the other three. I am not overly optimistic. Well established procedures tend to carry their own sanction, and to be supported by the natural conservatism of those who become involved in their use. Annual reports of labour departments suggest strong administrative support. Similarly, while both labour and management may complain about certain aspects, there is much support for the procedures on both sides. Management has generally either supported the system or refrained from serious criticism. Labour has complained about specific aspects, and a few unions, for example the Confederation of National Trade Unions and the United Automobile Workers, have urged that the system be radically altered or dropped. But generally labour has hesitated to denounce it entirely. Some unions have supported the policy. Even if we could achieve a concensus on the unsatisfactory state of conciliation, it is quite obvious that the conflict of interest over the basic relationship of labour and management, and over the substantive matters in dispute is too great to permit labour and management to agree on policies regarding conciliation. In the meantime, healthy evolution of the institutions of labour-management relations, and of the bargaining process are seriously frustrated.

NOTES

1. Hereafter Canadian *Federal* will be replaced by the term *Dominion* to avoid confusion between the two federal governments at Washington and Ottawa respectively.

2. The constitutional division of authority is contained in Sections 91 and 92 of the British North America Act of 1867. This act contains no reference to labour relations; the present allocation of jurisdiction therefore rests on judicial interpretation. Since 1925 and the *Snider* case which was decided by the Privy Council in England, the ascendancy of the provinces has been assured. Prior to that time, and especially from 1900 to 1925, the Dominion parliament had been assuming considerable authority and a national system appeared to be in the making.

3. For a detailed study of the Industrial Disputes Investigation Act, its amendments, and its fate in the courts, see B. M. Selekman, *Postponing Strikes*, New York, Russel Sage Foundation, 1927.

4. Noted at footnote 3.

5. H. D. Woods, "Canadian Collective Bargaining and Dispute Settlement Policy: An Appraisal," *Canadian Journal of Economics and Political Science*, November, 1953.

6. Strictly speaking British Columbia and Ontario in 1943 introduced legislation on Wagner Act lines with enforcing agencies, but this was aban-

doned in 1944 when the Dominion introduced its compulsory collective bargaining on a national scale.

7. Dominion I. R. D. I. Act, Sections 16 and 27.

8. Dominion I. R. D. I. Act, Section 32.

9. Dominion I. R. D. I. Act, Section 35.

10. Labor Management Relations Act, Section 201(b).

11. Dominion I. R. D. I. Act, Section 21.

12. British Columbia Labour Relations Act, Section 29.

13. British Columbia Labour Relations Act, Section 52.

14. Alberta Labour Act, Section 93.

15. Quebec Labour Relations Act, Section 14.

16. In Ontario the application for conciliation service goes first to the Labour Relations Board rather than to the Minister of Labour.

17. Ontario Labour Relations Act, Section 13.

18. Ontario Labour Relations Act, Section 30.

19. British Columbia Labour Relations Act, Section 43.

20. Report of the Department of Labour, Ontario, Fiscal Year Ending March 31, 1961, Table F-1.

21. Noted in footnote 20, Table F-2.

22. Annual Report, Department of Labour Nova Scotia, Fiscal Year Ending March 31, 1962, p. 19.

23. A. M. Ross and P. T. Hartman, *Changing Patterns of Industrial Conflict*, Wiley, 1960.

24. H. D. Woods and Sylvia Ostry, *Labour Relations Policy and Labour Economics in Canada*. MacMillan Company of Canada, Ltd., 1962, Chapter VII.

25. Ontario Department of Labour, *Time Lapses in Disputes Disposed of by the Conciliation Service*, Submission to the Select Committee on Labour Relations, Ontario Legislature, 1957.

26. In Canada it is probable that this has combined with a built-in legal bias toward small units to stall the natural evolution to larger bargaining units on both sides.

27. Quebec Public Service Employees Disputes Act.

M Industrial Peace in South Africa*

GARFIELD CLACK**

S OUTH AFRICA IS NOTED for gold, gaols, strong government, racial antipathies, growing unrest, and infrequent strikes. The remarkably low incidence of industrial strife has been attributed by government spokesmen to the nature of the labour legislation and the sense of responsibility of trade unions and employers. Others write of 'thorough-going repression on the non-white majority practised by nearly all white groups, and particularly the government,' adding that this repression has itself reduced the militancy of white workers.[1] Further suggestions range from 'economic factors of supply and demand'[2] to the view that 'South Africa is, generally speaking, not a very strike-conscious community.'[3] It is also noted that work stoppages by Africans are

---

* Reprinted by permission from the *British Journal of Industrial Relations*, Vol. I, No. 1, February 1963.

** Research Fellow, Department of Economics, University of Leeds.

often more 'protests against the established order'[4] than against employers, i.e. are 'stay-aways' rather than strikes. Systematic discussion seems worthwhile.

Strikes are widely defined. In the Industrial Conciliation Act of 1924, a strike was 'a suspension or temporary stoppage of work of any number of employees in order to compel their employer or to assist other employees in compelling the employers of such employees to agree to specific terms or conditions of employment', but subsequent amendments have amplified and refined this definition to include partial stoppages such as overtime bans or go-slows, obstructing or retarding the progress of work, refusal to resume work, and other breaches of contracts of employment.[5] Despite definitional problems, and those leading to under-reporting,[6] it is probable that the great majority of strikes of significant proportion have been included in the official records.[7] In any event, quibbles here over these problems are irrelevant when a doubling or trebling of the incidence would not seriously affect South Africa's status as a remarkably strike-free country.

By international comparison, strike incidence is extremely low. The proportion of workers directly and indirectly involved in strikes during the period 1950-56, expressed as a percentage of non-agricultural employment, was lower in South Africa than in fourteen other countries for which analogous figures are available. The number of working days lost per striker was similarly lower in South Africa than in the other countries. This is inexplicable by conventional considerations. In most countries, the incidence of strikes correlates positively with weak labour organisation, the presence of rival labour movements, and the degree of employer hostility. In South Africa it might be expected that protest symptoms would find significant expression in industry both for these reasons and others: the high rate of industrial development and attendant stresses, the diversity of cultures and languages implying misunderstandings and difficulties of communication, the pervasive importance of racial antipathies, and the severe limits placed on the fulfilment of non-white aspirations. Additionally, there is the tendency for strike-proneness to be a feature of relatively isolated, socially cohesive work communities, and rough or dirty manual labour,[8] both features of, for example, mining, dock work, and the unskilled labour to which most dark-skinned workers are confined.

The history of strikes can be simply summarised. Mining dominated the early period of industrialization, and strikes by white miners were national crises until the 1920's. Imported along with the skilled white workers had been an established tradition of labour organization, which drew its main orientation from Britain. Unions received little recognition from employers until World War I, and functioned without legislative protection or constraint until 1924. The major disputes of the period were characterized by violence, culminating in the Rand Strike of 1922 on the scale of a minor civil war in which about 230 persons were killed. These disputes involved issues of recognition, but more significantly, reflected opposition by skilled and highly paid whites to attempts by employers to make greater use of unskilled, unorganized, and low-paid Africans. The Industrial Conciliation Act then gave legal protection to the unions and encouraged collective bargaining, while restraining strike action. Since 1922, with the exception of one year,[9] despite industrial expansion and an increasing number of strikes, the total of man-days lost has never been more than one-sixth of the 1922 peak. Strikes have been of decreasing duration, and increasingly undertaken by Africans. During the period 1955-60, more than nine-tenths of all strikers were non-whites, most of whom were Africans.

The racial structure of the labour force and industrial relations makes analytical apartheid convenient, for many suggestions offered to account for infrequent striking by whites are very different from those which seem relevant to the low incidence amongst Africans, notwithstanding intricate interdependence of the races in economic production. That four-fifths of a total population of 16 millions are non-whites is reflected in the industrial classification of the labour force. Non-whites form proportions ranging from one-half of total employment in the civil service to nine-tenths in mining. Occupationally, most administrative, technical, clerical, and skilled work is done by whites. Only one per cent. of unskilled jobs are done by whites, while only six per cent. of jobs classified as skilled are done by Africans.[10] Racial dichotomy is as sharp in industrial relations arrangements: Africans are by definition excluded from membership of legally protected trade unions and from officially-sanctioned collective bargaining.

White Workers and Industrial Militancy

White workers in most industries are highly organized. The trade unions which function under statutory protection and control are of an industrial type yet exclude the unskilled. Unions which represent more than half the number of white or non-African workers in an industry may be empowered to negotiate minimum wages and conditions applicable to all workers in that industry, enforceable through the criminal courts. There are altogether about half a million union members organized into about 250 unions, including about 65 relatively small and unregistered unions with mainly African membership. Seven out of every ten trade unionists are whites, whilst only one is an African. Racially mixed unions have never been in the majority, but most Coloured and Asiatic trade unionists prefer to be in economically secure white-controlled unions and have resisted pressures making for racial separation between unions. Seven out of every ten unionists are in only 28 unions, most of which are all-white, and the three largest of which, together with some of the others, are for white-collar workers.

A high proportion of white-collar workers in the unions, and the white-collar attitudes of many skilled artisans who, by virtue of the occupational structure exercise supervisory functions over non-whites, adds to the disinclination of white workers to consider or undertake strike action. Attitudinal considerations reflect more than merely colour of collar, and the abrupt decline of strikes after the defeat of the unions in 1922 may be linked to changes in the composition of both union leaders and members. Time and phthisis killed off many of the old militants who had come from abroad[11] and led the struggle for union recognition. The early militancy was changing under the impact also of an agricultural revolution. Closure of the frontier, pressure of rural population, subdivision of land holdings, and the expansion of commercial farming, were factors which had been forcing whites with no industrial tradition or experience into towns and competition for jobs with non-whites with a lower standard of living, and their rural background was often associated with an authoritarian family structure. Public attention to the 'poor white problem' had given rise to an official Civilized Labour Policy. In the decade from 1925 many posts in central and local government services, on the state-owned railways, and to a lesser extent in manufacturing, became a form of sheltered employment for these unskilled whites, inducing an attitude of reliance on state aid hardly conducive to labour militancy.

Nor was communism espoused by white trade unionists. In 1921 a number of socialist groups had merged their identity in the Communist Party of South Africa. A communist 'Council of Action' usurped a leading role in 1922—many had dubbed the strike a 'Red Revolt'—and their actions had earned the party little esteem. In the years to 1925 the Party had approached and been rejected by white unions and the Labour Party, while an internal faction had succeeded in carrying an alternative policy aimed at organizing African workers into unions. The Party became inactive during most of the 1930's, and with a temporary softening of white attitudes to the organization of African workers, Party members obtained leading positions in some of the registered unions until they were evicted in 1950 with more public alarm and a greater show of force than was warranted. Left-wing radicals have in South Africa inflamed the conservatism of white workers rather than induced industrial militancy.

The Suppression of Communism Act of 1950 was described by a visiting delegation of the British T.U.C. as 'the greatest single threat to the trade union movement and to the entire democratic life of South Africa. . . . It has little or nothing to do with Communism.'[12] Yet the penalties in terms of banishment and social disability, the arbitrary nature of its application, and lack of recourse to the Courts are salient features.[13] By 1956, 75 trade union officials had been listed as communists, and 56 had been ordered to resign from their positions. No later figures are available, but press reports and private statements indicate increased use of the Act since then. It is now a constant source of second thought to leaders who may be contemplating action likely to incur government disfavour.

South African trade union history is littered with the corpses of defunct federations, nor is the fertility of the unions in this respect exhausted. There has never been a representative labour movement,[14] and there are now five political federations forming three main labour movements. The latest round of rupturing and re-alignment began in 1947, and can be attributed to substantive racial issues, parochialism, personality conflicts, and the activity of the Afrikaner nationalist movement. Afrikaners had suffered what Smuts, writing in 1898, had described as 'a century of wrong' at the hands of the British, and in the years between the World Wars, Afrikaner protest took shape in a comprehensive yet cohesive movement planned to capture the machinery of state. Organs of the movement set out to gather Afrikaner workers together, either to gain control of, or to form separate, trade unions in opposition to what was considered the dangerously communistic orientation of those into which they were being inducted, to muster electoral support, and in alarm at the tendency for colour bars to become blurred in the economic forces of industrialization. The movement wants unions to be 'Christian' and nationalized; rival labour movements are an interim result.

Rival labour movements are often a frequent source of strikes: the union structure most conducive to industrial peace is a unified national movement with strongly centralized control. Special features of labour movement rivalry in South Africa tend to off-set conventional expectations. Firstly, white workers have for long been well organized, and the rival movements are not competing for net additions to union membership, or for the allegiance of the unorganized. Racially exclusive membership is a major point at issue. Secondly, labour legislation did not facilitate until recently the formation of rival unions.[15] Where more than half the workers of any (non-African) race in an industry, area, or occupation were organized, no rival union could obtain registration, and the comprehensive coverage of most collective agreements discourages militancy as a tactic of rivalry. Finally, while rivalry between the white movements does not lead to strikes, many strikes of recent years can be related to the proselytism of the non-white movement, weak and comprised mainly of unregistered unions fighting desperately for recognition.

Employers are almost exclusively white and well organized, showing little hostility to white unions or unwillingness to bargain collectively. Bargaining is on an industry-wide scale although geographical and other factors often reduces it to regional proportions. The Industrial Conciliation Act encourages the voluntary establishment of standing joint industrial councils by registered unions and employers' organizations, and provides for voluntary arbitration where conciliation fails. There is close statutory control over the shape and conduct of bargaining councils but they may be given wide powers to impose and enforce agreements on non-parties in their sphere of jurisdiction. There are currently over 90 industrial councils in existence, of which thirteen negotiate agreements of national application. Agreements are lengthy, comprehensive, and legalistic public documents of usually two to three years' tenor, breaches of which are criminal offences. Grievances arising out of agreements are channelled through the councils thus reducing pressures which could make for plant bargaining and more frequent localized disputes.

The Act thus encouraged and extended a system of centralized bargaining: it also imposes compulsory delays on the calling of strikes or lockouts, extending an earlier and ineffective measure in this regard.[16] Strikes are illegal on matters covered by an agreement during its currency, or, if the issue in dispute is not so covered, before the parties have met to consider the matter. Where no council is in existence, strikes are illegal pending report by an *ad hoc* conciliation board or the passage of prescribed periods. Once more, voluntary arbitration may be resorted to, but is ultimately compulsory in the case of workers engaged on certain 'essential services' in urban areas, i.e. work connected with the supply of light, power, water, sanitary, transportation or fire extinguishing services. The earlier clauses providing for compulsory arbitration were later extended to include all workers employed by local authorities, and to all workers connected with the canning or preserving of perishable foodstuffs. The penalties which may be imposed for illegal striking are severe: in the original Act persons convicted could be fined up to £500 or imprisoned for two years, or both, although a later amendment reduced these maxima to £100 or one year's imprisonment, or both.

Legislation places other constraints, both direct and indirect, on striking, or union militancy. The Industrial Conciliation Act requires that no legal strike may take place unless a majority of the members of the union in good standing in the area and in the particular undertaking, industry, trade or occupation in which the action is proposed, have voted by ballot in favour. The Act is lengthy and intricate, and imposes controls on union government and administration ranging from elaborate record-keeping to procedures for the holding of meetings and the election of officials. These controls, taken together with strong centralized union government, have made for bureaucracy and attitudes of conservatism rather than crusade amongst union leaders.

The Industrial Conciliation Act was both symptom and support of a more general reaction to the period of violence which ended in 1922. It was drafted and passed in an atmosphere of shock and disillusion. Defeat of the strikers had been followed by capital sentences passed on eighteen of the participants, and the execution of four of these before public outcry and party-political tactics led to eventual amnesty. The events generated an ethos of industrial peace and an exaggerated concern with strikes as manifestations of industrial conflict which became entrenched in the legislation. There is little regard for the views of many who hold that strikes may not always be wholly or even mainly disadvantageous in their overall effects, or that 'man-days lost' is a meaningless measure of the economic impact of strikes. The continued uncritical propagation of industrial peace as an unmixed blessing has almost certainly had a significant (if indeterminate) effect on the general willingness to strike.

Similarly general considerations regarding the wage structure may be additional explanation of low strike incidence amongst white workers. In 1914 a government Commission[17] considered that skilled white workers on the Rand were better-off in real terms than their fellows anywhere else in the world, and although it was these workers who undertook the major strikes of the early period, the incidents were sparked off not by wage demands but by attempts to reduce wages or employ more unskilled labour. It is an axiom of South African industrial relations that 'State policy cannot allow free competition between peoples living on such widely different levels of civilization as the Natives and the white population'.[18] The gap between skilled and unskilled wage rates has always been large, and has tended to widen in recent years. Skilled wage rates in most trades are four to five times the unskilled rates, and in mining from eight to ten times. Whites have thrived not on industrial militancy but on economic expansion and racial restrictions. Nor are rising standards of living and widening wage differentials conducive to 'coercive comparisons' or intractable wage demands.

The African Majority

The majority of industrial workers are Africans, and it is in relation to these workers that strike incidence and other manifestations of industrial conflict are surprisingly low. African workers are weakly organized, poorly paid, and bear the brunt of racially discriminatory policies. Excluded from the statutory conciliation machinery, there have been no officially-sanctioned channels for making collective representation to employers, and the localized and informal or non-statutory bargaining which was increasing in some centres, particularly during the war, has been severely discouraged by the government over the past ten years. Africans have been required to rely on a system of state mediation machinery which allows for no organization other than works committees on a plant basis (which employers are not obliged to recognize), and for no bargaining. They are excluded from the industrial conciliation machinery because 'the official recognition of Native trade unions will be detrimental to the interests of South Africa . . . we can realize that if there is a strong, well-organized Native trade union movement in South Africa, and they utilize those trade unions as a political weapon, at a given time they can create chaos in South Africa.'[19] Africans are held to be mentally undeveloped, irresponsible, and open to incitement by left-wing agitators for personal and ulterior motives.[20]

Africans have been slow to organize to protect their interests. Reasons will be suggested below, but occasional collective action at work has been undertaken in support of wage demands or improved conditions since the early days of diamond mining. The largest of the strikes, and most notable for the orderly conduct of the strikers, involved mine-workers in 1913, 1920, and 1946. Police and soldiers were used to break them. Characteristic of strikes of Africans has been their limited size and short duration of from one to three days: sustained collective action is difficult without formal organization. The large-scale work stoppages which have occurred of recent years are only incidentally strikes, having been political demonstrations against general rather than industrial disabilities.

The first African labour organization was not formed until 1919. The Industrial and Commercial Workers' Union was amorphous in structure, loose in aim, and charismatic in leadership. Trade unions on more conventional lines were not formed until 1928, after the Communist Party had undertaken the task. African union membership reached its peak during World War II, had dropped heavily by 1950, and has been increasing slowly since 1955. There are today estimated to be about 60,000 African trade unionists, as against a probable 100,000 at the end of the War. African labour organization is thus less weak than minimal. Writing in 1948 of the decline of the Industrial and Commercial Workers' Union, one observer notes that 'persecution helped to kill it; but the forces of internal disruption were a more fundamental cause of its collapse. . . . Remembering the I.C.U., the Africans are wary'.[21] A government Commission attributed the postwar decline of the unions to inexperienced and dictatorial leaders, maladministration, lack of membership gratifications, over-confidence and the expulsion of white leaders with the competence they had contributed, and the restrictions on movement and meetings by Africans.[22]

With the onset of more systematic official hostility during the 1950's, similarly specific difficulties hampering the formation and operation of African unions may be listed: lack of legal protection for members and unions; inability to obtain or retain suitable office accommodation in either industrial or residential areas; police raids on union offices and the confiscation of records; banning of leaders under the Suppression of Communism Act; employer hostility induced or backed by government threats; victimization of unionists and their removal from urban areas under the complex of regulations controlling movement and residence. Check-off facilities have been in effect prohibited. The practicalities of the situation have required organization 'from above', and the centralized organizations are relatively more easily and seriously affected by official interference. But overshadowing these considerations has been their exclusion from statutory bargaining and grievance negotiation. Union membership had reached its peak when employers and government were granting administrative recognition. African unions can now grasp at little with which to gratify their members and grow.

Persecution, together with lack of experience, resources, and persons willing to assist in overcoming these obstacles, can account only in part for the slow development of social movements by Africans, and their ineffectiveness. There are other, less tangible, considerations. The mining industry adopted, adapted, and entrenched a migrant labour system which, buttressed by the unwillingness of whites to accept Africans in towns as permanent industrial workers, was extended by the growth of manufacturing industry. Migrants still form the great majority of mine-workers, and are an important proportion of workers in industries such as chemicals, explosives, iron and steel. Migrancy tends to scatter amongst the disjointed and often isolated areas which comprise African reserves or 'homelands', the protest induced by rapid industrialization. It tends also to reduce the tensions of transition to urban living: the mining industry uses the analogy of a bridge to justify continued reliance on the system.[23] But perhaps the major effect of the migrant system in this context has been the slowing down of the growth of more or less stable occupational groups on which viable organizations can be more easily founded.

Some of the factors which hinder organization also directly discourage striking. More sophisticated workers gravitate to better jobs, and in the South African context, job security is seriously jeopardized by trade union activity. Poverty and unsympathetic police are pervasive realities in the everyday activities of urban Africans,[24] and prospects of severe penal sentences, victimization, blacklisting, and forced removal from urban areas militate against incautious or impetuous action. But many of the strikes which do occur are of an emotionally-charged or spontaneous kind, and absence of organization and directly repressive measures are insufficient to prevent strikes. When Africans are willing to take collective action, degree of formal organization is not always important: in racial situations of this kind, colour may become a kind of membership card. Sustained and successful boycotts and the successful though necessarily short-lived stay-aways involving large numbers with little formal organization indicate the importance of motivational factors.

Transvaluational religion may be suggested as a general influence on the willingness of Africans to engage in industrial protest. Early missionary activity associated with the anti-slavery movement inflamed Afrikaners, but despite the concentration of most African education in the hands of missionaries until very recently, there is little evidence that they fostered a spirit of protest against general or specific non-white disabilities. By 1951, about three-fifths of all Africans belonged to Christian churches, and of these, one-third were members of numerous African separatist churches whose growth has been related to colour bars— agricultural, religious and industrial.[25] African Christianity has not the cohesion of Afrikaner Christianity, neither has it been mobilized behind a nationalist movement. Yet religious organizations have absorbed a significant proportion of the protest produced by industrialization and racial disability. Some African intellectuals[26] have maintained that missionaries have contributed to the propagation of the 'Great Lie' of racial inferiority of African peoples. The doctrine that the poor are worthy and will be rewarded in the next world may have been a powerful influence making for peace.

Many of the controls on African labour operate away from places of work and, by association, protest expressions are more diffuse than industrial. Docility at work motivated by willingness rather than sullen caution may be inferred from evidence on absenteeism and labour turnover. Staying away from work, and changing employers, are at least partly responses by workers to situations they regard as intolerable. Those studies which support the common belief that the absenteeism and turnover rates of African workers are high, either in relation to white behaviour or by international comparison, do not distinguish between the short-period contracting of migrants and the individually unexpected although aggregatively predictable mobility of committed workers who form an increasing proportion of the industrial labour force.[27] The most recent and comprehensive study[28] indicates that 'the average black industrial worker is not fundamentally more mobile than other industrial groups', and that 'absence and turnover levels compare favourably with those in industrial communities outside Africa', including Britain, United States, and Australia. African workers do not see their job or working conditions as intolerable: not only are they unwilling to change or avoid them, but they do not bring pressure to bear in the form of work-to-rule behaviour, nor have they yet indulged in industrial sabotage.

Poverty does not appear to stimulate protest at work. The poverty of urban Africans is well-documented and undeniable. Figures showing slowly rising real wages must often be deflated to allow for changes involved in the transition from patterns of consumption based on extended family units, or on other forms of subsidization, to sole reliance on wage-earning. Yet there are surprising indications that African workers do not interpret their occupational problems primarily in terms of low wages. Attitudinal studies[29] provide evidence that these workers, migrants excluded, have job attitudes similar to those of comparable groups of workers in the United States. Job satisfactions are related firstly to the nature of the job itself, and to working conditions, before the level of remuneration is rated as important. The single attitudinal category which differs noticeably in rank order from the American evidence, i.e. 'opportunity for job advancement', which Africans rank low in preference order, has been interpreted to mean that Africans know, and by implication accept, that opportunities for them are limited. Articulate Africans see redress of their grievances in terms of ballot boxes, or at most, a national minimum wage for unskilled work.

Prospects for Industrial Peace

There is little doubt that the rapid changes taking place in Africa, and not least in South Africa, are producing pressures making for re-assessment and modification of industrial relations policies and practices. Sophisticated personnel management is being extended to African workers, and the backwash of diffuse unrest, affecting employers, has given emphasis to the use of organization for purposes of control. Widespread recognition of poverty and an interest in the level of domestic purchasing power, have led to voluntary increases of unskilled wages by many employers, acting in concert with government policy in this regard. The statute against sabotage, passed in 1962 after a number of sporadic explosions damaging public property, is one response to a new phase of non-white protest. The net effect of these pressures is unlikely to increase strike incidence amongst white workers. Faced with external hostility and a sense of growing internal unrest, whites are drawing closer together behind government policy, whilst unions are under increased constraint. Statutory work reservation has been designed and administered to increase whites' feelings of job security and to shift the incidence of economic difficulties on to non-whites. Nor does there seem to be any immediate prospect of increased striking by non-whites.

The psychologistic phase of personnel management, introduced into South Africa shortly before World War II and largely confined to whites, was less a response to labour organization than to shortage of skills. It is one indication of a more sensitive approach to labour problems, and the immediate effect of its application to non-whites may be to delay the percolation of dissatisfaction into the workplace. But all of the organizations which now propagate personnel management avoid mention of or contact with trade unions or collective bargaining, and the effect is to relegate to the background consideration of, and prospects for, the extension to Africans of accommodatory machinery for the joint determination of wages and conditions of employment.

Labour organization is a universal response to industrialization: this is recognized by the government and most employers. Arguments are being conducted over the forms which this organization should take and the functions which it should fulfil. The government would turn all trade unions into welfare societies. Employers are divided on the issue of African labour organization, but few are willing to concede unions as effective centres of power. The moves to encourage works committees for Africans, by employers since 1958 and by the government since early 1961, are difficult to assess because of the differing aims of their sponsors. Works committees are to be channels of communication and control, are to drain off protest and act as counters to the existing African unions, as well as to foster the continued willingness of African workers. The government has indicated possible expansion of the mediatory regional Native Labour Committees into organizations 'which can give expression to the aspirations of the workers in the negotiation and enforcement of wage regulating measures',[30] but it is hard to believe that there is anything more immediate in mind than the creation of regional forums to advise the all-white Central Native Labour Board. Control is to remain in the hands of the state, and collective bargaining is not envisaged. On the other hand, some employers are planning that works committees in an industry should be linked together in a central council for direct negotiation over wages and conditions. It is not likely that employers will lack workers willing to participate in whatever form of organization is suggested, and the number of committees, small now, is likely to grow. They may well become foci of discontent, but there is little evidence to indicate this course as an immediate prospect.

While most whites in South Africa would say that most Africans are responsible workers who respect the superiority of white leadership, more neutral observers would attribute industrial docility to the caution of Africans in opposing the legal, administrative and customary constraints which beset them, their confusion in the face of conflicting appeals on their loyalties, and the conviction of many that their interests lie in accepting existing arrangements. Others, white and non-white, speak of force and fraud. However coloured by phraseology, the factors making for docility of African labour are not likely to last indefinitely. The government is committed to promoting industrial expansion, urbanization, and universal literacy, and the adaptations being made to absorb accumulating stresses associated with these developments have the appearance of temporary holding operations. There are few precedents or plausible arguments to support the view that personnel management, joint consultation, and the payment of higher wages of the order usually in mind will by themselves contribute significantly to the long term prospects of industrial peace. A more fundamental task is the formulation of new and acceptable social machinery to channel rather than choke the forces at work both in industry and a wider terrain.

NOTES

1. A. M. Ross and P. T. Hartman, *Changing Patterns of Industrial Conflict* (New York: Wiley, 1960), p. 159.

2. F. T. De Vyver, 'Labor Relations in South African Industry,' *Journal of Industrial Relations*, II, 2, October 1960.

3. *Ibid.*, citing 'one South African industrial relations expert.'

4. M. Arkin, 'Strikes, Boycotts—and the History of their Impact on South Africa,' *S. A. Journal of Economics*, XXVIII, 4, December 1960.

5. The definition of 'strike' in the Industrial Conciliation Act is reproduced in the Native Labour (Settlement of Disputes) Act of 1953.

6. The Central Native Labour Board, which mediates in the settlement of labour disputes involving Africans, is not obliged to, and in fact does not, publish reports on its work. A few brief paragraphs appear in the Annual Reports of the Department of Labour, but the information needs careful assessment, as the adequacy of the Board is a touchy political issue. During interview in October 1961, the Board admitted reporting less than 40 per cent of the number of work stoppages involving Africans which had come to its attention since 1954. It is probable that some stoppages do not come to its attention.

7. Bureau of Census and Statistics, *Union Statistics for Fifty Years* (Pretoria: Government Printer, 1960), G-18. See also comparative figures for 15 countries in Ross and Hartman.

8. Clark Kerr and A. Siegel, 'The Interindustry Propensity to Strike—an International Comparison,' in Kornhauser, Dubin and Ross, eds. *Industrial Conflict* (New York: McGraw-Hill, 1954).

9. The 1947 total of 1.4 million man-days lost arose primarily out of a seven-week strike by several thousand members of the all-white Mine Workers' Union in a successful attempt to unseat the union leadership.

10. Official figures reproduced in *A Survey of Race Relations in South Africa: 1957/8* (Johannesburg: S.A. Institute of Race Relations), p. 171. Many Coloured and Asiatic workers occupy intermediate positions in the skill hierarchy.

11. Biographical sketches of 36 white labour leaders, living and dead, had been compiled in 1926. They show that 27 were born in Britain, 6 were Australian born, one came from Holland, and only 2 were born in South Africa.

12. Trades Union Congress, *Trade Unions in South Africa*, March 1954.

13. On this Act, and similar legislation, see International Commission of Jurists, *South Africa and the Rule of Law* (Geneva: Studer, 1960).

14. The S.A. Trades and Labour Council, which existed from 1930-1954, was the most representative of all the labour movements. In 1946 at the peak of its affiliated membership, it had less than 170,000 members while the membership of registered unions alone was almost 350,000.

15. Act 18 of 1961 amended the Industrial Conciliation Act to make it easier for dissident members to break away from an existing union, but it is yet too soon to assess the practical significance of the amendment.

16. The first statute regulating labour relations was the Transvaal Industrial Disputes Prevention Act of 1909, itself a hurried importation of the Canadian Industrial Disputes Investigation Act of 1907. The latter was claimed by its originator, W. L. McKenzie King, to be the first legislation embodying the principle of compulsory delay on the right to strike. See some discussion of the Transvaal Act in Ellison Kahn, 'The Right to Strike in South Africa,' *S.A. Journal of Economics*, XI, 1, March 1943.

17. *Report of the Economic Commission*, U.G. 12/1914, par. 130.

18. *Report of the Native Economic Commission*, U.G. 22/1932, par. 845.

19. Statement by Minister of Labour, *Hansard*, Assembly, Vol. 82, August 4, 1953, cols. 865ff.

20. In November, 1961, a statement in these terms was addressed by the

Minister of Labour to the Natal Employers' Association, and is reproduced in their *Eighteenth Annual Report.*

21. E. Roux, *Time Longer than Rope* (London: Gollanz, 1948), pp. 204-5.

22. *Report of the Industrial Legislation Commission of Inquiry,* U.G. 62/1951, pars. 1540-1545.

23. Advanced as justification to a government Commission in 1948, it drew the retort that a bridge is meant to be crossed, not to serve as a permanent abode. *Report of the Native Laws Commission,* U.G. 28/1948, esp. pars. 59-65.

24. The number of criminal convictions involving Africans has been over a million a year since 1954, i.e. an annual figure more than ten per cent of the total African population. As most arrests and prosecutions are made in urban areas, it is not unlikely that several times this percentage of the urban African population makes annual acquaintance with police or prison cells, mostly for technical offenses. *Union Statistics for Fifty Years,* F—3.

25. B. M. G. Sundkler noted that 'the existence today of a considerable number of Independent Church leaders who prior to the enforcement of the Colour Bar Act [Mines and Works Act, 1926] were occupied as skilled artisans and craftsmen, seems to point to an important relation between these two phenomena in the life of Africans at the present time. It is pertinent to our subject to observe that these restrictions were most strongly felt on the Witwatersrand, the most important centre of the Independent Church movement.' *Bantu Prophets in South Africa* (London: Lutterworth Press, 1948), p. 34.

26. For example, Nosipho Majeke, *The Role of the Missionaries in Conquest* (Johannesburg: Society of Young Africa, 1952).

27. See, for example, S. T. van der Horst, 'A Note on Native Labour turnover and the structure of the labour force in the Cape Peninsula,' *S.A. Journal of Economics,* XXV, 4, December 1957; Hobart Houghton, *Economic Development in a Plural Society* (Cape Town: O.U.P., 1960), chap. 10.

28. Y. Glass, *The Black Industrial Worker* (Johannesburg: National Institute for Personnel Research, 1960). The same study indicated that white workers had higher absenteeism and turnover rates than Africans.

29. Summary findings reported by S. Biesheuvel in *Race, Culture and Personality* (Johannesburg: S. A. Institute of Race Relations, 1959), and in 'Some Characteristics of the African Worker,' *Journal of the S.A. Institute of Personnel Management,* XV, 5, January 1962.

30. Minister of Labour, as reported in the *Minutes* of a meeting of the Executive Council of the S.A. Federated Chamber of Industries, March 1961.

N Prosperity and British Industrial Relations

BY ARTHUR M. ROSS

[INDUSTRIAL RELATIONS in Britain do not involve much government interference. In his interesting article "Prosperity and British Industrial Relations" Professor Arthur M. Ross, now United States Commissioner of Labor Statistics, reviews government intervention attempting to set wage guidelines. This section of the article is reproduced below by permission from *Industrial Relations*, University of California, Vol. 2, No. 2, February 1963.—H.R.N.]

The TUC and the Labour Party

The TUC* has never had the dominant authority enjoyed by the Scandinavian union federations. It does not participate in collective bargaining; its policy pronouncements are not binding; and it interferes as little as possible in the domestic affairs of its affiliates. For example, it was only after a major national scandal

[* Trade Union Congress, the British equivalent of the AFL-CIO.]

had developed that TUC overcame its hesitation and took action against election-rigging by the Communist minority in the Electrical Trades Union.

One function of a trade union federation is to provide ideological leadership for constituent unions and their members. But although the TUC's General Council, in consultation with various unions, continues to examine the possibilities of extended public ownership, the fact is that socialist ideology has largely dried up as a political force in Britain. TUC, more socialist than the Socialists, has called for nationalization of steel, trucking, and parts of the machine tool and aircraft industries, but there is persuasive evidence that most union members do not feel deeply about this objective.

Another traditional function of trade union federations is to press for social legislation and to carry on relations with the government. The Method of Legal Enactment, as the Webbs described it, has always been a significant technique of the British labor movement, but persistent prosperity and rising consumption standards have tended to reduce its relative significance. Furthermore, it must be kept in mind that the Conservatives have now been in power for over a dozen years. While there has been nothing like open warfare between the TUC and the Conservatives, in the nature of things relations have not been intimate. And inasmuch as the Conservatives have largely retained and to some extent have expanded the welfare state programs of the previous Labour Government, social legislation has not been an important issue.

Finally, central labor federations serve as the connecting link between trade unions and labor or socialist parties. In Britain the connection between the TUC and the Labour Party has been close: the larger unions are all affiliated with the Party, they supply the bulk of its membership and funds, they elect a majority of the Party Executive, and they have approximately 100 Members of Parliament. Nevertheless, the strength of the bond seems to be diminishing. On the one hand, the unions are finding that many white-collar and professional workers who might desire economic representation are reluctant to affiliate themselves so closely to the Labour Party. Some white-collar unions such as the National Union of Teachers and the National and Local Government Officers Association have remained out of TUC for this reason. On the other hand, the Party finds the unions to be something of an embarrassment. Mr. Gaitskill believed that the Party, like the labor and socialist parties in Scandinavia, should abandon its traditional emphasis on public ownership and should concentrate on welfare state policies with broader appeal. However, his attempts to amend Clause 4, the public ownership provision in the Party constitution, have been turned back by opposition emanating from the unions. Instead, the 1960 Congress reaffirmed the principle of public ownership and called upon the General Council to prepare comprehensive plans for its extension.

Union unpopularity also tends to weaken the bond. According to Eric Wigham:

The more critical the public becomes of the unions, the more reluctant they are to entrust power to a party over which the unions exercise so much control. Labor's defeat in 1959 was attributed in some measure to this attitude. . . . After that year's election some voices on the political side were heard talking about the possibility of separating the two sections of the movement.[1]

If the Labour Party should regain political power, possibly a closer relationship with the TUC might be reconstructed. Up to the present, however, the link between the Party and the Council, as well as the authority of the Council over its constituent unions, has been growing weaker. The trend is in the direction of a more decentralized, less politically oriented, labor movement.

The Problem of Wage Policy

In recent years the British—like the Americans, the Germans, and the French—have been struggling inconclusively to develop "wage restraint" within a collective bargaining system. They have been searching for criteria, procedures, and sanctions; but although numerous ideas have been explored and several expedients have been tried, it cannot be said that the results have been decisive.

Lord Beveridge was one of the first to recognize the difficulty of maintaining full employment, price stability, and free collective bargaining at the same time. In *Full Employment in a Free Society*, he noted that "irresponsible sectional wage bargaining may lead to inflationary developments which bestow no benefits upon the working class; which spell expropriation for the old-age pensioner and the small rentier; and which endanger the very policy of full employment whose maintenance is a vital common interest of all wage-earners." He advocated that the TUC should undertake "a unified wage policy which ensures that the demands of individual unions will be judged with reference to the economic situation as a whole"; that wage disputes should be submitted to voluntary arbitration; that the State should adopt "a definite policy of stable prices" in return for a reasonable wage policy; and that "full information as to the financial condition of industry" be made available to unions and to arbitrators.[2]

Conditions in Great Britain did not favor a coordinated wage policy: the collective bargaining structure was not centralized and the labor and industry federations did not occupy authoritative positions in the economy. However, the Labour Government did experiment with "voluntary wage restraint" between 1948 and 1950, following the issuance of a White Paper on Personal Incomes, Costs, and Prices. The unions, although declining to participate in formal discussions of national wage policy, actually cooperated to a considerable extent, so that the experiment did serve to limit the upward movement of wages and prices in the next two years. "But, like the 'wage drift' in the Scandinavian countries, the haphazard influences of increases in earnings not associated with contractual changes led to increased tensions among the unions and greater dissatisfaction with a policy which had not had wholehearted support from the beginning."[3] In 1950 the TUC voted to discontinue wage restraint.

Between 1950 and 1955 the Conservatives relied for the most part on fiscal and monetary policies to restrain inflation. Some preliminary explorations were initiated to find ways and means of keeping wage movements in line with productivity changes, but these gestures were rebuffed by the TUC and accomplished little. The Government's own role in wage determination was rather ambiguous. In 1952 the Labour Ministry sought to reduce the increases recommended by about a dozen statutory Wages Councils, but backed down before a storm of protest. In 1951 and 1953 the Ministry intervened to obtain higher wage increases for railroad employees in order to prevent stoppages.

In 1956, as inflationary pressures mounted, the Government decided that it would have to abandon its generally neutral position with respect to wages. A new White Paper on the Economic Implications of Full Employment was issued, and Prime Minister Eden held a series of meetings with representatives of the TUC, the employer organizations, and the nationalized industries. Harold Macmillan, then Chancellor of the Exchequer, declared in May 1956 that "another round of wage increases could not be repeated without disaster." A number of private and nationalized industries expressed their agreement, but the TUC rejected the appeal on the ground that wage increases were justified by the rise in prices.

In 1957 the Government established a three-man Council on Prices, Productivity, and Incomes, similar to the Council of Economic Advisers in the United States. In its first report, published in February 1958, the "Cohen Council" presented a gingerly discussion of wage policy. Concerning the proposal that a percentage figure for allowable average wage increases should be announced, the Council stated: "We are conscious of the attractiveness of this proposal, offering as it does the hope of establishing a link between the rate of wage increases and the growth in overall productivity." But the Council went on to note the practical problems which were destined to haunt the Kennedy Administration's "wage guideposts" four years later: the arguments certain to be offered in favor of increases exceeding the "formula," the danger that the prescribed average would always be a bargaining minimum, etc. Nevertheless the Council did express the hope that "if any wage increases are granted in 1958, they will be substantially below the average of the last few years." By virtue of the mild recession of 1958, they were.

With full employment restored in 1960, concern over inflation was renewed. In its Fourth Report of July 1961, the Council—now headed by Lord Heyworth—once more discussed its proposed policies for controlling inflation. After dealing with the need to increase productivity and restrain demand, the Council turned to the problem of wage determination. Again the Council considered the possible uses of a figure projecting the anticipated increase in national productivity (nicknamed "the guiding light" in journalistic circles). This could be an important tool of economic planning:

Such a projection could be related to a planned investment pro-

gramme, and to forward assessments of manpower needs and resources. It . . . would be a guide for those responsible in their own
particular fields for the planning of production, the fixing of prices
and profit margins and the settlement of wages and salaries.

Two difficulties were recognized, one the method of calculat-
ing the projection and the other its acceptance by decision
makers.

It would not be prescribed as an absolute limit but its object would be
rather to make clear—what is not clear now—the line beyond which
particular decisions or settlements cannot go without the risk of being
inflationary or else gaining at the expense of others. . . . Particular industries would remain free to go beyond the limit, and some might do
so with good reason, but what their decisions meant for others would
be made apparent.[4]

In its tone the Fourth Report bears an interesting similarity to
the "guideposts for noninflationary wage and price behavior"
issued by the Council of Economic Advisers six months later. The
subsequent course of events was also similar. The Conservative
Government, like the Kennedy Administration, was not satisfied
with a "productivity formula" which served merely as a kind of
intellectual litmus paper to evaluate the wisdom of autonomous
decisions. A more active policy was pursued, but within the year
it seemed evident that the means were not adequate to the task
and that the government had bitten off more than it could chew.

Selwyn Lloyd, Chancellor of the Exchequer, addressed Parliament on July 26, 1961, concerning the need to make British industry more competitive and to improve the balance of payments. The climax of the speech was the promulgation of a
"wage pause." Mr. Lloyd thought Britain was heavily overdrawn
on its productivity account; that there should be a pause until
productivity could catch up and make room for further advances;
that the government would act accordingly in the areas directly
under its control; that the same policy should be followed both in
the private sector and in those parts of the public sector outside
the immediate control of government; and that meanwhile a new
long-term wage policy should be developed.

That policy is that increases in incomes must follow and not precede
or outstrip increases in productivity. (Ministerial cheers.) During the
pause we must work out methods of securing a sensible long-term re-

lationship between increases in incomes of all sorts and increases in productivity.[5]

The wage pause was initiated by reducing the size of a salary increase awarded to school teachers by an arbitration board. This was a rather unpopular move, since it was widely agreed that the teachers were underpaid. Space does not permit a detailed account of wage developments in Britain during the subsequent year. Suffice it to say that the wage pause has been highly controversial, to say the least.

About six months after the new policy had been announced, Mr. Hugh Gaitskill—speaking for the Labour Party—said that industrial relations in Britain had worsened; that the country might soon be involved in industrial conflict; and that all of this, "without a shadow of a doubt," was the result of "the extraordinarily clumsy and inequitable way in which the Government had tried to enforce their so-called pay pause."[6]

One of the central difficulties was the one-sided character of the wage pause. A successful national wage policy must have positive as well as negative aspects so that all the pressure will not appear to be directed against the workers. Moreover, wage restraint must be sought in an appropriate context of economic policies designed to achieve full employment, economic growth, and equality of sacrifice. This point was recognized even in conservative circles. Discussing the bitterness of the unions toward the wage pause, the London *Times* stated:

If the Chancellor can convince the union leaders that the Government is genuinely trying to [promote full employment and improve living standards], and that the policy he plans can reasonably be expected to have that effect and is socially and economically equitable he should therefore be assured of their cooperation. It would mean laying more emphasis on full employment and continuous expansion than on price stability and it would mean that restraint on incomes would have to include profits and capital gains as well as wages and salaries. It might mean more selective controls for instance on investment and imports. The Government will have to decide what price it is prepared to pay.[7]

At the beginning of 1962 the Government began to intensify its search for a long-term national wage policy. On January 13, Mr. Lloyd dispatched a letter to the TUC. Against the background of an estimated 2.5 per cent annual increase in productivity, comments were solicited on three alternative approaches: (1) tying wage changes to productivity changes in each industry; (2) limiting the gross amount of wage increases to a specified monetary sum; (3) holding the average percentage increase within the 2.5 per cent limit. Mr. Lloyd's letter did not spell out how the second and third alternatives might be implemented in practice; and in any case, TUC did not endorse any of the three.

A similar air of unreality has surrounded other discussions of wage policy in 1962. Thus, the *Economist* has argued against uniform or "pattern" increases in the national wage bargaining industries. Increases should be made only in those areas and occupations where additional labor is needed.[8] The Economic Editor of the *Observer* concurred, describing uniform wage settlements as "probably the most important single instrument of inflation." He also proposed that, in order to make the policy valid in the private as well as the public sector, the Government should be able to intervene in any wage negotiation to set maximum levels.[9]

Late in January 1962 Mr. Lloyd established the National Economic Development Council (NED), a rudimentary economic planning agency patterned somewhat after the French modernization commission. The TUC agreed to nominate six members of the Council. NED's principal tasks were to establish targets for increasing in gross national product, higher than the Treasury itself would approve, and to recommend policies needed to achieve such increases. Another task, according to the *Manchester Guardian Weekly*, was to "utter a truism: to say that if national production increases by only 3 or 4 per cent a year, total earnings can increase by only 3 or 4 per cent a year too, so that basic wage rates (which always rise more slowly than actual earnings) must go up by rather less." The *Guardian* added, "TUC has said that it will join NED only on condition that it need not utter that truism, or at least on condition that it can issue minority reports denying it."[10] In May the Council announced a five-year plan to expand Britain's GNP by an average of four per cent a year.

Two months later, Mr. Lloyd was replaced in a cabinet shake-up. It is too early to know what will be the effect on the program of the National Economic Development Council. It seems amply clear, however, that the wage pause contributed significantly to the growing unpopularity of the Conservative Party and to Mr. Lloyd's retirement. Likewise it seems evident that in Britain, as in the United States, the conditions of successful wage restraint in peacetime have not been thought through very carefully.

What are these conditions? To begin with, there must be public acceptance of an overriding national need justifying restraints on private behavior. Certainly there is a pressing need to improve the efficiency and competitive position of British industry, but it cannot be said that business and labor leaders are full of eagerness to confront the problem. Current ambivalence on the question of forming the Common Market parity reflects a reluctance to submit to the discipline of free competition with the industries of continental Europe, as well as concern over problems of the British Commonwealth.

As already noted, national wage policy must have affirmative as well as negative components if it is to be compatible with a system of free collective bargaining and must be developed in a context of effective planning for full employment and economic growth. Corporate autonomy, business unionism, resistance against planning, and dislike of controls may not be such powerful barriers in Britain as in the United States, but they are powerful enough. With such affluence and prosperity, who wants to face unpleasant problems aside from professional problem-mongers?

History shows that effective wage restraint cannot be imposed on the bargaining parties from the outside, but must be developed through intimate consultation between labor, industry, and the government. For this purpose, there must be a potent, competent consultative mechanism capable of producing an authoritative consensus. Obviously it is too soon to know whether the National Economic Development Council will be able to reach agreement in controversial areas. Like the President's Labor-Management Committee in the United States, which was established about nine months earlier, NED is an interesting experiment, but so far only that.

Finally, an influential national wage policy must be impregnated into the collective bargaining apparatus. Otherwise it will serve merely as a target or beacon for the weak unions without restraining the strong. There are several possible methods of incorporating a conscious wage policy into the collective bargaining system: (1) There might be a highly centralized bargaining structure, with leadership and coordination supplied by powerful labor and employer federations. This is the situation in Norway and the Netherlands, considered the most successful practitioners of peacetime wage restraint. (2) There might be a tripartite government board with mandatory power, such as the National War Labor Board of World War II. (3) The collective bargaining scene might be dominated by a few unions with centralized bargaining policies. If sufficiently secure from factionalism, rival unionism, and internal unrest, these unions might be amenable to government pressure. (4) Conceivably the public sector of the economy might be so large that the wage policies of the government, acting as an employer, would set the pattern for private industry as well.[11]

To list these possibilities is sufficient to indicate that the structural deficiencies of the British bargaining system, so far as implementation of conscious wage policy is concerned, are almost as great as those of the American bargaining system. Mr. Lloyd sought to rely on the fourth possibility, by making an example of the public sector, and found himself batting to a sticky wicket indeed.

It is interesting to note that since the Labour Party assumed power it has been no more able to convince the unions of the necessity of wage restraint than was its conservative predecessors.

NOTES

1. Eric Wigham, *What's Wrong with the Unions* (London: Penguin Books, 1961), p. 65.

2. William H. Beveridge, *Full Employment in a Free Society* (New York: W. W. Norton, 1945), pp. 199-201.

3. Mark W. Leiserson, "A Brief Interpretative Survey of Wage-Price Problems in Europe," Study Paper No. 11 (Washington: Joint Economic Committee, 1959), p. 47.

4. *Council on Prices, Productivity and Incomes, Fourth Report* (London: HMSO, 1961), p. 28.

5. *The Times* (London), July 26, 1961, p. 8.

6. *The Observer* (London), January 28, 1962, p. 1.

7. August 10, 1961, p. 9.

8. *The Economist* (London), February 19, 1962.

9. *The Observer* (London), January 28, 1962, p. 2.

10. *Manchester Guardian Weekly*, February 10, 1962, p. 5.

11. The preceding four paragraphs have been adapted from A. M. Ross, "Wage Restraint in Peacetime," presented before the Western Economic Association, August, 1962 (mimeographed).

INDEX

INDEX